Beyond Ecological Economics and Development

The interrelationship among development, environment, and human needs is one of the key issues being faced by the world today. The Chilean economist, Manfred Max-Neef, was a leading thinker on this dynamic, and this book provides both an introduction to and analysis of his work and ideas. Arranged in three main sections – "Human needs and well-being", "Development, growth and sustainability", and "Methodology of economics" – the chapters in this book contribute to on-going debates on issues as important as human development, the limits of economic growth, deep ecology, sustainable consumption, entrepreneurship, climate change, interdisciplinarity, and the methodology and practice of economics. The contributors to this volume provide a broad range of different critical perspectives on these issues, and the chapters are arranged in dialogue with each other to provide the reader with a rounded view of the legacy of Max-Neef. This book is vital reading for all those interested in ecological economics, environmental economics, development economics, methodology and philosophy of economics, and heterodox economics.

Luis Valenzuela is an assistant professor at the Institute of Economics of the Austral University of Chile. He holds a PhD in Economics from the University of Oxford, as well as a Master's degree in Economics from the University of Oxford and the Pontificia Universidad Católica de Chile.

His areas of interest are inequality, technological change, productivity, and the labour market, in addition to the philosophy and methodology of economics. He is an associate member of the Institute for New Economic Thinking at the University of Oxford and adjunct researcher at the Millennium Nucleus on the Evolution of Work (M-NEW). He has been a consultant for the World Economic Forum and advisor of different agencies at the Government of Chile.

María del Valle Barrera is an adjunct professor at the Institute of Economics of the Austral University of Chile. She holds a Master's degree in Rural Development from Austral University of Chile and a PhD in Political Science from Universidad de Cuyo in Argentina.

She teaches at the Master's Programme in Human Scale Development and Ecological Economics at Austral University of Chile. She worked with late Prof. Max-Neef on several projects since 2001, and has specialised in participatory processes of sustainable development and community engagement. As a UNDP consultant, María has worked on energy poverty, climate change, and local governments.

Routledge Frontiers of Political Economy

Socialist Economic Systems
21st Century Pathways
Steven Rosefield

COVID-19 and Economic Development in Latin America
Theoretical Debates, Financing Dilemmas and Post-Pandemic Scenarios
Monika Meireles, Bruno De Conti and Diego Guevara

Marxist Political Economy and Bourdieu
Economic and Cultural Capital, Classes and State
George Economakis and Theofanis Papageorgiou

New Institutional Economics as Situational Logic
A Phenomenological Perspective
Piet De Vries

Human Economics
Paradigms, Systems, and Dynamics
Sara Casagrande

The Knowledge Problems of European Financial Market Integration
Paradoxes of the Market
Troels Krarup

Beyond Ecological Economics and Development
Critical Reflections on the Thought of Manfred Max-Neef
Edited by Luis Valenzuela and María del Valle Barrera

For more information about this series, please visit: www.routledge.com/Routledge-Frontiers-of-Political-Economy/book-series/SE0345

Beyond Ecological Economics and Development

Critical Reflections on the Thought of Manfred Max-Neef

Edited by Luis Valenzuela & María del Valle Barrera

Routledge
Taylor & Francis Group
LONDON AND NEW YORK

First published 2024
by Routledge
4 Park Square, Milton Park, Abingdon, Oxon OX14 4RN

and by Routledge
605 Third Avenue, New York, NY 10158

Routledge is an imprint of the Taylor & Francis Group, an informa business

British Library Cataloguing-in-Publication Data
A catalogue record for this book is available from the British Library

ISBN: 978-1-032-46323-0 (hbk)
ISBN: 978-1-032-46326-1 (pbk)
ISBN: 978-1-003-38114-3 (ebk)

DOI: 10.4324/9781003381143

Typeset in Times New Roman
by KnowledgeWorks Global Ltd.

Contents

Contributors

Yerko Castillo Ávalos is an adjunct professor at the Institute of Earth Sciences, Universidad Austral de Chile. He holds an MSc in Water Resources (Universidad Austral de Chile) and Renewable Natural Resources Graduate (Universidad de Chile). Yerko was an academic assistant of Manfred Max-Neef between 2011 and 2018.

Patricio Belloy is an adjunct professor at the Institute of Economics at Universidad Austral de Chile, and former collaborator of Manfred Max-Neef. Patricio holds a PhD in Public Policy at UMass Boston's McCormack Graduate School. His work explores environmental, energy, and climate policies to promote needs-based community development.

Julio Boltvinik is a researcher and professor of economics at Colegio de Mexico, Mexico City. Formerly a politician for the Mexican PRI and PRD parties, he has specialised in poverty, human needs, and social policy. He has co-authored more than 28 books, 73 book chapters, and 86 academic articles and received national and international awards.

Lina Brand-Correa is an assistant professor at the Faculty of Environmental and Urban Change, University of York, Canada. She holds a PhD in Earth and Environment from University of Leeds. Her research interests include energy services, energy and development, human wellbeing, energy return on investment (EROI), participatory methods, energy poverty, demand and consumption, and democracy.

Ivonne Cruz is a resident scholar for the Center for the U.S. and Mexico at the Baker Institute, and Faculty on Sustainability topics at Rice University. She holds a doctorate and Master's degree in the field of Sustainable Human Development and Social Public Policy from the Universidad Politécnica de Cataluña.

Iñaki Ceberio de León is a professor and researcher at the Universidad Nacional de Chilecito, Argentina. He holds a PhD in Philosophy from the University of the Basque Country, Spain, and a postdoctoral degree in Environmental Philosophy under the direction of Manfred Max-Neef at the Center for Environmental Studies of the Universidad Austral de Chile.

Jean Pierre Doussoulin is an assistant professor at the Institute of Economics of the Universidad Austral de Chile and associate researcher at the study centre on the use of panel data in economics (Erudite) in Paris, France. He holds a PhD in Economics from the Université Paris-Saclay and Master's in Environmental Economics from Agroparistech.

Antonio Elizalde Hevia is the founder and rector emeritus of the Bolivarian University of Chile. He has researched and written extensively in Spanish and Latin American journals on issues of development, environment, poverty, education, ethics, and epistemology. He is one of the co-authors of Max-Neef's most well-known book, "Human Scale Development" (1991).

Felix Fuders is an associate professor at the Institute of Economics of the Universidad Austral de Chile. He holds a PhD in Economics and Social Sciences at the University of Erlangen-Nuremberg, Germany. He is the author and co-author of numerous publications on Regional Economic Integration, Regulatory Economics, as well as Ecological Economics and Monetary Policy.

Des Gasper is a professor emeritus of Human Development, Development Ethics and Public Policy at ISS of Erasmus University Rotterdam. He has more than 360 publications, covering a wide range of areas like development, climate change, migration, ethics, gender, and human rights. His focus is both theoretical and applied research.

Patrick Kletzka is a German economist, friend, and mentee of Manfred Max-Neef. He spent several years practicing "barefoot economics" in the slums of Nairobi (Kenya), directing grassroots development projects. His monograph *Inside Barefoot Economics* (2021) shares these experiences. Kletzka holds a doctorate in economics from the University of Wuppertal (Germany).

Clara Olmedo is a professor at the Universidad Nacional de Chilecito, Argentina. She holds a PhD in Sociology from the State University of New York at Binghamton, USA. She is an associate researcher at the Center for Environmental Studies, Universidad Austral de Chile. Her research interests include environmental sociology, eco-feminism, epistemologies of the South, decolonial studies, and labour market.

Roberto Pastén is an associate professor at the Institute of Economics of the Universidad Austral de Chile. He holds a PhD in Economics from the University of Alabama, USA. His research interests include models of economic growth and environmental quality, economic valuation of ecosystem services, risk and uncertainty, modern approaches to cost-benefit analysis, and economic analysis of law.

Andrés Solimano is the founder and Chairman of the International Center for Globalization and Development (CIGLOB). He holds a PhD in Economics from the MIT, USA. Formerly Dr. Solimano served as Country Director at the World Bank, Executive Director at the Inter-American Development Bank, and

Director of the Chile office of the Latin American School of Social Sciences (FLACSO).

Wenceslao Unanue is an assistant Professor at the Universidad Adolfo Ibáñez Business School, Chile. He holds a PhD in Economic Psychology and MSc in Applied Social Psychology from the University of Sussex, UK. He is a fellow of the British Psychological Society, Action for Happiness, and the International Positive Psychology Association. He is also a board member of the Instituto del Bienestar.

Yoann Verger is a professor agrégé in Social Sciences. He holds a PhD in Economics from the University of Versailles Saint-Quentin-en-Yvelines, France. His dissertation is titled "Sraffa and ecological economics: links and possibilities".

Gibrán Vita is an assistant professor in Environmental Sciences at the Open University Netherlands and a senior researcher on the Bioeconomy at the University of Kassel – Center for Environmental Systems Research. He holds an Erasmus Mundus MSc in Industrial Ecology and a PhD in Engineering and Integrated Environmental Modelling by NTNU Norway.

Acknowledgements

This book started as a virtual workshop that took place in October 2020, to reflect on the thought of economist Manfred Max-Neef, who had passed away the year before. It was organised at the Universidad Austral de Chile (Max-Neef's academic residency) by some of the authors of this book. It was a two-day programme involving 21 papers. Many of them made it into this book. Others were published elsewhere.

We are grateful to many people who participated in this book project, starting from the 2020 workshop, some of whom were not able to be part of the final book. We thank the support of Universidad Austral de Chile, which hosts both editors of this book. We also thank Anna Rios Wilks for valuable editing help.

1 Introduction

María del Valle Barrera and Luis Valenzuela

Manfred Max-Neef (1932–2019) was not only a prominent Chilean economist, thinker, academic, activist and short-term politician, principally associated with his theory of human needs, but also prolific and innovative in other areas of research. Being very critical of established development paradigms, he developed a career outside – usually in opposition to mainstream academic circles. This book reflects on the diverse ranging thought of Max-Neef. The reflection is not only descriptive but also critical. The book, recovering the state of the art of the major themes that the author addresses, describes them in a synthesised form for both familiar and unfamiliar readers. Each chapter provides insights highlighting not only Max-Neef's contributions but also shortcomings and gaps. Our contribution hopes to become a point of reference for discussion and dialogue in academic and research circles, in relation to Max-Neef's ideas. We hope it will contribute to developing theories, methodologies and approaches that shed light on current challenges which societies and humankind face.

Max-Neef's work and the debates he engaged in are intimately related to his biography and the circumstances of his work positions, displacements, the places where he lived and the circumstances he faced (see Chapter 2 for a short biography). Graduating as an economist from *Universidad de Chile* in the 1960s, he then worked for two decades as a consultant to United Nations agencies in development projects in Latin America, giving him first-hand experience on poverty, the role of development agencies and, even more, his role as an "expert". Around those years, he developed a critical approach to the contradictions that the supposed "progress" brought to the communities. He also raised an epistemological critique of economics and of the position economics places its object of study, devoid of history, values and subjectivity.

During the 1970s and 1980s, he connected with the European and Latin American debates that questioned the development model based on the exploitation of nature, with no regard for the biosphere's limits. He spent a stint at the Bariloche Foundation, an Argentinian think tank that sought to define an alternative development paradigm for Latin America. There Max-Neef met Carlos Mallmann, whose research on "human needs" would later inspire Max-Neef's thought.

In 1982, Max-Neef published his first major work, *From the Outside Looking in: Experiences in Barefoot Economics*, for which the Swedish Right Livelihood

DOI: 10.4324/9781003381143-1

Foundation awarded him the so-called Alternative Nobel Prize in 1983. The book compiled his experiences and critical reflections on the economics of development and the way of understanding the role of the economist.

He returned to Chile with the money from the prize and founded a research centre, CEPAUR (Centre for Alternative Development, in Spanish), with the goal of building an alternative development paradigm. The intellectual result was first published in an article (1986), and then in the form of a book (1989), re-edited many times and translated into many languages. Titled *Human Scale Development*, it is Max-Neef's most widely acknowledged publication, and where he first proposed his theory of fundamental needs and satisfiers, his most well-known theory in academic circles.

Throughout these years and until his death, Max-Neef was a prolific writer of academic articles (mostly outside the mainstream academic journal scene), newspaper articles, as well as gave many speeches and interviews. He created a Master programme, still in existence, which teaches his ideas. He was an activist for environmental causes and had a brief incursion into politics, running for president in 1993.

Max-Neef's thought has influenced heterodox academic circles, mainly in Latin America and Europe. However, his ideas did not permeate the traditional economics circles and teaching. There is a general disconnection between mainstream and heterodox economics, with weak and intermittent communication channels. This is due, in part, to the labels – imposed and self-imposed – that tend to keep people (including academics) in comfort zones and beyond criticism.

The lack of such communication channels motivates this book. It provides a critical review of his thinking in light of both the heterodox and the mainstream thought, creating a space for interdisciplinary dialogue on the human, economic, environmental and socio-cultural dimensions of development and well-being.

Inspired by his challenging way of thinking, this book is an introduction to an author who not only provides alternative answers to development problems but fundamentally also invites us to reformulate the questions and embrace innovative ways of thinking to obtain different results from those solutions that continue to generate frustration and dead ends in economics and sustainable development.

As editors of this book, we believe that some of Max-Neef's contributions, regardless of any weaknesses, can inform our theory and praxis against the crises, complexity and uncertainty that humanity faces. Max-Neef provokes and invites us to return to the human scale and establish as a measure the satisfaction of the needs that make us human and connect us with what we are and the places, times, cultures and environments we inhabit.

Contents of this book

The present one is an edited book written in collaboration with 19 invited authors, coming from various countries and disciplines. Some knew and also collaborated with Max-Neef during his career. Some belong to the disciplinary mainstream, and others have been trained in heterodox visions. All of them accepted our proposal to build bridges and deepen and challenge disciplinary links beyond affinities, recognising the shortcomings from which it is possible to move forward.

The book contains 17 chapters, after this introduction. The first one is a short biography of Max-Neef, to provide some context of his life and works. The last chapter is a comprehensive bibliography of his research, not available elsewhere. In between there are 15 chapters, grouped across three themes: (1) Human needs and well-being, (2) Development, growth and sustainability and (3) Methodology of economics.

The first part, entitled Human needs and well-being, contains five chapters covering Max-Neef's contributions to the theories of human needs. They discuss the historical contextualisation of Max-Neef's proposal, a comparative analysis with other needs theories, highlighting its novelties. These authors also address the potential of the needs approach in contexts of its use in the transition to sustainable societies, governance and public policy.

More specifically, Chapter 3, by Julio Boltvinik, undertakes a synthesis of the theory of fundamental human needs and addresses the conceptual distinctions between needs, goods and satisfiers. Boltvinik also critically reflects on the links that shaped the proposal since its historical conformation and presents a comparative analysis with other theories of needs, pointing out their similarities and differences.

The next chapter, by Des Gasper, builds on the analysis of his predecessor and explores the potential of the theory and its associated matrix methodology as a practical tool for diagnosing and supporting processes of social transition, overcoming poverty and including marginalised groups. Gasper analyses what is distinctive in Max-Neef's model and what is not, assessing Max-Neef's contributions as counter-language. At the same time, he warns us not to treat it as a reified doctrine.

Then, Wenceslao Unanue reflects on the experience he shared with Manfred Max-Neef and a group of experts in Bhutan in the 2011 United Nations initiative to create a New Development Paradigm. He draws on Max-Neef's contribution and concept of the good life as a source of inspiration for the group of experts. Unanue analogises Max-Neef's proposal with the eudaimonic models of happiness, where there is space for compassion and benevolence for living a good and sustainable life.

Following this reflection, Chapter 6, by Felix Fuders, asks whether spirituality should be added to the matrix of fundamental human needs. Fuders argues that development and well-being cannot be achieved, even under Max-Neef's proposed model of fundamental human needs, without including a spiritual dimension, which is absent in Max-Neef's original taxonomy. This chapter argues that practising spirituality is critical for feeling deep and abiding happiness, and thus, "spirituality" should be added to the matrix as the tenth axiological fundamental human needs to make it a complete theory.

Chapter 7, by María del Valle Barrera and Patricio Belloy, closes the first part of the book. The authors explore the contributions and shortcomings of the theory of needs for governance and public policy. The chapter takes up a little-explored dimension of the proposal in the model and political theory, albeit a crucial one, which would better define the achievement of Human Scale Development policies. Its contribution synthesises some elements and highlights those aspects where further research is needed. They raise some questions that Max-Neef, by omission, did not answer in his work.

The second part of the book, titled "Development, growth and sustainability", takes us from the more "micro" analysis of individuals' well-being to its "macro" implications in terms of economic growth as the backbone of the development model and the issue of sustainability and sustainable development as a challenge. Ultimately, the question is about what development means, as well as finding a proposal for "better development". This part of the book has six chapters that together address from a critical and constructive perspective Max-Neef's visions on these topics. These chapters combine perspectives from economics and ecological economics, contrasting dominant and critical development visions.

The first chapter of this second part is written by Manfred Max-Neef's close collaborator and co-author of many of his writings, the Chilean sociologist Antonio Elizalde Hevia. In Chapter 8, Elizalde reviews the ecological critique of economics as a discipline justified in a relationship of domination and exploitation of nature. For him, the discourses of developmentalism and neoliberalism have generated a language and a system of knowledge that have conditioned the possibility of understanding the actual complexity of development. Elizalde invites dialogue from a Latin American proposal of Degrowth, characterised by the diversity of spaces and local identities.

In Chapter 9, Ivonne Cruz examines the contribution that Max-Neef's Human Scale Development (HSD) model can offer to monitor and evaluate the achievement of the Sustainable Development Goals (SDGs) of the UN 2030 Agenda. According to her, Max-Neef's HSD framework has the potential to identify simultaneity, complementarity and synergistic outcomes across the proposed policies, mechanisms and strategies. At the same time, it can ensure a systemic approach to addressing the complexity and ambiguity of the SDGs.

The following three chapters have complementary perspectives on the ecological limits of sustainability and Max-Neef's contributions to the renewal of its analysis and solution. Ecological economics and deep ecology support the postulate that no economy is possible without the services provided by nature, a precondition that leads Clara Olmedo, Iñaki Ceberio and Yerko Castillo in Chapter 10 to analyse the complementarities of Rockström's proposal of planetary boundaries, and that of Kate Raworth, known as the doughnut economy. Chapter 11, by Lina Brand Correa, continues with Max-Neef's contributions to climate change and sustainability studies. She considers at least three forms of contributions: demand-side mitigation strategies, socio-cultural changes through how needs are satisfied and consumption takes place and systematic solutions through the questioning of the type of institutions needed to achieve the objective of not exceeding 1.5 degrees of global warming. Then, in Chapter 12, Gibrán Vita connects the theory of human needs with that of planetary limits to postulate a Human Scale Sustainable Development (HSSD), an extension of Max-Neef's HSD. Despite the benefits that the encounter between needs and sustainability may bring, the author does not ignore that a normative vision of consumption generates tensions between personal freedoms of choice and the search for environmentally sustainable satisfiers.

The last chapter of this second part deals with the so-called threshold hypothesis, one of Max-Neef's most renowned papers. The hypothesis, which links economic growth with quality of life, has generated multiple subsequent discussions in heterodox environments. However, in Chapter 13, Luis Valenzuela highlights the potential flaws of this hypothesis, both because of the lack of empirical robustness and that of theoretical foundations. The author argues that, if one is to be true to Max-Neef's conception of development, the hypothesis has not been properly tested yet, ending the chapter with a call for further research on the topic.

The third and last part of this edited book groups four chapters that discuss his ideological placement within the economic science, as well as the contributions to the author to the Methodology of economics – or more accurately, Max-Neef's critiques to mainstream economics. These chapters make an effort to build bridges between different perspectives within economics. They are all written by economists.

In Chapter 14, Andrés Solimano places Max-Neef's thought in a broader context of economic and social thought and recognises Max-Neef's efforts as an "alternative" economist who was critical of orthodoxy and sought a more humane and sustainable development. At the same time, it identifies some concepts that require further clarification and precision.

In the same dialogical tone of disciplinary encounter, Roberto Pastén, in Chapter 15, seeks to build a bridge between Max-Neef's theory of human needs and the neoclassical concept of exogenous preferences. On the one hand, Pastén challenges the cornerstone of neoclassical economics, which conceives material consumption as the key determinant of social well-being. On the other hand, he argues that the lack of a formal economic framework for Max-Neef's theory of needs limits the extent of the dialogue across discipline. Then, Pastén proposes a bridge connecting Max-Neef's vision of needs to the neoclassical approach to preferences. The result is a new "Max-Neefian theory of preferences".

In the next chapter, Jean Pierre Doussoulin and Yoann Verger argue that Max-Neef contests not only the ideas of mainstream economics but also those of many of the authors considered heterodox in the field of economics, highlighting spaces of potential encounter. Their contribution advances the comparison and confluences between the author's thought and the theory of value of Piero Sraffa, whose proposal is linked to post-Keynesian analysis and circular economy, on which the authors focus their research.

Finally, Chapter 17, by Patrick Kletzka, revisits the proposal made by Max-Neef in his 1982 seminal book *From the Outside Looking in: Experiences in Barefoot Economics*. Kletzka describes and analyses the epistemology of a positivist discipline such as economics and its language's repercussions on the way we understand and study reality. He considers Max-Neef's proposal as a dialectical phenomenology capable of overcoming the epistemological obstacles of the current prevailing positive economic methodological paradigm. In his perspective, the discipline requires pruning and recreation of language from words to things and back again to maintain its connection with real-life economics.

Future research

The above selection of topics is not exhaustive of Max-Neef's research and contributions. In effect, much more could have been written about Max-Neef's contributions to economics and other areas of science, for example, on topics like education, globalisation, power, philosophy and even art! To us editors, this edited book covers his key intellectual contributions to understand his worldview and influence. Chapter 18 closes the book with a complete bibliography of Max-Neef's publications, where readers can explore other topics on which Max-Neef worked on and that are not covered in this book.

All in all, we think the book reveals the importance and relevance of Max-Neef's contributions, whilst also exposing potential flaws, lack of coherence or lack of formalisation. It also highlights the wide gaps available for further research. We hope the book will inspire researchers across disciplines and ideologies to connect with Max-Neef's thought and make use of what they find good and interesting to help tackle societies' most pressing challenges.

2 Short biography of Manfred Max-Neef

María del Valle Barrera

Manfred Max-Neef was a Chilean economist and ecologist (environmentalist) who was known for his work in the field of human development and sustainability. He was born in Valparaiso, Chile, in 1932, in a German family that awakened his interest in economics and music.

He graduated in economics from the University of Chile in 1953. After a short stay in the private sector between 1954 and 1957, he studied for a postgraduate degree in Regional Planning and a Master in Economics at the School of Economic Studies of Latin America at the same University, graduating in 1960.

In the early 1960s, Manfred and his wife Gabriela de Amesti settled in California, USA, where he worked as a researcher and professor in the Department of Political Science at the University of Berkeley. During the following two decades, his career was oriented to fieldwork in local and rural development projects in indigenous and peasant communities in the context of poverty and vulnerability in Latin America. He was a consultant for FAO, OAS, UNICEF, UNESCO, and other UN agencies in Uruguay, Peru, Ecuador, Mexico, and Brazil. Towards the end of the 1970s, he joined the Bariloche Foundation, an Argentinian think-tank oriented to the search for alternative development models for Latin America.

In 1982, he published his book "From the outside looking in: experiences in barefoot economics", under the auspices of the Swedish Dag Hammarskjöld Foundation. The book contains intellectual reflections about his practice and experience in the 1960s and 1970s.

The principles of Barefoot Economics brought him the recognition of the Right Livelihood Foundation, which awarded him a prize sometimes known as the alternative Nobel prize. Due to this, he became a world reference in alternative visions of development. In 1983, he resettled in Chile and created the research center CEPAUR (acronym for Centre for Alternative Development, in Spanish), where he promoted projects and critical reflection on development. The relationships with collaborators such as Antonio Elizalde, Martin Hopenhayn, Hugo Herrera, Luis Weinstein, Jorge Jatoba, among others, enhanced his work at CEPAUR. Together, they formed a dynamic network dedicated to challenging conventional development paradigms and promoting sustainable, socially just approaches.

He is best known for his work on alternative economic development models, which he has advocated as necessary to achieve sustainability and human well-being. In the

DOI: 10.4324/9781003381143-2

late 1970s, Max-Neef began to develop a theory of "fundamental human needs". This approach is based on the idea that a finite set of universally shared human needs evolves with humankind. To Max-Neef, needs do not change from one culture to another but remain constant. What changes are the *satisfiers* (defined as everything that contributes to the satisfaction of human needs, like objects, institutions, practices, etc). According to Max-Neef, traditional approaches to economic development often focus on economic growth, which can lead to social and environmental degradation. In his view, instead of focusing solely on economic growth, the focus should be on meeting fundamental human needs. He published his theoretical and methodological model under the title "Human Scale Development: and option for the future", in 1986 (with expanded versions later on). This work, Max-Neef's most renowned publication, has been a theoretical reference in multidisciplinary fields.

In 1993, with the return to democracy in Chile, he presented his presidential candidacy, encouraged by humanist and ecological parties, presented as an "icon" of visibility of issues and of people usually invisible to traditional politics.

After this short political adventure, he returned to academic life at the *Universidad Austral de Chile*, where he served two consecutive terms as a rector from 1994 until 2002. At the end of this administration, he continued working in the Institute of Economics of this University as director, academic, and researcher. His teaching activity at the undergraduate and graduate levels ensured the transmission of his experience to several cohorts. It is worth mentioning the creation of the master's program in Human Scale Development and Ecological Economics in 2013 at the same University.

Max-Neef was a vocal critic of globalization, arguing that it often leads to increased inequality and environmental degradation. He advocated for more localized approaches to development, which he believed were more sustainable and equitable. In the 1990s and 2000s, he published in the journal Ecological Economics, where he was also an editorial board member. His most important publications are *Economics Growth and Quality of Life: A Threshold Hypothesis* (1995); *Human Ecology, Human Economy; a Review* (2002); *Human Ecology: Following Nature's Lead; a Review* (2003); and *Foundations of Transdisciplinarity* (2005). During this decade, his writings progressively shifted from human development issues to environmental and ecological considerations of development, making proposals to strengthen the links between well-being and sustainability.

Max-Neef had a long and distinguished – although unconventional – academic career, teaching at several universities in Chile and worldwide. As a guest of conferences and congress inaugurations, he traveled worldwide, giving hundreds of lectures and conferences. He was a loquacious and convincing speaker who could inspire reflection and action in his audiences.

Throughout his career, Max-Neef was recognized for his contributions to economic development and sustainability. He received numerous distinctions, among them the National Award for the Promotion and Defense of Human Rights in 1987, the University Award of Highest Honour by the Soka University of Japan in 1997, the University Excellence Gold Medal by the University of Santiago de Cali, Colombia in 2003, to mention a few. He was also awarded four doctorates "Honoris Causa": in 2002, by the University of Jordan of the Kingdom of Jordan;

in 2005, by the University of Antioquia in Colombia; in 2008, by the Universidad Nacional del Litoral in Argentina; and in 2009, by the University of San Francisco in Pennsylvania, USA.

In parallel to his academic work, Max-Neef was also involved in various non-governmental organizations and civil society groups. He was an honorary member of the Club of Rome and member of the Board of the World Future Council. In 2011, he participated in the United Nations high-level panel with a group of experts to build a new development paradigm based on the Gross Domestic Happiness Index from the kingdom of Bhutan.

Manfred Max-Neef passed away in August 2018 at the age of 86 in his house in the Chilean city of Valdivia.

Max-Neef's ideas have been influential in academic and policy circles, and his work remains relevant today. He inspired many people working in the field of economic development and sustainability, and his legacy will continue to shape how these crucial issues are confronted.

Part I

Human needs and well-being

3 On the contributions of Max-Neef et al. to the theory of human needs[1]

Julio Boltvinik

Introduction. The object of this chapter

This chapter has as its main object of study Max-Neef et al. (1986, chapters III, IV pp. 34–49) and Max-Neef (1991, pp. 23–37). I will refer to it as Max-Neef et al. "book" (MNEAB),[2] which is a highly creative and imaginative work. This object of study is approached from the perspective of theories and conceptions of human needs and not from the perspective adopted by MNEAB of Human Scale Development. My approach to human needs derives from my main objects of study: poverty and social policy (Boltvinik, 1984, 2004, 2008). This is reflected in how I analyse and evaluate contributions to human needs.

The contributions of MNEAB are multiple. A notable methodological one is the definition of multiple analytical spaces, in particular the original distinction (which does not always work well as shown later) between goods and satisfiers, and which should not be confused with the distinction between needs and satisfiers made also by other authors.

The main flaw of the book, from an academic point of view, is its lack of explicit foundations. The only authors they refer to, in very general terms, without referring to specific works, are Marx and Maslow.

My aim is to provide a clear idea of their contributions to the understanding of human needs, highlighting the valuable and original as well as the problems and limitations of what they wrote.

Conception of needs, satisfiers, and goods. Basic postulates

The authors indicate that the contributions presented in the second part of the book aim "to make understandable *and operational a theory* of human needs *for* development". These contributions can be expressed in the following postulates[3]:

1 *Development refers to people, not to* objects. This they consider the basic postulate of "Human Scale Development", their central proposal. This postulate generates the following questions and answers: "How can it be established that a certain development process is better than another?". They reject indicators of the *quantitative growth* of *objects,* such as GDP, and point out that *an indicator*

DOI: 10.4324/9781003381143-4

of the qualitative growth of people is required. "What could it be?" They respond by pointing out that "the best development process will be *the one that allows to raise most people's quality of life*", which in turn "will depend on the possibilities that people have to adequately satisfy their *fundamental human needs*". Finally, they ask "Which are the fundamental human needs?" and "Who decides which they are?". This last is left unanswered (p. 25)

2 *It is essential to distinguish* between *needs and satisfiers.* For example, food and shelter are *not needs but satisfiers* of the fundamental need for *subsistence.* Similarly, education (whether formal or informal), study, research, early stimulation, and meditation are satisfiers of the need for *understanding*. Traditional beliefs that human needs tend to be infinite, that they are constantly changing, that they vary from one culture to another, and that they are different in each historical period are incorrect, since *they are the product of the conceptual error* of not making explicit the basic difference between what are properly needs and what are satisfiers of those needs (p. 26)

3 *The person is a being of multiple and interdependent needs that function as a system.* Needs should be understood as a system within which they interrelate and interact. Simultaneities, complementarities, and trade-offs are characteristic of the dynamics of the process of need satisfaction (p. 26)

4 *There is a pre-system* threshold *in every need.* Although hierarchical linearities cannot be established between needs (as Maslow did in his prepotency hierarchy), it is necessary to recognise a pre-system threshold for each need, below which the urgency to satisfy it becomes an absolute urgency. The case of subsistence is the clearest. When this need is under-satisfied, all other needs are blocked, and a single impulse prevails. But the case is equally relevant for other needs: total absence of affection or loss of identity can even lead people to self-annihilation (p. 50)[4]

5 *Fundamental human needs are finite, few and classifiable and are the same in all cultures and in all historical periods* (p. 27)

6 *Needs make evident the constant tension of human beings between lacks and potentials.* Needs reveal the being of the person in the most pressing way: as lack and potential. Conceiving needs only as a lack implies restricting their spectrum to the purely physiological, which is the area in which a need assumes most strongly and clearly the feeling of lack of something. "To the extent that needs *commit, motivate and mobilise people, they* are also *potentialities* and, even more, they can become *resources*. The need to participate is potentiality for participation, just as the need for affection is potentiality for affection". "Thus, understood needs it is inappropriate to speak of needs that are 'satisfied'. As they *reveal a dialectical process, they constitute an incessant movement.* Hence, it is more appropriate to talk about *living and realizing needs ...* in a continuous and renewed way" (p. 34)[5]

7 *What is culturally determined is not fundamental human needs, but their satisfiers.* Each economic, social, and political system adopts different styles for the satisfaction *of the same fundamental needs*. In each system, these are satisfied through the generation of different types of satisfiers (p. 27)

8 *Definitions of satisfiers.* "Satisfiers are not available economic goods but are everything that, *by representing* ways *of being, having, doing and interacting*[6], contributes to the realisation of human needs". Here they specify what kind of elements satisfiers can be: "among others, forms of organisation, political structures, social practices, subjective conditions, values and norms, spaces, contexts, behaviours and attitudes". "Feeding is a satisfier, as can also be a family structure (e. g., of the need for protection) or a political order (of the need for participation)". A satisfier can also be defined, in the ultimate sense, as the "way in which a need is expressed" (p. 35)

9 *The introduction of satisfiers distinguishes humanist from mechanistic economics.* The construction of a humanist economics requires, in this context, facing an important theoretical challenge: to understand and unravel the dialectic between needs, satisfiers, and economic goods. To suppose a direct relationship between needs and economic goods leads to the construction of a mechanistic discipline, in which the central assumption is that needs are manifested through demand which, in turn, is determined by individual preferences in relation to the goods produced. Although in this last sentence, the word needs is not required,[7] from here they conclude that "the inclusion of satisfiers as part of the economic process implies asserting the subjective beyond the pure preferences regarding objects and artifacts" (p. 36). This implies understanding how needs are lived, how satisfiers and economic goods are related to the ways of feeling, expressing, and acting our needs, how satisfiers and goods limit, condition, distort or stimulate our possibilities of living our needs. Since ways in which we live our needs are ultimately subjective, positivists would conclude that any universalising judgement would be arbitrary. However, our authors reject the identification that positivism makes of the subjective with the particular and point out that, *when the object of study is the relationship between human beings and society,* the universality of the subjective cannot be ignored (pp. 36–37). Here they would seem to imply that the inclusion of satisfiers introduces the social dimension into the otherwise individual relationship between preferences and goods. That is why they continue to argue that *the social character of subjectivity is one of the axes of reflection on the concrete human being*. Therefore, the subjective can indeed be judged, they conclude. *They place preferences on the plane of the subjective-particular and needs on that of the subjective-universal* (p. 37)

10 *Definitions of goods.* "Goods are *strictly speaking* the means by which the subject enhances the satisfiers to live his/her needs". Previously they have identified goods as *objects and artefacts that allow to increase or decrease the efficiency of a satisfier,* and later they add: "thus altering the threshold for realizing a need" (p. 41)

11 *Each need can be met at different levels and with different intensities. Moreover, it is satisfied in three contexts: (1) in relation to oneself (Eigenwelt); (2) in relation to the social group (Mitwelt); and (3) in relation to the environment (Umwelt)* (p. 27)

12 *Needs change with the species' evolution and have a unique trajectory.* Of the nine needs listed, it can be argued based on common sense and some

anthropological knowledge that the following seven were present since the origins of *Homo habilis* and, undoubtedly, since the appearance of *Homo sapiens*: subsistence, protection, affection, understanding, participation, leisure, and creation. The need for identity probably emerged in a later evolutionary stage and, much later, that of freedom. The need for transcendence was not included, because it is yet not "sufficiently universal", but it will become so at some point. In conclusion, human needs change at the pace of the evolution of the species, have a unique trajectory, and are universal

Satisfiers evolve with history and have "a double trajectory": first, "they modify at the rhythm of history and, second, they diversify according to cultures and circumstances, that is, according to the rhythm of different histories" (pp. 37–38)

13 *Economic goods (artefacts, technologies) have a triple trajectory*: "they are modified at conjunctural rhythms", diversified with cultures and, within these, with social strata. Nowadays, they argue, the speed of production and diversification of artefacts is such that people increase their dependence and their alienation grows to such an extent that it is increasingly common to find economic goods (artefacts) that no longer enhance the satisfaction of any need but are transformed into ends in themselves (p. 38)

14 *Any unmet human need reveals a human poverty*. The traditional concept of poverty is limited and restricted, since it refers exclusively to the situation of those who can be classified below a certain income threshold. The notion is strictly economistic. We suggest not talking about poverty but about poverties. In fact, any fundamental human need that is not adequately met reveals human poverty. Subsistence poverty (insufficient food and shelter); protection poverty (inefficient health systems, violence); affection poverty … and so on (pp. 27–28)

15 *Poverties, once they exceed critical limits of intensity and duration, generate both individual and collective pathologies.* The authors illustrate pathologies with conditions generated by unemployment, foreign debt and inflation and comment that it is necessary to develop indicators for these pathologies (p. 28)

The authors' contributions are manifold. In general, I agree with the set of postulates, although I will express my disagreement (sometimes only nuanced disagreement) with some. Although only a few postulates are individually original, *the set is original.* The fact that the only references to other authors are to Marx and Maslow makes me think that the authors carried out a synthesis leaning on Marx and, more evidently, on Maslow (1943, 1987, 1999).

They adopt, like Maslow, the vision of the set of needs as a system (postulate 3). This is a positive trait present in very few authors. Among the possible relationships between needs, they dismiss that of precondition, an essential (but controversial and nuanced by him) feature in Maslow's theory. In doing so, they reject the theory of hierarchy, or prepotency scale, which is backed up with some strong empirical evidence.[8] On the other hand, they maintain the relations of concurrency, complementarities, and trade-offs, which are weaker and less defined.

The link with Marx is more implicit and less developed. From Marx, two main lines of thought are not appropriated by MNEAB: the dynamic relations between production and needs, and the vision of the human essence (where such dynamic is rooted). As their conception of need (postulate 6) is a unit formed by lack and potentiality it comes close to the Marxian notion of human essential forces (needs and capacities). As anticipated in endnote 5, if potentiality is matched with capacity, which is perfectly valid,[9] this closeness becomes more evident. When the authors say that needs, "reveal a dialectical process, constitute an incessant movement" (p. 34), the profound coincidence with the concept of essential human forces (by Marx-Márkus) becomes evident, but it also becomes evident that their conception remains short by not incorporating in it the conception of the human essence associated with work and production.

The set of postulates related to what Sen has called analytical spaces is their greatest contribution, which is summarised in Table 3.1. Within this set, several contributions can be distinguished: (1) the distinction between needs, satisfiers, and goods, and the definition of each of the three concepts; (2) the rates of change of each and their trajectories; and (3) their attempt to understand the dialectic between needs, satisfiers, and goods, which although not fully developed opens a promising research line.

On the first point, a systematic assessment will be presented in the next section. Their position, barely argued (postulates 12–14) on the rhythms of evolution and the trajectories of needs, satisfiers, and goods, seems flimsy. First, associating the evolution of needs with the evolution of our species, while consistent with a universalist theory, implies biological reductionism. It seems to me that in the context of the other theses by MNEAB, it would have been sufficient to indicate that the evolution of needs is very slow, similar perhaps in speed to biological evolution, without tying it to a biologistic conception. Regarding postulate 13, which I have rephrased so that the double trajectory of the satisfiers is read as "*at the rhythm* of universal history and local history", the thesis has the problem that only in a small part of human history one can speak of universal history.

Finally, regarding the dynamics of interrelationship between needs, satisfiers, and goods, this is a very promising issue discussed in the following section.

Matrix of needs and satisfiers

The highlight of this complex definition of spaces is the matrix of needs and satisfiers they construct (Table 3.2). Although they caution that *it is not a normative matrix* and that it gives only examples of satisfiers, it helps understand their scheme. The rows of the matrix contain "needs classified according to *axiological categories*": subsistence, protection, affection, understanding, participation, leisure or idleness, creation, identity, and freedom; and in the columns "needs classified according to *existential categories*": beingS, having, doing and being C; see endnote 6. Interpret existential needs as *the existential dimensions of axiological needs* 1,[10] *rather than as needs in themselves*, makes the matrix intelligible.

Table 3.1 Analytical spaces in Max-Neef et al.

Analytical spaces	*Definition or concept*	*Absolute or relative character and time variability*	*Classification, listing, or examples*	*Evaluation scheme and space in which it occurs*
Needs	Needs are both lacks and potentialities (they commit, motivate, and mobilise). They constitute a constantly moving system (simultaneities, complementarities, compensations). The authors reject the linear hierarchy but accept the existence of pre-system thresholds.	Absolute. They are the same in all cultures. They evolve with the species.	Axiological Classification: subsistence, protection, affection, understanding, participation, leisure, creation, identity, freedom. Existential classification: beingS, having, doing, beingC.	Although the possibilities of realising needs are indispensable for assessing a society, this is not enough. The dominant modality that a culture imprints on needs is defined at the level of satisfiers. The relationship between needs, satisfiers, and goods is central. In industrial society, goods have become ends in themselves. Life service of artefacts.
Satisfiers	1. Way in which a need is expressed. 2. Forms of beingS, having, doing, and beingC that contributes to the realisation of needs.	Relative. They are modified with history and culture. They are (like goods) historically constituted products that can be modified.	Examples. Feeding, education, political order, law, subjective conditions. Classification: Violators/ destroyers, pseudo-satisfiers, inhibitors, singular and synergistic.	
Goods	1. Means by which the subject enhances the satisfiers to live his needs. 2. Objects and artefacts that increase or decrease the efficiency of a satisfier.	Relative. They change with the conjuncture, cultures, and social strata.	Books, food.	

Table 3.2 Matrix of needs and satisfiers by Max-Neef et al.

Needs according to axiological categories	*Needs according to existential categories*			
	1. BeingS	*2. Having*	*3. Doing*	*4. BeingC*
1. Subsistence	Physical & mental health, balance, solidarity, mood, adaptability	Feeding, shelter, work	Feed, procreate, rest, work	Living environment, social environment
2. Protection	Care, adaptability, autonomy, balance, solidarity	Insurance systems, savings, social security, health systems, legislation, rights, family, work	Cooperate, prevent, plan, take care of, cure, defend	Vital contour, social environment, dwelling
3. Affection	Self-esteem, solidarity, respect, tolerance, generosity, receptivity, passion, will, sensuality, humour	Friends, couples, family, pets, plants, gardens	Make love, caress, express emotions, share, take care of, cultivate, appreciate	Privacy, intimacy, home, meeting spaces
4. Understanding	Critical awareness, receptivity, curiosity, astonishment, discipline, intuition, rationality	Literature, teachers, method, educational policies, communication policies	Investigate, study, experiment, educate, analyse, meditate, interpret	Settings of formative interaction, schools, universities, academies, groups, communities, family
5. Participation	Adaptability, receptivity, solidarity, disposition, conviction, dedication, respect, passion, humour	Rights, responsibilities, obligations, work	Become affiliated, cooperate, propose, share, dissent, obey, dialogue, agree, express opinions	Settings of participative interaction, parties, associations, families, churches, communities, neighbourhoods
6. Leisure	Curiosity, receptivity, imagination, carefreeness, humour, tranquillity, sensuality	Games, spectacles, parties, calm	Divagate, distract, daydream, long, fantasise, evoke, relax, have fun, play	Privacy, intimacy privacy, meeting spaces, free time, environments, landscapes

(*Continued*)

Table 3.2 (Continued)

Needs according to axiological categories	*Needs according to existential categories*			
categories	*1. BeingS*	*2. Having*	*3. Doing*	*4. BeingC*
7. Creation	Passion, imagination, will, intuition, audacity, rationality, autonomy, inventiveness, curiosity	Skills, abilities, method, work	Work, invent, build, ideate, compose, design, interpret	Areas of production and feedback, workshops, athenaeums, groups, audiences, spaces, expression, temporary freedom
8. Identity	Belonging, coherence, differentiation, self-esteem, assertiveness	Symbols, language, habits, customs, reference groups, sexuality, values, norms, roles, historical memory, work	Commit, integrate, confront, define oneself, know oneself, recognise, oneself, actualise oneself, grow	Socio-rhythms, everyday settings, belongingness settings, maturational stages
9. Freedom	Autonomy, will, self-esteem, passion, assertiveness, openness, determination, boldness, rebelliousness, tolerance	Equal rights	Disagree, choose, differentiate from, run risks, know oneself, assume oneself, disobey, meditate	Space-time plasticity

Source: Max-Neef et al., *Desarrollo a Escala Humana*, p. 42.

The authors say that feeding and shelter should not be considered needs, but as satisfiers of the subsistence need, as well as education, study, and research, are satisfiers of the understanding need. Curative systems, prevention, and health schemes in general, as well as insurance, legislation (including rights), are satisfiers of the need for protection.

In each cell, the authors list some relevant "satisfiers". For example, in the beingS dimension of subsistence, we find physical health and mental health (which are personal *conditions*), as well as mood (a transitory condition) and adaptability (a *virtue or character trait*), and solidarity (which can be a collective virtue or a trait of social relations). When reading vertically the "beingS" column of the matrix, it stands out that almost all "satisfiers" included are virtues, emotions, personal qualities, or character traits. Reading horizontally the subsistence need we find, in the column having, feeding and shelter (abstract formulations of necessary goods); and work (which is not a direct satisfier nor a universally required one); feeding appears as feed, and work is repeated, in the column doing, where procreate and rest are added but there is no term for shelter (it could be *to shelter oneself*). In the column, beingC "living environment" and "social environment (setting)" are included, introducing nature and society as the place of *estar* (beingC). By reading the first line (subsistence) horizontally, one perceives the diverse nature of the satisfiers, but social satisfiers are relatively absent. If we look at the *second line, protection*, we find again virtues or qualities in the first column (beingS). But now, in the second column, in contrast to what is found in subsistence, mostly social elements appear, referring either to the social organisation of production to satisfy the need (insurance systems, social security, health systems), or to current regulations (legislations, rights) or to institutions (family) or a labour related condition (work). In the "doing" column cell, there are activities, some of which are social (cooperating, planning), and others include family activities (take care, cure, defend).

Reading the entire column "having", we can conclude that the contents refer, dominantly, to possessions formulated in a general way so that they do not sound like possession of goods: feeding, shelter, games, spectacles, parties, rights, and relationships. Looking at the line understanding, we find *virtues* in the "beingS" column, while in the having column we find literature, teachers, and method, three elements of diverse nature. Literature is very close to the goods in which it is embodied (books, journals). Teachers can be read as a relationship and method is a skill (but skills should be in the column beingS). In the same cell, one finds elements of the state apparatus: educational and communication policies. Again, these social satisfiers are classified in the having, which seems odd. In the cell understanding/doing, only human activities appear and, in the understanding/beingC cell appears a single type of satisfier, which the authors call settings of formative *interaction*, where they list schools and universities. The relevant aspect here is not beingC *but interacting and participating*. The social dimension reappears here.

In the matrix presentation, the authors are very concise. They limit themselves to warning that *it is not normative*, that it is an example and that each human group can build and fill its own matrix. They also explain, using a single and exceptionally fortunate example, the way in which various economic goods can be derived from the satisfiers of each cell. They choose the cell that "indicates ways of doing to satisfy the need for understanding". They point out some of the activities identified as satisfiers: investigate, study, experiment, interpret, etc. and point out that these give rise to economic goods, according to the culture and its resources, such as books, laboratory instruments, and computers. They emphasise that in this example the definition of goods works well: "the function of these (goods) is certainly to *enhance the doing of understanding*" (p. 43). I analysed other examples to assess whether the definition works generally well. I started with the doing of subsistence and focus on feed. Certainly, from it, we could derive goods that would be the same as those derived from the satisfier feeding, located in the halving of subsistence: food and the goods to prepare, consume, and preserve food. If we were to add cooking in the subsistence doing column, it would be clear that goods like the gas stove or the refrigerator enhance the doing of subsistence. But in all these cases we would be referring *to goods that support an activity, in a similar way as computers or books do.* But when we derive food from the subsistence cell of having, this derivation looks like a simple change from feed to food and, therefore, the distinction between satisfiers and goods is diluted. The same thing happens when from literature, in the halving of understanding, we derive books and journals. In the case of beingC protection cell, one of the satisfiers is directly a good (dwelling). This is because there are goods that directly, without human activity, meet human needs. The best example is housing. It is enough to be passively in it for us to receive the protection it provides. That is why in the doing of protection there is no human activity that is related to the multiple (passive) protections that housing provides.

Drawing some conclusions from the semi-built complex world of analytical spaces in Max-Neef et al., I found the following: (1) The scheme is attractive and suggestive but insufficiently elaborated. (2) The concept of satisfier in the practical examples of the matrix goes beyond its definition, as this is constrained to the individual dimension, while the examples include also the social dimension (although in an individual existential format, in such a way that *health systems, for example, appear as something that the individual "has"*). (3) The distinction between satisfiers and goods functions well when the satisfier is a human activity that relies on goods to enhance itself, but in many other cases it seems artificial, since what is included as satisfier is simply a grammatical variation of what are called goods. (4) The idea of existential dimensions is fruitful in many ways. For example, it allows to relativise and criticise Sen's *functionings* for being unilaterally concentrated in the "doing" dimension, paying little or no attention to other dimensions. However, existential categories form a rigid scheme that, for example, leaves human relations misplaced, under having.

The dynamic interrelationships among needs, satisfiers, and goods

Another important contribution, outlined but not fully developed by the authors, is that of the dynamics between needs, satisfiers, and goods. In defining goods (p. 35), they add: "goods have become determining elements within industrial civilization". This phrase is complemented as follows: "the way in which the production and appropriation of economic goods has been organised throughout industrial capitalism has overwhelmingly conditioned the type of dominant satisfiers". (*Ibid.*) And further in the following paragraph:

> When the form of production and consumption of goods converts goods into ends in themselves, then the presumed satisfaction of a need *tarnishes* the potentialities of living it in its full breadth. This paves the way for the conformation of an alienated society that embarks on a meaningless productivist race. Life is then put at the service of artifacts rather than artifacts at the service of life. The question on the quality of life is concealed by the obsession with increasing the productivity of means.
>
> (*Ibid.*)

They outline a *cognitive challenge* for what they call the "construction of a humanistic economics": "to understand and unravel the dialectic between needs, satisfiers and economic goods". A critical theory must present satisfiers and economic goods as historically constituted and, therefore, as modifiable. A humanist economy assumes "forms of economic organisation in which goods enhance satisfiers to live needs in a coherent, healthy and full way". In it, it would no longer be a question of relating needs only to goods and services which are supposed to satisfy them, but also, of relating them to social practices, forms of organisation and political models.

This is an important text that one would expect to see backed up with historical examples. Consider the human need for transportation (which does not usually appear in the usual lists of needs, largely because it is an instrumental need, something we need to meet virtually all other needs). Let us define transport systems as the main satisfier of this need. Let us reflect on the dynamics between the need for transport, specific goods, and "transport systems". The dynamic element has always been, long before industrial capitalism, the development of new means of transportation (the wheeled cart, the sailing boat, the steamboat, the railway, the automobile, the plane). The need to travel itself has been produced by the means that make travel possible. At its time, each of these means of transport transformed the world. It is clear, for example, that the holding of world scientific congresses was facilitated by air transport. This example seems to show that *not only in industrial capitalism, as Max-Neef et al. claim, goods play the dominant role*. However, it is easy to think of a counterexample. Despite the development of many goods that enhance the satisfiers of human understanding, such as computers and the internet, school education remains the same as it was two centuries ago. In this case, the school, a satisfier, seems to be the dominant element, regardless of the mode of production or economic system.

A typology of satisfiers: From destroyers to synergistic satisfiers

Max-Neef et al. also make an additional important contribution by classifying satisfiers into five types: (1) violating or destroyers; (2) pseudo-satisfiers; (3) inhibitors; (4) singular; and (5) synergistic.

The *violating or destructive satisfiers* are defined as those which, applied under the pretext of satisfying the need for protection, not only annihilate the possibility of its satisfaction, but also make it impossible to adequately satisfy other needs. The examples presented by the authors are diverse: arms, national security doctrines, authoritarianism, or censorship, which clearly do not achieve their protective effect, or this turns out to be ambiguous, and which can clearly limit the satisfaction of other needs. In the case of exile, which can be very effective in providing protection (sometimes it is the only option), it can effectively have high costs in terms of other satisfiers. Finally, bureaucracy, which is also presented as a destructive satisfier, does not seem to be able to be associated uniquely with the need for protection.

Pseudo-satisfiers are those that stimulate a false sense of satisfaction of a certain need and that can, sometimes, annihilate, in a medium term, the possibility of satisfying the same need. The examples provided by the authors include satisfiers aimed at almost all needs. They include "mechanistic medicine" ("a pill for every ill"); "chauvinistic nationalism", formal democracy, prostitution, almsgiving, fashions. They are all elements that are open to criticism, of course, but it is not clear that in all cases they deny the possibility of satisfying the need in question.

Inhibitor satisfiers are those that they satisfy (usually over-satisfy) a certain need, seriously hinder the possibility of satisfying other needs. They tend to emanate from ingrained habits. Examples include paternalism, overprotective family, Taylorist-type production, authoritarian classroom, commercial television. In these cases, it is very clear how they limit the satisfaction of other needs. The authoritarian classroom, however, in my opinion does not satisfy even the need for understanding to which it is addressed, so it corresponds more to the group of pseudo-satisfiers.

Singular satisfiers are those that aim at the satisfaction of a single need, being neutral with respect to the satisfaction of other needs. They are almost always institutionalised and characteristic of development plans and programmes. Examples include curative medicine, housing assistentialist programmes, food supply programmes, insurance systems, voting, professional armies, gifts. The idea is quite clear.

Synergistic satisfiers are those that meet a given need, stimulate, and contribute to the satisfaction of other needs. Examples include cultural television, breastfeeding, and self-managed production.

The first four groups, the authors say, are exogenous satisfiers to a community of free people capable, potentially or in fact, of designing their own projects of living together. They are imposed, induced, ritualised, or institutionalised satisfiers driven from top to bottom. Synergistic satisfiers are endogenous and tend to be counter-hegemonic, even though they can also be driven by the state.

Regardless of its problems, the classification is very suggestive and useful for development projects.

A comparative analysis of Max-Neef et al. scheme of needs with other needs schemes

What follows is a comparison of Max-Neef et al. scheme of needs *vis à vis* the need schemes by Maslow, Fromm, Maccoby, Doyal-Gough, Nussbaum, Heller,

Malinowsky, and Deci-Ryan.[11] Although the conception of needs in Marx (including the interpretations by Márkus and Heller) is not included formally in the comparative table, as there is not a defined list or scheme of needs in Marx, it is the standpoint from which the comparative analysis is viewed (Boltvinik, 2021). The scheme by Heller included reflects her view rather than Marx's conception and it comes from a paper she wrote in 1961 (13 years before the original German edition of her book *The Theory of Need in Marx*), which to my knowledge has not been published in English but is included as an Appendix in the Spanish edition of the mentioned book.

I have organised the items listed (mostly *needs*, but also *capabilities* and *value-drives*) in Table 3.3, which is divided into two parts. In the first part, I compare Max-Neef's scheme of needs with those of Maslow, Doyal and Gough, Nussbaum's capabilities, Malinowsky, and Agnes Heller. Of them only Malinowsky derives his scheme from a conception of the "Human Essence" in which needs play an essential role. It is a biologistic limited conception of human essence where cognitive and emotional dimensions of human beings are absent.

All authors in both parts of the Table *regard the identified needs (or capabilities* or *value drives) as universal*, although there is a degree of ambiguity in Maccoby and Maslow, who avoids positing total universality. Max-Neef et al., while Doyal-Gough and Nussbaum strongly assert universality. Doyal-Gough base their concept of universal need on the idea that *serious harm* takes place when a need is not satisfied.

Martha Nussbaum expresses thus her *capability* approach: "The intuitive idea behind the approach is that certain functions are particularly central in human life in the sense that their presence or absence is typically understood to be a mark of the presence or absence of human life; and that there is something that it is to do these functions in a truly human way, not a merely animal way. *The core idea is that of the human being as a dignified free being who shapes his/her own life in cooperation and reciprocity with others,* rather than being passively shaped. A life that is really human is one that is shaped throughout by these human powers of practical reason and sociability. The idea of *human dignity* has *broad cross-cultural resonance and intuitive power*" (pp. 71–72).

The idea of cross-cultural universal values is the basis of Nussbaum's list of capabilities.

On the structure of needs postulated by each author, I have previously said that Max-Neef's and Maslow's schemes are the two which most explicitly posit a system of needs.

A very broad consensus in Table 3.3, first part, is found in the fact that all authors recognise (in most cases various items) associated with Max-Neef's subsistence needs. Malinowsky and Doyal-Gough have the greatest detail here. Malinowsky because his conception is focused on biological needs, which contrasts sharply with the absence in his scheme of any need related to Max-Neef's needs 3, 6, 7, 8, and 9. In the case of Doyal and Gough (1991), the reason for the detail is that I have included in the table what they call intermediate needs which, as they explain, is a less clumsy name for universal satisfier characteristics (which in its turn are "those properties of goods, services, activities and relationships which enhance physical

Table 3.3 First part. Comparative analysis of schemes of needs: Max-Neef et al.; Maslow; Doyal-Gough; Nussbaum; Malinowsky; Heller

Max-Neef et al. *(needs)*	*Maslow (basic needs)*	*Doyal-Gough (basic & intermediate needs)*	*Nussbaum (capabilities)*	*Malinowsky (basic, biological, needs)*	*Agnes Heller (existential and properly human needs*
1.Subsistence	1. Physiological	Nutrition; housing; non-hazardous physical and work milieus; health care; birth control; safe childbearing; physical health	1. Life 2. Bodily health	1. Metabolism 3. Bodily comfort and temperature control 6. Growth (care) 7. Health care (hygiene)	1. Nutrition
2. Protection	2. Safety (security)	Security in childhood; physical and economic security; physical health	3. Bodily Integrity	4. Safety (protection)	
3. Affection	3. Love, affection	Primary relations	5. Emotions 10. Environmental control		9. Friendship 10. Love
4. Understanding	6. Cognitive needs (knowing and understanding)	Basic education	4. Senses, imagination, & thought (D) 6. Practical reason	6. Growth (education)	8. Reflection
5. Participation	3. Belongingness		7. Affiliation A (relatedness)	2. Reproduction (kinship)	3. Social contact and cooperation
6. Idleness (leisure)			9. Play		5. Free time. 7. Play (in adults)
7. Creation (D)	7. Aesthetic Needs		4. Senses, imagination, & thought		8. Reflection 6. Cultural activity

(*Continued*)

Table 3.3 (Continued)

Max-Neef et al. *(needs)*	*Maslow (basic needs)*	*Doyal-Gough (basic & intermediate needs)*	*Nussbaum (capabilities)*	*Malinowsky (basic, biological, needs)*	*Agnes Heller (existential and properly human needs*
8. Identity					
9. Freedom					
10. Without clear-cut association to Max-Neef needs	4. Esteem (bases for self-esteem; reputation or: esteem by others) five. Self-actualisation.	Autonomy Critical autonomy	7. Affiliation B (social bases of respect 10. Environmental control 8. Other species	6. Growth (socialisation) 5. Movement; activity	2. Sexual satisfaction 4. Activity 11. Self-realisation in objectivation 12. Moral activity 13. Alienated needs: money, power, possession of more goods

health and autonomy [the only two basic needs in their scheme] in all cultures)" (p. 157). All other schemes (except Heller's) have some item related to *Protection*. In *Understanding*, there is also a consensus although formulated in very different terms, from the conventional *education* to the more profound formulations by Nussbaum (2000, pp. 78–79) ("Being able to use the senses, to imagine, think, and reason in a truly human way, a way informed by an adequate education"; and to Heller's "reflection").

The need in Max-Neef's scheme with the minimum level of consensus is *freedom*, which is absent in both parts of the table, and *identity* which is only present in Fromm's scheme (second part of the table). Although *autonomy* (present in Doyal-Gough and Deci-Ryan schemes), forcing a bit its meaning, could be associated with freedom, I have classified autonomy, in both parts of the table as not associated with any need in Max-Neef's scheme (last line). Also with a very low level of consensus is *leisure (idleness)*, which I equated with *Play* in Maccoby and *Play in adults and free time* in Heller. Heller classifies needs in three groups (Table 3.3, first part): (1) Existential needs (numbers 1, 2, 3, 4: nutrition, sexual satisfaction, social contact and cooperation, and activity); (2) Properly human, non-alienated, needs (numbers 5, 6, 7, 8, 9, 10, 11, and 12: free time, cultural activity, play (in adults), reflection or meditation, friendship, love, self-realisation in objectivation and moral activity; (3) Properly human alienated needs (number 13: money, power, possession of more and more goods). She makes some interesting remarks in reference to each group. She says that *existential needs* are ontologically primary as they are based on the self-conservation instinct. Non-alienated properly human needs have a *qualitative character* and "are distinguished by the fact that in the desires, in the intentionalities directed to their objects, the natural drive plays no role". Their development is not distinguished by an infinite accumulation of useful objects, but by the evolution of their multilaterality that Marx referred as "wealth". On the contrary, she adds, alienated needs have a *quantitative character* where the process of accumulation is infinite. *And she points a very important element: "the infinite accumulation induced by quantitative (alienated) needs can only be hampered by the development of qualitative needs, by their progressive dominion"* (*op. cit.*, pp. 170–172).

Finally, the lower line in Table 3.3, first part, which contains the unmatched needs to Max-Neef's scheme, includes all authors and the number of entries is large. On the one hand, we can identify *autonomy* that is also included in the second part of the table: and *critical autonomy* present only in Doyal-Gough's scheme. The same happens with Maslow's *self-actualisation* and *esteem* needs and Nussbaum's capability *Affiliation B (social bases of respect)*. Heller's *sexual satisfaction* in this first part and the clearly related Maccoby's *pleasure* have no match in MNEAB's list. Nussbaum includes pleasure in her capability *senses, imagination, and thought*: "Being able to have *pleasurable experiences, and to avoid non-necessary pain*" (*ibid.* p. 79).

The list of unmatched needs in the first part of Table 3.3 also includes two capabilities: *environmental control* (political and material) – which refers to participation in political choices, property rights, and freedom to seek employment – and

Table 3.3 Second part. Comparative analysis of schemes of needs: Max-Neef et al., Fromm, Maccoby, and Deci-Ryan

Max-Neef's et al. (Needs)	*Fromm (needs)*	*Maccoby (value-drives)*	*Deci and Ryan (psychological needs)*
1. Subsistence	A. Instinctive (animal) needs	Survival	Biological (or non-psychological needs)
2. Protection	Instinctive needs; C. Rootedness	Survival	
3. Affection	B. Relatedness (intimate relations); C. Rootedness	Relatedness	Relatedness
4. Understanding	E. Frame of orientation/ devotion	Mastery, information; meaning	Competence
5. Participation	Relatedness	Relatedness	Relatedness
6. Idleness (leisure)		Play (7)	Competence
7. Creation (D)		Mastery	
8. Identity	F. Sense of identity		
9. Freedom			
10. No clear-cut association to Max-Neef needs	D. Transcendence	Pleasure Dignity (F)	Autonomy

other species. This capability is absent in all other schemes. From Malinowsky's scheme, I could not match two items with Max-Neef's list: *growth* (socialisation) and *movement or activity*. This last one is also present in Heller's list. For Marx, activity, in the form of work, understood as an activity directed to the satisfaction of needs through mediations, *is the most important human need*: man is an active being which satisfies his needs by the active deployment of his capacities (see Márkus, 1978).

Malinowsky's *reproduction* is an item surprisingly absent in all other schemes. Malinowsky clearly states it as a species need, as an unavoidable condition for the existence of the species ([1944] 1960, p. 92). Nussbaum includes "choice in matters of reproduction" under the capability *bodily integrity*; Maccoby (1988, p. 243) acknowledges the absence of this item in his list, and Doyal-Gough posit "safe childbearing" as an intermediate need, but reproduction/childbearing is absent.

Malinowsky also includes *growth* as a *need* referring to the conditions imposed by human's beings' life cycle (growing up, maturity, and decay) on culture, which matches no item in MNEAB's scheme. In particular, he states that "no group could survive, nor its culture endure if the infant, immediately after birth, were left to its own devices, as is the case in many animal species" (*ibid.* p. 93). The only additional reference to age-group needs is *security in childhood* posited by Doyal-Gough. Heller includes *play*, present also in Nussbaum's and Maccoby's list, which is a specific form of activity, and according to Fromm manifests the presence of surplus energy ([1947] 1990, pp. 186–187). *Play* is associated with *movement or activity* in Malinowsky's list.

I could not match five items in Heller's (1978) list with any in Max-Neef scheme: *sexual satisfaction*, *activity*, two *properly human non-alienated needs: self-realisation in objectivation* and *moral activity;* lastly her properly human *alienated needs:* money, power, and possession of more goods. She considers *Sexual satisfaction* as an existential need, associated with the survival instinct. In Heller (1976, p. 91), she argues that *free time*, although originally an *elemental need*, becomes in capitalism, according to Marx's view, a *radical need*: "Marx is convinced that from a certain point onwards capitalism is incapable of shortening labour time any further: the need for free time then becomes in principle *a radical need*, which can only be satisfied with the transcendence of capitalism". This need is related to Max-Neef *idleness*.

In Table 3.3, second part, I have compared the needs included in the schemes by Fromm and Ryan-Deci, as well as what Maccoby calls *value-drives* with Max-Neef et al.'s list. Among the important differences in their theories of needs are the following: (1) Fromm is the only which, as Marx-Márkus, derives his vision of human needs in a rigorous fashion from his conception of the human essence, characterised by the existential dichotomies. In an ultra-synthetic fashion one, could express Fromm's conception of the human essence saying that, having been expelled from nature the human being becomes homeless and faces a central existential dichotomy: *he wants to live but knows he is going to die*; his only way out is therefore to try to build a new home, a human world that replaces the natural home he has lost, for which he has to satisfy not only his *physiological or instinctive, animal, needs*, but also the *specifically human needs* which derive from that dichotomy. Maccoby does not formulate a conception of the human essence. His *value-drives*, which can be reinterpreted as *needs* (understood as forces that propel us and as the harm we want to avoid). Ryan and Deci (2017) have developed self-determination theory, described as "an empirically based perspective on development and wellness". Their approach is a very interesting attempt at bringing together important aspects of *humanist psychology* and *behavioural theory*. Their list of psychological needs only includes those that can be regarded as universal and is not linked to a conception of the human essence.

(2) In terms of the structure of the set of needs, Fromm regards all five (non-instinctive) needs (see Table 3.3, second part) as equally crucial, as in all of them *total failure* means insanity (madness).[12] One could say that for Fromm *these five needs are co-realisable* as the cost of total failure in the satisfaction of any of them means madness. Maccoby accepts with reticence a hierarchy between survival and the rest of value-drives as he accepts that *survival might become dominant when fear of lay-offs and unemployment* prevails. Both Fromm and Maccoby seem to accept, at least a two-tier hierarchy of needs, reducing their differences *vis à vis* Maslow. Deci and Ryan maintain (within their psychological needs) a similar position to the one by Fromm within existential needs: "Deprivation of any of these three [needs] leads to decrements in growth, integrity and wellness irrespective of individual or cultural values for them". But, at least in the case of autonomy and competence,

they go even further and postulate mutual interaction (or complementarity) between them: "Perceived competence, or mastery, without perceived autonomy is not enough because being a competent puppet does not nourish humanness. In such competence, the essence of life is missing. Strivings for competence and autonomy together are thus complementary growth forces" (Deci & Flaste, 1996, p. 71).

In Table 3.3 (second part), some consensus among our four authors is found. *First*, all authors identify physiological needs although they call them by different names (survival, instinctive and biological needs). None of them acknowledges what Marx-Márkus have termed the *humanisation of animal needs*.[13] Although neither of the other three (apart from Maslow) specifically mention protection needs, in Fromm it appears (implicitly) within the instinctive needs (the survival instinct which makes us run or fight in the face of danger) and explicitly in the need for rootedness. Maccoby explicitly mentions it under the survival drive-value. Deci and Ryan exclude this dimension, and this could be an important gap for a theory of psychological needs. *Second*, there is consensus in the *need of relations with other persons* (that Max-Neef et al. include in two needs *affection* and *participation*) and which we share with animals. This item reflects the greatest level of consensus as all four authors include it, three of them with the same word: *relatedness*. The fact that we share this need with animals might be problematic for Fromm's division into instinctual and existential needs (these latter assumed to be exclusively human). In the *third place*, I identify a certain consensus around the *understanding* of need although formulated in very different ways. The weakest formulation in this case is that by Deci and Ryan who do not include it, but I have interpreted that their *competence* need includes understanding. In Maccoby's case, I have classified three value-drives under this heading: *mastery* (close synonym of competence) *information* and *meaning* which are clearly closely associated with understanding.

There are items without or partial consensus. In Fromm, there is nothing that can be clearly associated with *leisure, creation,* and *freedom*. But Fromm's *transcendence* need is described as "man is driven by the urge to transcend the role of the creature … *by becoming a 'creator'*" (1955, p. 36). It seems that Fromm should have included creation as a need in his scheme. On the other hand, there is no item in MNEAB's scheme close to Fromm's *transcendence*, which they discussed but excluded arguing that it is not yet a universal need. I have associated with Max-Neef's *creation,* Maccoby's *mastery,* which is equivalent to Deci-Ryan's *competence*. But I haven't found any match to Maccoby's *pleasure* and *dignity* in MNEAB. Maccoby (1988, p. 64) says that "Pleasure is also developed aesthetically as good taste, a love of beauty, and a sense of harmony". Neither have I found any item in Max-Neef's scheme that matches Deci-Ryan's *autonomy.*

In Maccoby (1988), we find an almost entirely solitary need: *play* (only matched by Heller). But play clearly finds a counterpart in MNEAB's leisure. Neither Fromm nor Deci-Ryan attaches sufficient importance to the ludic dimension of life to classify it as a human need. Maccoby (1988, p. 68) highlights the importance of play saying that in its "most developed forms, play merges with mastery to become creative work …". By separating *pleasure* as an independent need, Maccoby gives it an importance which is absent in the other schemes.[14]

Final words

The precedent text shows that Max-Neef et al. contain very important contributions to the understanding of human needs and opens up possibilities for using this improved understanding to improve human well-being through progressive policies. The main purpose of the text, to analyse critically these contributions might help as well those who want to stand on the shoulders of Max-Neef et al. and continue advancing our comprehension of human needs as part of necessary work towards human flourishing for all.

Notes

1 The first four sections are a translation of Chapter 5 of my Ph. D. Dissertation, Boltvinik (2005).

2 I write "book" in quotation marks because it is a special issue of a journal. The English version was published in 1988. A larger version is available in English, which omits the names of the four last authors and has a different subtitle: *Conception, application and further reflections*, Apex Press, New York and London, 1991. This includes a new Second Part with two chapters by Max-Neef. They are good examples of his critical and witty mind but are outside the topic of this chapter. This edition also includes an addition to what in the Spanish edition is the Second Part called "Development and Human Needs". It is a text called "A Note on Methodology", which explains how to use the needs and satisfiers matrix as an instrument to promote change in a neighbourhood, a village, a city, a state, or a country. The methodology focuses on building a matrix of destructive satisfiers affecting the society to which the methodology is applied, as well as a matrix of how the society ought to be for them to feel really satisfied, i.e. their utopian matrix. I do not deal with this addition as it doesn't add to the conceptual issues about needs in MNEAB that I broach. I follow mainly the Spanish edition and have used my own translation to English which I constantly contrasted with the published one. Pages quoted are from the Spanish edition.

3 The authors do not present most of what follows as explicit postulates. However, since the structure of their text is unsystematic, it seemed necessary to reorder the material following another logic *while strictly respecting their ideas.*

4 Their assertion that hierarchical linearities cannot be established is a critique of Maslow's hierarchy of needs, which they replace with a system of needs without a hierarchy between them, in which, however, any unmet need acquires absolute urgency. It is an interesting idea, which however, cannot answer the following questions: When a person has all needs unmet, will any of them dominate his body, his thought, his motivation, his action? If so, which of them will be dominant?

5 *Ibid.* p. 34. If in the previous text one changes the term *potentiality* by *capacity*, the similarities with the conception of Marx, as interpreted by György Márkus (1978), are highlighted. For an account of Márkus' philosophical anthropology, see Julio Boltvinik "Marx's Theory of Prehistory", chapter 2 in S. Ray and S. Gupta (Eds.), *Probings and Re-probings. Essays in Marxian Reawakening*, Aakar Books, Delhi, 2021. MNESB presents here the only (or almost only) references to other authors in this part of their work, but they do so in very general terms: "Accessing the human being through needs allows us to build the bridge between a *philosophical anthropology* and a choice of politics and policies; such seemed to be the will that animated the intellectual efforts of Karl Marx and Abraham Maslow" (*Ibid.*).

6 The Spanish word translated as interacting is "estar", translated also as "being", repeating the translation of "ser". *Ser* is what is meant when one says, "I am human" (*structural* sense of being), whereas *estar* is what one means when one says "I am hungry"

(*circumstantial* sense of being). I will translate *ser* as *beingS*, and *estar* as *beingC*. In the English edition of MNEAB, *estar* is translated as *interacting*, far away from the meaning of "estar".

7 Indeed, later (p. 37) they point out that economic theory, from neoclassical to monetarist, avoids the term needs and refer only to preferences.

8 For a detailed analysis of Maslow's theory and a discussion of some criticisms to it, see Chapter 3 of my previously quoted Ph.D. Dissertation (endnote #1).

9 The Spanish Dictionary of the Real Academy (DRAE) includes, among the meanings of *potentiality*, (1) *capacity to* execute something or produce an effect; (2) in philosophy, passive capacity to receive the act; *capacity to become*. *Potentiality*, in one of its two meanings, is "potential capacity, *independent of the act*". *Capacity*, on the other hand, is "aptitude, talent, quality that disposes someone for the good exercise of something". It is clear, then, that potentiality and capacity are remarkably similar terms, although potentiality is broader since it means not only what a person can do, but what he/she can become.

10 By calling them *axiological*, the authors express their intention to emphasise the values or aims that one pursues in satisfying needs, rather than on the impulses behind them. But they do not elaborate this point.

11 The analysis in this section follows, to some extent, the one realised in Boltvinik (2020), except that in the present section, the scheme to which all other schemes are compared is the one by MNEAB, whereas in the referred book the pivotal scheme was Maslow's.

12 An important additional difference between Fromm and most other authors of theories of human need is the fact that Fromm conceives for each of his five non-instinctual needs a continuum from positive to negative ways of meeting the need. For instance, the sense of identity might be achieved by an advanced sense of individuality or, in the other extreme, by "herd conformity". The herd conformity way of meeting this need might explain why most people do not become insane: a negative way of meeting needs implies maintaining sanity.

13 Nevertheless, Maccoby separates eating in two parts, one included in survival and the other, which he calls *tasty food (and drinks)* under pleasure. Tasty food or eating for pleasure is a form of humanisation of the need for food.

14 Nevertheless, Fromm does indeed pay attention to pleasure and has written a wonderful text on pleasure and happiness (Fromm, [1947] 1990, pp. 172–197). In that text, Fromm develops the difference between *pleasure of abundance* and *pleasure of scarcity*. While the latter is mainly the relief of tension and is associated with satisfaction of physiological needs and *is a condition for happiness*, the first is associated with the realm of abundance which is essentially a human phenomenon and is *associated directly with happiness, with joy*. It is "the realm of productiveness, of inner activity", says Fromm (p. 187). "Happiness (joy) is proof of partial or total success in the art of living" (p. 191).

References

Boltvinik, J. (1984). Satisfacción desigual de las necesidades esenciales en México. In R. Cordera & C. Tello (Eds.), *La desigualdad en México*. Siglo XXI editores.

Boltvinik, J. (2004). Métodos de medición de la pobreza. Una tipología. Limitaciones de los métodos tradicionales y problemas de los combinados. In J. Boltvinik & A. Damián (Eds.), *La Pobreza en México y el mundo. Realidades y desafíos*. Siglo XXI Editores.

Boltvinik, J. (2005). *Ampliar la Mirad a, Un nuevo enfoque de la pobreza y el florecimiento humano*. Centro de Investigación y Estudios Superiores en Antropología Social-Occidente.

Boltvinik, J. (2008). Evaluación crítica del enfoque de 'capabilities' de Amartya Sen, Primera Parte. *Mundo Siglo XXI*, Revista del Centro de Investigaciones Económicas,

Administrativas y Sociales del Instituto Politécnico Nacional, 12: 43–55. Segunda Parte, 13: 19–41.
Boltvinik, J. (2020). *Pobreza y florecimiento humano. Una perspectiva radical*. Universidad Autónoma de Zacatecas y Editorial Ítaca.
Boltvinik, J. (2021). György Márkus memorial lecture. Marx's theory of prehistory. In S. Ray & S. Gupta (Eds.), *Probings and re-probings: Essays in Marxian reawakening*. Aakar Books. In Spanish in *Estudios Sociológicos*, 40(120), 2020, El Colegio de México. io de México.
Deci, E. L., & Flaste, R. (1996). *Why we do what we do. Understanding self-motivation*. Penguin Books.
Doyal, L., & Gough, I. (1991). *A theory of human need*. Macmillan. Spanish Edition: (1994), *Teoría de las necesidades humanas*. Icaria, Barcelona.
Fromm, E. (1955). *The sane society*. Henry Holt and Company.
Fromm, E. ([1947] 1990). *Man for himself: An inquiry into the psychology of ethics*. Henry Holt and Company.
Heller, A. (1976). *The theory of need in Marx*. Allison and Busby.
Heller, A. (1978). Teoría, praxis y necesidades humanas, Appendix in Agnes Heller, *Teoría de las Necesidades en Marx* (Theory of Needs in Marx). Ediciones Península.
Maccoby, M. (1988). *Why work: Leading the new generation*. Simon and Schuster.
Malinowsky, B. ([1944] 1960). *A scientific theory of culture and other essays*. Universidad de Oxford. Edition in Spanish (1981), *Una teoría científica de la cultura*. Edhasa, Mexico.
Márkus, G. (1978). *Marxism and anthropology. The concept of 'Human Essence' in the philosophy of Marx*. Modem-Verlag.
Maslow, A. (1943). A theory of human motivation. *Psychological Review*, *50*, 370–396.
Maslow, A. ([1954] 1987). *Motivation and personality*. Harper and Row. Spanish edition: (1991), *Motivación y personalidad*. Díaz Santos, Madrid.
Maslow, A. ([1968] 1999). *Toward a psychology of being*. John Wiley & Sons. Edición en español: ([1973] 1995), El hombre autorrealizado: Hacia una psicología del ser, prólogo de Richard Lowry, Kairós, Barcelona.
Max-Neef, M. (1991). *Human scale development. Conception, application and further reflection*. Apex.
Max-Neef, M., Elizalde, A., Hopenhayn, M., with the collaboration of Herrera, F., Zemelman, H., Jatobá, J., & Weinstein, L. (1986). Desarrollo a escala humana. Una opción para el futuro. *Development Dialogue*, Special issue, 1986, Cepaur and Foundation Dag Hammarskjöld, Santiago de Chile and Uppsala, Sweden.
Nussbaum, M. (2000). *Women and human development. The capabilities approach*. Cambridge University Press.
Ryan, R. R., & Deci, E. L. (2017). *Self-determination theory. Basic psychological needs in motivation, development and wellness*. The Guilford Press.

4 Understanding Max-Neef's model of human needs as a practical toolkit for supporting development work and societal transitions

Des Gasper[1]

Introduction

Manfred Max-Neef (1932–2019) is perhaps best known for his model of human needs, a system of linked categories that has served as a set of flexible and stimulating work-formats for many development analysts and practitioners around the world. The system was stated in the 1980s, relatively briefly, as a section of a 1986 manifesto in Spanish published as a special journal issue (Max-Neef et al., 1986), translated to English in 1989, and subsequently slightly elaborated in publications in English (e.g., Cruz et al., 2009; Max-Neef, 1991, 1992) and Spanish.[2] It became and continues to be quite frequently used across a range of contexts, as we see later.

The model contains at least the following aspects: first, a matrix of fundamental needs and diverse satisfiers, based on a number of propositions; second, a theorisation of satisfiers; third, a methodology for satisfier specification, for use in diagnosing current systems, sketching preferred alternative systems, and considering how to move from one towards the other. Boltvinik (2023, Chapter 3 in this volume) gives a detailed exposition and systematic assessment of issues under the first aspect and briefly refers to the second. He also interprets Max-Neef's work in relation to earlier and contemporary needs theories.[3] Different theorists have different purposes here, reflecting their different contexts, audiences, and ambitions. This chapter aims to give a fuller understanding of Max-Neef's model's specific context, purposes, and significance. It complements Boltvinik's analysis through attention also to the second and third aspects just mentioned (the theorisation of satisfiers and the system for satisfier specification, situation diagnosis and design of alternatives), to the purposes behind the enterprise, and to its diverse applications.

Part One of the chapter notes the context of emergence of Max-Neef's model. It arrived after his initial book on *Experiences in Barefoot Economics* (1982), as an instrument to pursue that book's agenda, and was presented as a section, co-written with Antonio Elizalde and Martin Hopenhayn, within a treatise on *Human Scale Development* (1986, 1989, 1991).[4] It continues in use 35 years later, now in a variety of settings.

Part Two locates the model in terms of different modes in needs theory: descriptive, explanatory, evaluative, prescriptive, and in relation to the corresponding understandings of needs as lacks or as potentials or as requirements or as

DOI: 10.4324/9781003381143-5

entitlements. It focuses on what is distinctive, and distinctively valuable, in the model and what is not distinctive. Max-Neef did not introduce the conception and specification of fundamental needs, nor the distinction between needs and satisfiers. He was especially influenced by work from the 1970s in Argentina and elsewhere, such as at the Bariloche Foundation by authors like Carlos Mallmann (1977a, 1977b, 1980), as well as by others in the 1985–86 project that generated the "Human Scale Development" book. That book's distinctive contribution was to enrich thinking about satisfiers by considering multiple existential modes and the impacts of satisfiers on multiple needs. As a practical man, Max-Neef looked not at concepts in isolation from life but instead at patterns of living, viewed as systems of needs, satisfiers, and goods. The concepts were practical tools, none of them perfect, but serving to look at life-situations actively, holistically, and creatively. Similarly, while he did not consistently distinguish between needs as drives or as desiderata, he was aware of the distinction and looked at both, confident that human needs as desiderata for living well could often at least potentially correspond to certain drives, which he therefore sought to promote and channel. His concepts of pseudo-, inhibitor-, and violator- satisfiers reflected an awareness however that drives can sometimes be misdirected or destructive.

Part Three of the chapter looks at intended and attainable functions of the various components of the model, conscious that it was intended for use in practical development work not in academic philosophy or psychology. It notes some of the range of applications, for diverse levels and topics; by Max-Neef himself and close collaborators, and by various recent authors not connected to Max-Neef or ecological economics.

Max-Neef was an activist, not a pure theoretician. He inspired much work by others. In that spirit, this chapter does not restrict itself to line-by-line examination of his texts and comparison with other texts but looks also at work that he inspired and that uses and extends his proposed tools.

Part One: Emergence of a tool for promoting local sustainable development

Max-Neef's Human Scale Development (HSD) approach, centred on understanding and promoting human needs fulfilment, was explicitly articulated in relation to dilemmas of development in Latin America and his advocacy of a self-reliant people-centred path rather than either state-led or market-led economic growth. It grew out of the disillusioning years as an economist working for international organisations, as described in the 1982 book subtitled *Experiences in Barefoot Economics* (Max-Neef, 1982, Preface). He looked for a human-centred reality-based approach, not the alienated and megalomaniac economics he had been trained in and had practised. Having rejected also the notions that poor people are ignorant, don't know their own problems, and need to be conscientised before any action is worth attempting (1982, pp. 30–31), he looked to horizontal communication between localities as a source of learning and critique, rather than to reliance on outsiders with often dangerously misconceived or unbalanced ideas. So he sought tools with which to encourage and support local analysis, communication, planning, and action. The 1982 book contained as yet, however, little use of needs language, and no needs model.

We might say that Max-Neef had become a Schumacherian Green, an advocate of "integral ecological humanism" (1982, p. 54), affiliated neither to conventional economics nor to Marxist alternatives (1982, Theoretical Interludes I & II). He had concluded that sustainability and social justice concerns could not be added as marginal refinements in existing forms of social organisation, for he saw those forms as being rooted in profoundly anthropocentric conceptions and in rule by dominant classes who are largely indifferent to the poor (1982, p. 45, 115ff.). The conceptions are flawed by blindness to the physical world, to waste production and entropy, and by resulting fantasies of endless economic growth. Required instead are fundamental alternatives, a "humanist eco anarchism" (1982, p. 55). "Anarchist" here meant radically decentralised and community-centred (1982, p. 56). His 1971–72 work in Ecuador had convinced him that this is possible – except perhaps politically; the Ecuadorian central authorities had intervened to stop the experiment because, in his view, of its success.

This ECU-28 Project in remote and extremely poor areas of NW Ecuador – its full name was "Planning of Zonal Programmes for the Modernization of Rural Life in the Andes" – planted seeds for his later model of needs. "Each community manifests a clear awareness of a number of problems affecting it, and its members express the felt need that the solution of these problems is often a matter of the greatest urgency" (1982, p. 64). But each locality thought only of its own situation, had no idea of shared problems and causes, and had no systems for cross-locality discussion. Max-Neef and his team proposed a bottom-up regional development planning process. Despite profound scepticism in advance from most officials and technicians, the 54 local situation reports prepared by local committees and checked by local consultations proved surprisingly rich and profound (1982, p. 70ff, "Wisdom unveiled"). Studying them was a humbling and transformative experience for the project staff, who prepared a book containing extracts and then a synthesis document: the Regional Felt Diagnosis. These were followed-up by extended consultations ("Encounters") in Quito in 1972, involving 300 peasant participants, that fostered a broader regional consciousness and a reasoned set of project proposals, not a pile of traditional village-specific petitions. Nineteen days of meetings led to six reports for each of three provinces, then a synthesising meeting involving a representative from each of the 54 self-studied localities. This produced a proto-regional plan and instituted a planning commission to proceed further. But next, counterforces within and via the new military regime blocked phase 2, arranged Max-Neef's expulsion from the country, confiscated all project documents, and demolished the institutions that the project had created.

The 1982 book describes also a second major generative project experience. In 1979–81, Max-Neef established and led a small team for revitalisation of Tiradentes, a historic small town in SE Brazil. The Argentinians Carlos Mallmann (1928–2020) and Oscar Nudler (1934–) were important advisers (1982, p. 125), and one can see needs theory themes emerging. "I should like to make the proposal, … that there are at least four functions expected of a city: it should provide its members with sociability, well-being, security and culture. Such functions can only be fulfilled as long as human communication between citizens is satisfactory and genuine, and participation is complete, responsible and effective" (Max-Neef, 1982, p. 134). Similarly, when reflecting on the relation between spaces and identity, Max-Neef prefigured his later adoption of identity as eighth axiological need.[5] He was greatly struck by the impact of a sub-project that mobilised households to contribute local photographs between 1880 and 1980 and that then exhibited them widely. He proposed that felt identity of persons is better built or safeguarded in small towns or in cities that contain systems of small localities having their own identities.

The 1982 book was looking for tools to advance autonomous local action, approaches that can mobilise especially the poor and the young, their energies, knowledges, and commitment.[6] It opposed elephantine standardised national or global programs (1982, pp. 203–204); "if national systems have learned to circumvent the poor, it is the turn of the poor to learn how to circumvent the national systems" (1982, p. 117). In 1982, Max-Neef did not yet use needs language. But major work on basic needs theory had been done in Argentina and elsewhere in the 1970s (see, e.g., Lederer et al., 1980; Mallmann, 1977a, 1977b), supported by for example the Bariloche Foundation, and Max-Neef encountered this (see, e.g., Guillén-Royo, 2016, p. 48). He became close to the Foundation and to Argentinian researchers, notably Mallmann and Nudler, from the late 1970s. They and others influenced the 1985–86 project co-funded by the Dag Hammarskjold Foundation that generated the 1986 *Human Scale Development* volume. Already by 1983, Max-Neef articulated his list of fundamental human needs.[7] It can be seen as a modification of Mallmann's lists (e.g., 1977a, pp. 8, 24; 1977b, p. 256). By 1986, he had emphatically adopted a needs approach in which he added a different way of working creatively with such a list, by recognition of a plurality of existential modes. This step took Max-Neef beyond Mallmann's work.[8]

Not surprisingly, the character of his needs model flowed from his bigger project. He considered, for example, needs both as lacks and as potentials or drives, stressing the mobilisation of "non-conventional resources" such as solidarity, commitment, knowledge and creativity, resources that are not depleted by use (1991, pp. 78–81) and are essential elements in HSD. Part Two will now elucidate distinctive features of the model and their roles in the overall project.

Part Two: Characteristics of Max-Neef's needs model

Elements of the model

I suggest seven main (sets of) elements or features of the model, in the list below. I add cross-references to Boltvinik's itemisation of elements (Boltvinik, 2023).

A Broad specification of needs: nine axiological categories (Boltvinik: #3, 5, 12)
B Needs as both lacks and potentials (Boltvinik: #6)

C A contrast between needs, satisfiers, and goods (Boltvinik: #2, 7, 8, 10, 12–13)
D Plural existential modes, which together with elements A and C generate the famous matrix
E Theory of satisfier types and interactions
F A methodology for using elements A–E in situation analysis and planning
G Stress on needs ideas as tools for examining an integral life-reality; "needs as a system" Boltvinik: #3)

Some important elements are not itemised by Boltvinik, notably from areas D, E, and especially F in my list, though he gives some attention later to area E, the theory of satisfier types. Within area F, the methodology for application, Max-Neef insisted that any needs model should be: (1) Understandable to the intended users, (2) Operational, (3) Critical (e.g., it helps to identify where candidate satisfiers don't work), (4) Propositional, and (5) Combine scope with specificity (1991, p. 29). He then proffered suggestions on how to fulfil these criteria.[9]

Many authors reproduce the matrix with all the illustrative satisfiers suggested in the 1986, 1989, 1991, and 1992 expositions; as could Max-Neef himself (e.g., Smith & Max-Neef, 2011, p. 143; see also Table 3.2 in this volume). However, he warned that the satisfiers mentioned in those expositions are merely illustrative. Thus, Guillén-Royo (2016, 2020) reproduces only the outline of the matrix, i.e., the titles row and titles column, since the matrix is intended for use as an exploratory tool for thinking and discussion, not for their inhibition. I do so too, slightly extended (Table 4.1).

Transcendence is added here provisionally. Max-Neef noted it (e.g., 1992, p. 203) but considered it had not yet sufficiently emerged to be included in the matrix. However, one might disagree with that judgement; further, for his sustainability agenda, transcendence values could be essential (cf. Chapter 12 in this volume).

Table 4.1 Matrix for discussion of fundamental human needs and possible satisfiers

		Existential categories			
		Being	*Having*	*Doing*	*Interacting*
Axiological categories	Subsistence				
	Protection				
	Affection				
	Understanding				
	Participation				
	Idleness/Recreation				
	Creation				
	Identity				
	Freedom				
	(Transcendence)				

What is distinctive in Max-Neef's model and what is not

The degree of originality and sources of attraction of Max-Neef's needs model are perhaps often partly misunderstood. Still, for nearly all the issues that we will discuss, the model appears to incorporate major relevant insights, whether or not original, and to use them in complex ways, enriching much.

Let us look in turn at the elements or areas, A through G.

A – *A broad specification of axiological needs* (i.e., types of fundamental value)[10] is not original and Max-Neef's is similar to Maslow's which included seven sets of needs.[11] Like Maslow, Max-Neef was careful to make his list of intermediate length: not crudely brief, but not so long as to be hard to remember and too unwieldy to function as a flexible and stimulating tool for thinking.[12]

A broad specification of needs helps us "escape the 'tyranny' of *economic* needs as the main measure of well-being" and the corresponding tyranny of economic growth criteria (Cardoso et al., 2021, p. 9; emphasis added). Stressing plurality and diversity of needs brings openness to basic realities of human existence, in contrast, for example, to the ridiculously impoverished treatment of work in conventional economic theory. "Work constitutes much more than a factor of production: it fosters creativity, mobilises social energy, preserves communal identity, deploys solidarity and utilises organisational experience and popular knowledge for the satisfaction of individual and collective needs" (Max-Neef, 1991, p. 77, cf. Gasper, 2009a).

The explicit broad specification of needs means that Max-Neef is more effective than, for example, Amartya Sen in describing and responding to "lack in the midst of [modern] abundance" (Regan, 2021, p. 274). Like nearly all writers on development ethics, he considered those people who are excluded or marginalised from the fruits of modernity, but also, like only some writers, the people who are not fully satisfied by that material abundance.

Many authors praise Max-Neef for departing from the model of prepotency associated with Maslow (e.g., Cardoso et al., 2021). However, Maslow himself always allowed for some co-occurrence of needs, prepotency is true to some extent, and Max-Neef too provided room for it. While psychological research has found much co-occurrence of felt needs, and little support for presence of five or more different stages or levels, it may suggest not just one level but two or three that contain different relative emphases (e.g., first on physiological and safety needs, later on affective needs, and then on other needs; Lea, 1987). Max-Neef acknowledged the priority of subsistence but noted that in fact for all needs there may be a threshold level below which there is intense preoccupation with the deficiency (1992, pp. 211–212). Consequently, one must not assume poor people are focused only on material subsistence; searches for meaning are important at all material levels of living, and arguably they are sometimes even more intense amongst the poor.

B – Needs as both lacks and potentials. In formal analysis of needs language, we must distinguish at least three modes: (1) Descriptive/explanatory usages – "Needs" as various sorts of positive entity, e.g., strongly felt wants or prepotent wants or the general drives that underlie wants and/or behaviour; (2) Instrumental usages – "Needs" as requisites for attaining an objective; and (as a subset of #2) (3) Evaluative/prescriptive usages – Needs as ethically approved requisites for attaining ethical priority objectives (Braybrooke, 1987; Doyal & Gough, 1991; Gasper, 1996a, 1996b, 2004, 2005, 2007, 2009b; Taylor, 1959). It is not clear whether Max-Neef used these distinctions consciously. Cardoso et al. (2021, p. 5) claim that: "In [Max-Neef's] framework, all interpretations coexist but some need our attention more than others at different times and places".

Max-Neef and his colleagues moved across this territory by talking of needs both as lacks and potentials.[13] On the latter: "to the degree that needs engage, motivate and mobilise people, they are a potential and eventually may become a resource" (Max-Neef, 1992, p. 201). Guillén-Royo argues that Max-Neef's model brings together both concerns: "Until the nineteen eighties human needs in international development had mainly been addressed either as motivations for action or as deprivations (Gasper, 1996a, 1996b; Jackson et al., 2004) [Modes 1 and 2/3 respectively]. Approaching human needs both as deprivation and potential, aligns with the democratic and empowering vocation of the HSD … [It brought a belief that needs could] stimulate creative strategies in the pursuit of their satisfaction both at the personal and group levels" (Guillén-Royo, 2016, p. 44). Such analyses were present already in 1970s "Basic Human Needs" discourse (e.g., Galtung, 1980; Green, 1978; Lederer et al., 1980), but we will see how HSD provided a format for seeking to activate them.

C – The needs-satisfiers distinction is not original to Max-Neef. It was emphatically stated by, for example, Galtung (1980) and Mallmann (1980), and was implicit in the work of Taylor (1959), Doyal and Gough (1984), Sen and others.[14] How Max-Neef discussed satisfiers is more distinctive though: as the ways that needs are expressed in a particular society, and as forms of activity to (seek to) express/actualise/fulfil needs. Economic goods are commodities that may be used in those forms of activity. He emphasised the trio needs-satisfiers-goods, not only the duo needs-satisfiers (e.g., 1992, p. 201–202), partly in order to show goods as only one type of satisfier, in contrast to in economic theory, and as in fact often pseudo-satisfiers.[15] Boltvinik (2021, p. 12) adds that a Satisfiers-Goods distinction works only sometimes. Indeed, all these distinctions are not universally applicable perfect blueprints but are instead imperfect tools to be applied situationally; and sometimes they must be multiply, recursively, used. When we try to order and understand complex life-situations then a single contrast (need versus satisfier) or even two (need versus satisfier versus good) will often not suffice.

Max-Neef's theory is perhaps more original and value-adding in regard to the following aspects.

D – *Plural existential modes, resulting in a matrix*. In the words of Cardoso et al. (2021, p. 9), the nine axiological needs each "manifest themselves differently according to four 'existential' categories: they may entail being in a certain state, having a certain asset, doing a certain action or interacting with a certain setting. These categories cover the spectrum of need satisfiers as emerging, respectively, from individual attributes, available economic goods, personal or collective agency and societal interaction, which come together and interact, …". In Max-Neef's own words "satisfiers are forms of Being, Having, Doing and Interacting, related to structures …" (1992, p. 204).[16] For readers who find this partly unclear or questionable, I suggest that the four existential categories can also be seen as suggestive prompts rather than as exact ontological building-blocks. The addition of the existential categories serves to bring us to a matrix not a list, allowing the treatment of satisfiers to become suitably rich. The use of a matrix makes people think and be more active in discussion.

An existential contrast between Being and Having brings to mind the thinking of Eric Fromm, amongst others. Balyejjusa (2017a, p. 8) compares Max-Neef's (1991) existential categories and Allardt's (1976) earlier basic needs classification (having, loving and being).[17] But in fact Allardt's list refers to types of axiological category, and Max-Neef's set of existential categories thus included instead Doing and Interacting. There has been discussion over the adequacy of the label "Interacting".[18] I would suggest though that the English word can open productive territory. One might perhaps also use "occurring" or "being situated", but the labels may not matter too much if the role is to serve as a discussion prompt.[19] Labels, and language in general, cannot be perfect; they serve to construct relevant contrasts through which we seek to somewhat better order complexity.

E, the *exploration of multiple types of satisfiers*, is very fertile and could well be original. It appeared a generation before the discovery of similar ideas by the political philosophers Jonathan Wolff and de-Shalit (2007), which were then circulated by Martha Nussbaum (2011). We discuss it in the next section.

F, *use of the needs model as a tool in group investigation* not as a revered academic construct. Max-Neef insisted on using tools accessible to ordinary people, regardless of any philosophical imperfections. In his Tiradentes project, for example: "A central preoccupation… was to find a way to secure the participation of children in the revitalisation process. It seemed to me that if children could be made to reveal freely their visions of society, of school, of authority, of work and of the worst, best and most likely futures, then the most fundamental and pressing problems of their society could be exposed in the purest possible way" (1982, p. 171). He hired an assistant to interview 107 children of ages from 7 to 12 and reported that the results were very illuminating. Cardoso et al. contrast theories for use by external observers and those for use by situation participants. Their own adaptation of Max-Neef for urbanism is "devised as a flexible roadmap able to be locally adapted by participatory communities and policymakers rather than a general model to apply analytically" (2021, p. 6).

G, *needs seen as a system*, is not original but is fundamental. Boltvinik (2021, p. 5) notes that we find both in Max-Neef and "Maslow the vision of the set of needs as a system (postulate 3). This is a positive trait and one which is present in very few authors". Perhaps another way of saying this is that the Max-Neef model treats needs-ideas as a set of complementary tools for looking at complex life realities, not as Platonic concepts. (He was an exponent and theorist of transdisciplinarity (2005) and his needs theory reflected that and tried to contribute to it.) As a result, when Cardoso et al. (2021, pp. 6–8) compare various approaches in terms of a set of desiderata for a needs theory, they suggest that the Max-Neef approach satisfies all the desiderata; for example, sensitivity to both objective and subjective conceptions of need.

Theorising satisfiers

Max-Neef presented five categories of satisfier: singular, synergic, inhibiting, pseudo, and violator. He provided many examples for each type (e.g., 1992, tables 7.2–7.6), with indication too of the needs that were being promoted, inhibited, violated, or only apparently promoted.

The last three categories can be discussed as a set of "negative satisfiers [,] that over-satisfy certain needs (*inhibiting*), [or] generate a false sense of satisfaction (*pseudo*-satisfiers) or eliminate the possibility of satisfying the need in question while reducing the possibility of meeting other needs (*violators*)" (Guillén-Royo, 2020, p. 116; italics added). Presumably "false" here means fleeting and/or unsustained, or later regretted. More fully: "the satisfiers that are often in place in societies that prioritise material production, such as competition, materialist values, consumerism and acquisition, are often considered by people participating in HSD workshops as pseudo or inhibiting satisfiers without synergic or needs fulfilling characteristics" (Guillén-Royo, 2016, p. 167). Max-Neef himself remarked that: "*Inhibiting* satisfiers are those which by the way in which they satisfy (generally over-satisfy) a given need seriously impair the possibility of satisfying other needs" (1992, p. 209); and that *violators* appear often to be misguided responses to needs for protection, that in fact undermine both protection and other values (1992, p. 208).[20]

These categories add to the toolbox of socioeconomics and ecological economics. Beyond ideas about the "externalities" impacts of one's consumption on other people, they help us to consider the impacts on ourselves and to understand the distinction between economic goods and genuine satisfiers. Economic goods are not automatically genuine satisfiers.[21] For example, "Contrary to common understandings of mobile phones, televisions, tablets, laptops, broadband, or Internet as 'necessities' or needs (Røpke 2003), ICT-related products are considered here as economic goods that [can] support [or inhibit or even violate] the role of satisfiers" (Guillén-Royo, 2020, p. 122). They can not only support fulfilment of important fundamental needs, but they can also support withdrawal from other people and foster persecution fantasies and hate speech, etc.

Singular satisfiers serve a single need, whereas *synergic* (or synergistic) satisfiers satisfy more than one need, without harming other needs (Guillén-Royo, 2020). Elsewhere Guillén-Royo adds that "synergic satisfiers [are] those that contribute positively to more than one human need *now and, in the future*" (2016, p. 66; italics added) and offers as an example "extensive cycle lanes in urban areas". Max-Neef saw identification of synergic satisfiers as key for HSD: "fundamental human needs can and must be realised from the outset and throughout the entire process of development. In this manner, the realisation of needs becomes, instead of a goal, the motor of development itself. This is possible only if the development strategy proves to be capable of stimulating the permanent generation of synergic satisfiers" (Max-Neef, 1991, p. 53). Use of the needs model is itself considered to be a synergic satisfier (1992, p. 201).

Gradually he came to see synergic satisfiers as central too for sustainability, HSD that respected following generations. In Guillén-Royo's words: "harmful satisfiers like consumerism have negative consequences both for people and the environment ... [whereas, in contrast,] synergic satisfier[s]...are sustainable as they cannot satisfy more than one need if they destroy or harm the natural environment. ... [So] by targeting human needs fulfilment and not economic growth, societies can progress towards [sustainability]. Societies need to provide the population with the means to identify synergic satisfiers and support their production and consumption..." (Guillén-Royo, 2016, p. 27).

Guillén-Royo adds a term (2016, p. 59): "*synergic bridging satisfiers* (those that would enable a society or community to transition from a situation dominated by harmful satisfiers to another characterised by synergic ones)". Workshop participants should be asked to seek these and to note those that must come from outside a particular community and those that can be mobilised from inside it. In her case studies, "Cooperating, sharing, exchanging, accepting, appreciating, integrating, restructuring, finding personal spaces and connecting with nature were ways of Doing describing the processes behind most synergic bridging satisfiers" (2016, p. 177).

Part Three: Using Max-Neef's needs model as an exploratory toolkit

I will note three types of use seen in recent literature. First, simple uses that employ the list of nine fundamental axiological needs to give more adequate pictures of the life-situations of the poor and marginalised. Second, use of all aspects of the model in the ways envisaged by Max-Neef to investigate and promote local development, preferably local sustainable development. Third, uses in new areas of policy evaluation and design.

Situation assessment/diagnosis of lives of the poor and marginalised

The format of the matrix of needs and satisfiers offers a manageable and vivid way of addressing complexity and interconnections in the lives of any group and in the systems encasing them. One sees it employed by various analysts to try to deal with this complexity, especially for groups who are particularly marginal and vulnerable. For example, Balyejjusa (2017b) analyses the felt well-being of Somali refugees in Kampala by reference to their perceptions of the fulfilment of their needs viewed in terms of Max-Neef's axiological categories.[22] Boshuijzen-van Burken et al. (2020) similarly consider the treatment of refugees in the Netherlands. Schenk et al. (2020) use the framework to look at the structural vulnerability of day labourers in South Africa.[23]

In all the cases mentioned, the role of ideas from Max-Neef appears to be to promote attention to multiple dimensions of life. Other frameworks could do this too, but Max-Neef's has an extra richness through its second dimension, the set of existential categories. Yet the studies mentioned above focus on the list of nine fundamental needs (the axiological categories) rather than the existential categories. For example, for Schenk et al. "*Max-Neef's matrix consisting of the finite nine Fundamental Human Needs (FHN)* was used to be able to conduct a multidimensional analysis and to order and describe the data" (2020, p. 144; italics added). In contrast, Max-Neef's own usage was more dynamic and change-oriented. As Boshuijzen-van Burken et al. themselves note, for example, in "order to emphasize that the poor are not mere passive receivers of development or charity, Max-Neef uses the term actualize instead of satisfy: you actualize your need for understanding when you take steps to find out what is going on" (2020, p. 171).

Local sustainable development: Using the model in participatory workshops

The 1989 English version of the HSD book contained a new section on using the model in participatory workshops (1989, pp. 40–43), which was then considerably enlarged in the 1991 book (pp. 39–49). This extended treatment used examples from Colombia (indicating a society dominated by fear), Britain (showing a plurality of poverties and unhappiness amidst overall material wealth), Sweden (a society of many lonely people), Bolivia, and Argentina. The model was seen to be operationalisable and able to generate unexpected insights.

As shown by those examples, Max-Neef advocated use of his needs model not only in localities but for analyses at regional and national levels too (1992, p. 211; Jolibert et al., 2014 is another example), and indeed even at global level. No doubt attempted uses at such levels produce new challenges. His 1991 book highlighted the ideas of Argentinian ecologist Gilberto Gallopin (1939–) which largely anticipated the core concepts and title of The Great Transition Initiative (GTI; Raskin et al., 2002) regarding possibilities for a global sustainability transition. Max-Neef insisted though that regional and higher level work must "recognize the primacy of local wishes and realities and [seek] to find ways of helping them to be realized" (1991, p. 214). He appeared closer to what the GTI calls an eco-communalist path rather than to its own eclectic proposed transition path.

Mónica Guillén-Royo's (2016) book surveys needs-centred HSD work from the following 25 years, covering desk uses as well as workshops. The "HSD approach to human needs has been drawn on by the transition town movement in Europe; it has inspired the ecovillage movement in Sweden and peasant associations in Latin America (Smith & Max-Neef, 2011)" (Guillén-Royo, 2016, p. 58).[24]

She proposes that, used as a workshop methodology, the model has "emerged as a flexible tool that could be used to reach many interlinked goals such as achieving a deeper understanding of specific development challenges; a greater engagement of people in social transformation processes; or an increased awareness of what was important in community development" (p. 59). Underpinning this greater engagement, such workshops are found to work against downwardly adapted preferences of resignation to poverty, injustice, and unsustainability, and to contribute to various forms of felt empowerment (pp. 49, 76). She confirms that the workshops can function as synergic satisfiers (Ch. 8). Reflecting on satisfiers, life-elements, and their relation to fundamental needs leads to more insight, including on the

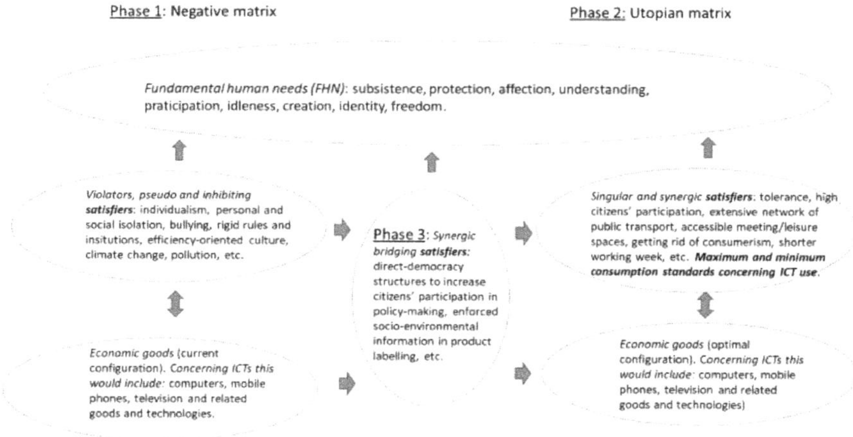

Figure 4.1 A fundamental human needs (FHN) perspective on sustainable consumption and ICTs

"well-being dividend" (how less GDP growth can bring both higher well-being and less environmental damage), more creativity, and more resolve.

The workshop methodology outlined by Max-Neef called for inputs from very many people. Guillén-Royo therefore developed a modified, simplified, more widely feasible version. A core idea is to focus on identifying "a set of satisfiers with synergic characteristics that can bridge [between] the negative and the utopian scenarios" that are produced in a workshop (pp. 65–66), in other words to show how to move from a diagnosed actual negative trajectory to a preferred path. Figure 4.1 makes clear the three-stage procedure (Guillén-Royo, 2020, p. 122).

Guillén-Royo follows up Max-Neef's idea that "the system of synergic satisfiers emerging from needs-based workshops unveils a supportive structure on which to base sustainable development policies" (2016, p. 6) and reviews experiences with preparing and using such analyses. To give an example, her 2010 workshops in Lleida (Catalonia) identified as one synergic bridging satisfier the rationalisation of daily schedules and timetables and the flexibilisation of work times (2016, pp. 84, 99). She concludes that "Through discussions on satisfiers, people deepen their exploration into the structures that define the functioning of their society and they come up with personal, collective and higher-level changes that have to be in place for the system to become better suited to satisfy needs" (2016, p. 75).[25]

Her book offers a synthesising case study from her work on relations between consumption and well-being in Lima, Peru. The HSD toolkit proved very useful, for four reasons which she suggests are widely applicable (pp. 175–176). First, people understood the language of needs, for it connects to everyday life. Second, Max-Neef's classification of satisfiers served well in helping people to explore their own lives and to consider how to improve them by searching for synergic satisfiers that serve more than one need. In particular, third, the search for violator, inhibitor, and synergic satisfiers gives people tools to think about interconnections and the socio-ecological systems in which they live. Fourth, not least, the notion of synergic satisfiers leads people into active concern for sustainability, to not damage their environment and hence their own need-fulfilment and that of others now and in the future. Overall, the HSD needs model helped for considering the plurality of needs, the variety of satisfiers, and the systems of interconnection that structure life-patterns.

Guillén-Royo's Chapter 6 discusses in detail workshop formats that combine HSD ideas with insights from sustainability-promotion approaches (e.g., The Natural Step framework and Theory U),[26] and studies that have used or adapted HSD methodology in order to address sustainability (e.g., Cuthill, 2003; Guillén-Royo, 2010; Jolibert et al., 2014). Her Chapter 7 summarises how HSD ideas are used by various sustainable communities; and notably "how different community initiatives such as eco-municipalities, ecovillages and the transition movement have linked to the fundamental needs approach of the HSD proposal" (2016, p. 126). She highlights the work of Inez Aponte with the Transition movement in the UK (https://transitionnetwork.org/) for sustained use of HSD ideas plus a major addition: "To the standard HSD approach, I added a fundamental condition for needs satisfaction: a Living Earth" (Aponte, 2016, p. 137).

Aponte (2016) notes that "Transition projects often intuitively meet many of the nine fundamental human needs in a synergic way" (p. 138), but that awareness of the HSD model can substantially improve this. "A Transition approach that worked consciously with the nine fundamental needs would quickly make it clear that action must take place on [all three of] the personal, community and global/state levels" (p. 140). She has used this approach with many hundreds of participants and found it fruitful. Many sustainability activists experience economics language as off-putting; whereas the language of human needs and satisfiers allows them to discuss the economy not in alienated monetised terms but more concretely.

Guillén-Royo (2020, p. 123 ff.) discusses also important limits of the HSD workshop format for sustainability analysis; for example, when combining groups with very different views, not only environmental activists. She suggests possible responses too. "One way of adapting the HSD methodology to reach [people's] 'inner dimension' when [participants] do not [already] have similar values or goals is to give them the opportunity to reflect on needs and satisfiers on a personal level before engaging in a collective discussion. This was the strategy followed by Jolibert and colleagues" (Guillén-Royo, 2016, p. 159).

Policy design

One finds a wide diversity of applications of the HSD needs model, even if most of Max-Neef's own work might be described as Small-is-Beautiful radical populism. His *Barefoot Economics* book declared that its "two basic leitmotivs are smallness and self-reliance" (1982, p. 19). The interest of the FHNs model appears not dependent though on adopting Max-Neef's philosophy. Salado and Nilchiani (2014), for example, adopt his needs concepts for design engineering. They consider that his list of fundamental needs can help engineers to generate more adequate specifications of requirements, to guide systems design, rather than only looking at assumed desirable design attributes or at the specifications in contracts.

Let us consider more fully two recent applications: one for urban design, and one for development policy design more broadly.

Designing and managing cities

Max-Neef largely focused on rural areas and towns. A generation or two later, in a now predominantly urbanised world, Cardoso et al. (2021) use his ideas for situation diagnosis and design engineering in regard to the challenges of city planning and management. The overwhelming predominance of economic measures of performance has brought a bias in urban studies and urban policy towards very large cities, and too little systematic attention to aspects of life other than the market economy. Max-Neef's model provides a usable framework to remedy this.

> ...we argue that, among several approaches to human needs, a suitable model which responds to the theoretical challenges of the [urbanism] discipline and can tackle the problem in cities already exists, namely the Human Scale Development theory of Max-Neef (1992). We highlight the nexus between the properties of this framework and the processes of human needs satisfaction in cities.
>
> (Cardoso et al., 2021, p. 4)[27]

Cardoso et al. admire the framework's effort to be comprehensive and systematic and yet at the same time manageable. Their paper outlines how to adapt and operationalise the framework "to assess and envision how cities may satisfy [or frustrate] human needs" (Cardoso et al., 2021, p. 4). They "'urbanise' the list of human needs" (p. 17), by identifying distinctively urban satisfiers and dissatisfiers, and then propose corresponding indicators.

Cardoso et al. are aware of other approaches to need-satisfaction in cities but after comparison suggest that Max-Neef's is superior.[28] They rely on his 1992 chapter in the remarkable edited collection *Real-Life Economics* that Paul Ekins and he produced, and appear unaware of his 1982 book that reflected on urban social systems. Although that book considered small towns not big cities, and did not yet articulate a needs language, its discussion of towns as living (and sometimes dying) social systems could enrich their work.

Designing development policies; counteracting "perspectivity"

Mahlert (2020) addresses metropolitan power-centres' overgeneralisations about and for other actors. She treats this danger by using Max-Neef's needs model and vocabulary, together with insights from functionalist theory in sociology and the theme of perspectivity: "the quality or condition of being limited by or confined to a particular mental perspective or point of view" (https://en.oxforddictionaries.com ' definition ' perspectivity).[29] She looks especially at overgeneralisations about democracy and civil society, and gives attention also to the complex influence of needs for identity and recognition.

> … this paper draws three features of satisfiers that can help dealing with three potential fallacies arising from perspectivity [i.e., framing], including (a) unduly narrowing down the range of conceivable means for achieving a goal; (b) depicting something as beneficial in itself by ignoring the potential variability of its context specific effects; (c) evaluating in dichotomic ways, i.e., seeing something in a rosy light only while regarding something else as exclusively deficient.
>
> (2020, p. 3)

The three features that she draws from Max-Neef's model to counteract these potential fallacies are his principles that, in Mahlert's words:

1 Satisfiers for the Same Needs Vary across Groups and over Time
2 A Candidate Satisfier Can Enable or Hamper the Fulfilment of a Need, Depending on Which Other Potential Satisfiers It Connects with
3 A Satisfier Can Simultaneously Fulfil Some Needs and Fail to Fulfil Other Needs, and This Holds Both for the Needs of One Person and of Different Groups (Mahlert, 2020, p. 6)

For example, regarding the second feature: "If a satisfier is 'transplanted' from one context into another it might interlink with different 'local' satisfiers and might hamper instead of fulfilling needs as a result. Therefore, this second feature of satisfiers can be a tool for discerning whether a policy framework reifies strategies as inherently beneficial, thereby drawing attention to its potential negative effects" (2020, p. 7).

Mahlert applies these insights in critiques of three international development reports: a regional Human Development Report (HDR) for Africa, "*Towards a food secure future*" (UNDP 2012); a global-level HDR on democracy, "*Deepening democracy in a fragmented world*" (UNDP 2002); and the final report to the UN Secretary-General by the Commission on Human Security (CHS 2003), "*Human Security Now*". The third fallacy – evaluating dichotomously: treating A as ideal in all ways and B as flawed in all ways – is seen in a recurrent idealisation of democracy and participation and often in an underestimation of "traditional" arrangements. "In the reports, this fallacy becomes manifest through [their] highlighting the merits of the proposed institutions (e.g., equal citizenship rights, 'accountable authorities'), while pointing [only] to weaknesses of 'traditional' institutions" (2020, p. 13) in overly simplistic fashion.[30]

Max-Neef himself thought hard about overgeneralised social science and policy discourses. In his remarks on "Fads and Biases in Development Discourse", he regretted "the feverish and obsessive doings of the technocrats who design solutions before having identified where the real problems lie… [and who] seek the justification of the models in the models themselves…" (1991, p. 12). Mahlert's article shows use of needs-satisfiers theory to investigate this concern and facilitate an alternative approach.

Conclusion

Max-Neef theorised with a pragmatic orientation and an insistence on the limits of theory. He did not become bewitched by words or imagine that there is one correct specification of needs. The *Human Scale Development* book bemoaned "the utilization of simplistic theories for the interpretation of social complexity, the impoverishment of our language" (1991, p. 94), and our enslavement by the language of mainstream economics. In reaction, he enriched needs theory as a counter-language, providing some tools to explore the complexity of life and to respond to it. As explained in Part Two of the chapter, the resultant needs model should not be treated as a reified doctrine. Instead, if used with emphases on Doing and Interacting, the examples noted in Part Three have suggested that it can serve us as itself a synergic satisfier.

Notes

1 I am grateful to participants in the Max-Neef book project of the Universidad Austral de Chile for stimulation and especially to Julio Boltvinik, Mònica Guillen-Royo, María del Valle Barrera, and Luis Valenzuela for detailed suggestions, and to Mirtha Muñiz Castillo for advice on translation from Spanish.
2 This chapter focuses not on the original version (1986 journal special issue in Spanish), but on the later versions in English (1991 book, 1992 chapter, 2009 article), precisely because they are later and since Max-Neef can be considered bilingual between English and Spanish. He had intensively studied and worked in English, including at Berkeley and for various international organizations, universities, and projects.
3 Including Karl Marx, Bronislaw Malinowski, Abraham Maslow, Eric Fromm, Agnes Heller, Michael Maccoby, Len Doyal and Ian Gough, Martha Nussbaum, and Edward Deci and Richard Ryan.
4 The 1986 and 1989 special issues listed Elizalde and Hopenhayn as second and third authors. For the expanded and amended 1991 book, they have a "with contributions by" status but are listed as full co-authors of the chapters on needs theory.
5 Max-Neef suggested "I am part (object/element) of a space that is my space, because as long as I contribute to its creation just by being present and make it definable through my presence, by being an element that, in it *is,* I attain and acquire identity" (1982, p. 140).
6 He later added (1992, p. 198): "The creation of a political order which can represent the needs and interests of a heterogeneous people is a challenge to both the state and civil society. The most pressing question, not only for a democratic state but also for a society based on a democratic culture, is how to respect and encourage diversity rather than control it. In this regard, development must nurture local spaces, facilitate micro-organizations and support the multiplicity of cultural matrixes comprising civil society".
7 See his acceptance speech for the Right Livelihood Award, https://rightlivelihood.org/speech/acceptance-speech-manfred-max-neef/. In addition to subsistence, "protection, affection, understanding, participation, leisure, creation, identity and freedom are extremely fundamental human needs". I am grateful to María del Valle Barrera for this reference.

8 Mallmann's (1977a, 1977b) papers contain matrices for types of need. The axiological categories are close to those in the model presented by Max Neef et al. in 1986 but the second dimension is "according to the means whereby they are principally satisfied" (1977b, p. 254), grouped under three headings: psycho-somatic, psycho-habitational, psycho-social. In Max-Neef's matrix, the specification of means/satisfiers is instead more fruitfully generated by the combination of the axiological type and the type of existential mode.

9 Boltvinik also specifies other, important but perhaps less central, elements. For example, his elements #14 and 15, that each inadequately satisfied fundamental human need represents a poverty and can generate pathologies; "poverties are not only poverties. Much more than that, each poverty generates pathologies" if it corresponds to a fundamental need (Max-Neef, 1991, pp. 18–19). Such pathologies can include "collective pathologies of fear" (p. 21).

10 Boltvinik, note 10: "By calling them axiological, the authors express their intention to emphasise the values or aims that one pursues in satisfying needs, rather than on the impulses behind them".

11 Julio Boltvinik (personal communication) notes that Maslow specified five sets of needs within his prepotency hierarchy and two sets of needs outside it: cognitive needs and aesthetic needs.

12 For comparisons with other needs theories see, besides Boltvinik's intensive analysis, Guillén-Royo (2016) which connects to the work of Amartya Sen and Martha Nussbaum. Sen's influential writings lack though an adequate treatment of needs theory (Gasper, 2020, section 5).

13 A lack is assessed by (1) a description of a situation, (2) a theory that states that this situation will lead to an outcome, which (3) is normatively judged as unacceptable, with reference to particular value(s) and a threshold. The threshold may be converted into (4) a prescription for public provision/guarantee. A potential, concerning a desirable outcome which can or will result from removal of a lack, is diagnosed in terms of an explanatory theory such as in (2). A potential might be understood instead as a (latent) drive, a motivating force that conduces to generate attempted action; often this action will correspond to a lack that the action attempts to lessen.

14 Mallmann (1980, pp. 37–38): "Satisfier: an element whose use or consumption human beings require in order not to become ill", i.e., in order to fulfil a need; "Need: generic requirement that all human beings have in order not to be ill". Paul Taylor (1923–2015), later a famous environmental ethicist, wrote a seminal 1959 paper on needs language that was clear on the distinction between two roles: (1) something-that-is-needed as a necessary means to the attainment of (2) a goal of a person who is said to have a need (1959, p. 107), although he did not use the term "satisfier" for (1). Braybrooke (1987 and earlier) likewise distinguished four levels: (1) Universal requirements, (2) Matters of universal need, (3) Derived needs (i.e., implications of 1 and 2 in specific contexts), (4) Specific forms of provision. See also, e.g., Wiggins (1987); Doyal and Gough (1991); Gasper (1996a, 1996b).

15 For example: "The speed of production and the diversification of objects have become ends in themselves and as such are no longer able to satisfy any need whatsoever. People have grown more dependent on this system of production but, at the same time, more alienated from it" (Max-Neef, 1992, p. 204).

16 Max-Neef (1992, 207 fn.): "The column of BEING registers attributes, personal or collective, that are expressed as nouns. The column of HAVING registers institutions, norms, mechanisms, tools (not in a material sense), laws, etc. that can be expressed in one or more words. The column of DOING registers actions, personal or collective, that can be expressed as verbs. The column of INTERACTING registers locations and milieus (as times and spaces). It stands for the Spanish ESTAR or the German BEFINDEN, in the sense of time and space. Since there is no corresponding word in English, INTERACTING was chosen *à faut de mieux*".

17 For Allardt (1993, p. 91), "loving" referred to "the need to relate to other people and to form social identities".

18 Boltvinik too considers the term "interacting" only an inferior equivalent for "estar" or "befinden". However, "interacting" alludes to the idea that every entity exists in a system of relations to other entities, existing-in-situ; and further, tools can evolve beyond the original intentions of their creators.

19 Cardoso et al. (2021, p. 18) call for work to explore how "the being-having-doing-interacting axis of our matrix closely relates to the distinction between the four qualities of life defined by [the prominent well-being researcher] Veenhoven (2000): (1) The attributes entailed in Being play a similar role in the set to that of the Satisfaction/Perception quadrant in the four qualities model. (2) The economic goods categorised in Having are related to the elements of the Liveability/Environment dimension. (3) The individual and collective actions of Doing have their parallel in the carriers of the Capability/Ability quadrant. (4) The societal relations and progress relevant for Interacting are implied in the Utility/Externality dimension of Veenhoven's matrix". Exploration and testing of these proposed equivalences might help deepen the HSD framework.

20 For example, in a series of workshops involving students, researchers, and other staff at the University of Oslo, in their matrix diagnosis of current situations "Participants discussed the use of ICTs... in connection with various negative satisfiers particularly detrimental to the needs for protection, affection, understanding, and freedom"; whereas "in the context of the utopian matrix [showing a desired future], ICT use emerged as [potentially] enabling singular and synergic satisfiers" (Guillén-Royo, 2020, p. 121).

21 "Economic goods" refers here to commodities that may be physical goods or services or a combination.

22 In contrast, Glasman's (2020) book on humanitarianism and needs ignores Max-Neef and seems focused only on deficiency needs in regard to subsistence.

23 Schenk et al. link Max-Neef's concepts to the notion of structural vulnerability as articulated by Du Toit (2005), seen as "embedded in the social, political and economic organisation of a society, with the result that it will be extremely difficult for the person to escape poverty. The person will be unemployed, without any income, without any assets and thus very little social capital. The structurally vulnerable will also be exposed to unequal power relationships, social injustices, marginalisation and restrictive policy frameworks" (Schenk et al., 2020, p. 144).

24 See also Spiering and del Valle Barrera (2020, 2021) for two other wide-ranging discussions of using and extending the HSD methodology.

25 Later she proposes "the concept of 'necessary' synergic satisfiers, those that seem to be present in societies or communities where needs are optimally actualised and the negative environmental impacts of human activity minimised" (p. 126). E.g., under "Being": inner strength and authenticity (p. 142); and "participatory conflict resolution schemes, volunteering, cooperating and direct experience of nature are put forward as [other] examples of interdependent necessary synergic satisfiers" (p. 146).

26 See: https://thenaturalstep.org/approach/ and Scharmer (2016).

27 To see the "nexus" proposal, see Cardoso et al. (2021, p. 10, table 1).

28 Cardoso et al. (2021, p. 8) propose: "Moving beyond the limitations of the still-popular 'pyramid' approach and its offspring, as well as from some existing approaches discussed earlier which we see as too specific and normative, we argue that a good candidate is the human needs framework by the Chilean economist Manfred Max-Neef".

29 We can perhaps equally speak of "framing". For Mahlert herself defines "Perspectivity... as the phenomenon of perceiving the empirical world through pre-established interpretative frameworks that are shaped by the social contexts in which they are employed and/or have been created and modified" (2020, p. 4).

30 For a similar earlier discussion, see Gasper (1996b).

References

Allardt, E. (1976). Dimensions of welfare in a comparative Scandinavian study. *Acta Sociologica, 17*, 227–239. https://doi.org/10.1177/000169937601900302

Allardt, E. (1993). Having, loving, being: An alternative to the Swedish model of welfare research. In M. Nussbaum & A. Sen (Eds.), *The quality of life* (pp. 88–94). Clarendon.

Aponte, I. (2016). Fundamental human needs and the transition movement. In M. Guillen-Royo (Ed.), *Sustainability and wellbeing: Human-scale development in practice* (pp. 137–141). Routledge.

Balyejjusa, M. (2017a). *Human needs and human wellbeing: Some evidence from Somali refugees, Kampala* [Working Paper]. Uganda Christian University.

Balyejjusa, M. (2017b). The wellbeing of Somali refugees in Kampala: Perceived satisfaction of their human needs. *Journal of Science & Sustainable Development, 6*(1), 94–111. https://doi.org/10.4314/jssd.v6i1.6

Boltvinik, J. (2023). On the contributions of Max-Neef et al. to the theory of human needs. Chapter 3 in this volume.

Boshuijzen - van Burken, C., Goede, R., & van Niekerk, A. (2020). Reflections on the Humanitarian Logistics for Refugees in the Netherlands from Three Perspectives: Maslow, Max-Neef, and Dooyeweerd. *Philosophia Reformata*. 85. 157–180. 10.1163/23528230-8502A004.

Boshuijzen-van Burken, C., Goede, R., & van, N. (2020). Reflections on the humanitarian logistics for refugees in the Netherlands from three perspectives: Maslow, Max-Neef, and Dooyeweerd. *Philosophia Reformata, 85*, 157–180.

Boshuijzen-Van, B. Goede, R., & van N. (2020). Reflections on the humanitarian logistics for refugees in the Netherlands from three perspectives: Maslow Max-Neef and dooyeweerd. *Philosophia Reformata, 85*(2), 157–180. https://doi.org/10.1163/23528230-8502A004

Braybrooke, D. (1987). *Meeting needs*. Princeton University Press.

Cardoso, R., Sobhani, A., & Meijers, E. (2021). The cities we need: Towards an urbanism guided by human needs satisfaction. *Urban Studies, 59*(13), 2638–2659 *(20211007)*. https://doi.org/10.1177/00420980211045571

Cruz, I., Stahel, A., & Max-Neef, M. (2009). Towards a systemic development approach: Building on the human-scale development paradigm. *Ecological Economics, 68*(7), 2021–2030. https://doi.org/10.1016/j.ecolecon.2009.02.004

Cuthill, M. (2003). From here to utopia: Running a human-scale development workshop on the Gold Coast, Australia. *Local Environment, 8*(4), 471–485. https://doi.org/10.1080/13549830306666

Doyal, L., & Gough, D. (1984). A theory of human needs. *Critical Social Policy, 4*(1), 6–38. https://doi-org.eur.idm.oclc.org/10.1177/026101838400401002

Doyal, L., & Gough, D. (1991). *A theory of human need*. Macmillan.

Du Toit, A. (2005). *Chronic and Structural Poverty in South Africa: Challenges for Action and Research* (University of the Western Cape (UWC), Programme for Land and Agrarian Studies (PLAAS) Working Paper 6).

Galtung, J. (1980). The basic needs approach. In K. Lederer, J. Galtung, & D. Antal (Eds.), *Human needs: A contribution to the current debate* (pp. 55–125). Oelgeschlager Gunn & Hain.

Gasper, D. (1996a). Needs and basic needs – A clarification of foundational concepts for development ethics and policy. In G. Köhler & C. Gore (Eds.), *Questioning development* (pp. 71–101). Metropolis. Also: Working Paper 210, Institute of Social Studies, The Hague. http://repub.eur.nl/res/pub/18952/

Gasper, D. (1996b). Essentialism in and about development discourse. *European Journal of Development Research, 11*(2), 149–176. https://doi.org/10.1177/1049732312468251
Gasper, D. (2004). *The ethics of development – From economism to human development.* Edinburgh University Press.
Gasper, D. (2005). Needs and human rights. In R. Smith & C. van den Anker (Eds.), *The essentials of human rights* (pp. 269–272), Hodder & Stoughton.
Gasper, D. (2007) Conceptualising human needs and wellbeing. In I. Gough & J. A. MacGregor (Eds.), *Wellbeing in developing countries: New approaches and research strategies* (pp. 47–70), Cambridge University Press.
Gasper, D. (2009a): Capitalism and human flourishing? – The strange story of the bias to activity and the downgrading of work. In J. B. Davis (Ed.), *Global social economy – Development, work and policy* (pp. 13–41), Routledge. Also: Working Paper 469, Institute of Social Studies, The Hague, http://repub.eur.nl/res/pub/18724. Based on the keynote address, 12th World Congress for Social Economics, University of Amsterdam, June 2007.
Gasper, D. (2009b). Chapter 46: Human needs and wellbeing. In J. Peil & I. van Staveren (Eds.), *Handbook of economics and ethics* (pp. 348–357). Edward Elgar. http://repub.eur.nl/res/pub/17959/
Gasper, D. (2020). Human development thinking about climate change requires a human rights agenda and an ontology of shared human security. In A. Crabtree (Ed.), *Sustainability, capabilities and human security* (pp. 135–168). Palgrave Macmillan. https://link.springer.com/book/10.1007/978-3-030-38905-5
Glasman, J. (2020). *Humanitarianism and the quantification of human needs*. Routledge.
Green, R. H. (1978). Basic human needs: Concept or slogan, synthesis or smokescreen? *IDS Bulletin, 9*(4), 7–11. https://doi.org/10.1177/1049732312468251
Guillén-Royo, M. (2010). Realizing the 'wellbeing dividend': An exploratory study using the human scale development approach. *Ecological Economics, 70*(2), 384–393. https://doi.org/10.1016/j.ecolecon.2010.09.010
Guillén-Royo, M. (2016). *Sustainability and wellbeing: Human scale development in practice*. Routledge.
Guillén-Royo, M. (2020). Applying the fundamental human needs approach to sustainable consumption corridors: Participatory workshops involving information and communication technologies. *Sustainability: Science, Practice and Policy, 16*(1), 114–127. https://doi.org/10.1080/15487733.2020.1787311
Jackson, T., Wander, J., & Stagl, S. (2004). *Beyond Insatiability: Needs Theory, Consumption, and Sustainability* (Working Paper Series, 2004/2), Centre for Environmental Strategy, University of Surrey.
Jolibert, C., Paavola, J., & Rauschmayer, F. (2014). Addressing needs in the search for sustainable development: A proposal for needs-based scenario building. *Environmental Values, 23*, 29–50. https://doi.org/10.3197/096327114X13851122269007
Lea, S. (1987). *The individual in the economy: A survey of economic psychology*. Cambridge University Press.
Lederer, K., Galtung, J., & Antal, D. (1980). *Human needs a contribution to the current debate*. Oelgeschlager Gunn & Hain.
Mahlert, B. (2020). Needs and satisfiers: A tool for dealing with perspectivity in policy analysis. *European Journal of Development Research*. https://doi.org/10.1057/s41287-020-00294-9
Mallmann, C. (1977a). *Holistic Knowledge and Research Priorities* (Paper for UNESCO programme on 'Investigacion y necesidades humanas'). http://accmallmann.org/pdfs/documentos-cm-y-sus-colaboradores/1977-Mallmann-Research-priorities-and-holistic-knowledge-SPA.pdf

Mallmann, C. (1977b). Moving toward synergy. *Impact of Science on Society*, 27(3), 253–258. UNESCO: Paris. https://unesdoc.unesco.org/ark:/48223/pf0000023052.nameddest=23052

Mallmann, C. (1980). Society, needs, and rights: A systemic approach. In K. Lederer (Eds.), *Human needs: A contribution to the current debate* (pp. 37–54). Oelgeschlager, Gunn and Hain Publishers.

Max-Neef, M. (1982). *From the outside looking in experiences in barefoot economics*. Dag Hammarskjold Foundation. The edition cited here was published by Zed Books, London, 1992. http://www.daghammarskjold.se/wp-content/uploads/2014/08/From_the_outside_looking_in.pdf

Max-Neef, M. (1991). *Human scale development: Conception, application, and further reflections*. Apex Press. With contributions from A. Elizalde, M. Hopenhayn.

Max-Neef, M. (1992). Development and human needs. In P. Ekins & M. Max-Neef (Eds.), *Real-life economics*. Routledge.

Max-Neef, M. (2005). Foundations of transdisciplinarity. *Ecological Economics*, *53*, 5–16. https://doi.org/10.1016/j.ecolecon.2005.01.014

Max-Neef, M., Elizalde, A., & Hopenhayn, M. (1986). Desarrollo a escala humana. Una opción para el futuro. *Development Dialogue,* Special issue, 1986.

Max-Neef, M., Elizalde, A., & Hopenhayn, M. (1989). Human scale development: An option for the future. Special section of *Development Dialogue*, 1989(1), 5–81.

Nussbaum, M. (2011). *Creating capabilities*. Harvard University Press.

Raskin, P., Banuri, T., Gallopín, G., Gutman, P., Hammond, A., Kates, R., & Swart, R. (2002). *Great transition: The promise and the lure of the times ahead*. Stockholm Environment Institute and Tellus Institute.

Regan, M. R. G. (2021). Treading between joy and grief: *Gaudium et Spes*, Louis-Joseph Lebret, and the challenge of modernity. *Journal of Global Ethics*, *17*(2), 243–259. https://doi.org/10.1080/17449626.2021.1958903

Salado, A., & Nilchiani, R. (2014). A categorization model of requirements based on Max-Neef's model of human needs. *Systems Engineering*, *17*(2), 348–360. https://doi.org/10.1002/sys.21274

Scharmer, C. O. (2016). *Theory U: Leading from the future as it emerges* (2nd ed.). Society for Organizational Learning.

Schenk, R., Blaauw, D., & Mathee, M. (2020). Max-Neef en die strukturele kwesbaarheid van dagloners in Mbombela en Emalahleni, Suid-Afrika (Max-Neef and the structural vulnerability of day labourers in Mbombela and Emalahleni, South Africa). *Tydskrif vir Geesteswetenskappe*, *60*(1), 142–163. https://doi.org/10.17159/2224-7912/2020/v60n1a11

Smith, P. B., & Max-Neef, M. (2011). *Economics unmasked*. Green Books.

Spiering, S., & Barrera, M. (2020). *How to? Practical knowledge for transformative science – Facilitation guidelines for two applications of the human scale development approach*. https://www.ufz.de/export/data/global/240323_DP_3_2020_SpieringBarrera.pdf

Spiering, S., & Barrera, M. (2021). Testing the quality of transformative science methods: The example of the human scale development approach. *Sustainability Science*, *16*, 439–457. https://doi.org/10.1007/s11625-021-00966-3

Taylor, P. (1959). "Need" statements. *Analysis*, *19*(5), 106–111. https://doi.org/10.2307/3326899

Veenhoven, R. (2000). The four qualities of life. *Journal of Happiness Studies*, *1*(1), 1–39. https://doi.org/10.1177/1049732312468251

Wiggins, D. (1987). *Needs, values, and truth*. Oxford University Press.

Wolff, J., & de-Shalit, A. (2007). *Disadvantage*. Oxford University Press.

5 A new development paradigm based on happiness and well-being

Max-Neef's contributions for building a better world

Wenceslao Unanue

Introduction

I feel extremely grateful. I met Manfred Max-Neef personally. Max-Neef was an exceptional man, blessed with key scientific and human qualities. I would like to highlight three of them. First, he knew different disciplines and fields and was able to integrate them in solid conceptual frameworks. Second, his high critical thinking allowed him to question the world and the prevailing views on it. Max-Neef's vision and intuition also allowed him to anticipate social changes several decades before renowned international organisations, academics from the broadest spectrum, governments and civil society did. For example, despite the fact that he was not the first researcher exploring "the limits to grow" (Meadows et al., 2013), Max-Neef made important contributions to *ecological economy* at the time when the field was hardly understood. Only in recent years have we begun to realise that the paradigm of "unlimited growth" is impossible on a planet with finite resources (Stiglitz et al., 2010) and that the indiscriminate use of resources makes incompatible human happiness and environment conservation (Crompton & Kasser, 2009). Human beings, according to Max-Neef, should achieve a state of harmony and build a new relationship with nature. Otherwise, we would go directly into a "collision" that will put on risk the future of the planet (Max-Neef et al., 1991; Smith & Max-Neef, 2012). Third, Max-Neef tended to propose novel solutions to the problems he was detecting. For instance, he was one of the first economists who introduced the concept and spoke about the importance of *compassion* for building a better and more sustainable world (Smith & Max-Neef, 2012). Indeed, as Max-Neef claimed, compassion has been found to be not only a central determinant of altruistic behaviour but also a fundamental element of individual and societal quality of life (Fuders & Nowak, 2019; Ricard, 2015).

The need for a new development paradigm

The storm is coming: The world on a collision course

There is strong consensus that during the last decades, we have witnessed unimaginable progress in various areas of development (income, health, technology, consumption etc.), which has improved the quality of life of millions of the world's

DOI: 10.4324/9781003381143-6

inhabitants (Sachs, 2012). However, it has also become strongly recognised that this progress has reached only a few people, and that the majority belong to the so-called developed world (NDP, 2013; Royal Government of Bhutan, 2012).

Serious problems of poverty, inequalities, mental health and environmental sustainability are putting our planet at risk. Indeed, we are living in times of enormous contradictions, and the world is now at a "crossroads" (Royal Government of Bhutan, 2012, p. 92). Our current model of development, mainly based on economic growth and income, has reached its limits: focusing excessively on gross domestic product (GDP) as a measure of progress and consumption has led the world to unsustainable ecological, social and economic crises. Unfortunately, humanity is facing several major challenges (Unanue, 2014a, 2014b):

First, poverty. We are facing an unacceptable number of humans living in poverty and misery. According to the World Bank (2022a), 685 million people were living in extreme poverty (i.e., living on less than US$1.90 per day) by 2022. Even worse, several global problems (the negative effects of the Covid-19 pandemic, rising food and energy prices, conflicts such as the war in Ukraine etc.) have led to project that 7% of the world's population (approximately 574 million people) will be still living in extreme poverty by 2030 (World Bank, 2022a).

Second, inequalities. According to the World Bank (2022b, p. 27), "the world is marked by a very high level of income inequality and an extreme level of wealth inequality". For example, in terms of income distribution, the global bottom 50% captures a very small share of 8% of the global income, whereas the global top 10% earns 52% of the total income. In terms of the global wealth distribution, the situation looks even worse. For example, "the poorest half of the world population owns just 2% of total net wealth, whereas the richest half owns 98% of all the wealth on earth" (World Bank, 2022b, p. 27).

Despite previous data, research has consistently shown that higher economic inequalities are associated with a whole range of health and social problems, such as higher rates of homicide, teenage births, obesity and mental illness, as well as lower rates of trust, children's well-being and life expectancies (Unanue, 2014a, 2014b; Wilkinson & Pickett, 2011). Importantly, reducing inequalities is central to building better lives and more sustainable societies, and to overcome poverty. For example, "simulations suggest that an increase of just 1% in within-country inequality would result in 32 million people living on less than $1.90 a day in 2021" (World Bank, 2022c).

Third, mental health. Economic progress and affluence have created their own disorders, increasing the prevalence of several mental and physical health problems. Overconsumption and materialism have put enormous pressure on the health of the population, resulting in the appearance of psychiatric and psychosomatic symptoms, such as unprecedented increases in the rates of obesity, stress, depression, suicide, alcoholism, drug addiction, anxiety and self-medication (Kasser, 2016; Sachs, 2012; Unanue, 2014a, 2014b).

Fourth, climate change and global warming. The environmental crisis has become one of the hardest challenges for the 21st century. Overproduction and overconsumption have played a crucial role in the current environmental crisis, reducing the possibilities of well-being for current and future generations (IPCC, 2022; Sachs, 2012). Indeed, the most recent report on climate change developed by the International Panel on Climate Change "provides a framework for understanding the increasingly severe, interconnected and often irreversible impacts of climate change on ecosystems, biodiversity, and human systems; differing impacts across regions, sectors and communities; and how to best reduce adverse consequences for current and future generations" (IPCC, 2022, p. 7). The report also recognised the negative impact already introduced by humans and identified 127 key risks for the planet and all life on Earth. ¡We need to act now!

The roots of the coming collision

International organisations, such as the United Nations, have recognised the urgency for tackling the problems that are leading us to the mentioned collision. Interestingly, United Nations (2011) has also recognised that part of the reasons and origins of the problems are rooted in the way in which we have been understanding and measuring "progress" and well-being. That is because we have been living with an economic system where its "golden standard" of progress is the growth of GDP, or the so-called economic growth. Indeed, economic growth is constantly used by countries as the main measure of social progress. Human beings and public policies have taken it as a back seat (UN, 2011). As a consequence, we have a strong desire to promote unlimited economic growth on a planet that, as we already know, has finite resources (IPCC, 2022; Sachs, 2012). However, despite the popularity of this view, it has been extensively questioned in recent times. To assume that rising GDP in turn always leads to higher well-being (or even happiness) is wrong (Easterlin et al., 2010; Stiglitz et al., 2010; UN, 2011). For instance, even though current GDP per capita in the United States is more than three times higher than it was in the 1960s, the satisfaction with the average life of Americans (a key indicator of happiness and well-being) has remained almost constant during the last 50 years (Sachs, 2012). One of the most revolutionary and challenging concepts regarding this paradigm has been proposed by Richard Easterlin and his famous paradox (see Easterlin et al., 2010). The authors have consistently found that the positive relationship between happiness and income only occurs in the short term, and never in the long run (see Gasper, 2007 for alternative views). More evidence can also be found in Diener and Oishi (2000) and Myers (2000). Additional limitations of GDP as a measure of progress and well-being may be found in Diener et al. (2009), Stiglitz et al. (2010) and Unanue et al. (2017a, 2017b).

In short, our current development model has led us to an unsustainable ecological, social and economic crisis (NDP, 2013; Royal Government of Bhutan, 2012; Unanue, 2014a, 2014b). Thus, the challenge and the solution to our problems could go through rethinking and redefining what is important in our lives. Following UN (2011), a new model of development should focus on happiness and well-being instead of on economic growth, money and materialism.

Max-Neef's prediction about the collision

Only recently, the World Bank (2022d) stated that "Climate change, poverty, and inequality are the defining issues of our age". Yet, Max-Neef not only anticipated these and other key problems several years ago. For example, he spoke about the exponential increase in climate change, the end of cheap energy, the exhaustive depletion of key resources for well-being (drinking water, soil, energy diversity etc.) and a gigantic speculative bubble. As causes of these problems, Max-Neef highlighted the excessive focus on GDP, the promotion of consumerism as a pathway to happiness, the annihilation of traditional cultures, ignorance of planetary limits and overpopulation (Smith & Max-Neef, 2012). For Max-Neef, we were facing not only an economic and environmental crisis but also a crisis of humanity. He suggested that we must urgently move from "efficiency" to "well-being" and replace the dominant values of greed, competition and materialism with solidarity, cooperation and compassion (Smith & Max-Neef, 2012), which are key dimensions of happiness and the NDP (2013) – to be discussed later on.

Can we avoid the collision? Happiness as part of the solution

Nowadays, there is a growing consensus on the need and urgency for a new model of development which will help to protect the future of our natural environment, as well as reduce poverty and inequalities, decrease mental and physical health problems and enable people to be happier and flourish. In fact, as stated by the former Secretary-General of the United Nations, the old model is broken; thus, we need to create a new one. Furthermore, it is time to recognise that we need to change our lifestyles to move towards a model of sustainable development: a sustainable model of development with a main focus on the happiness of all life on Earth (Ki-moon, 2012; Royal Government of Bhutan, 2012).

Following previous arguments, several international organisations have supported the proposal of using happiness indicators to complement the information provided by GDP (Diener et al., 2009; Helliwell et al., 2012; Layard, 2011; OECD 2022; Stiglitz et al., 2010; UN, 2011). Just as an example, Stiglitz et al. made a specific call to incorporate measures of happiness and well-being when assessing the progress of nations given that so far, we have been mismeasuring our lives (2010).

Why does happiness matter? Recent research has shown that sustainable development is closely linked to happiness (Layard, 2011; Layard et al., 2012; Unanue, 2014a, 2014b; Unanue et al., 2017a, 2017b). As we will discuss in detail later, happiness has been conceptualised mainly from two approaches: hedonic and the eudaimonic views. Whereas the hedonic view understands happiness as the presence of pleasure and the absence of pain, the eudaimonic view argues that happiness is far more than only pleasure and conceptualises it as the optimal human functioning through, for example, the actualisation of human potentials (Ryan & Deci, 2001). From a hedonic perspective, Diener and Tay (2017) conducted an extensive review of correlational, longitudinal and experimental studies into the link between happiness and several individual and societal outcomes. The authors found that higher levels of happiness lead individuals to become healthier, to live longer, to follow good health practices and to function better. In addition, higher levels of happiness would also lead people to become more sociable, friendlier and more cooperative. Moreover, people scoring higher in happiness would have better social relationships, higher levels of trust and community involvement, and greater willingness to support people in need. Therefore, happier people are more likely to fight harder against poverty and inequalities, to have better physical and mental health and to protect their communities. In addition, happiness tends to be associated with higher environmentally responsible behaviour, which shows that happiness and sustainability may be complementary (Kasser, 2017). From a eudaimonic perspective, research has found similar results. For example, happiness has been associated with better indicators of mental and physical health, more pro-social behaviour, altruism and benevolence, higher levels of cooperation and trust, and enhanced meaning and positive emotions (see Ryan & Deci, 2017; Unanue 2014b).

Previous evidence shows the positive and transformative power of happiness. Thus, happiness should be at the centre of public policies, in order people, communities, organisations, nations and the planet can flourish and reach their maximum potential, giving sustainability to both present and future generations (see Nowak & Fuders, 2019; Seligman & Csikszentmihalyi, 2000a, 2000b).

Conceptualising happiness: Feeling good, functioning well and doing good

Psychologists have played a key role in the conceptualisation of happiness, which has significantly influenced several fields, such as economics, sociology and neuroscience (see Helliwell et al., 2012; Layard, 2011). To date, the most scientifically accepted paradigms for the construct of happiness are the so-called the hedonic and the eudaimonic models (Unanue, 2014a). Additionally, in recent years, dimensions that had not been directly considered by the two previous paradigms have taken on more and more strength. Specifically, constructs, such as compassion, altruism and benevolence, have emerged as fundamental dimensions of happiness and well-being (Oriol et al., 2022; Unanue et al., 2021).

The hedonic model of happiness

The hedonic model states that happiness mirrors the pursuit of pleasure and the avoidance of pain. A happy person believes and feels that his/her life is desirable, satisfying and rewarding (Diener & Tay, 2017). The words "beliefs" and "feelings" are not random. While beliefs are associated with our cognitions, feelings are associated with our emotions. Therefore, a happy person is a person who thinks that his life is going well (cognitions) and who experiences feelings (emotions) according to this evaluation (Diener, 1984).

In order to measure hedonic happiness, Ed Diener developed the construct of subjective well-being (SWB; Diener, 1984). SWB includes three key "hedonic" blocks: life satisfaction, positive emotions and negative emotions. Based on the above, a hedonically happy person would have a high level of SWB, which implies that they have high satisfaction with life, a high amount and intensity of positive emotions and only occasional negative emotions (Diener & Tay, 2017). Diener model of SWB is by far the most cited model of hedonic happiness.

The eudaimonic model of happiness

The eudaimonic paradigm states that happiness does not only consist of pleasure and positive emotions. True happiness should reflect, for example, the actualisation of human potentialities, a meaningful life and self-realisation (Ryan & Deci, 2001). That is why the eudaimonic model defines happiness as "functioning optimally" in our lives. There are different models of eudaimonic well-being, one of the most influential models comes from the self-determination theory (SDT; Ryan & Deci, 2000, 2017) and its basic psychological needs theory (BPNT).

Ryan and Deci (2000, 2017) claim that humans, like plants, need nutrients to flourish and function optimally. Just as plants need water and mineral salts, humans would need them too. In the case of individuals, these basic nutrients were called basic *psychological* needs: autonomy, competence and relationships. Satisfying the need for autonomy implies feeling that our behaviour is free and meaningful, that we are the initiators of our own actions, that our actions are in accordance with our deepest values, and that our behaviour is the product of a high level of reflection. Satisfying the need for competence implies feeling that we are effective and efficient in our actions and that we are capable of facing challenges successfully. Satisfying the need for relationships implies feeling that we are connected to others who are important to us, feel that we are appreciated and understood by those who matter to us, and that we have intimate and meaningful relationships (Ryan & Deci, 2017; Unanue 2014a, 2014b). Research has consistently shown that satisfying the needs for autonomy, competence and relationships are the essential ingredients for human happiness. Previous results have been found cross-culturally, across the life span and in several dimensions of life (see Ryan & Deci, 2017 for review).

Beyond feeling good and functioning well: The importance of doing good

For decades, the two paradigms mentioned above have co-existed. However, only in recent years, dimensions of human nature that had not been directly considered by the two previous models have taken on more and more importance: this is the case of dimensions such as compassion towards others (Khoury, 2019; CTO), altruism (Ricard, 2015) and benevolence (Martela & Ryan, 2016). CTO refers to the experience of caring, concern and tenderness for others (Oriol et al., 2022). Benevolence refers to feeling and believing that we are contributing to building a better world and has been proposed as a fourth basic psychological need of SDT (Martela & Ryan, 2016).

Research has found that altruistic behaviour (motivated for example by compassion) leads to significant increases in benevolence, which in turn has been associated not only with a higher quality of life but also with a greater sense of purpose, meaning and more pro-sociality (Fuders & Nowak, 2019; Martela et al.,

2021, Unanue et al., 2021). In other words, goodness is recognised today as a key dimension of happiness, being closely related to the role of compassion (as a motivator) and altruism (as a concrete behaviour). Therefore, happiness is not only feeling good (hedonism) or functioning well (eudaimonism). Happiness is, above all, "doing good". Importantly, doing good not only leads to happiness. Happiness is a kind of divine reward for doing good, and for contributing to the well-being of all (Fuders & Nowak, 2019). Previous findings have led to talk about the virtuous circle between happiness and altruism (Ricard, 2015; Unanue et al., 2021).

The model Bhutan model of happiness

The above models are individual-centred models. However, there are also models that are centred on the society as a whole. Within the latter, the most recognised one to date is the Bhutan model, known as the Gross National Happiness (GNH) model. The GNH model consists of four pillars: good governance, sustainable socio-economic development, cultural preservation and environmental conservation. The four pillars were then classified into nine domains: psychological well-being, health, education, time use, cultural diversity and resilience, good governance, community vitality, ecological diversity and resilience, and living standards. The nine dimensions of the Bhutan model guide all their public policies.

The GNH model has not only used insights provided by the research on hedonic and eudaimonic happiness but has also supplemented it with Buddhist wisdom and has been technically supported by the University of Oxford through the OPHI (Oxford Poverty and Human Development Initiative). The multidimensional model of happiness seeks to achieve a harmonious balance between material well-being and the spiritual, emotional and cultural needs of society (OPHI, 2022).

Bhutan's model (Royal Government of Bhutan, 2012, p. 107) "integrates inclusive economic growth with strengthening communities, protecting the environment, providing universal access to health services and education, and preserving traditional culture and heritage". Indeed, Bhutan "is putting before us a framework for a New Economic Paradigm, based on principles of happiness and well-being, ecological sustainability, efficient use of resources, and fair distribution". For Bhutan, public policies need to understand that "people are the real wealth of nations". Interestingly, "Bhutan's ancient legal code of 1629 stated that, if the government cannot create happiness for its people, then there is no purpose for government to exist". GNH is thus developed with values (GNH Centre, 2022).

Importantly, despite the GNH societal model being probably the best known attempt to put happiness and sustainability at the centre of the debate, several other efforts have been made with a similar goal. Examples are, among others, the World Happiness Report (https://worldhappiness.report), the OECD better lives initiative (https://www.oecdbetterlifeindex.org), the World Database on Happiness (https://worlddatabaseofhappiness.eur.nl) and the Happy Planet Index (https://happyplanetindex.org).

Max-Neef understandings of happiness and well-being

Smith and Max-Neef (2012) discussed largely de Sismondi and Hyse (1991) thoughts about a "good economic system". They considered him one of the oldest and most distinguished defenders of well-being for having reacted strongly against the abuses, misery and injustice caused by the prevailing economic model of his time (today the precursor of neoliberalism). For Smith and Max-Neef (2012), it was de Sismondi's human compassion – now recognised as one of the greatest keys to happiness – that set them apart from the rest, providing both authors with an illumination of what the central goal in economic science should be: the well-being of people. These thoughts strongly influenced how Max-Neef understood happiness.

Following de Sismondi and Hyse (1991), Max-Neef (Smith & Max-Neef, 2012) agrees that governments should create the conditions in order for people to find happiness and well-being. Public policies should assure that all people (poor and rich) may find happiness with equal chances. This, in part, would be achieved by eliminating human suffering, where compassion plays a fundamental role. Max-Neef also argues that the economy could be a key pillar to improve the destiny of humanity if it manages to move away from all utilitarian thinking that is only an obstacle to understanding and promoting a good life. In this sense, he proposes that his "Needs and Satisfiers Matrix" (Max-Neef et al., 1991; see Chapter 3 of this volume) could become a powerful basis for creating a new and more holistic model of development based on the well-being of people: a model that not only attends human needs but also the physical and animal needs of every living being. In this new model, justice, human dignity, compassion and reverence for life must be the guiding values of development, which may help the world to be a better place to live (Smith & Max-Neef, 2012).

Yet, Max-Neef not only had a great intuition regarding the role of compassion and benevolence for living a good and sustainable life. There is an impressive match between Max-Neef theory of human needs (Max-Neef et al., 1991) and Ryan and Deci's (2000, 2017) eudaimonic model of happiness. As discussed previously, SDT, and in particular its BPNT, posits that the satisfaction of basic psychological needs for autonomy, competence and relationships are one of the main determinants of a good life, well-being and sustainability in different domains of our existence. Please note that lately, the need for benevolence is also taking on extraordinary strength as another potential fundamental psychological need.

Looking at the Needs Matrix proposed by Max-Neef, it can be seen that the need for affection, which includes elements such as generosity, taking care of others, care for nature, intimacy and friendship, is closely linked to the SDT benevolence and relationship needs. The need for creation, which includes elements such as abilities, skills and techniques, is closely linked to the SDT need for competence. The need for freedom, which includes elements of autonomy and passion, is in-line with SDT need for autonomy. Interestingly, both SDT and GNH approaches have a non-hierarchical consideration of needs such as Max-Neef's theory of needs. Indeed, the three models give the same weight to the different categories they include, with a non-linear and non-hierarchical view of the satisfiers.

Max-Neef was correct when he proposed that his matrix of needs and satisfiers (Max-Neef et al., 1991) could be the starting point for a new model of development with a focus on well-being. Indeed, a few scholars have made important efforts to integrate Max-Neef model of needs and happiness (e.g., Papachristou & Rosas-Casals, 2015; Royo, 2007) and even an index of development based on human needs has been proposed: the Human Scale Development Index (see Fuders et al., 2016).

Integrating different visions of happiness

As discussed previously, happiness has been studied using different approaches. For example, on the one hand, the hedonic and eudaimonic models are considered individual-centred models. Importantly, despite the starting point being the happiness of the individual, research has consistently shown that both hedonic and eudaimonic happiness have a large positive impact on people, groups, organisations and the planet (Diener & Tay, 2017; Ryan & Deci, 2017). On the other hand, there are models that are centred on the society as a whole such as the Bhutan GNH model. Yet, in spite of its starting point in the society, the GNH model dimensions include individual aspects (e.g. psychological well-being, spirituality). Thus, the holistic definition of happiness would correspond to a vision of individual, collective and social happiness, defined as a deep sense of harmony with the natural world and with other human beings, where (a) basic human needs and (b) compassion, altruism and benevolence may play a key role. In this way, true happiness would be achieved with several dimensions such as good health (mental and physical), with knowledge and constant learning, with peace and security, with justice, with equality and equity, with interconnected communities, with meaningful relationships with others, with appreciation and respect for our culture and our roots, with good governance, and with respect and care for the environment and our ecological diversity. Previous happiness dimensions are indeed strongly linked to Max-Neef theory of fundamental human needs (Max-Neef et al., 1991) and thoughts.

The proposed new development paradigm based on happiness and well-being

On July 13, 2011, inspired by Bhutan, the United Nations adopted the A/65/L.86 resolution: *Happiness: towards a holistic model of development* (UN, 2011). Approved by the plenary session of its members, this resolution made a formal and concrete call to the governments of the world to place the happiness of its inhabitants at the centre of their public policies. United Nations proposed happiness as a fundamental objective to be pursued and invited "Member States to undertake the development of new measures that better reflect the importance of the pursuit of happiness and well-being in development with a view to guiding their public policies" (p. 1). To the United Nations, happiness could be, thus, part of the solution to the dilemmas (poverty, inequalities, mental health, climate change) that humanity is currently facing.

Then, with the support of the United Nations, Bhutan organised a High-Level Meeting on Happiness and Well-being at the UN headquarters. The event was attended by almost 1000 international leaders from the public, academic, spiritual and civil society spheres. After this meeting, Bhutan was asked to lead a process to rethink a new development model, where the happiness of human beings and the well-being of all life forms on Earth were at the centre of the model. From that moment, Bhutan formed a working team with a group of world-renowned professionals to collaborate in formulating the foundations of this new model. The group included experts from various disciplines (economics, psychology, neurosciences, environment, education and philosophy, among others) and received the name *International Expert Working Group* (IEWP). Max-Neef was part of the group.

After a few months of collaborative work, Bhutan and the IEWG published a report, proposing a New Development Paradigm based on happiness and well-being (NDP, 2013): *Happiness: Towards a New Development Paradigm* (see NDP, 2013). Given the relevance of the work, and the relevance for the moment that humanity was living, the report was delivered to the Secretary General of the United Nations, requesting its circulation to all the member states, the president of the 68th session of the UN General Assembly, and the administrator of the United Nations. This report was also officially presented at the United Nations as a means of contribution to the discussion agenda on the Millennium Development Goals post-2015. Additionally, the group continued working together for more than five years and published a book called *Happiness: Transforming the Development Landscape* (see Ura, 2017).

Max-Neef's contributions to the NDP

I propose that Max-Neef's thoughts played a crucial role in the development of the NDP report. The limited space of this chapter does not allow to go into detail, but I try to summarise two key points (for detail, please see NDP, 2013).

First, Max-Neef theory (Max-Neef et al., 1991), together with other visions about needs (material, psychological etc.), led to the recognition that the starting point of the NDP should be *human needs*. Indeed, "the vision of societal happiness is taken as a wider lens to view human progress within planetary limits, thus fulfilling the needs of *all* humans rather than the 'wants' of just a few. Having this more accurate focus on real needs, it is possible to detail a holistic development agenda" (NDP, 2013, p. VI). This is a key challenge for more standard visions of progress and development. In short, aiming to stop "miss-measuring our lives" (Stiglitz et al., 2010), the NDP stated that people are by far more important than materialistic/economic aspects.

Second, Max-Neef deeply inspired the atmosphere and the spirit of the IEWG proposal. Since the beginning, he was very emphatic in the importance of his so-called Five Postulates and Value Principle (Max-Neef, 2013). Max-Neef's five postulations are the following. First, the economy is to serve the people and not the people to serve the economy. Second, development is about people, and life in general, and not about objects. Third, growth is not the same as development, and development does not necessarily require growth. Fourth, no economy is possible in the absence of ecosystem services. Fifth, the economy is a subsystem of a larger and finite system: the biosphere. Hence permanent growth is impossible. His Value Principle is that "no economic interest, under any circumstance, can be above the reverence for life". I must say that, with the passing of the days in Bhutan, the IEWG was deeply inspired and convinced of the powerful message Manfred was giving us. Indeed, both the report (NDP, 2013) and the book (Ura, 2017) we published are strongly rooted in Max-Neef's (2013) principles and values.

Possible challenges for the NDP

The NDP proposes a completely new way of understanding development and progress. Thus, it is very likely that it will face several challenges. Indeed, the report itself highlights three possible challenges related to realizing and adopting an NDP. First, in terms of which dimensions should be included in the NDP. Second, which process should be followed (e.g. who could take the leading role). Third, how to implement the NDP in practice (for more details, see NDP, 2013, p. VIII–IX).

Despite these likely challenges, and that the changes are taking longer than expected, there was an agreement regarding that business-as-usual – that has led to the current crisis we are facing – is no longer acceptable. Because of this, the proposed NDP offers a "brighter and more uplifting future with potential for experientially rich, decent, healthful and fulfilling lives for all" (NDP, 2013, p. VIII–IX). Fortunately, just very recently, the World Well-being Movement (WWM; see https://wellbeing.hmc.ox.ac.uk/world-wellbeing-movement) has been launched at the University of Oxford. The WWM "is a coalition of global leaders from business, civil society, and academia that have come together to help put well-being at the heart of decision-making in both business and public policy". The movement's main goals are to design a universally acceptable standard for measuring well-being and happiness (metrics and dimensions) as well as to share best practices to improve well-being, creating positive change for people, organisations and the planet. I hope the WWM may help to tackle the challenges faced by the proposed NDP almost ten years ago.

Concluding remarks

Manfred Max-Neef deeply inspired key proposals for changing our current model of development, mainly based on economic growth and materialism, to a new one focused on a good and sustainable life where "no economic interest, under any circumstance, can be above the reverence for life" (Max-Neef, 2013, p. 1). He also encouraged us to think about the importance of compassion, altruism and benevolence as engines for building a better world, which was brave and challenging. But above all, Max-Neef was a person with a compassionate heart and an outstanding vision of the future.

References

Crompton, T., & Kasser, T. (2009). *Meeting environmental challenges: The role of human identity* (pp. 1–93). WWF-UK.

Diener, E. (1984). Subjective wellbeing. *Psychological Bulletin, 95*, 542–575. https://psycnet.apa.org/doi/10.1037/0033-2909.95.3.542

Diener, E., Lucas, R., Schimmack, U., & Helliwell, J. (2009). *Wellbeing for public policy*. Oxford University Press.

Diener, E., & Oishi, S. (2000). Money and happiness. In E. Diener, & E. M. Suh (Eds.), *Culture and subjective well-being* (pp. 185–218). MIT Press.

Diener, E., & Tay, L. (2017). A scientific review of the remarkable benefits of happiness for successful and healthy living. In K. Ura (Ed.), *Happiness: Transforming the development landscape* (pp. 90–118). The Centre for Bhutan Studies and GNH.

de Sismondi, J.-C.-L. S., & Hyse, R. (1991). *New principles of political economy: Of wealth in its relation to population*. Transaction Publishers.

Easterlin, R. A., McVey, L. A., Switek, M., Sawangfa, O., & Zweig, J. S. (2010). The happiness-income paradox revisited. *Proceedings of the National Academy of Sciences, 107*(52), 22463–22468.

Fuders, F., Mengel, N., & Barrera, M. (2016). Índice de desarrollo a escala humana: propuesta para un indicador de desarrollo endógeno basado en la satisfacción de las necesidades humanas fundamentales. In *Seguridad Alimentaria, Actores Territoriales y Desarrollo Endógeno*. Laberinto Ediciones.

Fuders, F., & Nowak, V. (2019). The economics of love: How a meaningful and mindful life can promote allocative efficiency and happiness. In Steinebach C., & Langer Á. (Eds.), *Enhancing resilience in youth*. Springer. https://doi.org/10.1007/978-3-030-25513-8_17

Gasper, D. (2007). Uncounted or illusory blessings? Competing responses to the Easterlin, Easterbrook, and Schwartz paradoxes of wellbeing. *Journal of International Development: The Journal of the Development Studies Association, 19*(4), 473–492. https://doi.org/10.1002/jid.1383

GNH Centre (2022). *History of GNH*. Retrieved from https://www.gnhcentrebhutan.org/history-of-gnh/

Helliwell, J. F., Layard, R., & Sachs, J. (2012). Some policy implications. In J. F. Helliwell, R. Layard, & J. Sachs (Eds.), *World happiness report* (pp. 90–96). The Earth Institute, Columbia University.

IPCC, International Panel on Climate Change (2022). *Climate change 2022. Impacts, adaptation, and vulnerabilities. Summary for policymakers*. Retrieved from https://www.ipcc.ch/report/ar6/wg2/

Kasser, T. (2016). Materialistic values and goals. *Annual Review of Psychology, 67*, 489–514. https://doi.org/10.1146/annurev-psych-122414-033344

Kasser, T. (2017). Living both well and sustainably: A review of the literature, with some reflections on future research, interventions, and policy. *Philosophical Transactions of the Royal Society A: Mathematical, Physical and Engineering Sciences, 375*(2095), 20160369. https://doi.org/10.1098/rsta.2016.0369

Ki-moon, B. (2012, May 17). *High-level thematic debate on The State of the World Economy and Finance and its Impact on Development*. http://www.un.org/en/development/desa/newsletter/desanews/feature/2012/06/

Khoury, B. (2019). Compassion: Embodied and embedded. *Mindfulness, 10*(11), 2363–2374. https://doi.org/10.1007/s12671-019-01211-w

Layard, R. (2011). *Happiness: Lessons from a new science* (2nd ed.). The Penguin Press.

Layard, R., Clark, A., & Senik, C. (2012). The causes of happiness and misery. In J. F. Helliwell, R. Layard, & J. Sachs (Eds.), *World happiness report* (pp. 58–89). The Earth Institute, Columbia University.

Martela, F., Gómez, M., Unanue, W., Araya, S., Bravo, D., & Espejo, A. (2021). What makes work meaningful? Longitudinal evidence for the importance of autonomy and beneficence for meaningful work. Longitudinal evidence for the importance of autonomy and beneficence for meaningful work. *Journal of Vocational Behavior*, *131*, 103631. https://doi.org/10.1016/j.jvb.2021.103631

Martela, F., & Ryan, R. M. (2016). The benefits of benevolence: Basic psychological needs, beneficence, and the enhancement of wellbeing. *Journal of Personality*, *84*(6), 750–764. https://doi.org/10.1111/jopy.12215

Max-Neef, M., Elizalde, A., & Hopenhyan, M. (1991). *Human scale development: Conception, application, and further reflections*. The Apex Press.

Max-Neef, M. (2013). *Short background contribution by IEWG member to this report.*

Meadows, D. H., Randers, J., & Meadows, D. L. (2013). *The limits to growth* (1972). In *The future of nature* (pp. 101–116). Yale University Press.

Myers, D. G. (2000). The funds, friends, and faith of happy people. *American Psychologist*, *55*(1), 56. https://doi.org/10.1037/0003-066X.55.1.56

NDP, Steering Committee and Secretariat (2013). *Happiness: Towards a New Development Paradigm.* Report of the Kingdom of Bhutan.

Nowak, V., & Fuders, F. (2019). Education as the key to facing today's challenges: How we can generate a more resilient environment and promote a paradigm shift in economics. In de Christoph Steinebach, & Álvaro I. Langer (Eds.), *Enhancing resilience in youth* (pp. 189–217). Springer.

OECD (2022). *Better Life Initiative: Measuring wellbeing and progress*. Retrieved from https://www.oecd.org/wise/better-life-initiative.htm

OPHI (2022). *Bhutan's Gross National Happiness Index.* https://ophi.org.uk/policy/gross-national-happiness-index/

Oriol, X., Unanue, J., & Unanue, W. (2022). *Compassion toward others and its longitudinal relationship with subjective wellbeing: Is beneficence a good candidate to explain this relationship?* Manuscript in preparation. Universidad de Girona.

Oriol, X., Unanue, J., & Unanue, W. (2022). The longitudinal link between compassion toward others and subjective well-being: The role of beneficence as an underlying psychological process to explain this relationship. *Current Psychology*, 1–15. https://doi.org/10.1007/s12144-022-03490-4

Papachristou, I. A., & Rosas-Casals, M. (2015). Making the neighbourhood a better place to live. A SWB approach implementing fundamental human needs. *On the Waterfront*, *40*(2), 31–50.

Ricard, M. (2015). *Altruism: The power of compassion to change yourself and the world.* Little, Brown.

Royal Government of Bhutan (2012). *The report of the high-level meeting on wellbeing and happiness: Defining a new economic paradigm*. New York: The Permanent Mission of the Kingdom of Bhutan to the United Nations. Thimphu: Office of the Prime Minister.

Royo, M. G. (2007). Happiness and Consumption in Peru: Exploring Basic Needs, Social Comparison, Social Integration and Hedonism. *In Conference Policies for Happiness* (pp. 1–31).

Ryan, R. M., & Deci, E. L. (2000). Self-determination theory and the facilitation of intrinsic motivation, social development, and wellbeing. *American Psychologist*, *55*(1), 68.

Ryan, R. M., & Deci, E. L. (2001). On happiness and human potentials: A review of research on hedonic and eudaimonic wellbeing. *Annual Review of Psychology, 52*, 141. https://doi.org/10.1146/annurev.psych.52.1.141
Ryan, R. M., & Deci, E. L. (2017). *Self-determination theory: Basic psychological needs in motivation, development, and wellness*. Guilford Publications.
Sachs, J. (2012). Introduction. In J. F. Helliwell, R. Layard, & J. Sachs (Eds.), *World happiness report* (pp. 2–9). The Earth Institute, Columbia University.
Seligman, M. E. P., & Csikszentmihalyi, M. (2000a). Positive psychology. *American Psychologist, 55*(1), 5–14.
Seligman, M. E. P., & Csikszentmihalyi, M. (2000b). Happiness, excellence, and optimal human functioning [Special issue]. *American Psychologist, 55*(1), 5–183.
Smith, P. B., & Max-Neef, M. (2012). *Economics unmasked: From power and greed to compassion and the common good*. Green Books.
Stiglitz, J.E., Sen, A., & Fitousi, J. (2010). *Mismeasuring our lives: Why GDP doesn't add up*. New York: New Press.
United Nations (2011). UN General Assembly Resolution A/65/L.86. https://digitallibrary.un.org/record/715187?ln=es#record-files-collapse-header
Unanue, W. (2014a). *Materialism, Personal Well-being and Environmental Behaviour: Cross-national and Longitudinal Evidence from the UK and Chile* (PhD Thesis). University of Sussex.
Unanue, W. (2014b). ¿Por qué felicidad? In J. C. Oyanedel & C. Mella (Eds.), *Debates sobre el Bienestar y la Felicidad* (pp. 55–75). Ril Editores.
Unanue, W. (2017a). Subjective well-being measures to inform public policies. In K. Ura (Ed.), *Happiness: Transforming the development landscape* (pp. 118–155). The Centre for Bhutan Studies and GNH.
Unanue, W., Martínez, D., López, M., & Zamora, L. (2017b). El Rol del Bienestar Subjetivo para Medir el Progreso de las Naciones y Orientar las Políticas Públicas. *Papeles del psicólogo, 38*(1), 26–33. https://doi.org/10.23923/pap.psicol2017.2818
Unanue, W., Barros, E., & Gómez, M. (2021). The longitudinal link between organizational citizenship behaviors and three different models of happiness. *International Journal of Environmental Research and Public Health, 18*(12), 6387. https://doi.org/10.3390/ijerph18126387
Ura, K. (2017). *Happiness: Transforming the development landscape. The Centre for Bhutan Studies and GNH.*
Wilkinson, R. G., & Pickett, K. (2011). *The spirit level*. Bloomsbury Press.
World Bank (2022a). 2022: The year in review. Retrieved from https://www.worldbank.org/en/news/immersive-story/2022/12/15/2022-in-nine-charts?cid=ECR_GA_worldbank_EN_EXTP_search_YearInReview&gclid=Cj0KCQiA5NSdBhDfARIsALzs2EBzlXWs769CjK4KYTXuBathnQVcpl1FFG7vzDLAS6YCggfhqgZuEmEaAno9EALw_wcB
World Bank (2022b). World Inequality Report 2022. Retrieved from https://wid.world/document/world-inequality-report-2022/
World Bank (2022c). COVID-19 leaves a legacy of rising poverty and widening inequality. Retrieved from https://blogs.worldbank.org/developmenttalk/covid-19-leaves-legacy-rising-poverty-and-widening-inequality
World Bank (2022d). Climate change. Retrieved from https://www.worldbank.org/en/topic/climatechange

6 The Human Scale Development approach

Is 'spirituality' a fundamental human need?

Felix Fuders

Introduction: Happiness despite facing the most adverse situation?

In 2013, I attended a conference on smarter cities in Manila, Philippines.[1] Roberto Mayorga, the then Chilean ambassador to the Philippines, presented a project that he had initiated some years earlier. This project was called 'Calidad Humana Project'. Mayorga asked the question, what good are concepts for 'smarter cities' if people are increasingly less happy and less human, showing less affection and compassion for each other? In the Philippines, he said, most people (still) seem to give priority to 'concern for others' rather than material things; most people in the Philippines (still) possess[2] what in Spanish would be called 'Calidad Humana', that is human compassion, humanity, humility, a human tone. Being overwhelmed by the special traits of Philippine people, so different from people in many other countries, and with the deep desire to help to preserve this 'Calidad Humana' he started the 'Calidad Humana Project'.

The 'Calidad Humana Project' had by the time of the conference become a sort of *corporate identity* of the Philippines. The project receives support from multinational companies as well as from governmental and non-governmental organisations and universities. It aims to highlight what in Spanish is called the 'Calidad Humana' of Filipinos, a 'human quality' characteristic that they possess and that seems to exist in few other countries. At the conference, the Chilean ambassador indicated that 'Calidad Humana' was reflected in the faces of people who seem to almost smile constantly. As part of the project, a photo contest was carried out called *Smiles for the World*. These photos show mostly (financially) poor people **in the most adverse situations smiling**. Children who do not even have clothes to wear are smiling. And these are not the artificial smiles of people posing for a photo; rather they are smiles that convey happiness and warmth. Apparently, even in dire poverty, it is possible to be happy. This begs the question, does happiness depend on development?

The Human Scale Development approach and happiness

In their *Human Scale Development* (HSD) approach, Max-Neef et al. (1991) proposed a matrix of nine *axiological* (subsistence, protection, affection, understanding, participation, idleness, creation, identity, and liberty) fundamental human

DOI: 10.4324/9781003381143-7

needs that are each viewed in four *existential* modes (being, having, doing, and interacting) as an instrument to be able to identify potential satisfiers, and through this to contribute to the achievement of a development that serves people, helping them to satisfy their needs. Usually, there is a significant gap between the matrix that describes the *status quo* and the utopian matrix where all needs would perfectly be satisfied (Max-Neef et al., 1991). The HSD approach is designed to be a tool that serves to build this 'bridge' (Max-Neef et al., 1991) between the current and the desired situation, i.e., it can help development planners to identify how to best develop a city or region.

But would we automatically be happy if we were to develop our society such that the fundamental needs in each cell of the human needs matrix defined by the *Human Scale Development* HSD approach were perfectly satisfied, if this was possible?[3] If, as already the ancient Greek philosophers (Aristotle 1995a, 1995b; Plato, 2011) argued, felicity (*eudemonia*) is to be regarded as the highest aspirational good, then the ultimate objective of development can only be to come as close as possible to this state. However, it is not clear if development, even if we define it alternatively as the state as close as possible to all fundamental human needs being perfectly satisfied, would automatically mean that we are happy, fulfilled, or have reached felicity.[4] This chapter will inquire deeper on this aspect. The aim is to articulate the idea that spirituality is key for achieving true and abiding happiness and therefore could be considered a human need which should be included in the HSD approach matrix.

Proceeding

This paper first defines briefly what could, for the purpose of this text, be understood by 'true happiness'. It will then discuss whether development is key to reach true happiness. I will be concluded that it is not, at least not by itself, and that instead, spirituality is the key for reaching true happiness. If, as most people would agree, happiness is the ultimate objective in life, then spirituality should be considered a fundamental human need. As such this paper proposes that it should be integrated in the fundamental human need matrix of the HSD approach of Max-Neef et al. (1991). If we enhance the matrix with the need of spirituality, then HSD and happiness will go hand in hand. That is, if all fundamental human needs, including the need of spirituality, are perfectly satisfied, then we will reach true happiness. Finally, this chapter will discuss, based on a review of existing studies, which religion or religious practices seem to be the best satisfiers for the need of 'spirituality'.

Does happiness depend on development?

What is happiness?

Happiness and the philosophy about how to best achieve it is not a new issue. Plato (2008) and his scholar Aristotle (1995b) discussed the origins and circumstances they believed to be necessary to achieve felicity. Also, Utilitarianism (based on

Bentham, [1780] 1986 and Mill, [1861] 2003), which seeks as its ultimate objective happiness, is centuries old. Nevertheless, until today after a millennium of philosophical dispute, still there is no clear delimitation of terms such as 'happiness', 'felicity', 'felicitousness', or simply 'well-being'. Not seldom are these expressions are used in a synonymous way in one and the same text. Happiness is a feeling that everyone can feel; however, it is very difficult to define. To seek an exact definition of each of these terms could easily fill a book of its own and is not necessary for our discussion. In the following, I will just refer to 'true happiness' as a deeper sense of inner fulfilment of life different from the material, short-lived, and superficial satisfaction we receive, e.g., eating a good meal or go hiking. Yes, the latter also makes us happy, but it is not long-lasting and true happiness. In the following sections, it will be explained why spirituality, if rightly practised, can be key to achieve this 'deeper sense of inner fulfilment'.

Happiness and GDP growth

Since 1972, Bhutan's government has been taking measures to increase the country's Gross National Happiness instead of its gross domestic product (GDP) (Ura et al., 2012). The GDP is the sum of all values (goods and services) produced in one period (usually one year). Bhutan was the first country to understand that neither total GDP nor GDP growth necessarily makes people happy. Accordingly, the government tries to take actions to increase national happiness instead of GDP. The rest of the world seems to have begun to realise that GDP growth does not necessarily lead to happiness only just recently, for example, France started measuring the Gross National Happiness in 2009 (Hall, 2009) and Germany in 2011 (Lachmann, 2011). In 2011, the United Nations issued a Resolution to develop an annual World Happiness Report (Wikipedia, 2021),[5] and in 2012, United Nations convened a conference, chaired by the prime minister of Bhutan, on the subject 'happiness' in 2012. Former UN Secretary-General Ban Ki-moon said in his remarks at a high-level meeting at the UN Headquarters in New York that 'Gross Domestic Product (GDP) has long been the yardstick by which economies and politicians have been measured. Yet it fails to take into account the social and environmental costs of so-called progress' (UN News Centre, 2012). Robert F. Kennedy once said that a country's GDP measures 'everything except that which makes life worthwhile' (Costanza, 2014).

The fact that economic growth does not make people happy is widely known as 'Easterlin paradox' (Easterlin, 1974; for further references, see Wallburg & Fuders, 2013) and can be understood intuitively. If, for example, we cut down all the trees in all of Chile's forests and sold them as chips to China, GDP could grow to a higher level. But our well-being, at least for most people, would not be greater (Fuders & Mora Motta, 2021). Economic growth, as our esteemed colleague Manfred Max-Neef had explained in many of his publications, is not the same as development. Economic growth is quantitative, while development is qualitative[6] (Max-Neef et al., 1991, pp. 16 ff., 53 f., 58 f., 91, 100 f.; Max-Neef, 1992, pp. 34, 51, 133; Max-Neef, 2007, p. 48 ff.; see also Daly & Farley, 2011, p. 233 ff.; Lietaer et al., 2013, p. 83).

This observation can be corroborated by the fact that countries with the highest GDP per capita are not necessarily the ones with the happiest people, at least not according to the famous **Happy Planet Index**, according to which the happiest 25 countries are not those we usually consider having the highest living standards or the highest level of 'development' (New Economics Foundations [NEF], 2022). One might now object that this index does not purely measure happiness but, instead, it mixes three variables, while the subjective perception of happiness is only one variable next to life expectancy and the ecological footprint. However, the Happy Planet Index does give a rough idea of which countries are happier than others. Polls conducted by the Gallup group have suggested similar. Of the ten countries in the world in which the highest percentage of the population experiences positive emotions, almost all are in Latin America (Gallup, 2022).

Happiness and Human Scale Development

We can conclude so far that what we measure with the GDP is not development. In fact, even those indices that try to measure development alternatively (i.e., by not just taking into account the GDP per capita or GDP growth rate) have in my point of view still a quite **materialistic focus** since they use arbitrarily chosen variables to measure development, variables that the respective authors of the indices believe to represent what they believe to be 'development' (see Fuders et al., 2016; Pastén et al., 2020), such as, e.g., the number of physicians per capita or the access to potable water. Is the number of physicians per capita really an adequate indicator of development? If people live in the middle of nature, their healthy lifestyle may require less physicians. We could even argue the other way around that the number of physicians per capita could be interpreted as an indicator for the sickness of a society. Likewise, we can question if access to potable water is really a useful variable for measuring development when people may be instead living in nature with freshwater from a glacier next to their houses (water that is cleaner and purer than the chlorine- and fluoride-treated drinking water in our cities).

Maybe using the HSD matrix (Max-Neef et al., 1991) would be a much better way of measuring development. Human needs in the HSD concept are seen as ontological, i.e., stemming from the condition of being human. They are few, finite, and classifiable, and they do not vary across human cultures and historical time periods, unlike what economics defines as 'wants', which are infinite and insatiable.[7] What do change over time and among cultures are the strategies through which these needs are satisfied (Max-Neef et al., 1991, p. 33 ff.). Hence, a development index based on this theory would provide a way to measure development based on fundamental human needs rather than arbitrarily chosen variables. The idea of using the HSD Matrix as a basis for identifying development and to build an indicator out of this approach has been taking shape in my mind since I first heard of the theory. An HSD *Index* would measure development as the subjectively perceived satisfaction of each need in each dimension in the fundamental human needs matrix (Fuders, 2011; Fuders & Mora Motta, 2021; Fuders et al., 2016).[8]

However, even if we measured development based on human needs instead of arbitrarily chosen material objects, it is **still doubtful that development and happiness go together** in a perfectly synchronised manner. This is because development, even when measured according to the satisfaction of fundamental human needs, is most likely not the **only variable** that explains happiness. That is, even if we used a development index based on human needs as proposed above, the Philippines would probably still not appear as one of the most developed countries in the world but nevertheless seem to have quite happy people. Apparently, regardless of whether a country is in dire poverty and suffering major disasters, people can still be happy. Roberto Mayorga raised a very interesting question in his speech at the Smarter Cities Conference: Could it be that true happiness has to do with faith in God, rather than the physical development of a country? The next paragraph will explore this question.

Faith in God as the true origin of happiness?

Happiness and its connection to humility

Coming back to the example of the Philippines. Most Filipinos seem to be **humble**. I use the word humble here to refer to humility in the original sense of the word. Humility is contrary to arrogance. Roberto Mayorga, an ex-ambassador and having lived for many years in the Philippines, told us that Filipinos know how to listen and do not act as if they were the owners of the truth. Filipinos generally (of course there might be exceptions) accept their situation in life and feel less envious of people who do (materially) better than them, at least this was his impression. They seem to accept whatever happens, not with resignation but with a positive outlook, with hope for a better future and without envy. This humility is probably an important characteristic that **makes it easier to be happy**, especially in a country with so much inequality. This last point is particularly interesting, given the existence of studies that conclude that the intensity of inequality in a country is inversely correlated with the population's perceived well-being.[9] This seems not to be true for the Philippines.

Happiness and its connection to religiosity

In fact, being happy is supposed to be an attribute of Christians. Once I found a brochure in a church bearing the title *The happiness of Christians*. In short, it tells us that a major aspect of the Christian faith is to be happy, even in difficult life situations, and to accept tribulations as a means of purifying the souls of those who would otherwise be lost.[10] In a study using data of 100 countries from 1981 to 2014, religious persons, especially Roman Catholics and Protestants, were found to be happier and more satisfied with their lives compared with other groups (The Conservation, 2021). It seems no coincidence that the Philippines is a highly religious country. For example, many children in the Philippines learn to pray the Rosary when they are in kindergarten. On buses and taxis, you can frequently find messages like 'Jesus loves you' or 'God is Love'. This is something that sometimes can also be seen in Chile, but much less so than in the Philippines; it is almost never seen in Europe.

Happiness and its connection to the love for-one's-neighbour principle

As an example of Filipinos' 'Calidad Humana', Roberto Mayorga explained in his presentation at the Conference on Smarter Cities that in the Philippines, the habit of offering one's seat on public transportation to an elderly person or a woman is not yet lost. These are customs that are becoming more and more out of fashion in Chile as well as in many other countries. Medardo Márquez, the winner of the *Smiles for the world* photo contest, emphasises that 'Calidad Humana' means prioritising human beings over material things, and taking care of others instead of just yourself. This attitude, in his opinion, is a choice that is made every day. In this way, it is not something genetic or innate, as some might argue. 'Calidad Humana' thus is the expression of altruistic behaviour, of the **love-one's-neighbour** principle.

In this context, I would like to share with you a personal experience that illustrates the special 'human qualities' of Filipinos. On the plane on my way back to Chile, a Filipino sat next to me. When the plane landed in Tokyo and everyone stood up, one of the passengers carelessly took his briefcase from the overhead compartment, hitting the Filipino who had sat next to me. The Filipino's reaction amazed me. He turned, smiled at the guy who had hit him with his briefcase, and said, 'At least I'm awake now'. Many other people probably would have been angry with the person who hit their face by accident. Forgiveness, of course, is a trait associated with loving one's neighbour.

Loving one's neighbour and happiness

In the 2012 UN conference on happiness mentioned above, where Bhutan's aspiration to measure national happiness instead of economic growth was made known to a wider public, a poster[11] was shown saying:

If you want happiness…

- For an hour – take a nap
- For a day – go fishing
- For a month – get married
- For a year – inherit a fortune
- For a lifetime – help someone else

This statement means that, if we aspire truly and long-lasting happiness, we should aim to constantly help and serve others. Here, I do not refer to happiness as the superficial, materialistic joy we feel after having bought new possessions (e.g. a car) or eating a delicious meal, but to a deep sense of inner fulfilment that might come from the intuitive knowledge that you are doing the right thing, that you 'do what you have to do' as Manfred Max-Neef frequently used to encourage his students on graduation celebrations.[12] Similarly, Bhutan's Prime Minister once remarked that true abiding happiness 'comes only from serving others, living in harmony with nature, and realising our innate wisdom and the true and brilliant nature of our own minds' (Ura et al., 2012, p. 7). Helping and serving others means loving our neighbour, and this in turn makes us happy.

Love for one's neighbour translates into treating others as we would like to be treated; not to do unto our neighbour what we would not want to be done on us (Matthew 7:12). One could say that loving our neighbour is the perfect realisation of Immanuel Kant's **categorical imperative** (Kant 1868). Neighbourly love is not just reserved for helping people in distress, proselytising, and observing the Ten Commandments. Neighbourly love also compels us to **make use of our individual talents** for the benefit of the common good. Part of the realisation of neighbourly love is therefore also to find our vocation and make it our profession or a life's work, so that we may earn our daily bread with our skills (Fuders & Nowak, 2019).

Love for one's neighbour and humility are key for achieving happiness

Love for one's neighbour is the **first law of Christianity** (Bible, Lev. 19:18; Deut. 6:5; Matt. 22:37–22:39; Galat. 5:14), as well as of other religions (for Islam see Koran, Surah 42:23; for Judaism see Tanakh, Lev. 19,18). Jesus Christ said that the most important laws are to love God and your neighbour as yourself, and that all other laws hang on these two commandments (Mt 22:37–40; Mk 12:29–31). In fact, the Ten Commandments[13] can be seen as a concretisation of the meta-law to love one another. To love one another means that we should treat others as we would like to be treated; not to do unto our neighbour what we would not want to be done on us (Matthew 7:12). A person who respects this law will not kill, nor steal, nor lie, etc.; the Ten Commandments would indeed be superfluous if everyone perfectly loved one another. In this understanding, a great person is not one who is served by many but one who serves many (Warren, 2002, p. 208) and 'serving' translates into best making use of our talents for the common good, and not to work only for the sake of economic benefit (Fuders, 2017; Fuders & Nowak, 2019).

Some might say that the idea that the Filipinos' happiness comes from their strong Christian faith is wrong, since not all Filipinos are Christians. But the fact that not all Filipinos are Christians **does not contradict** the assertion that it is faith in God that distinguishes the Philippines from other countries of the world. The Muslim faith dominates in some parts of the Philippines, but Muslims believe in same God, creator of heaven and earth, as Christians and Jews and as mentioned, love for one's neighbour is a key attitude in Islam (and Judaism) too.[14] And even the few who do not believe in any religion in the Philippines (less than 0.1% of the population, see Wikipedia, 2022a, 2022b) are not necessarily very far away from faith. The Bible says: 'Everyone who loves has been born of God and knows God.

Whoever does not love does not know God, because God is love' (NIV, 1 John 4:7–8). According to this definition, persons who are not consciously Christian could still be filled with the Holy Spirit due to their practice of neighbourly love. In the gospels, it is preached that the **acts or fruits are what make us recognise a Christian** (e.g., Mt. 7, 15–20; Lc 6, 43–45).

Perhaps we could establish the following hypothesis: **The greater the faith in God[15] you find in a country, the greater the humility, love for neighbours and happiness of its people.** Happiness defined above proposed a deeper sense of inner fulfilment. Already Émile Durkheim back in 1897 presumed that spiritual commitment and religiousness might promote emotional well-being, as it provides a source of meaningfulness (Durkheim, 1897). Many studies corroborated this hypothesis and found a positive correlation between spirituality, especially the faith in God, and happiness (Walsh, 2017). For example, a study conducted in 2015 by the London School of Economics together with the Erasmus University Medical Center in the Netherlands found that participating in a religious organisation was the **only** social activity associated with sustained happiness (Stanek, 2015; Walsh, 2017). The PEW research centre corroborated this study and found that actively religious people are more likely than their less-religious peers to describe themselves as 'very happy' (Marshall, 2019).

It has to be admitted that not all studies come to such a clear conclusion. For example, some studies conclude that religion could bring meaning, but not necessarily happiness to people's lives, even if it provides us with other benefits (Suttie, 2020). And often it is discussed whether it is the faith in God itself or rather its 'social support network that is fulfilling', such as a church, a synagogue, and a Bible study group (Quinn, 2014). In this context, however, it is especially interesting that another study found that while religious organisations boosted happiness, joining any **other type of community organisation actually led to decreased happiness** over time (Stanek, 2015). The different conclusions might also be due to different definitions of what is understood as 'religious person', 'participating in religious organisation', 'religiousness', or 'spirituality'.[16] Most probably, not all forms of spirituality bring the same desired effects.[17]

Spirituality as the tenth axiological need

If happiness is the ultimate goal of life[18] and if happiness itself is connected with spirituality, especially the faith in God and the two key attitudes 'love for one's neighbour' and 'humility' associated with it, then it makes sense to include spirituality as a tenth axiological need to the matrix of fundamental human needs. In this way, development, defined in terms of satisfaction of fundamental human needs, and happiness would be reached **simultaneously**. And even if happiness is not the ultimate goal, then it is still an important aspect of well-being and as such should be included in the matrix. A question remains, what are the satisfiers for the need for 'Spirituality' in each of the four dimensions (being, having, doing, and interacting)? According to Max-Neef et al. (1991), there are five types of satisfiers (see Table 6.1).

Table 6.1 Types of satisfiers

Type of satisfier	*Description*
Singular satisfiers	They aim at the satisfaction of a single need, being neutral with respect to the satisfaction of other needs.
Synergistic satisfiers	While satisfying a given need, stimulate and contribute to the simultaneous satisfaction of other needs.
Destroyers	They are elements of paradoxical effect to be applied with the intention of satisfying a given need. They not only annihilate the possibility of its satisfaction in the medium term but also make impossible, by their collateral effects, the adequate satisfaction of other needs.
Pseudo-satisfiers	Stimulate a false sensation of satisfaction of a determined need. Without the aggressiveness of the violators, they can sometimes annihilate, in a medium term, the possibility of satisfying the need they originally aimed at.
Pseudo-satisfiers	By the way in which they satisfy (generally over-satisfy) a determined need, seriously hinder the possibility of satisfying other needs.

Source: Based on Max-Neef et al. (1991).

Considering what has been outlined above, the faith in God (and here especially Christianity) could perfectly serve as *singular* or even as *synergic* satisfier, while other forms of spiritualism and spiritism, especially New-Age Spiritualism, 'Old-Age' Spiritualism, and other forms of occultism or satanism (even though painted in white as 'white magic'), could be seen as pseudo-satisfiers or even destroyers. Naturally, followers of these types of spiritualism will not straight away subscribe to this point of view. But, in fact, there are many pseudo-satisfiers that give a feeling of (superficial) comfort, calmness, or inner balance that lasts for some time but does not give long-lasting (and much less eternal) and true inner fulfilment and happiness. Not seldom times those forms of spirituality even lead, after some time to suicide (BBC, 2018; Heathcote et al., 1999; Stiel & Madea, 2002), while organisational religiousness and daily spiritual experiences of especially Christianity are associated with decreased risk for thinking about suicide (Kopacz et al., 2016), committing suicide (Gearing & Alonzo, 2018; Lawrence et al., 2016) as well as lower attachment insecurity, depression severity, and social anxiety (Adams et al., 2020).

This goes hand in hand with the finding described above that religion has the power to produce deep and abiding happiness in people. A bibliometric study that analysed 1745 studies on the relation between religion and suicide showed that the risk to commit suicide compared to other religions and atheists is especially low in Jews and Christians, and among the Christians lower among Catholics and Baptists Protestants than other Protestants (Gearing & Alonzo, 2018). Hindus have higher probability to commit suicide than Muslims and Christians (Gearing & Alonzo, 2018; Ineichen, 1998; Thimmaiah et al., 2016). This finding goes hand in hand with the hypothesis that man-made religions[19] are pseudo-satisfiers. Table 6.2 enhances

Table 6.2 Max-Neef's human needs matrix with tenth need 'Spirituality'

Need	*Being (qualities)*	*Having (things)*	*Doing (actions)*	*Interacting (settings)*
Subsistence	physical and mental health	food, shelter, work	feed, clothe, rest, work	living environment, social setting
Protection	care, adaptability, autonomy	Social security, health systems, work	cooperate, plan, take care of, help	Living environment, social setting
Affection	respect, sense of humour, generosity, sensuality	friendships, family, relationships with nature	share, take care of, make love, express emotions	privacy, intimate spaces of togetherness
Understanding	critical conscience, capacity, curiosity, intuition	literature, teachers, policies, education	analyse, study, meditate, investigate	schools, families, universities, communities
Participation	receptiveness, dedication, sense of humour	responsibility, duties, work, rights	cooperate, dissent, express opinions	associations, parties, churches, neighbourhoods
Leisure	imagination, tranquillity, spontaneity	games, parties, peace of mind	daydream, remember, relax, have fun	landscapes, intimate spaces, places to be alone
Creation	imagination, boldness, inventiveness, curiosity	abilities, skills, work, techniques	invent, build, design, work, compose, interpret	spaces for expression, workshops, audiences
Identity	sense of belonging, self-esteem, consistency	language, religions, work, customs, values, norms	get to know oneself, grow, commit oneself	places one belongs to, everyday settings
Freedom	autonomy, passion, self-esteem, open-mindedness	equal rights	dissent, choose, run risks, develop awareness	anywhere
Spirituality	happy, feeling self-actualised, fulfilled	churches, priests, sacred locations for praying, personal relation to God, sense of plenitude	praying, attending holy mass, applying talents in daily work	praying together, helping others, visiting the ill, listening, altruism, charity

Source: Based on Max-Neef et al. (1991, p. 32 f.; for the nine needs) and own considerations.

the matrix of fundamental human needs (Max-Neef et al., 1991) with the need of 'spirituality'.

Some readers might be willing to argue that 'spirituality' is not necessarily to be considered as a fundamental human need itself but, instead, as a satisfier of the need 'leisure' or 'participation'. However, the final end of this text is to articulate my strong conviction that spirituality is more than a nice way to pass time (satisfier of leisure or participation) but is key for reaching inner fulfilment and thus true and abiding happiness. Therefore, it should be considered a fundamental human need that everyone intuitively seeks to fulfil. Faith in God, the creator of heaven and earth, and its related practices and attitudes, especially humility and the love-for-thy-neighbour principle as discussed above, could be the satisfiers.

In this context, it is noteworthy that Manfred Max-Neef himself mentioned in a publication together with Paul Ekins (Ekins & Max-Neef, 1992) that in some future time, it may be necessary to include a need of 'Transcendence' to the matrix of fundamental human needs. In words of Ekins and Max-Neef (1992)

> … it is likely that in the future the need for Transcendence, which is not included in our proposal, as we do not yet consider it universal, will become as universal as the other needs. It seems legitimate, then, to assume that fundamental human needs change with the pace of evolution. That is to say, at a very slow rate. Therefore, fundamental human needs are not only universal but are also entwined with the evolution of the species. They follow a single track. (p. 203)

However, this assumption contradicts Christian as well as Jewish and Muslim doctrine, which assumes that the person was created by God and for God, and therefore with an innate desire for God (for Christian doctrine see Catechism of Catholic Church, number 2003; for Muslim doctrine see Koran: 7:172; 51:56; Phillips, 2009; for Jewish doctrine see: Reichman, 2016). That is, spirituality is according to these three world religions, a universal need by default.

Conclusions and final reflections

If we agree with Aristotle that happiness is the highest aspirational goal, then **desirable human development is one that leads us to happiness**. Since powerful arguments and even empirical evidence exist that spirituality is key for achieving deep, abiding, and long-lasting happiness, spirituality should enter as the tenth axiological need in the matrix of fundamental human needs in the HSD approach. In this way, happiness and development – development defined in terms of the satisfaction of fundamental human needs – would go hand in hand.

The conclusion that a certain degree of spirituality seems to be positively correlated with 'happiness' brings up the following questions: does **the obsession with efficiency and materialism** found today in many countries find its origin in the loss of faith and spirituality? Could it be that people, especially in the northern hemisphere, are trying to compensate for a lack of spirituality, replacing values that really matter with materialism and consumerism? materialism and consumerism are very much related to the obligation of economic growth – which is inherent in our financial system (Fuders & Max-Neef, 2014a, 2014b). However, it could well be argued that the metaphysical reason for excessive materialism finds its roots in a lack of spirituality and that the invention of our financial system, a system that makes it possible to hoard money (which the money interest rate as a reward for abstaining from liquidity eventually arises (Keynes, 1936), is just a symptom of this materialism.

Notes

1 International Conference on Smarter Cities, Manila (2013), organised by the School of Urban and Regional Planning, University of Philippines.
2 Of course, there are exceptions; the Philippines is not a paradise.
3 Arguments exist that a perfect fulfilment of all needs is not possible (Elizalde et al., 2006).
4 On the Connection between felicity and fundamental human needs, see Chapter 5 in this book.
5 The *World Happiness Report* is an annual measure of happiness published by the UN Sustainable Development Solutions Network. It is based on a resolution passed by the UN General Assembly in 2011 inviting member countries to participate in measuring the happiness of their people and to use this information to help guide their public policies (Wikipedia, 2021). The United Nations convened a conference, chaired by the prime minister of Bhutan, on the subject 'happiness' in 2012.
6 In this context, it seems incomprehensible that even the World Happiness Report, prepared annually by the UN Sustainable Development Solutions Network, uses a logarithm of GDP per capita as the first variable for explaining (and defining) happiness (Helliwell et al., 2013, p. 19). Is it surprising that the happiest countries, according to this report (ibid, p. 22), are those with highest per capita GDP, especially northern European Countries?
7 In textbooks on microeconomics, it is taught that one of the assumptions about consumer preferences is 'the more the better' (Frank, 2015). That this is false is indicated by the 'law of diminishing marginal utility' which too is taught in economics (often even in the same microeconomics textbooks), and which relates to the fact that the more we have consumed of a good, the less we will value the next unit.
8 On first attempts to apply this index and some conclusions drawn, see Fuders and Mora Motta (2021).
9 See more references on this topic in Wallburg and Fuders (2013).
10 If we understand that by accepting sufferings and offering them as sacrifice, we can save souls (metaphorically said, we help Jesus to carry His cross), then this makes it easier to stand tribulations, we might even bear them in love and in joy.
11 The phrases on the poster were taken from a label you can find in the 'Federal Palace Restaurant' in Hong Kong.
12 If we 'do what we have to do', we contribute to correctly put together the big 'puzzle of neighbourly love' and, thus, build an 'economy of neighbourly love' (Fuders, 2017; Fuders & Nowak, 2019).
13 The Ten Commandments are a set of principles relating to ethics and worship that can be found in the Tora (Judaism) and the Old Testament of the Bible (Christianity) in the books of Exodus (20: 2–17) and Deuteronomy (5: 6–21). The Ten Commandments are: 1. You shall have no other gods before Me 2. You shall make no idols. 3. You shall not take the name of the Lord your God in vain. 4. Keep the Sabbath day holy. 5. Honour your father and your mother. 6. You shall not murder. 7. You shall not commit adultery. 8. You shall not steal. 9. You shall not bear false witness against your neighbour. 10. You shall not covet.

14 The Koran is based on the Bible, which is why the Koran asks to consult the Bible in case of doubts (Koran: 10,94). The Holy Scripture of Judaism (Tanakh) is the first part of the Bible (Old Testament).
15 With 'God', I refer to the God of the Christians, Jews and Muslims, who according to their belief is the creator of heaven and earth.
16 Faith in God, religiousness, religiosity and spirituality are often used as synonymous and there is no exact, universally accepted definition of the term 'spirituality'. Widely spoken, spirituality refers to people who believe in the presence or existence of something greater than the self (Gearing & Alonzo, 2018).
17 Some forms of spirituality here, especially those human-invented forms of spirituality, such as New-Age practices or Hinduism (I would call it 'Old Age' spiritualism), occultism (even though it might be painted in white as 'white magic'), satanism, yoga, breathing practices and meditation, might not lead to long-term happiness and neither to a life in plenitude, even though it could help to relay, to relax and to give us some sense of (probably superficial) calmness.
18 Personally, I would not subscribe to this point of view. As I pointed out earlier (Fuders, 2017; Fuders & Nowak, 2019), the pursuit of happiness as an end in itself might even be considered superficial as the pursuit of money or recognition. Rather, in my opinion, the ultimate goal of life and deeper sense of our existence is the realisation of neighbourly love while true happiness is the compensation, we receive for achieving the goal. This can also be derived from the German word for felicitousness (Glückseligkeit), in which the words 'happiness' (Glück) and 'soul' (Seele) are combined. Felicitousness is the state in which the soul is happy.
19 Hinduism shares similar thoughts and practices as so-called New-Age Spiritualism, only that it is some centuries years older.

References

Adams, G. C., Wrath, A. J., Le, T., Adams, S., De Souza, D., Baetz, M., & Koenig, H. G. (2020). Exploring the impact of religion and spirituality on mental health and coping in a group of canadian psychiatric outpatients. *Journal of Nervous & Mental Disease*, 918–924. https://doi.org/10.1097/NMD.0000000000001243

Aristotle (1995a). Politik 1st book. In *Aristoteles Philosophische Schriften in Sechs Bänden. Band 4*. Felix Meiner Verlag.

Aristotle (1995b). Nikomachische Ethik. In *Aristoteles Philosophische Schriften in sechs Bänden. Band 3*. Felix Meiner Verlag.

BBC (2018). *Were occult practices behind India's 'house of mass hangings'?* [Online] Available at: https://www.bbc.com/news/world-asia-india-44844617

Bentham, J. (1986). *An introduction to the principles of morals and legislation*. Legal Classics Library.

Costanza, R. (2014). Development: Time to leave GDP behind. *Nature*, *505*, 283–285. https://doi.org/10.1038/505283a

Daly, H., & Farley, J. (2011). *Ecological economics – Principles and applications*. Island Press.

Durkheim, E. (1897). *Suicide: A study in sociology*. Routledge.

Easterlin, R. (1974). Does economic growth improve the human lot? Some empirical evidence. In P. David & M. Reder, Hrsg. (Eds.), *Nations and households in economic growth: Essays in honor of Moses Abramovitz* (pp. 89–122). Academic Press.

Ekins, P., & Max-Neef, M. (1992). *Real-life economics – Understanding wealth creation*. Routledge.

Elizalde Hevia, A., Martí Vilar, M., & Martínez Salvá, F. A. (2006). Una revisión crítica del debate sobre las necesidades humanas desde el Enfoque Centrado en la Persona. *POLIS, Revista Latinoamericana* [Online], 15. https://polis.ulagos.cl/index.php/polis/article/view/465

Frank, R. (2015). *Microeconomics and behaviour*. McGraw-Hill/Irwin.

Fuders, F. (2010). Alternative concepts for a global financial system : an answer to the present world financial crisis. *Estudios Internacionales, Vol. 43* (166), p. 45–56. https://doi.org/10.5354/0719-3769.2010.12642

Fuders, F. (2011). *Política Económica – Class manuscript*. Universidad Austral de Chile.

Fuders, F. (2017). Neues Geld für eine neue Ökonomie – Die Reform des Geldwesens als Voraussetzung für eine Marktwirtschaft, Die den Menschen Dient. In *Finanzwirtschaft in ethischer Verantwortung – Erfolgskonzepte für Social Banking und Social Finance* (pp. 121–183). Springer-Gabler.

Fuders, F. (2021). The role of money for a healthy economy. In *Urban health and wellbeing programme – Policy briefs: Vol. 2* (pp. 17–22). Springer Nature.

Fuders, F., & Max-Neef, M. (2014a). Local money as solution to a capitalistic global financial crisis. In *From capitalistic to humanistic business*. Palgrave Macmillan.

Fuders, F., & Max-Neef, M. (2014b). Dinero, deuda y crisis financieras. Propuestas teórico-prácticas en pos de la sostenibilidad del sistema financiero internacional. In *Economía Internacional. Claves teórica-prácticas sobre la inserción de Latinoamérica en el mundo*. Latin.

Fuders, F., Mengel, N., & Barrera, M. (2016). Índice de desarrollo a escala humana: Propuesta para un indicador de desarrollo endógeno basado en la satisfacción de las necesidades humanas fundamentales. In *Seguridad Alimentaria, actores Terretoriales y Desarrollo Endógeno* (pp. 63–106). Laberinto.

Fuders, F., & Mora Motta, A. (2021). El Índice de Desarrollo a Escala Humana: una primera evaluación. In C. Oyarzún, P. Donoso, & J. J. Nuñez, Hrsg. (Eds.), *Historia natural, Servicios Ecosistémicos y Perspectivas de Desarrollo de la Cuenca de Llancahue* (pp. 173–194). Kultrun.

Fuders, F., & Nowak, V. (2019). The economics of love: How a meaningful and mindful life can promote allocative efficiency and happiness. In *Enhancing resilience in youth mindfulness-based interventions in positive environments* (pp. 259–277). Springer.

Gallup (2022). *People worldwide are reporting a lot of positive emotions*. Available at: https://news.gallup.com/poll/169322/people-worldwide-reporting-lot-positive-emotions.aspx

Gearing, R. E., & Alonzo, D. (2018). Religion and suicide: New findings. *Journal of Religion and Health*, *57*(6), 2478–2499. https://doi.org/10.1007/s10943-018-0629-8

Hall, B. (2009). *France to count happiness in GDP*. Available at: https://www.ft.com/content/1af2194c-a12f-11de-a88d-00144feabdc0

Heathcote, H., Gmeiner, A., & Poggenpoel, M. (1999). Adolescents previously involved in satanism experiencing mental health problems. *Curationis*, *22*(2), 56–61. https://doi.org/10.4102/curationis.v22i2.730

Helliwell, J., Layard, R., & Sachs, J. (2013). *World happiness report (2013)*. Sustainable Development Solutions Network.

Ineichen, B. (1998). The influence of religion on the suicide rate: Islam and Hinduism compared. *Mental Health, Religion, and Culture*, *1*, 31–36. https://doi.org/10.1080/13674679808406495

Kant, I. (1868). Metaphysik der Sitten – Erster Theil. Metaphysische Anfangsgründe der Rechtslehre. In *Immanuel Kant's sämmtliche Werke – In chronologischer Reihenfolge, Bd. VII* (pp. 1–173). Leopold Voss.

Keynes, J. M. (1936). *General theory of employment, interest, and money*. Harcourt.
Kopacz, M. S., Currier, J. M., Drescher, K. D., & Pigeon, W. R. (2016). Suicidal behavior and spiritual functioning in a sample of veterans diagnosed with PTSD. *Journal of Injury and Violence Research*, *8*(1), 6–14. https://doi.org/10.5249/jivr.v8i1.728
Lachmann, G. (2011). *Bundestag forscht jetzt nach dem Glück der Deutschen*. Available at: https://www.welt.de/politik/deutschland/article12203004/Bundestag-forscht-jetzt-nach-dem-Glueck-der-Deutschen.html
Lawrence, R. E., Oquendo, M., & Stanley, B. (2016). Religion and suicide risk: A systematic review. *Archives of Suicide Research*, *20*(1), 1–21. https://doi.org/10.1080/13811118.2015.1004494
Lietaer, B., Arnsperger, C., Goerner, S., & Brunnhuber, S. (2013). *Geld und Nachhaltigkeit – Von einem überholten Finanzsystem zu einem monetären Ökosystem. Ein Bericht des Club of Rome/EU-Chapter*. Europa Verlag.
Marshall, J. (2019). *Are religious people happier and healthier? Our new global study explores this question*. Pew Research Center.
Max-Neef, M. (1992). *From the outside looking in. Experiences in barefoot economics*. Zed.
Max-Neef, M. (2007). *La dimensión perdida – La deshumanización del gigantismo*. Icaria.
Max-Neef, M., Elizalde, A., & Hopenhayn, M. (1991). *Human scale development – Conception, application, and further reflections*. Apex.
Mill, J. S. (2003). *Utilitarism*. Daidalos.
NEF, New Economics Foundations (2022). *Happy planet index*. Available at: http://www.happyplanetindex.org
Pastén, R., Nazal, N., & Fuders, F. (2020). Subsidizing green deserts in southern Chile – Between fast growth and sustainability of forest management. In *Ecological economic and socio-ecological strategies for forest conservation – A transdisciplinary approach focused on Chile and Brazil* (pp. 59–78). Springer-Nature.
Phillips, B. (2009). *Why did God create mankind? (Part 1 of 4): The worship of god*. Available at: https://www.islamreligion.com/articles/336/viewall/why-did-god-create-mankind/
Plato (2008). *The republic*. Forgotten Books.
Plato (2011). Politeia. In *Platon – Sämtliche Werke Band 2* (pp. 211–537). Rowohlt.
Quinn, S. (2014). *Religion is a sure route to true happiness*. Available at: https://www.washingtonpost.com/national/religion/religion-is-a-sure-route-to-true-happiness/2014/01/23/f6522120-8452-11e3-bbe5-6a2a3141e3a9_story.html
Reichman, Z. (2016). *Flames of faith – An introduction to Chasidic thought*. Kodesh Press.
Stanek, B. (2015). *Study: The key to 'sustained happiness' is religion*. Available at: https://theweek.com/games/1012369/the-best-starting-wordle-word-has-been-revealed
Stiel, M., & Madea, B. (2002). Satanism and suicide in adolescence. *Archiv fur Kriminologie*, *210*(3–4), 76–82. https://doi.org/10.1177/1049732312468251
Suttie, J. (2020). *How does religion affect happiness around the world?* Available at: https://greatergood.berkeley.edu/article/item/how_does_religion_affect_happiness_around_the_world#:~:text=While%20it%20makes%20sense%20that,tends%20to%20make%20people%20happier
The Conservation (2021). *Are religious people happier than non-religious people?* Available at: https://theconversation.com/are-religious-people-happier-than-non-religious-people-87394
Thimmaiah, R., Poreddi, V., Ramu, R., Selvi, S., & Math, S. B. (2016). Influence of religion on attitude towards suicide: An Indian perspective. *Journal of Religion and Health*, 2039–2052. https://doi.org/10.1007/s10943-016-0213-z

UN News Centre (2012). Available at: https://news.un.org/en/story/2012/04/407782#.VDU_5il5NFs

Ura, K., Alkire, S., Zangmo, T., & Wangdi, K. (2012). *A short guide to gross national happiness index*. The Centre for Bhutan Studies.

Wallburg, C., & Fuders, F. (2013). *Relación entre la Distribución del Ingreso y el Bienestar Subjetivo – Thesis presented by Christian Wallburg and directed by Felix Fuders*. Universidad Austral de Chile.

Walsh, B. (2017). *Does spirituality make you happy?* Available at: https://time.com/4856978/spirituality-religion-happiness/

Warren, R. (2002). *La Vida Conducida Por Propósitos? Para Que Estoy Aquí En La Tierra?* Zondervan.

Wikipedia (2021). *World happiness report*. Available at: http://en.wikipedia.org/wiki/World_Happiness_Report

Wikipedia (2022a). *Bhutan*. Available at: https://en.wikipedia.org/wiki/Bhutan#cite_note-clock-3

Wikipedia (2022b). *The Philippines*. Available at: https://en.wikipedia.org/wiki/Philippines

7 Addressing fundamental human needs

Exploring the Human Scale Development proposal for governance and policymaking

María del Valle Barrera and Patricio Belloy

Introduction

The Human Scale Development (HSD) approach, conceived by Manfred Max-Neef in collaboration with Antonio Elizalde and Martin Hopenhayn, is a comprehensive theory that proposes a frame for individuals and groups to achieve higher levels of well-being and long-term sustainability in their communities. Unlike the conventional understanding of development as a certain amount of per capita income, the HSD suggests that the path to human development should be supported by three pillars: the adequate satisfaction of human needs; the attainment of growing levels of self-reliance; and the organic articulation among civil society, the state and its institutions, and nature (Max-Neef et al., 1991, p. 8).

Within the HSD, the theory of fundamental human needs (FHN) – and the methodological proposal of a matrix of needs and satisfiers derived from it – is undoubtedly the most renowned and cited, due not only to its originality but also to the broad spectrum of uses and applications worldwide (Barrera et al., 2022). In contrast, the other two pillars have notoriously had less theoretical and practical exploration and analysis. Policymakers, scholars, and practitioners have paid less attention to Max-Neef's proposals to reimagine the relationships between the community and the political, the articulation between social and state power, and the self-reliance of subnational governments as drivers for human well-being.

Contrasting with the scholarly work around the FHN theory, only a handful of studies have analysed the type of governance and policymaking that the HSD proposes in order to achieve sustainable societies (Azkarraga et al., 2011). This gap prevents us from answering some key questions currently being raised by researchers and politicians alike: what is the role of the state and governments in human and sustainable development processes? How much is self-reliance of communities or regions (sometimes read as self-determination) possible and tolerable without threatening national identity, territorial integrity, and trust in long-time institutions? What are the principles that would define human development policy that address and integrate the pillars of HSD and what would be the practical consequences?

These are vital questions at the moment of evaluating the applicability of the HSD approach in governance and policymaking, and we can discuss some possible answers based on Max-Neef's ideas and publications. However, the lack of

DOI: 10.4324/9781003381143-8

analysis and application of this political dimension of the HSD can lead to the simplification of the answers to those questions, many times responding with binary dogmatisms of right and left and making more difficult the elaboration of conclusions and further interpretations.

The objective of this chapter is to reflect on the explicit and implicit definitions of the HSD model for governance and policymaking, and hopefully lay the foundations to understand it as a political theory and an alternative model to achieve human and sustainable development. In this scenario, the proposal should aim at elaborating a political definition to achieve social change. In part, such a definition must be grounded in an understanding of the political reality and the governance models necessary to implement the HSD principles and ideals. The reflection on explicit and implicit definitions and the author's shortcomings may contribute to constructing a theoretical framework that satisfactorily articulates the HSD's principles.

The political dimension of HSD

In its original manuscript, the HSD approach does not neglect the larger political dimension but confines it to empowering civil society to pursue higher levels of participatory democracy, oriented to the satisfaction of the FHN.

> It is not the purpose of this document to propose a state model that promotes Human Scale Development. Rather, our emphasis is on empowering civil society to nurture this form of development. This is not to minimize the importance of the State but to develop further the potential role of social actors, of social participation and of local communities. Our preoccupation is a 'social democracy' (or rather a 'democracy of day-to-day living'), which does not imply a lack of concern for 'political democracy' but a firm belief that only through rediscovering the 'molecular' composition of the social fabric (micro-organizations, local spaces, human scale relations) is a political order founded on a democratic culture possible. We believe that in order to avoid the atomization and the exclusion of people – be it in political, social or cultural terms – it is absolutely necessary to generate new ways of conceiving and practicing politics. Thus, this book attempts to open up a space for critical reflection on the way we live and, more importantly, on the urgent need to develop a new political praxis.
>
> (Max-Neef et al., 1991, p. 11)

In a previous book, Max-Neef elaborates more extensively on aspects related to political philosophy, mainly based on the critique of ideologies and political models of development (Max-Neef, 1982). However, as seen in the previous quotation, Max-Neef's original work purposively avoids the discussion about the role of states and governments, perhaps missing the opportunity to advance the definition of a political proposal to achieve human development based on the HSD principles. We argue that the historical context of the emergence of the HSD – e.g., a dictatorial period in Chile and other parts of Latin America and an ailing civil society – constitutes a powerful reason both to exclude reflections on the political model and to encourage the revitalisation of the community and civil society.

However, we also see how Max-Neef leaves room for an interpretation of civil society democracy, in the form of an endeavour that can be carried out independently from the activities of the state. While conventional theories suggest that policymaking is an activity restricted to state institutions, there is increased divergence from theories and historical and empirical studies. Pluralist theories of power and studies of governance, particularly environmental governance, have contributed to highlight the role of stakeholders that sustain intertwined network of relationships that, under specific rules, lead and enable political action (Koelble, 1995; Lowndes & Roberts, 2013).

In this sense, although the HSD does not provide a theoretical or doctrinal political option that supports its implementation, the theory does propose political and normative ideas, alongside methodological reflections, for conducting empirical research and practice that addresses political action. In the next section, we analyse the normative principles and political ideas of the HSD proposal. Some of them are derived from its own postulates and values and others from its critical stance on orthodox development. Then, we present shortcomings and gaps that the author could have addressed and that remain open spaces for further discussion.

HSD's political ideas and principles

Since ancient times, philosophers and their political theories have addressed fundamental questions concerning the fate of humankind and societies, particularly about their ability to conform to a political community governed by rules, practices, and institutions in the pursuit of a common good. We believe that HSD responds to some of the critical questions that underpin a philosophical and theoretical perspective of politics, but leaves others unaddressed. In the next paragraphs, we will describe how Max-Neef's HSD approach provides alternatives to governance and policymaking that can further improve human well-being.

A conception of an empowered human being

Max-Neef, as a humanist, is one of several authors who advocate for the reorientation of the social and economic systems to achieve the advancement of the human being. Through a fundamental postulate, he claimed that human dignity is the principle and end of political and economic activity, stating that true societal development is about people and not about objects (Max-Neef et al., 1991, p. 18). Subsequently, the human person and his or her needs are the basis of the social, economic, and political development model for an HSD approach. As stated by the author in the original work presenting the HSD theory:

> Human needs, self-reliance, and organic articulations are the pillars which support Human Scale Development. However, these pillars must be sustained on a solid foundation, which is the creation of those conditions where

> people are the protagonists in their future. If people are to be the main actors in Human Scale Development, both the diversity as well as the autonomy of the spaces in which they act must be respected.
>
> (Max-Neef et al., 1991, p. 9)

Max-Neef argues that humans are conscious of themselves, how they actualise their needs and how they conduct their relations with nature and other human beings by means of culture. In addition, for the HSD, people are not only the object of development and political action but should also participate as active subjects in this process. The type of social democracy portrayed in the text is based on the legitimacy of people's participation in the decisions that affect them and the search for the satisfiers that enhance quality of life. Accordingly, the proposal legitimises direct democracy that is nurtured by the active role of the members of a political community in defining their own future.

The purpose of politics and the source of legitimacy of power

Development, as a historical process, has systemically interrelated social, political, and economic dimensions. In the same tradition, the purpose of an HSD process mainstreamed into politics and the economy is people's quality of life.

Max-Neef spent several decades denouncing the instrumentalisation of science and politics – embodied in development models – that have lost their moral and humanistic dimensions. He repeatedly insisted that the economy (and politics) must be at the service of people and not the other way around. In Max-Neef's views, the source of legitimacy of politics is action at the service of people and the satisfaction of finite series of universally shared human needs. It shares with theories of political liberalism that the foundation of politics is the search for a common good, which is more than the sum of individual interests.

More precisely, well-being or a good life as an end of politics is achieved through the satisfaction of needs, materialised in the form of a government that is culturally oriented to the search for solutions or *satisfiers* that achieve the simultaneous satisfaction of multiple needs. Such task would require considering people in their multidimensionality, without reducing their needs to aspects of biological and material deficiencies that they satisfy through consumption. In this sense, human needs according to Max-Neef are not only deficits and problems but a constant source of motivation for achieving human potentials that forge a better life. Using this interpretation, we find that the idea of quality of life should orientate and condition both the economy (the market) and politics (the state and its institutions) as the measure of good government.

The protection of rights and freedoms

The HSD defines the FHN as a set of shared characteristics of human beings in all historical periods and cultures. In this sense, they can be equated to the fundamental human rights proper to the Western and liberal traditions present in the universal human rights declaration. FHN, as defined by Max-Neef, share with the conceptual definitions of human rights the characteristics of (i) inalienable, (ii) interdependent, and (iii) universal.

FHN are inalienable because they are linked to human existence and are inherent to the human condition. This is also true to human rights approaches, although while some might bind the state towards the individual, the FHN focus on the multidimensional reality of the human condition (Rauschmayer et al., 2011). To support this point, the theory states that – with the sole exception of the need for subsistence as a precondition to exist within a system – human needs are indivisible, interdependent, and interrelated. As with the case of human rights, the FHN are part of an interdependent system where simultaneities, complementarities, and trade-offs occur. This view is opposed to a hierarchy of needs, typical of Maslow's scheme (Maslow, 1954).

Perhaps the most common element that binds Max-Neef's human needs and conventional understanding of human rights is that both sets are universal and, therefore, applicable to all people worldwide. Each individual is entitled to their human rights and FHN without distinction of racial or ethnic background, colour, gender, sexual orientation, physical ability, language, religion, political opinion, nationality or social origin, birth, or any other status. In a lifetime, it is not possible to renounce our own human needs.

On the other hand, for the HSD theory, the actualisation of the FHN is not only a right for individuals but also for groups. This is because optimal FHN satisfaction takes place in social and environmental settings. As explained by the Max-Neef:

> Needs are satisfied within three contexts: with regard to oneself (Eigenwelt); with regard to the social group (Mitwelt); and with regard to the environment (Umwelt).
>
> (Max-Neef et al., 1991, p. 21)

To this list, Spiering and Barrera (2022) suggest posterity (Nachwelt) as a fourth context of need satisfaction that adopts a longer term perspective on needs and sustainability. As discussed in Chapters 10 and 12 of this volume, this future-looking dimension of the FHN can potentially become the north of development policy, constituting the minimum conditions through which quality of life is sustained and political action is legitimised. On the other hand, this "compass for policymaking" can be supplemented by the idea of ecosystem services provided by nature and the planet's carrying capacity as outer limits for development and economic growth (Raworth, 2017).

The scale of power and political action

In the original theory, Max-Neef does not inquire about the best form of government to achieve the HSD in an exclusionary manner. Instead, he questions state technocracy and its developmental growth to justify a return to the human scale.

In his writing, the author expresses concern about unlimited economic growth and the fetish of gigantism that drives society. In line with this criticism, he later developed a reflexive argument that derives from the search for a "critical dimension" of organisations, according to their egalitarian or hierarchical structures, that considers a capacity of influence in communication and the agility in their response (Max-Neef, 2007). In there, Max-Neef maintains that the structures that grow above their critical dimension lose influence (valence), which tends to degradation or dispersion of their missions and, therefore, their structures.

Inspired by Leopold Kohr's *Breakdown of Nations* (1957) and E.F. Schumacher's *Small is Beautiful* (1973), Max-Neef proposes that, for each activity, there is an appropriate scale. This means that, the more active and intimate the activity, the smaller the number of people that can participate and the greater the number of relationships that need to be established. In relation to this point, Max-Neef suggested that large groups tend to organise in authoritarian structures.

This reasoning leads to the vindication of the small and local communities and local governments, not only as economical but also as political options for achieving human and sustainable development. On the other hand, by noting the naturalised tendency towards infinite growth and concentration of power, Max-Neef's claims for decentralisation, diversification, organic articulation, and interdependence, as he objects to the centralised vision of a unitary national state composed of marked hierarchical power relations.

> Every type of environment – economic, spatial, political, cultural and natural – may have both an optimum dimension and a critical dimension. I identify the first as "humanising" and the second as "alienating".... Within one, a person feels the consequences of whatever he or she does and decides; within the other, the human being resigns himself to letting others act and decide for him. In the first the development of people is possible; within the second, only the development of objects.
>
> (Max Neef, 1982, p. 132)

In his view, extreme concentration of power and political decisions is counterproductive to the active role that should be given to individuals and communities in defining their own paths of development. It propels them to exceed the scale where human needs can be adequately satisfied. As expressed in the book, this concentration may fractally reinforce inequality among countries, regions, and communities:

> Economic concentration along with the centralization of political decisions generates and reinforces dependencies among these different levels. Poor countries are subjected to the will of the rich countries; and within poor countries the same pattern exists, where local and regional realities seem doomed to subordinate their development to the decisions of centralized political and economic interests.
>
> (Max-Neef et al., 1991, p. 58)

This fresh perspective brought by Max-Neef in terms of considering the scale as a key element to assess optimal governance and policymaking dynamics has granted him a place among the key critical thinkers in community development (Westoby et al., 2020). It ties his ideas to those of other authors who share the struggle to decentralise and relocate power in communities (including discursive power) as a means to generate increased economic and social well-being.

In sum, the scale of governance and policymaking is relevant to the extent that it allows people to take responsibility for the pursuit of a dynamic balance between their activities and their impact on the natural environment. According to Max-Neef, this is only possible when human beings, both collectively and individually, feel directly responsible for the consequences of their actions, and this can only occur if the dimension of that environment is kept within the human scale.

The relationship with nature: Interdependence and organic articulation

In his political doctrinaire definition, Max-Neef draws a significant difference with liberal and conservative doctrines, and even with socialism, in terms of their relationship with and conception about nature as a common feature. As expressed in his earlier book, (i) all of them accept growth as indispensable, even though they differ as to the forms and mechanisms most appropriate for the distribution of its output; (ii) all of them limit their primary philosophical-political concerns to power relationships among people while ignoring the direct power that both nature as well as technology, at the existential level, are capable of exercising on the destiny of humankind; and (iii) they are all agreed that one of the unavoidable means of achieving a superior human destiny lies in the domination and control of nature, for which technology again becomes a primordial weapon (Max Neef, 1982, p. 40).

In that line, HSD questions the certainties that fields such as economics or sociology have used to model a reality where nature is given and subject to domination. On the contrary, HSD emphasises the interdependence of human systems and natural conditions, reconfiguring the relations of governance and policymaking with the environment. In his work, Max-Neef adopts two key concepts from political ecology, which are based on empirical biological support in normative precepts of power relations: self-reliance and organic articulation. Regarding the first, he states:

> We understand self-reliance in terms of a horizontal interdependence and in no way as an isolationist tendency on the part of nations, regions, local communities, or cultures. Interdependence without authoritarian relationships can combine the objectives of economic growth, social justice, personal development and freedom in much the same way that a harmonious combination of such objectives can achieve both the collective and individual satisfaction of the different fundamental human needs.
>
> (Max-Neef et al., 1991, p. 58)

Accordingly, Max-Neef rejects a Manichean vision of power that validates the domination of one over others, producing a binary confrontation of opposites. For the HSD, power relations in nature and society operate as a network of interconnected relations, acknowledging the interdependence of central and local levels.

On the other hand, when referring to organic articulation, Max-Neef claims for the construction of coherent and consistent relations of interdependence among given elements. Articulation, in this sense, refers to the complexity of a process composed by parts considered opposites, where dynamic equilibrium can be achieved simultaneously. Thus, the relation between nature and human beings – and their activities – requires an articulation between the personal with the social, of the micro with the macro, of autonomy with planning, and of civil society with the state. Therefore, success in this articulation depends on the promotion of a participatory process that encourages social creativity, a fair distribution of wealth, and tolerance for the diversity of identities.

The political doctrine that would emerge from this approach is a mixture of ecologism and humanism, not far from the idea of Deep Ecology (Naess, 1988), but with an enhanced vision about human development labelled as *integral ecological humanism* (Max Neef, 1982, p. 54).

Policy strategies and styles of development

In Max-Neef's views, a policymaking process that supports HSD entails the replacement and abandonment of destructive or inhibitory actions, and the consequent search for adequate practices or *synergistic satisfiers* that stimulate and contribute to the satisfaction of a system of interdependent and dynamic human needs, in a way that is respectful of human beings and nature.

Central to his approach is that needs are understood and the role and attributes ascribed to the possible satisfiers must determine public policy strategies aimed at improving people's quality of life. Max-Neef includes two guiding principles for these policy strategies: systemic vision and synergy. The former is opposed to a linear vision of policymaking, while the latter to a false search for efficiency. The systemic vision of needs that is synergic diverges from a reductionist vision of development as only overcoming material poverty, broadening this view.

For Max-Neef, any unsatisfied need generates poverty. Although the need for subsistence is a priority, considering it as the only important human need leads to an impoverishment of understanding, language, and room for action.

> Fundamental human needs must be understood as a system, the dynamics of which do not obey hierarchical linearities. This means that on the one hand, no need is more important per se than any other; and that on the other hand, there is no fixed order of precedence in the actualization of needs.
>
> (Max-Neef et al., 1991, p. 49)

Accordingly, for the HSD, the political choice between linearity or a systemic vision is a determining factor in the style of development and the type of public policies stimulated by the state.

> If linearity is favored, the development strategy will most probably establish its priorities according to the observed poverty of subsistence. Programs of social

> assistance will be implemented as a means of tackling poverty as it is conventionally understood. Needs will be interpreted exclusively as deprivations and, at best, the satisfiers that the system may generate will be singular satisfiers.
>
> (Max-Neef et al., 1991, p. 50)

Evidently, the HSD's systemic and interrelated vision of human development is opposite to how the modern state is divided and departmentalised into ministries, dependencies, and administrative bureaucracy. It is also an argument for the difficulties faced today by the public administration and its jurisdictions in dealing with transdisciplinary crises such as systemic poverty, migration, and the environmental and climate crises (Johnson et al., 2021; Max-Neef, 2005; Reid, 2014).

Political pathologies and negative political satisfiers

For Max-Neef, every unsatisfied need generates poverty, and not addressing them leads to collective pathologies. In his work, he describes the effects of inhibiting and annihilating satisfiers, whose presence hinders the satisfaction of FHN and, therefore, the improvement of quality of life. In this sense, at least three negative satisfiers stand out with respect to governance and policymaking: fear, instrumentalisation, and co-optation.

Max-Neef named the results of the binary confrontation in a friend/enemy political logic as "pathologies of fear". These pathologies are evidenced in ideological manipulation, marginalisation of political actors, and exclusion, subjugating alternative human development projects to the logic of the winner. According to the HSD theory, the way to overcome this scenario of confrontation is the recognition of the autonomy and diversity of individual and collective life projects, and mainstreaming the cooperation based on interdependence and self-reliance into public policy.

> Self-reliance means considering development not as an expression of a predominant class or of a single political project controlled by the state, but as the outcome of a diversity of individual and collective projects capable of empowering one another.
>
> (Max-Neef et al., 1991, p. 62)

The acceptance of political diversity promotes greater control of the mechanisms of exploitation and coercion that are generated in the confrontational logic of friend/enemy. The role of the state, then, is to open spaces for the participation of different social actors.

A second political inhibitor of well-being is political instrumentalisation, which Max-Neef links to dehumanisation. This occurs when people are seen as objects and not as active subjects and participants in their own development, causing politics to lose its ethical dimension.

> It is necessary to counter a logic of economics, (and politics) which has inherited the instrumental reasoning that permeates modem culture with an

> ethics of well-being…The state's vertical management and the exploitation of some groups by others must give way to a social will encouraging participation, autonomy and the equitable distribution of resources. It is absolutely necessary to do away with a priori categories and assumptions which, thus far, have not been questioned at the levels of macro-economics and macro-politics.
>
> (Max-Neef et al., 1991, p. 64)

For Max-Neef, the search for the self-reliance of individuals and communities in the definition of their own development faces another challenge in the form of a political threat: the co-optation by those who operate within the logic of absolute power. The problem of co-optation is the loss of control over one's own destiny and definition of the future.

> Micro-organizations frequently neutralized by a political landscape dominated by pyramidal structures in which struggles for hegemony are constantly taking place. The problem of cooptation is critical in shaping the articulations between local organizations and global processes. Cooptation is achieved through the identification and political manipulation of the social actors. This invariably leads, not only, to a loss of their identity, but also, to actions that ultimately defeat their endogenous objectives.
>
> (Max-Neef et al., 1991, p. 75)

This practice occurs in both authoritarian and democratic states, although frequently less pronounced in the latter. It implies a conditioned allocation of resources for individuals and organisations, or the idea of "strings attached", which does not guide but rather manipulates people and interest groups.

To address these obstacles and encourage greater participation and democratisation in the distribution of resources necessary to achieve HSD, Max-Neef summarises the main normative contributions to the formulation of a political theory compatible with the HSD principles. Table 7.1 summarises the contributions that the author and the HSD make to the formation of a political theory by addressing FHN as the aim and purpose of politics.

Shortcomings and pitfalls

Despite the normative definitions described above, which help guide political action, the HSD proposal is still far from becoming a political theory applicable to modern representative democracies. The proposal is self-limiting in defining participatory democracy in a merely civil society sphere. It focuses on criticising state models but may not provide a clear definition of government organisation at the national, regional, or local level.

Despite the vindication of decentralisation of power, its position must be clarified or completed. For example, complementary to the HSD, the field of political ecology is oriented towards the decentralisation of the state as the most effective

Table 7.1 Max Neef's contributions to a political theory of HSD

Anthropological vision	The human being is the basis and foundation of political activity towards development. Human dignity is the principle and end of political and economic activity. Individuals are entitled to self-determination and are also responsible to others, to the environment, and to future generations.
Purpose of politics and power	Human progress depends on the adequate satisfaction of a dynamic system of needs. The measure of their fulfilment is qualitative and is called quality of life.
Protection of rights and freedoms	Fundamental human needs (FHN) (finite, limited in number, and classifiable) Universal Inalienable Interdependent Satisfied at three levels, individual, collective, and environmental.
Policy	Construction of the future "people are the protagonists in their future". Creative process Respect for diversity and people's autonomy that is possible on a small scale.
Scale of power	Decentralised Emphasis on social, community, and local power. Optimal "humanising" dimension that provides a sense of identity and integration. The scale of power (and of the polis) where it allows maintaining influence capacity.
Orientation of the governance	Towards self-reliance Autonomy and interdependence Responsibility in individual and collective interaction with the environment and technology. Only possible in environments with a human and humanising scale.
Political (development) process	Democratic- participatory Ascendant (button up) Systemic and synergetic search towards the best satisfiers.
Political pathologies Inhibitory satisfiers	Fear (violence – frustration) Instrumentalisation Cooptation Unlimited growth leads to alienation, dehumanisation, loss of identity, and sense of cohesion (integration).
Affiliated ideologies	Humanism Ecologism Anarchism Power relationship with nature and technology differentiating liberal, conservative, and socialist doctrines.

means to reduce human impact on the biosphere. Dobson and Lucardie (2002) state that the relationship between decentralisation and sustainability lies in the fact that decentralisation may favour the satisfaction of needs with local resources and the reduction of dependence on large trade and transport networks, whose enormous energy expenditure is rarely reflected in prices. It also facilitates the encounter between production and consumption points, reducing expenditure and enhancing self-sufficiency. In this regard, an improvement in decision-making processes would be to ensure that the people who are closest to the effects of harmful actions can make or influence decisions, alongside a devolution of power that allows communities to implement the necessary measures for environmental stewardship.

Although these ideas are consistent with the HSD, there are discrepancies among political ecologists about the role that the central state should take in human development processes. From a more radical perspective, the central state must tend to disappear, as suggested by the school of thought of bioregionalism (Boisier, 2001). For more moderate views, the state should be maintained to guide and promote decentralisation, returning some legislative and planning prerogatives and increasing local self-confidence without reaching an expert communal policy. For Dobson (2000), the central political idea is that no decision should be made at a certain level if it can be made at a lower level.

From a methodological point of view, the HSD leaves many of these issues unanswered. One of them is escalating from particular cases to achieve generalisations that are applicable beyond a community or group. The application of the theory has proven helpful at the local level, but it does not represent more than a snapshot of the situation of a specific group that is not representative to others. Undoubtedly, the role of local politicians cannot be reduced to mere catalytic action, nor can the community be attributed a magical capacity to aggregate interests by unifying a shared vision of a desired future. In Max-Neef's work, other important issues guiding governance and policymaking that are excluded from the analysis are: how to acquire power? how to distribute it? and how to conserve it?

Besides these difficulties, others derive from the epistemological contradiction of quantifying reality through indexes or indicators, alongside the possibility to fall into the same reductionist criticism that is raised for indicators like GDP. Nevertheless, there is ample opportunity to continue broadening the philosophical and theoretical/epistemological discussion of a political theory that is compatible with the HSD approach.

Concluding remarks

We acknowledge that a number of aspects concerning governance and policymaking are not addressed by Max-Neef's more cited contributions. His work may lack a proposal for a robust political theory that defines, for example, the scalability from local scenarios, the methodological application in national scale schemes, and the best structure of state and government to achieve an improved quality of life and well-being. However, our review also finds that the HSD approach has several characteristics and tools that support political practices aiming at the same end.

The HSD's methodological proposal facilitates collective processes and planning to guide social change towards sustainability, building trust, and shared meaning in the search for a joint vision of the future. Its normative proposal, based on a humanistic vision, legitimises political action to satisfy FHN and active citizen participation.

The needs-based approach to policymaking for sustainable human development allows the construction of intersubjectivities, the sharing of knowledge, and the recognition of others as valid actors of knowledge towards shared vision building and to guide processes of transition and transformation (Spiering & Barrera, 2022). In the words of Max-Neef:

> The aim is to transform the traditional, semi-paternalistic role of the Latin American State into a role of encouraging creative solutions flowing from the bottom upwards.
>
> (Max-Neef et al., 1991, p. 8)

Finally, beyond the FHN framework, the HSD approach proposes a drastic redistribution of power through the organisation of horizontal integration, at the same time passing from destructive giantism to creative smallness (Max-Neef, 1982). We believe this is the basis for further discussions about the contributions of Max-Neef's ideas and work to formulate better governance and policymaking practices towards human well-being.

References

Azkarraga, J., Max-Neef, M., Altuna, L., & Fuders, F. (2011). *La evolución sostenible. (ii) apuntes para una salida razonable*. Mondragon Unibertsitatea. Humanitate eta Hezkuntza Zientzien Fakultatea.

Barrera, M. del V., Belloy, P., Mougenot, B., & Doussoulin, J. P. (2022). The international impact of Manfred Max-Neef's scholarship: A bibliometric approach. *International Journal of Sustainable Development*, *25*(1–2), 1–29. https://doi.org/10.1504/IJSD.2022.126458

Boisier, S. (2001). Biorregionalismo: la última versión del encuentro del traje del emperador. Territorios: *Revista De Estudios Urbanos Y Regionales* (Santafe De Bogotá), 05, 115–142.

Dobson, A. (2000). *Green political thought* (3rd ed.). Routledge. https://doi.org/10.4324/9780203131671

Dobson, A., & Lucardie, P. (2002). *The politics of nature: Explorations in green political theory* (1st ed.). Taylor and Francis.

Johnson, M. P., Belloy, P., MacLean, H., & Kandel, S. (2021). *Climate and housing crisis: A research agenda for urban communities*. Lincoln Institute of Land Policy.

Koelble, T. A. (1995). The new institutionalism in political science and sociology. *Comparative Politics*, *27*, 221–244.

Kohr, L. (1957). *The breakdown of nations*. Kegan Paul.

Lowndes, V., & Roberts, M. (2013). *Why institutions matter: The new institutionalism in political science*. Bloomsbury Publishing.

Maslow, A. H. (1954). The instinctoid nature of basic needs. *Journal of Personality*, *22*, 326–347.

Max-Neef, M. A. (1982). *From the outside looking in: Experiences in "barefoot economics"*. Dag Hammerskjöld Foundation.
Max-Neef, M. A., Elizalde, A., & Hopenhayn, M. (1991). *Human scale development: Conception application and further reflections*. Apex Press.
Max-Neef, M. A. (2005). Foundations of transdisciplinarity. *Ecological Economics*, *53*(1), 5–16. https://doi.org/10.1016/j.ecolecon.2005.01.014
Max-Neef, M. A. (2007). *La dimensión perdida: la deshumanización del gigantismo*. Nordan Ed.
Naess, A. (1988). Deep ecology and ultimate premises. *Ecologist*, *18*, 128–131.
Rauschmayer, F., Omann, I., & Frühmann, J. (Eds.). (2012). *Sustainable development: Capabilities, needs, and well-being*. Routledge.
Raworth, K. (2017). *Doughnut economics: Seven ways to think like a 21st-century economist*. Chelsea Green Publishing.
Reid, H. (2014). *Climate change and human development*. Bloomsbury Publishing.
Schumacher, E. F. (1973). *Small is beautiful: Economics as if people mattered*. Perennial Library.
Spiering, S., & Barrera, M. D. V. (2021). Testing the quality of transformative science methods: The example of the Human Scale Development approach. *Sustainability Science*, *16*(5), 1439–1457.
Westoby, P., Palmer, D., & Lathouras, T. (2020). *40 critical thinkers in community development*. Practical Action Publishing.

Part II

Development, growth and sustainability

8 Overcoming the development discourse

Max-Neef and economic growth

Antonio Elizalde Hevia

Introduction[1]

The current paradox in which we live is that all the institutions, norms, values and beliefs of our current civilisation had their origin in the imaginary of a world without limits, and that it is necessary to transform them to account for the finiteness of the planet we inhabit. In effect, universal recognition of planetary boundaries is a matter of recent date. The consequences of these boundaries for our civilisation are now being debated. One dimension of that debate occurs in the field of development: should be promote green growth, zero growth or degrowth?

Among these, the concept of degrowth has only recently been coined and incorporated into a tradition of several decades of reflection on development. However, the notion or idea of degrowth was implicit in the debates that have been going on for several decades.

This edited book discusses the intellectual contributions made by Manfred Max-Neef (hereafter MMN). And yet, degrowth is a topic on which MMN never explicitly wrote or lectured. I can state this responsibly because I systematically went through all his publications looking for any explicit reference to the subject and found nothing. Does this mean that he had nothing to do with the evolution of thinking about the problem of development and its necessary conclusion in the degrowth proposal? This chapter intends to demonstrate that the answer to this question is a resounding no. MMN's intellectual work from his beginnings in international organisations in the late sixties and early seventies, as well as his time at the Bariloche Foundation and the subsequent creation of CEPAUR (standing for Centre for the Study of Urban and Rural Development Alternatives in English), led to his most well-known publication *Human Scale Development*, in which I was a co-author. His incorporation and participation in various intellectual collectives and his academic work at the Universidad Austral de Chile were marked by his permanent criticism of the hegemonic growth discourse and his efforts to recover the notion of development and differentiate it from the idea of economic growth.

In this way, he made an important contribution to challenging the dominant notion of human needs (dominant in mainstream economics as well as other disciplines), understood as infinite, ever-growing and ever-changing, and constituted

DOI: 10.4324/9781003381143-10

as the key concept installed in the imaginary of today's society, which has led to confusing consumption with happiness (see Chapters 3 and 4 in this volume). This notion of human needs is also shaped as the psychosocial basis of the functioning of a *chrematistic economy* that pushes people, through advertising, to consume goods disguised as necessities, to achieve its ultimate goal: the maximisation of utility and thus the maintenance or increase of the rate of profit of capital. Its logic is to turn everything into an object of profit, so that everything that is abundant becomes scarce and can thus be assigned prices that make it possible to commodify it. **Permanent growth is in its DNA; it cannot stop growing.**

Max-Neef's basic intuition was that everything in the known universe has limits, so that infinite growth is a physical and biological impossibility, and the permanent transgression of those limits is a stupid way to live and is leading us to ecological destruction and thus to collective suicide.

I will first give an account of the main conceptual contributions of MMN regarding economic growth and its limits, and second, of the school that has been called the degrowth theorists.

Manfred Max-Neef and economic growth

It is not easy to summarise MNN's intellectual life and contributions to the world of ideas. However, I will allow myself to describe it as a quest and effort to put human beings and nature back at the centre of interest in economics.

In most of his reflections, he sought to answer the question of the appropriate size of things, trying to account for and denounce the immoderation, the gigantism, the excessive and the disproportionate in our ways of life.

He brought us highly original ideas, as well as conceptual distinctions of profound significance. As I had the good fortune to work with Manfred for many years, I will list the ideas and notions that I consider most relevant to what was being debated and constituted the state of the art at the time when I was first able to read, hear or discuss them from and with him.

1 The invisible actors of history. MMN maintains, like the one that History and the historical account have been carried out from the perspective of those who hold power and the winners in case of conflicts, making the true actors, the great dominated and invisible majorities
2 The original myth and its derivations. MMN affirms that the founding myth of the western Christian tradition of the expulsion from paradise has been translated into a cultural norm that justifies the relationship of domination and exploitation over nature
3 The theory of fundamental human needs. Unlike the hegemonic vision that thinks of needs as particular, infinite and always growing. MMN et al. maintain that these are universal, finite and limited, introducing the notion of satisfier as the medium or cultural artefact that articulates needs and economic goods, thus accounting for (updating) the emergence of need before consciousness as a desire

4 The language systems. MMN introduces the notion of language systems to account for the profound transformations experienced in the last century in the patterns of consumption and the exercise of political and economic power
5 The knowing and understanding. A substantive contribution made by MMN in the epistemological field is this distinction that makes it possible to understand the complexity of the act of knowing when getting involved in the observed phenomenon.
6 The value of diversity. MMN summarised this substantive value for the existence of life in the following statement: "The vulnerability of any living system is inversely proportional to the diversity it contains"
7 The *ecoson* and threshold point concepts. The concept of *ecoson* as the entropic weight of the existence of any human being, coined by MMN during his stay at the Bariloche Foundation, gave rise to the notion of threshold point, produced in the heat of long conversations while we were working at CEPAUR. Operationalising this notion was possible when Daly and Cobb coined the Index of Sustainable Economic Well-being and various works applied this concept in various countries

MNN's thought begins in his early works with a critique of the styles of growth, denouncing the transgression of the scales of operation and the immoderation of the culture we have built up in the last two centuries of human history, and it is necessary to recognise the great influence that the likes of Schumacher and Leopold Kohr had on his intellectual work. Manfred himself emphasises this, referring to Schumacher:

> Ever since I read his book, I have wanted to meet him, or at least to establish contact with him. contact with him. I wrote him a letter, but as fate would have it, he died two days after I put it in the post. He died of a heart attack, last year (1977), while travelling on a train in Switzerland. E.F. Schumacher was a master. From his book *Small is beautiful* I open the fifth chapter entitled: "A question of size." I read and, in my mind, I translate extracts freely.
> (Max-Neef, 2007, p. 63)

In dealing with the problem of dimension, Max-Neef puts it this way:

> The size or magnitude of systems, especially of artificial systems such as businesses, firms, and other types of enterprises, as well as cities, has been an issue in economics only in relation to the efficiency of the producing unit. So-called economies of scale and the corresponding law of diminishing returns are conspicuous cases in point. Economies of scale, in the name of efficiency, tend to favour large and, in many cases, gigantism.
> (Max-Neef et al., 1986, p. 149)

He also states, referring to the economy:

> ...[it] has worshipped efficiency and, in the name of efficiency, we have evolved from economies of scale to what I would call "diseconomies of

uncontrollable dimensions." The economic efficiency of these processes is undeniable if measured with a purely economistic approach. But, equally undeniable is their irrational predatory power of natural resources, their terrifying capacity to pollute and their remarkable contribution to the increase in cardiovascular death rates. Unfortunately, large-scale economic systems, once consolidated, can only evolve to the extent that they become even larger. The economic system thus becomes confused with society itself, dominates and determines it, to the point where its expansion no longer occurs to satisfy people's consumption needs, but where people consume more and more to satisfy the system's growth needs.

(…) As alienation, natural depredation, pollution and, in short, dehumanisation, are not measured as costs of the process, the process remains positive, efficient and successful according to the traditional standards by which it is measured.

It should be recognised once and for all that measures such as Gross National Product per capita are highly misleading. It is a poor measure of quality of life and standard of living because it includes any activity, regardless of whether it is beneficial to society. On the other hand, there is already powerful evidence that the improvement of living standards (basic needs and luxuries) constitutes a diminishing fraction of each new unit of GNP per capita increase; the rest is spent on the changes required by growth itself, on its side effects and on waste management. It should be clear, then, that the ever-increasing scale of economic activity is not only destructive of the environment and alienating for those who participate in it but reaches the characteristics of a veritable process of auto-anthropophagy.

The enthusiasm for gigantism has taken root in economic theory. Economies of scale, it is argued, have a stronger impact on economic growth. On the other hand, it has always been argued that economic growth is good for society and people, which is, moreover, perfectly true. The problem does not lie there. Rather, it lies in identifying good as synonymous with more and more. This obsession has led to a new mechanistic concept of social justice. It has come to be confused with growth itself. It is not – so it seems – a matter of better distributing a cake that is already big enough, so that those who have less receive a bigger slice. On the contrary, it is about making an even bigger cake so that everyone, while keeping the proportion assigned to them by the system, receives a bigger slice than they had before. With such a vision, it is obvious that the vicious circle never ends. But that is not all. The issue is even more serious. It has given rise to catchphrases that many people swallow in good faith. "Only with more growth will the poor be able to have more." "You cannot distribute what does not exist." And so on. And good people are convinced, especially if such phrases have been uttered by an "authority" on the subject.

> If things were that simple and that mechanical, the poor would be a minority, or at least declining. The evidence, however, is exactly the opposite. Moreover, contrary to what many economists have argued – and still argue – higher growth does not lead to better distribution. Even tax and fiscal measures that may be adopted for redistributive purposes do nothing to benefit the poorest sectors of a developing society. The reasons for this are glaringly obvious. If there are people living in self-subsistence conditions, in the informal sectors that the economic statistics do not register, marginalised from the labour market and the exchange market, they are obviously also marginalised from tax and fiscal effects.
>
> (Max-Neef, 2007, pp. 48–50)

It provides us with profound reflections that call us to value the spaces we inhabit and to develop the capacity to recognise the wonders they provide us with and which we are usually incapable of appreciating. This beauty is contained in the concept of "the small":

> I am surrounded by all forms of life and death, love and anguish, glory and decay, humility and vanity, despondency, and hope. The laws of nature are here, or it is here that their inflexible effects are reflected. Human laws are here, or it is here that their fallacies are reflected. This infinitely small grain of the universe is, after all, a Universe. I discover that the Universe is unravelling to repeat itself in infinite Universes of personal scope. To know the world means above all to know the house in which we live, its paths, its garden. Because if it is true that all the houses and all the paths and all the gardens make up a world, it is also true that the world unfolds to find a total place in each house, in each path, in each garden. All immensity is contained in the small. The small is nothing other than immensity on a human scale.
>
> (Max-Neef et al., 1986, p. 183)

Referring to the small town in Brazil where he lived and carried out an urban revitalisation project, he notes the following:

> The true dimension of Tiradentes – the dimension discovered – is the human dimension. And the case of Tiradentes is repeated in thousands of small towns. In the planners' designs they become anonymous little dots, without identity, despite the fact that they may well be the last places in the world where people have managed to preserve their identity. Is this not one of the most valuable human conditions we could recover? So why not do it in those places where it still exists?
>
> (Max-Neef et al., 1986, p. 184)

After the publication of his first books, *Barefoot Economics (1982)* and *Human Scale Development: an option for the future (1990?)*, his discourse had become increasingly radical, with a consistent critical reflection on the institutions and practices of developmentalism and neoliberalism, even proposing the concept of *economic crimes against humanity* (Max-Neef, 2014), referring to the 2008 financial crisis caused by the real estate bubble:

> When asked who is responsible for the crisis, the most frequent answer is the markets. The truth, however, is that these so-called *markets* have a name. These are those who advocated the unchecked liberalisation financial markets, the executives and companies that benefited from the excesses of the market during the financial *boom*; those who permitted their practices and those who now allow them to emerge unscathed and robust with more public money, for nothing. Companies like Lehman Brothers or Goldman Sachs, banks that allowed the proliferation of junk loans, auditors who were supposed to guarantee the accounts of the companies, and people like Alan Greenspan, head of the Federal Reserve during the Clinton and Bush administrations, a staunch opponent of financial market regulation.
>
> (Max-Neef, 2017, p. 173)

He also carried out a profound critique of the discourses and systems of language and knowledge in which today's societies operate, especially the economistic language that has hegemonised the collective imaginary:

> In economics – certainly the most arrogant and dangerous of all the disciplines of our time – the divorce between the human economy and the economy of the earth has led to catastrophic results. That it is considered positive that a Human Product is achieved at the cost of the decline, and even the extinction, of a Natural Product, is an absurdity.
>
> (Max-Neef, 2017, p. 132)

Finally, he arrives at a very absolute and radical critique of our ways of life, describing them as a form of collective suicide, progressively coinciding with the proposals of degrowth:

> For me there is no difference between a public good and a private good: it is all part of nature. I don't care whether it has an owner, no owner, or many owners. What matters is the characteristic of that asset and what the function of that asset is, not the concept of ownership behind it. And then, as I said before, it is a question of understanding that we are absolutely integrated with nature. So, we must understand that these goods are an integral part of a whole. Any action of ours that has to do with the destruction of that asset is an action of collective suicide. You are committing suicide and society is committing suicide to the extent that you destroy the goods of nature that cannot be replaced.
>
> (Max-Neef, 2015, in https://revistaentorno.cl/entorno/manfred-max-neef/)

His diagnosis of the crisis our civilisation is facing can be summed up in what he called the quadruple convergence (Max-Neef, 2017, p. 158):

1. An exponential increase in human-induced climate change that is already affecting all regions of the planet
2. The end of cheap energy, which will have a dramatic effect on all economies
3. The exhaustive depletion of key resources fundamental to human well-being and production, such as clean water, genetic diversity, forests and woodlands, fisheries, wildlife, soils, coral reefs, and most of the elements that make up the local, regional and global commons
4. The gigantic speculative bubble, which is 50 times bigger than the real economy of goods and services

The main criticism and absence in the intellectual work carried out by MMN is that despite his systemic discourse, while we worked together, he always rejected the idea that the material and immaterial dimensions of reality were part of the same system and consequently interpenetrated. But it is clear that a consumerist society like the one that exists now affects both dimensions, by impoverishing the human mind or soul. Hence, an excessive increase in goods – as stated not only by Gandhi, but also by many authors such as Bauman, Lipovestky, Illich, Gorz, among others – reduces and impoverishes the human spirit, generating various pathologies. This fact is beginning to be recognised by various currents within mainstream economic thought itself, in works that, recognising the physical limits to continuous growth, introduce the topic of intangibles, human capital, the knowledge economy, the metaverse, etc. In other words, the dematerialisation of the economy, although the issue of the internal logic of capital which requires continuous and permanent growth remains pending.

Theories of degrowth

The observation of these problems, to which MNN referred in his works, as well as many other problems that characterise today's societies and their respective criticism, has been carried out for several decades by a group of diverse authors,[2] who have been shaping a theoretical current that has been called the degrowth perspective, which goes far beyond the theory of economic degrowth that defends economic sustainability as compatible with the preservation of natural resources only if the consumption of goods and energy is reduced.

As pointed out by Giacomo D'Alisa, Federico Demaria and Giorgos Kallis:

> Degrowth resists a simple definition. Like freedom or justice, degrowth expresses an aspiration that cannot be enclosed in a phrase. Degrowth is a framework in which different lines of thought, imaginaries or courses of action coincide. We interpret this versatility as a strength. That is why we decided to represent degrowth in a (loose) dictionary form. The vocabulary of

> degrowth is a network of ideas and conversations, primarily based on radical and critical traditions, but at the same time open and open to multiple connections.
>
> (D'Alisa et al., 2018, p. 22)

The pillars of degrowth

One of the best known exponents of degrowth theories, Serge Latouche, defines the basic criteria of degrowth theory:

1 The re-evaluation of individualistic and consumerist values and their replacement by cooperative ideals
2 The reconceptualisation of today's lifestyle
3 The restructuring of production systems and social relations in accordance with the new scale of values
4 The relocation of economic activities to reduce the impact generated by intercontinental transport of goods and to simplify local management of production
5 Redistribution of wealth
6 Reducing consumption and simplifying people's lifestyles
7 A return to small and simple tools and techniques that are adapted to the needs of use, easy to understand, interchangeable and modifiable
8 Re-use and recycling and extending the life of products to avoid waste
9 The rejection of obsolescent product design and generation

For his part, another renowned degrowth theorist, Carlos Taibo, points out the principles and values contained in the degrowth proposal:

a the primacy of social life over the frenetic logic of production, consumption and competition
b creative leisure, as opposed to forms of leisure always linked to money, consumption and advertising.
c the reduction of working time and work-sharing
d the downsizing of many productive, administrative and transport infrastructures
e the recovery of many of the elements of local life in the face of the logic of ongoing globalisation
f decentralisation and decomplexation to revive rural life in the face of the megalopolises
g in the individual field, sobriety and voluntary simplicity

Giacomo D'Alisa, Federico Demaria, Giorgos Kallis, editors of the book *Degrowth. A vocabulary for a new era* (2014) point out that:

> Degrowth has multiple interpretations. Quite different people come at it from different to it from different angles. Some because they see limits to growth. Others, because they consider that we are entering a period of economic

> stagnation and that we should find ways to maintain prosperity without growth. Still others, because they believe that a truly egalitarian society can only be one that is free from capitalism and its insatiable quest for expansion, a society that learns to limit itself collectively and that works without constantly calculating selfish utility. And others, finally, because they find the term "degrowth" very consistent with their way of life.
>
> (D'Alisa et al., 2018, p. 9)

Degrowth, like other conceptualisations of alternative proposals to the hegemonic model, cannot be defined in a straightforward way. Like concepts such as justice, freedom, democracy or welfare, degrowth expresses an aspiration that cannot be enclosed in a phrase. Degrowth is an epistemic matrix in which different lines of thought, imaginaries or proposals for action converge and coincide. This versatility is one of its main strengths.

Although there is an intransgressible defining framework, in the words of Carlos Taibo:

> The so-called degrowth perspective tells us in essence that if we live – and we do live – on a planet with limited resources, it does not seem to make much sense for us to aspire to continue to grow limitlessly.
>
> (D'Alisa et al., 2018, p. 9)

He states further:

> (…) At the end of the decade Ivan Illich invited some of his friends to ask themselves: After development, what next? The result of the conversations was the *Dictionary of Development: a guide to knowledge as power.* We began to talk about post-development. It was thus possible to immediately disqualify the Bruntland Commission's new slogan, as "sustainable development" was about sustaining development, not nature or culture.
>
> (D'Alisa et al., 2018, p. 10)

He argues that, in Latin America, numerous currents of thought and action have emerged that dissociate themselves from all variants of development and seek their own path. In contrast to the path towards the *American way of life*, imposed by the developmentalist enterprise, they recognise the immense variety and richness of the real world, embrace radical pluralism and denounce the folly of adopting a universal definition of the good life that is unviable, unsustainable and the absurd imposition of a single way of inhabiting the human.

Good living, living well, living to the full, the good life, the worthy life, right living, good way of being, sweet life, austere life lubricated by affection, Spanish expressions like these began to be used to distance themselves from the prevailing winds. These translations of indigenous expressions such as *sumak kawsay* (Quechua) and *suma qamaña* (Aymara) reflect the propensity to find inspiration in those who have managed to resist colonial domination over 500 years. With them, one learns a sense of community respectful of Mother Earth and the cosmos, which opposes the inevitably individualistic and predatory breath of development (D'Alisa et al., 2018, p. 11).

It also emphasises Latin American societies in this movement. The theorists of degrowth and its practical derivations converge in a commitment to forms of communal self-limitation, thus explicitly challenging dominant patterns and giving full meaning to the concerns expressed as early as the 1970s about resource limits and the destruction of nature and societies in the name of economic growth.[3]

He concludes that we are facing the greatest crossroads in history, for we have discovered that we cannot continue a path that puts our survival as a species and even that of all life forms on the planet, at risk. Because at the present juncture, the destruction of nature is leading us to barbarism in social relations and a criminal updating of all kinds of fascism.

Conclusions

Although the degrowth proposal originated, as has already been stated, in the industrialised countries of the North, an important critical and practical reflection on developmentalist theories has been developed in Latin America, one of the main exponents of this intellectual current being MNN and the theoretical proposal he promoted with others: the proposal for Development on a Human Scale.

This contains at its core content a profound critique of the vision of the meaning of the human needs which underpin conventional economics. It proposes (a) understanding needs as universal, few and finite, and with a double character not only of *lack*, but also of *potentiality*; (b) distinguishing between needs and the satisfiers that account for them; (c) enriching the impoverished and reductionist conception of human nature that characterises the economic thinking underlying macroeconomic theories; (d) introducing a new view of resources; (e) placing life, human and of all forms of life, at the centre of the economic endeavour.

Similarly, he proposes five fundamental postulates and one inalienable value that he left as his legacy:

1. The economy is there to serve people, not people to serve the economy
2. Development is about people, not objects
3. Growth is different from development, and development does not necessarily require growth
4. No economy is possible without ecosystem services
5. The economy is a subsystem of a larger, finite system – the biosphere – so permanent growth is impossible

The inalienable value is that no economic interest, under any circumstances, can be above reverence for life (Max-Neef, 2017, p. 147).

Finally, in one of his latest works, Max-Neef points out (coinciding with degrowth, post-development and apologist proposals for the pluriverse) a reaffirmation of the essential value of identities and local spaces, claiming the need for diversity:

> Even though neoliberalism is the dominant model in the world today, those who consider an alternative indispensable and urgent, must avoid at all costs devising another global model. What is required is diversity. That is, economic systems that are coherent with local and regional realities that have their own cultures, traditions, ways of life and worldviews. Diversity is necessary to strengthen living systems and generate innovation and creativity, which are fundamental components of true development.
>
> (Max-Neef, 2017, p. 189)

Notes

1 All quotes included in this chapter are originally in Spanish. Translations are mine.
2 Possibly, as Pepa Gisbert (2007, p. 21) points out, "The idea of degrowth was born from thinkers critical of development and the consumer society, among them Ivan Illich, André Gorz, Cornelius Castoriadus or François Partant, including in this critique the failure of development in the Third World, with authors such as Vandana Shiva, Arturo Escobar, etc." Similarly, in the field of economics, following the Club of Rome report, voices critical of the growth model appeared. Herman Daly, an American economist who received the alternative Nobel Prize in 1996, proposes the idea that a stable economy is possible, with stationary conditions of population and capital, so-called zero growth. Serge Latouche, who appears as the most visible face of this school of thought, points out that degrowth implies unlearning, letting go of a mistaken way of life, incompatible with the planet. It is about seeking new forms of socialisation, of social and economic organisation. The fundamental aim of degrowth is to abandon the senseless objective of growth for growth's sake, whose driving force is none other than the unbridled pursuit of profit for the owners of capital.
3 Reference is made here to two landmark documents, the Report to the Club of Rome "The Limits to Growth" by Donella H. Meadows, Dennis L. Meadows, Jorgen Randers, and William W. Behrems and published by Universe Books of New York in 1972. Similarly, the 1975 paper "What now. Another development" report prepared by the Dag Hammarskjöld Foundation on the occasion of the Seventh Special Session of the UN General Assembly.

References

D'Alisa, G., Demaria, F., & Kallis, G. (2018). *Decrecimiento. Un vocabulario para una nueva era*. Icaria/Fundación Heinrich Boell.

Gisbert, P. (2007). Decrecimiento camino hacia la sostenibilidad. *El Ecologista*, *55*, 20–23.

Max-Neef, M. (1986). *Economía descalza. Señales desde el mundo invisible*. Nordan, Estocolmo.

Max-Neef, M. (2007). *La dimensión perdida. La deshumanización del gigantismo*. Nordan/Icaria.

Max-Neef, M. (2014). The good is the bad that we don't do. *Ecological Economics*, *104*, 152–154. https://doi.org/10.1016/j.ecolecon.2014.02.011

Max-Neef, M. (2015). La obsesión por el crecimiento es un disparate. *Revista Entorno*, *1*, disponible en https://revistaentorno.cl/entorno/manfred-max-neef/
Max-Neef, M. (2017). *Economía herética. Treinta y cinco años a contracorriente*. Icaria.
Max-Neef, M., Elizalde, A., & Hopenahyn, M. (1986). *Desarrollo a escala humana: una opción para el futuro, Development Dialogue*, Número especial 1986. Cepaur/Fundación Dag Hammarskjöld.

9 How Human Scale Development can help to achieve the Sustainable Development Goals for the 2030 agenda

Ivonne Cruz

Introduction

As the ambition grows to tackle the so-called Sustainable Development Goals (SDGs), there is still little knowledge and a lack of means to push an overall global strategy to help resolve the pressing challenges of eradicating poverty, protecting fragile ecosystems, greening the economy, promoting social justice and developing just economies. Certainly, the SDGs have redefined the way we address development practice globally and at a local level as we see an emerging trend in measuring their interactions specifically localising the goals and measuring progress through their numerous targets.

The SDGs claim to be systemic, multidimensional, comprehensive, context-specific and prevention-oriented (Hegre et al., 2020). These aspects suggest the possibility for the Human Scale Development (HSD) approach to potentially demonstrate progress by revealing people's participation and self-reliance in the process and through the valuation of actions and/or policies implemented to advance the goals, as synergistic, constraining or destructive. Only to mention a few examples.

Max-Neef *et al.* defined human needs as universal, interrelated, interactive, and interdependent; systemically interacting with culturally specific satisfiers. His fivefold categorisation of satisfiers (1. violators/destroyers, 2. pseudo satisfiers, 3. inhibiting satisfiers, 4. singular satisfiers, 5. synergic satisfiers) could help identify certain actions towards SDG achievement specially to avoid negative outcomes when potential trade-offs and specific synergies are fundamental for ensuring that progress in one direction does not threaten progress in others. Simultaneity, complementarity and trade-offs are features of the process of needs satisfaction under the HSD approach representing a creative, holistic multidimensional scheme to assess wellbeing within the framework of the global goals.

The goals allude to an intrinsic indivisibility and complementarity among the multiple suggested targets and indicators refraining for any hierarchical system. This is a so-called indivisible agenda, aiming to achieve progress across the economic, social and environmental dimensions of sustainable development integrated by set of global priorities and objectives emphasising an intrinsic interdependency.

Amongst the goals, there is a range of positive and negative interactions that need to be uncovered to ensure that progress made in some areas is not made at the

DOI: 10.4324/9781003381143-11

expense of progress in others. However, the interactions across the SDG domains depend largely on coherent and effective decision-making, as well as they are context-specific and contingent on the policy options and strategies chosen to pursue them. The challenge to grasp all dimensions entailed under the SDG scope is huge and past work on the multidimensionality aspect of the human development (HD) approach has brought some light in measuring progress on wellbeing accounts.

The HSD, on the other end, serves as an evaluation framework to help participatory processes aligned with people's aspirations to ensure the satisfiers chosen within the existential dimension of being, having, doing and interacting are coherent with their environmental and societal aspirations.

This chapter covers a retake on the HD multidimensionality debate as a refresher of the purpose of the SDGs and an overall description of their scope, interrelations and interdependence. The main objective, nonetheless, is the introduction of the HSD and the classification of satisfiers to assess key actions, policies, spaces, laws, mechanism etc., when addressing the goals.

By having these two approaches looking at each other, this chapter aims to help understand possible trade-offs as well as synergistic relations between the different SDGs as crucial for achieving long-lasting sustainable development outcomes.

After all, the SDGs present 17 areas of closely connected challenges (eradicating hunger, loss of live and biodiversity on land and in water, pushing for climate action, equal opportunities, for employment and paid jobs, only to mention a few). For this reason, an integrated approach to policy- and decision-making that focuses not merely on individual components but also takes into consideration the interrelatedness and interdependencies of the entire system (or relevant parts of it) is crucial to success in achieving results.

Human development definitions, dimensions and their relevance to the Sustainable Development Goals

In the wake of the publication of the 1990 United Nations HD Report (HDR), attention was stirred to find a new conceptual paradigm for governments and international agencies to better define, evaluate, measure and address development. The HD paradigm motioned an important ethical, methodological and theoretical shift to a new point of departure in the development discourse: development *of* the people, *by* the people and *for* the people.

This paradigm shift centred on the fact that HD converted the development process into a multifaceted humanistic practice displacing reductionist, quantitative approaches like the gross domestic product (GDP), which were premised on narrow materialist measures of development that was conceptually blind to qualitative, social and spiritual aspects of human lives.

A very much-needed people-centred approach was thereafter adopted confirming that indeed development is a process of enlarging people's choices in a vast range of possibilities. The Human Development Index (HDI) was then introduced and calculated by a series of composite indicators focused on the choice to live a long and healthy life, to be educated and to have access to resources for a decent standard of living (UNDP, 1990).

A development with a human face, people centered, and not based on economic means and material goals became essential on shifting the subjective reality of the human condition into objective means. Thereafter, HD focused on advancing the right conditions to open up opportunities for progress in different aspects of people's lives where people are able to "be" and "do" desirable things in life (Haq, 1995). This approach to human flourishing, HD or wellbeing originated from the capabilities approach (CA) focused on people and their opportunities and choices available (Sen, 1999). This normative framework became fundamental in the comprehension and definition of a person's wellbeing in the terms of her capabilities to function and served not only as a particular line of reasoning (Sen, 2003), but also as an alternative tool to conceptualise and evaluate poverty, inequality and wellbeing in the last two or three decades of development economics theory advancement.

Human capabilities are the real opportunities and the set of choices that individuals have to increase their freedom and agency (Sen, 1992). *Functionings* on the other end are the *beings* and *doings* (being well nourished, being able to take part in the political life, etc…) available to people which serve a twofold purpose in the process. These 'functionings' not only provide information about the quality of life but also determine the capability of a person to function and chose according to their individual social arrangements. A capability set available to a person is a subset of combinations of *doings* and *beings* describing a multidimensional way of life open to the individual that the person can choose among and therefore underlining freedom as the key element in this process. Many of these concepts and definitions opened Pandora's box in development and wellbeing economics during the late 1990s, pushing scholars and development practitioners to define the multiple dimensions of HD in advancing the new notion of HD and its operationalisation.

The importance of dimensions

The HD theory turned the debate into a more complex perception of wellbeing. The aim was to universalise the notion that people are not regarded as passive beneficiaries of services provided to meet basic needs, but instead, people are seen as active agents of change (Fukuda-Parr & Kumar, 2003). For this reason, the definition of HD aimed to be a more practical approach rather than philosophical agreement, which was instrumental in the socialisation and acceptance of the HDI as a novel indicator without being blind to social aspects of human lives (contrarily to GDP).

The school of thought promoting the expansion of the HD notion and debate kept publishing on the relevance of dimensions and incorporating the importance of measuring aspects pertaining the protection of human, ecological and social rights. The latter work expanded on the publication of the 1996 HDR where aspects such as participation, sustainability, gender and equity matters became central to the systematic debate (UNDP, 1996).

The HDRs had beforehand defined five different dimensions of HD in the effort to explain the notion of human flourishing to its largest extent: Empowerment,

Cooperation, Equity, Sustainability and Security (UNDP, 1996). These dimensions depicted the overarching definition of development as freedom. HD is the people's capabilities to increase their choices and freedom (*empowerment*), considering the relevance on people's sense of belonging (*cooperation*), access to opportunities (*equity*), intergenerational equity (*sustainability*) and freedom of chronic economic and environmental uncertainty (*security*) (Fukuda-Parr & Kumar, 2003). Despite the acknowledgement of these dimensions, it was not very clear how they were addressed throughout active development policies.

According to Alkire's work on dimensions of HD (Alkire, 2002), the importance on specifying dimensions relies in securing empirical footing to the multidimensional objective of HD and because of the intrinsic value of considering all possible angles of evaluating trade-offs. The later responded to the need within the academic and practitioner's community to define multidimensionality within the study of HD, since after all, human life is too complex to be captured by only 'the process of enlarging human choices' (Gasper, 1996).

Some questions came forward. Why is adding dimensions crucial to the deconstruction of the HD notion? Was it to widen up the HD study and scope? Was it about addressing simultaneities in practical terms? Was it a tool to study the constant overlapping of wicked problems pertaining human agency? Or all of the above.

Over the years, after the first publication of the HDR and the HDI, further work has been proposed pushing for more inclusive quantitative measures of HD. Alkire's work and the conception of the Global Multidimensional Poverty Index (MPI) (Alkire & Jahan, 2018) became mainstream in measuring HD achievement, by implementing multidimensional aspects of poverty, wellbeing and inequality, but overall by capturing simultaneous deprivations in health, education and living standards by addressing multiple aspects of poverty at the same time (UNDP, 2007). A great achievement of this work has not only been its breadth of country-coverage and its international comparability but also the introduction of a new unified methodology on poverty measurement with improved indicators potentially used to better monitor the SDGs (UNDP, 2018).

Strictly speaking, the MPI it is not global, covering all countries in the world, yet it focuses on developing regions designed to reflect acute multidimensional poverty in these countries. The MPI foresees that national contexts and policy priorities differ, hence, the dimensions and indicators used in national MPIs are tailored to each country (UNDP, 2018).

Further efforts such as the inequality-adjusted HD index or IHDI, are also worth mentioning. This index became well known by development economists accounting for inequalities missed within the HDI searching for possibilities to advance measures beyond traditional one-dimensional approaches (Foster et al., 2005).

Not only the qualitative tools had become key to assess progress on HD. The United Nations 2030 Agenda came into action in 2015 claiming the need to end poverty, protect the planet and ensure lasting peace and prosperity. Can HD thinking inspire a new generation of analysis, measurement and decision-making to revolutionise global development agenda once again?

The global goals come to fore

The Millennium Development Goals (MDGs) were initially launched in the year 2000 with considerably less ambitious targets than the current so-called SDGs. The MDGs aimed to represent the commitments of UN members to reduce extreme poverty, hunger, disease, gender inequality, lack of education and access to basic infrastructure throughout a 15-year timeline. These were consequently criticised for not being ambitious enough to be effective agents for progress; for lacking solid analytical background and reasons that these particular objectives were chosen, and others left out. All in all, for being 'goals' without means.

For some, the glass was half-full, for others, the glass remained half-empty since the overall goal was only to reduce the issue through a very constricted unilateral perception of the problem. Societal stakeholders were not included in the consultation process. Moreover, the MDGs adopted a simplified concept of development as 'meeting basic needs', yet, not taking into consideration any complex interactions affecting the cultural settings and, moreover, overriding institutions and their intrinsic responsibility in addressing inequalities and deficient governance practices.

The critique focused on the millennium goals being relatively vague, without precise indicators for within-country issues like income disparities, while excluding important dimensions of sustainable development such as environmental sustainability, consumption and access to resources, etc. (Kabeer, 2010). Most of the MDGs were donor-driven, which implied that government policies towards these goals were heavily located in so-called developing countries interested in child survival, basic education, promoting women's rights and halving world poverty and hunger in a very short amount of time – 15 years.

When the 2015 deadline arrived, the MDGs were approached with great frustration. The international community was in disbelief of adapting a new framework. However, the new proposed agenda aimed at eradicating very complex problems in all its variants (UN, 2021). The proposed list of universal goals included an inherent systemic approach to development by addressing a large list of tasks: reducing inequalities, increasing economic growth, providing decent jobs, sustainable cities and human settlements, industrialization, repair fractured ecosystems and slow climate change, sustainable consumption and production as well as building peace and strengthening justice and institutions. All of the above presented with the opportunity to be addressed through nationally owned and country-led strategies, with freedom to establish a local framework in achieving the SDGs.

The SDGs were presented in 2015, filling a long-time void in the operationalisation of what the literature had labelled as sustainable HD (Haq, 1995). Under the 2030 Agenda for Sustainable Development, the global community depicted an all-encompassing plan to protect universal fundamental human rights for sustainable development through an ambitious programme to tackle economic growth, social justice and environmental stewardship under a peace framework aiming for inclusive development (UNGA, 2015).

Five principles defined the SDGs' scope: People, Planet, Prosperity, Peace and Partnerships. There principles are organised under 17 goals: (1) No Poverty,

(2) Zero Hunger, (3) Good Health and Well-Being, (4) Quality Education, (5) Gender Equality, (6) Clean Water and Sanitation, (7) Affordable and Clean Energy, (8) Decent Work and Economic Growth, (9) Industry, Innovation and Infrastructure, (10) Reduced Inequality, (11) Sustainable Cities and Communities, (12) Responsible Consumption and Production, (13) Climate Action, (14) Life Below Water, (15) Life on Land, (16) Peace, Justice and Strong Institutions and (17) Partnerships to Achieve the Goals.

For once, the global goals addressed the malpractice of separating human well-being and environmental sustainability omitting the intrinsic connection of profound roots of poverty in environmental degradation, bad governance and social injustice issues. Together with a planetary assumption on the peace element as intrinsic need to sustainable development and ultimately realising that 'peaceful, just and inclusive societies are free from fear and violence' (UNGA, 2015). All actions within the SDGs would thus need to make provision for an overarching societal responsibility rather than just the average wellbeing of individuals. In other words, embracing what others have called the *Ubuntu*. Translated in Zulu as 'people depend on people to be people' or 'I am because we are' 'humanity towards others'.[1]

Under this rationale, the goals project the need for societal stakeholders to understand, manage and make use of the systemic interrelations between SDGs. This phenomenon known as the 'nexus challenge' (Tulder, 2018) relates to the alignment of actions, policies and progression to achieve success in certain problem areas. The focus is not merely on individual components, but in the interrelatedness and interdependencies of the entire system aiming to reduce trade-offs and identify synergetic connections.

For all the above, dimensions become intrinsic to understanding the nature of the goals. The SDGs are 'integrated and indivisible' and all SDGs interact with one another. Their objectives are fundamentally interdependent. Understanding the range of positive and negative interactions among SDGs are key to unlocking their full potential at any scale, as well as to ensuring that progress made in some areas is not made at the expense of progress in others. The nature, strengths and potential impact of these interactions are largely context-specific and depend on the policy options and strategies chosen to pursue them (International Council for Science [ICSU], 2017). Plenty of efforts are stirred in this direction and several examples of good practices and regional taskforces can be consulted in the United Cities and Local Governments (UCLG) site and elsewhere.[2]

There is indeed an intrinsic connection within both definitions of HD and the SDGs overarching principles; hence, the HD notion prevails at the forefront of the 2030 Agenda. It is an approach appealing to be universal, yet, the two are fundamentally different things: the SDGs represent a comprehensive framework to assess development progress multidimensionally and provide somehow a 'development destination' (Conceição, 2019). Meanwhile, HD stands for a philosophy allowing people to design the route to get there by actualising those freedoms that will expand their capabilities. Undeniably, it represents a process that will raise people's quality of life that depends directly on the possibilities available to that person.

The HSD approach could furthermore add that this should happen through a process of synergistically satisfying people's fundamental human needs and overcoming *poverties* (see below) neglecting their human flourishing and self-reliance (Max-Neef, 1998).

The HSD approach: A practical methodology to measure SDG progress under different unconventional dimensions

Max-Neef's approach on the Human Scale Development (HSD) and the elaboration of his matrix on human fundamental needs represents a great example of the relevance of including multidimensionality in the study and operationalisation and progress measurement within frameworks of HD and the SDGs. His work has been largely socialised and further details on his matrix are described in Table 9.1 and in other chapters of this volume.

Max-Neef stressed on the relevance of defining dimensions in terms of how human beings establish their relations with their environment (Max-Neef, 1992). Max-Neef's depiction of HD explains how development happens inside people, as a consequence of what happens between people and their life supporting systems, as they strive to synergistically satisfy their fundamental human needs by fashioning an infinite range of diverse satisfiers.

Under this rationale, if HD happened as a result of the relations maintained within their economy, spatial, political, cultural and natural environments, all the above, must entail not only an *optimum* dimension but also a *critical* one. As Max-Neef explains, the former humanises, while the latter alienates. In the first case, people are able to achieve a sense of identity and integration; the person embraces the consequences in whatever they do and decide. Within the *optimum* dimension, development of people is possible, and a dynamic equilibrium takes place. People feel responsible for the consequences of their actions within their environment, and this can only happen if the dimensions of this environment remain within the human scale (Max-Neef, 1992, pp. 132–133). On this dimension, people can choose to either actualise their individual integrity or resign to letting others act and decide for them. However, within the *critical* dimension, development of objects is intrinsic to the process. Human involvement is neglected, and a process of self-reliance is deserted. Therefore, they participate less and less, allowing to be led more and more. Ultimately realising that development of individuals and communities is no longer about self-reliance and agency, but dependency.

Within the HSD perception, the actualisation of human needs is not only the goal but also the motor of development itself. Needs are to be lived, achieved or realised throughout the whole development process. Needs could also represent deprivation or potential meaning that, for example, the need for participate is the potential for participation, consequently understanding that needs are never seen as passive but the opposite.

According to the HSD approach, any system of unsatisfied needs reveals a form of human poverty. This brings about the different perceptions of poverty versus poverties, suggesting that every culture or society could be rich in certain aspects of life and poor in others, depending on the specific circumstances (Cruz et al., 2009).

Table 9.1 Max-Neef's matrix on needs and satisfiers (Max-Neef et al., 1991)

Needs according to axiological categories	*Needs according to existential categories*			
	1. BeingS	*2. Having*	*3. Doing*	*4. BeingC*
1. Subsistence	Physical and mental health, balance, solidarity, mood, adaptability	Feeding, shelter, work	Feed, procreate, rest, work	Living environment, social environment
2. Protection	Care, adaptability, autonomy, balance, solidarity	Insurance systems, savings, social security, health systems, legislation, rights, family, work	Cooperate, prevent, plan, take care of, cure, defend	Vital contour, social environment, dwelling
3. Affection	Self-esteem, solidarity, respect, tolerance, generosity, receptivity, passion, will, sensuality, humour	Friends, couples, family, pets, plants, gardens	Make love, caress, express emotions, share, take care of, cultivate, appreciate	Privacy, intimacy, home, meeting spaces
4. Understanding	Critical awareness, receptivity, curiosity, astonishment, discipline, intuition, rationality	Literature, teachers, method, educational policies, communication policies	Investigate, study, experiment, educate, analyse, meditate, interpret	Settings of formative interaction, schools, universities, academies, groups, communities, family
5. Participation	Adaptability, receptivity, solidarity, dis-position, conviction, dedication, respect, passion, humour	Rights, responsibilities, obligations, work	Become affiliated, cooperate, propose, share, dissent, obey, dialogue, agree, express opinions	Settings of participative interaction, parties, associations, families, churches, communities, neighbourhoods

(*Continued*)

Table 9.1 (Continued)

Needs according to axiological categories	*Needs according to existential categories*			
	1. BeingS	*2. Having*	*3. Doing*	*4. BeingC*
6. Leisure	Curiosity, receptivity, imagination, carefreeness, humour, tranquillity, sensuality	Games, spectacles, parties, calm	Divagate, distract, daydream, long, fantasise, evoke, relax, have fun, play	Privacy, intimacy privacy, meeting spaces, free time, environments, landscapes
7. Creation	Passion, imagination, will, intuition, audacity, rationality, autonomy, inventiveness, curiosity	Skills, abilities, method, work	Work, invent, build, ideate, compose, design, interpret	Areas of production and feedback, workshops, athenaeums, groups, audiences, spaces, expression, temporary freedom
8. Identity	Belonging, coherence, differentiation, self-esteem, assertiveness	Symbols, language, habits, customs, reference groups, sexuality, values, norms, roles, historical memory, work	Commit, integrate, confront, define oneself, know oneself, recognise, oneself, actualise oneself, grow	Socio-rhythms, everyday settings, belongingness settings, maturational stages
9. Freedom	Autonomy, will, self-esteem, passion, assertiveness, openness, determination, boldness, rebelliousness, tolerance	Equal rights	Disagree, choose, differentiate from, run risks, know oneself, assume oneself, disobey, meditate	Space-time plasticity

Understanding the latter is key to stress that the HSD proposes an inflection point when the continuous deprivation of one or more of the fundamental human needs will create a collective social pathology and eventually result in the complete collapse of the whole system and death to people and living systems that sustain a given society(ies) (Cruz, 2011). The deprivation of various needs and the collapse of the system might not immediately occur in the present but could rebound in future generations.

In this regard, favouring singular and/or destructive satisfiers will perhaps attempt to achieve temporary human and environmental wellbeing but in the end, different types of povert*ies* will emerge as a result of the fractional strategies (namely satisfiers) that a society has prioritised through specific policies through time.

Introducing the HSD approach as a way forward in addressing system issues and wicked problems such as the ones posed by the 17 SDGs is an attempt to search for more coherence on sustainable development policy-making and to prevent these policies to fall under unidimensional operationalisation.

For the latter, it is important to distinguish between satisfiers and how often these have been interpreted as basic needs creating great confusion in terms of development goals and ends. To illustrate this, oftentimes, food, clothing and shelter are considered basic needs under a normative framework. However, under the HSD approach, these are all singular satisfiers to fulfil the needs of subsistence and protection. Another example similar to this is the misconception of seeing schools, books, formal education programmes as needs, when in contrast these elements are all satisfiers of the need of understanding in as much traditional cultural knowledge is, for example, a satisfier of the same need in grassroots communities.

Overall, partial satisfaction of the system of human needs is not justifiable. Wellbeing, HD and the realisation of fundamental human needs entail the systemic interaction throughout the four existential dimensions. For the latter, the cultural and social settings are so important to be considered in the process to thereafter enhance or inhibit personal and collective qualities and freedoms.

The relevance of the existential values of satisfiers (being, having, doing, interacting): an example with SDG 2

One particular objective of this work is to shed light on the specific role of satisfiers and the overall usage of its characterisation as synergetic satisfiers, violating or destructive, singular, pseudo satisfiers and inhibiting satisfiers as evaluation parameters. Satisfiers can be interpreted as organisational structures, political systems, social practices, norms, values, spaces, opportunities available, contexts, behaviour and attitudes and oftentimes could define the generation of commodities or goods.

This section applies this framework to SDG 2 (*End hunger, achieve food security and improved nutrition and promote sustainable agriculture*). The aim is to assess a system of satisfiers put forward in satisfying the system of fundamental human needs when addressing the issue of eradicating hunger. This is a simple example of interchangeably using the HSD matrix and values to evaluate an overall issue that entails evident multidimensionality and complexity.

Ending poverty and eradicating hunger are central to the 2030 Agenda recognising the multiple interdependencies entailed under this complex goal. That is achieving food and nutrition security, and increasing agricultural production and income for farmer workers, while achieving resilient and sustainable food systems will be challenging to achieve simultaneously under sustainable practice considering the amount of water and land required for this purpose.

Social scientists are currently aiming to address the complexity of these so-called interactions moving towards multi-level governance and multi-stakeholder partnerships. In addition, working on capacity development from the institutional to the individual level, mobilising resources towards research, innovation and technology development to mitigate trade-offs and supportive policies and investments needed to realise the full potential of the different targets and goals (International Council for Science [ICSU], 2017).

A potential policy goal will be depicted as follows: eradicating hunger and ensuring food security is a bottom-line requirement for achieving sustainable development and wellbeing for SDG2.

This will require a careful and context-sensitive assessment of the needs and critical trade-offs that may occur with other goals and targets such as water access, life on land constrains, fair wages and gender, inequality issues related to farm-workers, only to mention a few.

Conducting a thorough human needs assessment of a specific society facing food scarcity and vulnerability, malnutrition, poor agricultural yields and productivity and overall havoc of their food production system, the rationale under the HSD approach will represent something like the analysis given below.

Eradicating hunger will synergistically fulfil the needs of subsistence, protection, participation and freedom. Nonetheless, how to identify those synergistic *satisfiers* under the existential categorisation of *being, having, doing and interacting* is key in the elaboration of appropriate policies and action plans towards this goal. Therefore, the exercise of scrutinising potential actions/policies/strategies/ relevant for people to be active actors in pursuing their development goals, a thorough analysis of their choices could be conducted under the HSD approach, and considering the following dimensions as evaluation spaces. For example:

The *BEING* – What are some of the personal of collective attributes of this specific society? How does a particular society identify itself (culturally, economically, ethnically wise)?

Examples could be:

- Predominantly rural, farm workers (agricultural-based communities)
- Internally displaced peoples
- A community suffering of low life expectancy at birth
- A community struggling with finding access to appropriate nutritious food options etc.

The *HAVING* – Which institutions, norms, mechanisms, tools are there available to prevent hunger?

Examples at a global level:

Available programmes to those community global organisations include UN Food and Agriculture Organization (FAO), the International Fund for Agricultural Development (IFAD), the United Nations Children's Fund (UNICEF), the World Food Programme (WFP) and the World Health Organization (WHO).

Available programmes at the local level: Ministry of agriculture, social development, other local campaigns against hunger (civil society, churches etc.) customary law and communal land ownership benefits etc. National initiatives such as *Fome Zero* in Brazil (Zero Hunger) or *Bolsa Família* (Family Allowance), *One Acre Fund* or *Mercy Corps* in different countries in Africa and *Bienestar* (wellbeing) in Mexico.

The *DOING* – What are personal or collective actions in place to prevent hunger?

Examples of synergetic and singular satisfiers (actions):

Communities or local governments organise themselves launching initiatives such as: Climate smart agriculture crops, sustainable agricultural practices for climate adaptation and mitigation (such as improving soils and land quality, genetic diversity and bioenergy). Fostering gender equality in agricultural practices, reducing food waste strategies (converting biomass and agricultural waste as potential sources of renewable energy), disaster risk reduction plans, controlling infestations and crop infections, enhancing crops with bio-fortification. Enhanced water governance to manage growing and competing demands on water resources etc.

Sometimes also being victims of the introduction of *destructive, inhibiting satisfiers and pseudo-satisfiers* (giving the false sensation of satisfying fundamental human needs).

Communities or local governments are victims of large investments in agricultural research, trade and market development, which can pose trade-offs between the agricultural economies versus sustainability-focused targets. For example, yield gaps are particularly high in places like sub-Saharan Africa for some of the region's major staple crops (World Bank, 2008). Closing these gaps through agricultural productivity improvement can, however, constrain the sustainability of agriculture (International Council for Science [ICSU], 2017).

Or investment in rural infrastructure development which oftentimes does not pay attention to the needs of smallholder food producers as well as local biodiversity protection; only to mention a few.

Finally, the *INTERACTING* dimension – Determining which spaces and environments are available for communities suffering from hunger and malnutrition to advance the achievement of the goal to end hunger and food security?

For example: Are there opportunities for fair-trade farming certification and capacity building for co-ops?

Are there microcredit opportunities available for farmworkers? Schooling or paid jobs for women in agriculture? Spaces for innovative agricultural practice such as urban agriculture and vertical farming models to reduce stress from farmworkers in rural areas etc. See Table 9.2 for summary.

As depicted above through the examination and assessment of SDG 2 (eradicating hunger), the complexity and wickedness entailed in these types of valuations

Table 9.2 Analysing SDG 2 – Eradicating hunger under the Human Scale Development four existential dimensions spectrum

Being	*Having*	*Doing*	*Interacting*
What are some of the personal of collective attributes of this specific society? How do a particular society identify itself (culturally, economically, ethnically wise)	Which institutions, norms, mechanisms, tools are there available to prevent hunger?	What are personal or collective actions in place to prevent hunger?	Spaces and environments are available for communities suffering from hunger and malnutrition to advance the achievement of the goal to end hunger and food security.
• Predominantly rural, farm workers (agricultural-based communities) • Internally displaced peoples • A community suffering of low life expectancy at birth • A community struggling with finding access to appropriate nutritious food options	*Global*: Available programmes to that community under UN, WB, regional agencies etc. <u>Local</u>: Ministry of agriculture, social development, other local campaigns against hunger	*Examples of synergetic and singular satisfiers (actions):* Sustainable agricultural practices for climate adaptation and mitigation fostering gender equality in agricultural practices, reducing food waste strategies Water governance programmes etc. <u>Examples of destructive, inhibiting satisfiers and pseudo-satisfiers:</u> Large investments in agricultural research, trade and market development compromising agricultural sustainability-focused targets. Or Investment exclusively in rural infrastructure development attempting to needs of smallholder food producers and local biodiversity protection	Opportunities for fair-trade farming certification and capacity building for co-ops etc. are their availability for microcredit opportunities, schooling or paid jobs for women in agriculture, spaces for innovative agricultural practice such as urban agriculture and vertical farming models to reduce stress from farmworkers in rural areas etc.

Source: Self-elaboration.

appears challenging to apply. An integrated approach towards goal achievement is utterly what countries are willing to account or see. However, if 'development is about people and not about objects', as Max-Neef repeatedly asserted, people's participation in decision-making processes has become more important than ever. This will utterly allow communities to consider certain strategies and with insightful discrimination, reject others and search for further opportunities available to opt for strategies that are more coherent with the type of the development they are willing to pursue.

Additional policy actions could be drawn from analyses like the above example to briefly characterise actions to be *propositional* and *systemic* in time rather than destructive or only partially wholesome (as proposed in previous work Cruz et al., 2009). The idea behind this illustration is to represent an ideal form of isolating cultural attributes, policies, existing or lacking norms, created or missing spaces and individual or collective behaviours to stimulate and direct or re-direct development strategies so that it is authentically **of** the people, **by** the people and **for** the people.

The SDGs are considered integrated, indivisible and fundamentally interdependent. There is a range of positive and negative interactions among the full range of SDGs entailing that the potential impact of these interactions are largely context-specific and depend on the policy options and strategies chosen to pursue them. The more dimensions that come into play (political, economic, social, legal, technological and environmental dimensions) represent the structural complexity on the SDGs. The more 'systemic' a problem is, the more elements one should take into account to grasp it, and in this regard, synergistic satisfiers will need to be advanced to address this so-called interdependency.

As the SDGs represent challenges at a global scale, national policymakers are working towards achieving progress across the economic, social and environmental dimensions within the systemic nature of the 2030 Agenda. The so-called localising process of the SDGs has included the involvement of not only local governments but also civil society organisations, the private sector, academia and individual citizens in the implementation and monitoring of the SDGs.[3]

Further index development and operationalisation practices are part of the debate on how to measure progress across the board with interesting insights and methodologies in the SDG evaluation sphere.[4] Nevertheless, whether we talk about expanding people's capabilities, satisfying fundamental human needs or enhancing quality of life and wellbeing, by definition, these concepts must be defined within particular culturally related contexts. This attribute emphasises how certain social and cultural settings, as well as development patterns, enhance or inhibit personal and collective freedom, autonomy and wellbeing. The latter reveals how people realise their human needs in terms of their own space of rationality (*Eigenwelt)* with respect to others and their community (*Mitwelt)* and respecting their environment *(Umwelt)* (Max-Neef et al., 1991).

Even though all nations have agreed on embarking in the SDG train, it is for each nation to pursue the goals according to their own priorities and eventually turning the potential for synergies into reality through effective governance systems, institutions, partnerships and intellectual and financial resources. The SDGs interacting models and evaluating frameworks use this language of trade-offs, interactions and synergies, as these are crucial to address their interrelations. The SDGs however, adopted some kind intergenerational, crosscutting and cross-geographical scale. Overall 'SDG implementation determines the number and types of people affected and consequently the potential outcomes for other SDGs'.[5] It is imperative that some action towards an SDG may result in trade-offs at a local scale while contributing to progress at larger scale affecting either positively or destructively to goal achievement. And this will remain one of the biggest questions in addressing the wickedness of the goals.

Building on the sustainable human development notion

The intrinsic intergenerational solidarity reflected in the sustainability query and implicit within the SDGs refers to the achievement of sustainable development under a social rationale addressing not only intergenerational equity but also tackling the problem of intergenerational justice. Anand and Sen (2000) expand on the latter referring to the ethical dimension intrinsic to sustainability policies and how the moral value of sustaining what we now have, depends on the quality of what we own. This approach to sustainable development directs us as much towards an understanding of the present as of the future and time.

The Brundtland Report defined sustainable development in relation to societies' capacity to meet their human needs, under an elusive definition of them:

> Sustainable Development is the development that meets the needs of the present without compromising the ability for future generations to meet their own needs.
>
> (WCED, 1987)

The classic representation of needs within the Brundtland Report described needs from people, mostly from developed countries for food, shelter, clothing, jobs, energy, water and sanitation – physical or material commodities/goods. Max-Neef's framework, however, explains that such a conservative view of 'needs' are actually satisfiers of the fundamental human needs for subsistence and protection, to mention a few. This is just a bare example how Brundtland definition falls short in describing sustainable development as a value, as a political ideology, a normative path, an ethical position and a way forward (including our perception towards future generations) compared to the HSD existential values (Rauschmayer et al., 2011).

How we actualise human needs through the generation of synergistic, multidimensional and integral satisfiers and the expansion of human capabilities in the pursuit of a 'sustainable human development' becomes in many ways an overarching universal goal. Adding the notion of sustainability to the wellbeing notion enlarges the view and enhances the discourse of HD.

The inherent intra-generational justice discourse reminds us that wellbeing of a society can influence the wellbeing of others in both positive and negative ways making evident how the wealth of many nations and societies have taken a toll on poor countries suggesting that sustainability pertains, perhaps, more to a collective deed.

The tragedy of the commons and the precautionary principle must prevail to prevent future generations from enjoying meeting their needs although these are ultimately related to lack of access to resources that are vital for our human subsistence such as water, clean air and the right to a sustainable and healthy environment. Destructive satisfiers, indeed, hinder environmental goals and will also prevent indicators to rise in other HD achievements that entail social and environmental impacts.

Except for the need of subsistence, many needs do not require material goods to be fulfilled (the need for identity, idleness, participation or freedom). The responsibility for choosing one strategy over another aiming for a sustainable HD lies more on the hands of societal actors and less on individuals, even if it is ultimately the lifestyle of individuals that seem to prevail upon the realisation of wellbeing worldwide now and in the future (Spillemaeckers et al., 2011).

The global goals, hence, seem instrumental in societies with cultural connections to pursue collective agency and achieve collective capabilities in the synergetic realisation of their fundamental human needs. But also, as societies gain this so-called agency (Sen, 1985) (the individual freedom to act in pursuit of goals other than self-interest), the notion of sustainable HD therefore will be constructed under the premises of taking others into account.

The SDGs achievement should improve the realisation of the needs of *affection*, *protection*, in as much as they motivate *participation* and consequently enhancing *identity* and *freedom*. At the same time, the goals are aiming to accomplish people's *subsistence* satisfiers and *understanding* as societies embrace the value of the resources available for their ultimate wellbeing and human flourishing and stressing on the importance of stable institutional settings and spaces (for example, through SDG 16 – Peace, Justice & Strong Institutions).[6]

The perpetual deprivation of various needs systemically and across our societies has claimed the destruction of our environment, our cultural references, fair markets and distribution of shared benefits. These 'poverties' have emerged because of fractional strategies and satisfiers that a society or as individuals have prioritised through a particular policy (Cruz, 2011). Corrupt and illegitimate States have perpetuated unsustainable actions by preventing others to meet their needs and hindering people's capability sets. So, by favouring singular or inhibiting/destructive satisfiers (or strategies based on pure material goods) results in the collapse of the system of needs, not in the present but for future generations and, therefore, undermining opportunities for self-reliance and human flourishing.

The human dimension of global environmental change has shaped current wellbeing debates. There is still a lack of understanding of socioeconomic uncertainties that oftentimes dominate biophysical worries that also have big impacts on global issues. Human consequences of global change shows that they are due at least as much to the social systems that produce vulnerability as to environmental changes themselves (National Research Council, 1999). Approaches such as the HSD addressing the social-environmental dichotomy also embrace how cultural forces, values and beliefs can shape institutions and policies, and interactions among issues such as food security, deforestation, energy consumption, economic and technological development, gender inequality, peace and participation.

For all of the above, building on a sustainable HD definition must take into consideration how certain strategies, material and none material goods, policies, spaces, institutions, norms, mechanisms, collective actions and so forth can contribute to attain aspirational goals such as the SDGs.

Conclusions and possible ways forward

As less than ten years remain to achieve the SDGs, it is imperative to increase the effectiveness of all efforts directed to respond to the over 300 targets of the 17 globally agreed goals.

It is becoming ever more relevant to incorporate integrality and multidimensionality in aspects related to sustainable development policymaking. A prevailing debate regarding human needs, human capabilities and/or wellbeing frameworks will continue framing evaluation schemes. Nonetheless, the ethical and aesthetical aspect of any political exercise must prevail under the overarching goal of achieving human sustainable development in the terms described in this work. The ethics refers that each social group should define what is valuable to their own cultural, political, economic, technological and geographical context, as the SDGs have worked hard on localising the SDGs through regional work. Whereas the aesthetics aims to pursue more than mere survival but a sustainable development path that enhances overall wellbeing and the quality of life, it must also translate into ensuring people's true capacity to participate, influence and shape decision that affect them (Stahel et al., 2005).

Achieving the goals on protecting life below water and on land (SDGs 14 and 15), participating in the energy transition and embrace climate action (SDGs 7 and 13) will depend on existing policies frameworks and cooperation at regional and national levels.

There is an instrumental role of culture in providing opportunities for decent work, poverty reduction, social resilience, gender equality and other aspects of the 2030 UN agenda that will need to be acknowledged in the process of achieving the SDGs. A key question then will be how do we ensure sure these aspects of the human experience are part of the complex exercise of recognising synergies and trade-offs to achieve the goals?

The HSD approach is indeed a complex analytical framework, yet a humanistic approach 'based on the satisfaction of fundamental human needs, on the generation of growing levels of self-reliance, and on the construction of organic articulations of people with nature and technology, of global processes with local activity, of the personal with the social, of planning with autonomy and of civil society with the state' (Max-Neef et al., 1991). The SDG conception covers many of these aspects, yet lacking the importance of people creating these conditions and becoming protagonists of their future and as main actors in the process bringing it to a human scale so that the diversity as well as the autonomy of the spaces in which they act must be respected.

The 2030 Agenda represents the remake of many and several conventions, resolutions and landmarks in bringing the so-called *development with a human face* to the centre of the policy exercise. Making the SDGs a reality under the premises of justice, peace, social equity, good governance and inclusive environmentally minded societies will push the global community to advocate for synergetic strategies, policies and actions (in other words – satisfiers) to 'embrace' people's most intrinsic values, beings, doings and societal aspirations now and for the generations to come.

Notes

1 New World Encyclopedia. The meaning of Ubuntu. https://www.newworldencyclopedia.org/entry/Ubuntu_(philosophy)
2 World Organization of United Cities and Local Governments – UCLG https://www.uclg.org and Local 2030, https://www.local2030.org/library/shelves
3 Global Taskforce of Local and Regional Governments (Global Taskforce – GTF). Roadmap for localising the SDGS: Implementation and monitoring at subnational level. 2016. https://sustainabledevelopment.un.org/content/documents/commitments/818_11195_commitment_ROADMAP%20LOCALIZING%20SDGS.pdf
4 SDG Report. https://www.un.org/sustainabledevelopment/progress-report/
5 Global Taskforce of Local and Regional Governments (Global Taskforce – GTF) Roadmap for localising the SDGS: Implementation and monitoring at subnational level. 2016.
6 Promote peaceful and inclusive societies for sustainable development, provide access to justice for all and build effective, accountable and inclusive institutions at all levels.

References

Alkire, S. (2002). *Valuing freedoms: Sen's capability approach and poverty reduction*. Oxford University Press.
Alkire, S., & Jahan, S. (2018). *The new global MPI: Aligning with the sustainable development goals*. Human Development Report Office (HDRO). https://hdr.undp.org/system/files/documents//2018mpijahanalkirepdf.pdf
Anand, S., & Sen, A. (2000). Human development and economic sustainability. *World Development*, *28*(12), 2029–2049. https://doi.org/10.1016/S0305-750X(00)00071-1
Conceição, P. (2019). *Human development and the SDGs - June*. Human Development Report Office, UNDP. Available at http://hdr.undp.org/en/content/human-development-and-sdgs
Cruz, I. (2011). Human needs frameworks and their contribution as analytical instruments in sustainable development policymaking. In F. Rauschmayer, J. Frühmann, & I. Omann (Eds.), *Sustainable development: Capabilities, needs & wellbeing*. Routledge.
Cruz, I., Stahel, A., & Max-Neef, M. (2009). Towards a systemic development approach-building on the human-scale development paradigm. *Ecological Economics*, *68*(7), 2021–2030. https://doi.org/10.1016/j.ecolecon.2009.02.004
Foster, J. E., Lopez-Calva, L. F., & Szekely, M. (2005). Measuring the distribution of human development: Methodology and an application to Mexico. *Journal of Human Development*, *6*, 5–25. https://doi.org/10.1080/1464988052000342220
Fukuda-Parr, S., & Kumar, S. (2003). *Readings in human development*. Oxford University Press.

Gasper, D. (1996). Questioning development. In G. Kohler, C. Gore, U. P. Reich, & T. Ziesemer (Eds.), *Need and basic needs* (pp. 71–99). Metropolis Verlag.

Haq, M. (1995). *The advent of the human development report*. Oxford University Press.

Hegre, H., Petrova, K., & von Uexkull, N. (2020). Synergies and trade-offs in reaching the sustainable development goals. *Sustainability*, *12*(20), 8729. MDPI AG. Retrieved from http://dx.doi.org/10.3390/su12208729

International Council for Science (ICSU) (2017). *A guide to SDG interactions: From science to implementation*, Available at https://council.science/publications/a-guide-to-sdg-interactions-from-science-to-implementation/

Kabeer, N. (2010). *Can the MDGs provide a pathway to social justice? The challenges of intersecting inequalities*. UN MDG Achievement Fund, New York and Institute of Development Studies.

Max-Neef, M. (1992). *From the outside looking in. Experience in barefoot economics* (2nd ed.). Zeb Books.

Max-Neef, M. (1998). Ética, economía y desarrollo a Escala Humana. In C. Parker (Ed.), *Ética, Democracia y Desarrollo Humano* (pp. 249–258). LOM CERC-UAHC.

Max-Neef, M., Elizalde, A., & Hopenhayn, M. (1991). *Human scale development: Conception application and further reflections*. Apex Press.

National Research Council (1999). *Global environmental change: Research pathways for the next decade*. The National Academies Press. https://doi.org/10.17226/5992

Rauschmayer, F., Omann, I., & Frühmann, J. (Eds.). (2011). *Needs, capabilities and quality of life. Refocusing sustainable development*. Routledge.

Sen, A. (1985). *Commodities and capabilities*. Oxford University Press.

Sen, A. (1992). *Inequality reexamined*. Clarendon Press.

Sen, A. (1999). *Development as freedom*. Oxford University Press.

Sen, A. (2003). Development as capability expansion. In S. Fukuda-Parr et al. (Eds.), *Readings in human development*. Oxford University Press.

Spillemaeckers, S., Ootegem, L. V., & Westerhof, G. (2011). From individual wellbeing to sustainable development. A path where psychologist and economist meet. In F. Rauschmayer, I. Omann, & J. Fruhmann (Eds.), *Sustainable development (Capabilities, needs, and wellbeing)*. Routledge.

Stahel, A., Cendra, J., & Cano, M. (2005). Desarollos Sostenibles. In *Sostenible? What is sustainability?* (Vol. 7, pp. 73–92). Cátedra UNESCO en Sostenibilidad, UPC.

Tulder, R. (2018). *Business & the sustainable development goals: A framework for effective corporate involvement*. Rotterdam School of Management, Erasmus University.

UN (2021). *Our common agenda – Report of the secretary-general*. United Nations Publications, New York. Available at https://www.un.org/en/content/common-agenda-report/

UNDP (1990). *Human development report*. Oxford University Press.

UNDP (1996). *Human development report*. Oxford University Press.

UNDP (2007). *Human development report*. Oxford University Press.

UNDP (2018). *Human development report*. Oxford University Press.

UNGA (2015). *Resolution adopted by the general assembly on 25 September 201570/1. Transforming our world: The 2030 Agenda for Sustainable Development*. United Nations General Assembly (UNGA), New York. Available at https://sustainabledevelopment.un.org/index.php?page=view&type=111&nr=8496&menu=35

WCED (1987). *Our common future. World commission on environment and development*. https://www.un.org/ga/search/view_doc.asp?symbol=A/42/427&Lang=E

World Bank (2008). *World development report: Agriculture for development*. Washington, DC. http://hdl.handle.net/10986/5990 License: CC BY 3.0 IGO.

10 Climate change and planetary boundaries

An overview from the biocentric perspective of Max-Neef

Clara Olmedo, Iñaki Ceberio de León, and Yerko Castillo Ávalos

Introduction

The 2021 United Nations Conference on Climate Change (COP26) was held under the slogan: "Uniting the world to tackle climate change." A conference full of demagogic speeches, lacking real commitments to mitigate climate change (CC henceforth).

From critical perspectives of the ecological crisis such as those of Max-Neef and the Norwegian ecophilosopher Arne Næss with his Deep Ecology, this scenario is not new. Both authors agreed that mainstream studies consist of dropping a large body of valuable scientific data on CC to explain the phenomenon, without asking for the philosophical and sociocultural questions, where the roots of the ecological crisis lay.

Even though the problem of CC was not always at the forefront of Max-Neef's work, it is his holistic perspective on the ecological crisis that serves us as an epistemological frame to guide our work. In this line, we approach CC from the framework of planetary boundaries (PB henceforth), which was proposed by Rockström et al. (2009). The study, titled *Planetary Boundaries: Exploring the Safe Operating Space for Humanity*, alerted that,

> Anthropogenic pressures on the Earth System have reached a scale where abrupt global environmental change can no longer be excluded. We propose a new approach to global sustainability in which we define planetary boundaries within which we expect that humanity can operate safely. Transgressing one or more planetary boundaries may be deleterious or even catastrophic - to planetary scale systems. (p. 1)

Based on the relationship that Max-Neef established among economy, society, and nature, we bring into our analysis the perspective of Raworth (2012, 2017), who introduced the social dimension in the analysis of PB, as one lost but necessary piece to move from knowing to understanding the problem, as Max-Neef (2005b) suggested.

We assess the problem of CC by addressing two questions: (1) How this complex problem could be tackled? (2) Why is a real solution not yet offered?

DOI: 10.4324/9781003381143-12

This chapter offers some answers. The first two sections aim to underline the contribution of the Max-Neef framework to understand the complex problem of CC and give some explanation to the lack of solutions. The final two sections introduce the ethical and philosophical dimension through a dialogue between Max-Neef and Raworth and the transdisciplinary approaches in order to mutually strength those critical perspectives and underline the importance of those approaches in understanding CC as one of the PB.

Climate change as a planetary boundary: The contribution of Max-Neef to understanding and tackling the problem

What are the contributions of Max-Neef's work to analyse the CC and the lack or real solutions? Even though the issue of climate change was not at the forefront of Max-Neef's analysis, the connection, along his entire work, among economy, nature, and society, established the foundations with which to elaborate a critical argument on the causes of one of the planetary boundaries we have already exceeded: CC (Persson et al., 2022). In particular, Max-Neef's perspective on the principles over which the economy should be governed and the transdisciplinary methodology provide us enough guidance to approach this global problem, a "tragedy of the commons" in words of Hardin (1968), with no technical solution. In his frame, we highlight four aspects to orient our analysis of climate change, three of which are centred around an ethical dimension in the perspective of Max-Neef.

In the first place, we need to consider that from the perspective of Max-Neef, the ecological crisis is, overall, an ethical problem, linked to a lifestyle that equates consumerism with human happiness, without considering the deep social inequalities over which the consumer society is built. According to Max-Neef, we need to "replace the dominant values of greed, competition, and accumulation for those of solidarity, cooperation, and compassion" (2010, p. 201).

From this perspective, Max-Neef claimed that a new economic paradigm is urgently needed. A paradigm that, for instance, allows economists to raise questions like where was the money that suddenly came to save the private banks during the 2008 world financial crisis. Why economists and government keep saying that there are not enough resources to overcome poverty? For Max-Neef, we live in "a world accustomed to the fact that there is never enough for those who have nothing, but there is always enough for those who have everything" (Max-Neef, 2010, p. 200). A world where the dangerous environmental and social costs are still denied by mainstream economics. A denial related to a quadruple convergence over which a double crisis (human and ecological) is underpinned: increase of human-induced climate change; the end of cheap energy; the depletion of key resources (fresh water, genetic resources, forest, fisheries, wildlife, soils, and so forth); and the gigantic speculation bubble of exchange goods and services (Max-Neef, 2010). Among the consequences of this convergence, Max-Neef highlighted the global warming, the decimation of traditional cultures (language, values, rituals, and so on), and the cosmovision of indigenous people, with higher costs for poorer countries.

At the centre of the double crisis are three principles of the mainstream economics: the growth obsession and consumerism; the assumption of externalities that exempt economic processes and companies from accountability; and the macroeconomic aberration of accounting the loss of patrimony as increase of income. A combination of principles that "have devastating consequences for nature and society" (Max-Neef, 2014, p. 152).

In a co-authored book *Economics Unmasked: From Power and Greed to Compassion and the Common Good* (2011), Smith and Max-Neef underlined the inner links between the neoliberal economic system and the ecological crisis. As they said, "it is a direct consequence of the view of life, human, and non-human, fostered by neoliberal economic thinking" (p. 13). The obsession with economic growth and consumerism is poisoning the biosphere at an increasing rate with pollutants, among which are the rampant CO_2 emissions, a main greenhouse gas that causes climate chaos across the world. For Max-Neef, climate chaos is a global problem with devastating local, social, and cultural consequences, specially, for poor people and countries. Many poor people will be forced to abandon their territories, becoming the so-called climatic displaced persons, forced to emigrate and suffer the cruelties of these processes: discrimination, violence from illegal immigrant smuggling networks, etc. (Francis, 2015; Max-Neef, 2010).

In the second place, a key question in Max-Neef overview: Why classical and neoclassical economic approaches are not providing real solutions to the ecological and humanity crises, despite abundant scientific evidence regarding the climate change and its consequences? This question reveals a great deal of disappointment by Max-Neef with the discipline he was formed in. In particular, he was concerned with the insignificant results that economics offers to the problems of society. "Decades of development, growing poverty and ecological problems led me to reevaluate my role as economist", he said (1992, p. 24). It led him to recognise that economics is not a science, it is rather a discipline based on principles that are so far away from rationality. For him, this [I]rationality explains a great deal of the failures of international summits that, year after year, are limited to outlining goals that countries and governments never meet. Meanwhile, the climate chaos strikes at the very heart of life across the planet.

From this critical understanding of the discipline, Max-Neef began to think about an economics that serves the people and life, and not the other way around. In this path, he criticised the notion of development, laying down the foundations for what latter will be the Human Scale Development (HSD) approach, that he presented for the first time in 1986, in a paper co-authored with Antonio Elizalde and Martin Hopenhayn. From the framework of HSD, Max-Neef criticised the notion of growth national product (GNP) and the misleading ideas that human needs are infinite. Those critiques were not based on purely economic thinking. Instead, they were framed in a philosophical and ethical perspective, going deep into domains of ethics and values. In this way, he transcended the fields of economics and ecology to point out philosophical questions like the place of human beings in nature; the limits of human intervention in the biosphere; our responsibility in the ecological crisis; and the actions needed to solve this crisis.

In the third place, we come to the political milieu to address some of the solutions to the crisis Max-Neef has proposed, aware of that humanity faces a global problem whose effects materialise at the local level. Thus, the solutions will inevitably come from the territories and the people affected by the climate change. Indeed, in hundreds of places, many of those solutions are already being implemented, led by grass-root movements, which are very much dismissed by the media, as Smith and Max-Neef (2011) argued. In this path, the authors found very inspiring local experiences that guided them into the task of thinking and proposing a new paradigm based on the principles of solidarity, cooperation, and compassion, where the principle of reverence for life would be the axis of human actions. Some of these experiences are described in the last chapter of the book *Economics Unmasked* (Smith & Max-Neef, 2011).

Those suggestions are framed in Max-Neef's beliefs that we need to transcend the field of thinking to act, to do something! Urgent social, political, economic, and ideological changes are needed instead of looking forward only to improve the economic-human wellbeing (Bugallo, 2015; Max-Neef, 1992). This urgency was always at the centre of the intellectual, philosophical and political trajectory of Max-Neef. Even more, it led him to break with the economic establishment and embraced "barefoot experiences" with indigenous and Black people at the Ecuadorian jungle and with Brazilian artisans living in poverty (Max-Neef, 1992).

In the fourth place, and intimately related to those barefoot experiences of Max-Neef, we reach the methodological aspect. He proposed transdisciplinarity; a methodological approach that calls for a respectful dialogue among science, scientists, knowledge, and people who inhabit outside the academia. These could be social movements, community leaders, unionists, or politicians, under the belief that they can contribute with relevant knowledge (Lanz, 2010; Max-Neef, 2003, 2005a, 2005b; Olivé, 2011). A dialogue across different types of knowledge (scientific or non-scientific) can help us moving from knowing to understanding, where understanding implies getting involved in the problems we address. Because "when the Subject that searches and observes becomes inseparably integrated with the Object searched and observed" (Max-Neef, 2005a, p. 15).

Being "part of" means a new ontology that challenges the traditional or Cartesian epistemology, where scientists (representing the mind) must be separated from the object/problem (representing reality) they study (Jolibert et al., 2011). It also implies an ethical dimension, where the respect for all forms of life and respect for any kind of knowledge must guide our thinking and actions.

Shallow ecology and climate change: Dealing with the epistemological reductionism in scientific studies and the lack of real solutions

Since man stepped on the moon, in 1969, there were events and crucial moments that led us to acknowledge that the Earth is our only home. International summits and conferences began discussing the environmental problems. In the 1970s, the Club of Rome published *The Limits to Growth*, a Club in which Max-Neef will later participate. The report concluded that if the current level of development is maintained, society will reach the absolute limits of growth in 100 years (year 2070). So, limits to human growth were established and the concept of sustainability began to take shape, it was later developed in the Brundtland report (1987).

Meanwhile, greenhouse gas emissions kept increasing, and CC was just considered a hypothesis until 2007, when the Intergovernmental Panel on Climate Change (IPCC, 2018), together with former North American Vice President Al Gore (2006), released alarming information through various media platform on climate change, recognising anthropic causes. Since then, the data provided by scientists indicates that each passing year, the scenario becomes more dramatic. Nonetheless, scientists embrace certain optimism in a possible reversion of this trend. But this optimism contrasts with the absence of concrete measures to reduce emissions of greenhouse gases. And what is more compelling is the persistence of ideologies and principles that foster unsustainable practices (Max-Neef, 2016; Max-Neef & Smith, 2014; Smith & Max-Neef, 2011).

In general, the dimension of ideology and principles is a missing peace in scientific studies that analyse the ecological problems, all of them convinced that the solutions will come from science and technology. These are the type of studies that fall into epistemological reductionisms, with a deep faith in science and strictly scientific knowledge, where ethics has no room. Approaches that we identify with the shallow ecology (Naess, 1973) in the sense that they are just concerned with the effects of the ecological crisis, disregarding the values and ideologies that foster unsustainable practices and lifestyles.

A good example of an epistemological reductionism is the latest book by Gates (2021) which compiles abundant scientific evidence indicating that there are no ways of reaching "zero" emission of greenhouse gases. The possible solutions that Gates "imagines" come from technological inventions. However, at this point, there is no certainty that science will capture gases from the atmosphere.

On the other hand, we have the PB frame (Leach et al., 2013; Rockström et al., 2009; Wang-Erlandsson et al., 2022) that addresses the pressure of human activities on the physical variables of the earth system (ES). CC is one of the PB boundaries we have already exceeded, as shown in Figure 10.1 (Persson et al., 2022; Steffen et al., 2015).

From a critical perspective, this PB approach also falls into epistemological reductionisms. And a key contribution to overcome this reductionism is the biocentric perspective, "that holds that all living things are morally considerable, whereas many people hold that only human beings are so" (Attfield, 2016, p. 1). At the centre of this perspective is the notion of "reverence of life", long time ago proposed in the classical book of Albert Schweitzer, *Civilization and Ethics* (1923). Biocentrism is considered a worldview, analysed in diverse studies addressing the ecological crisis (Agar, 2001; Max-Neef, 2014; Naess, 1973; Rolston III, 1989; Sessions & Naess, 1986; Taylor, 1983), and it becomes the axis to transcend the epistemological reductionisms in the conventional approaches of the CC and PB.

In a more comprehensive line, we have the work of Kate Raworth (2012, 2017), who differentiates "external" (physical) and "internal" (social) limits that are

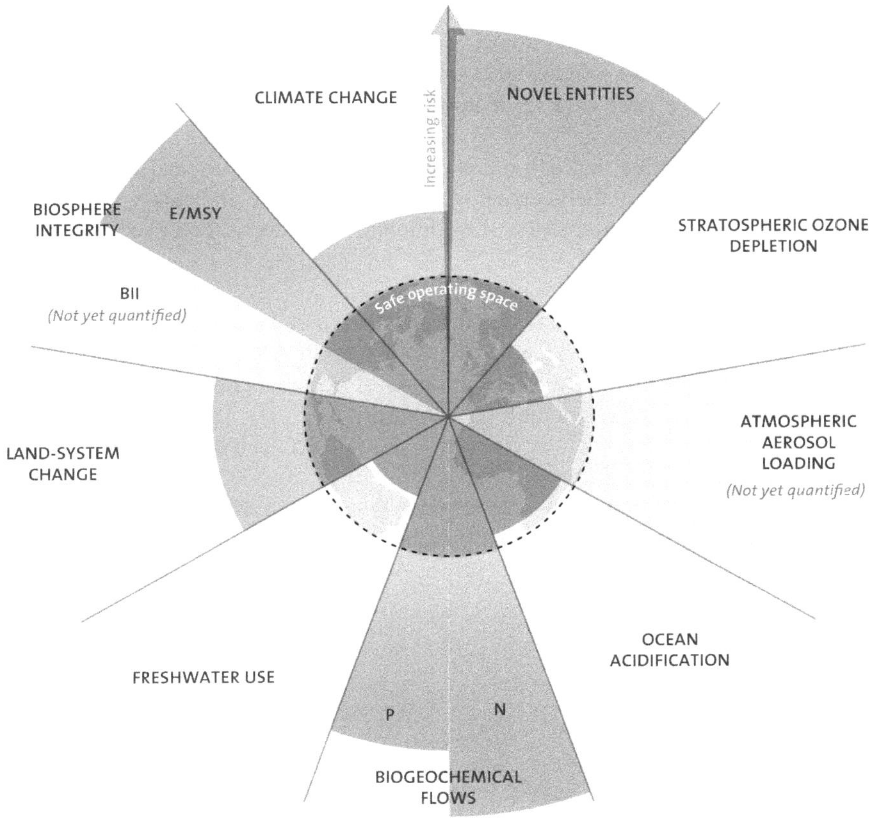

Figure 10.1 The planetary boundaries framework

conspiring against the sustainability of our planet and analyses them from a relational perspective. This work shows us that the current analyses of the PB only consider the "external/physical" limits. The internal limits, which refer to the resources each person need to meet their human rights (food, water, health, and energy) as Raworth (2012, 2017) argues, remain unaddressed in those analyses. We aim to tackle a theoretical as well as philosophical gap in the analysis of CC by integrating the insights of Max-Neef and Kate Raworth.

Integrating approaches: The fundamental human needs of Max-Neef and the doughnut economics of Raworth

As mentioned before, the work of the economist Kate Raworth (2012, 2017) offers a more comprehensive analysis of the complex interactions of external (physic) and internal (social) boundaries in the ES. In this sense, we see an interesting connection between the perspectives of Raworth and Max-Neef. Indeed, Raworth mentions the importance of Max-Neef's and Schumacher's views in introducing the ideas of human scale and ethics in the field of economics. "Thinkers such as these have for centuries offered alternative visions of what the economy is for, but their ideas have been kept far from the eyes and ears of economics students" (Raworth, 2017, p. 41).

This is a perspective that can be read under the epistemological lens of Max-Neef, in particular the relationship among economy, society, and nature from where we must understand the interaction of the internal and external boundaries Raworth proposes to analyse CC.

> Combining the inner limits of social boundaries and the outer limits of planetary boundaries in this way creates a doughnut-shaped space within which all humanity can thrive by pursuing range of possible pathways that could deliver inclusive and sustainable development.
>
> (Leach et al., 2013, p. 85)

Figure 10.2 is the doughnut-shaped space where the author shows that society faces two types of limits: (1) the external limits that define the ecological ceiling;

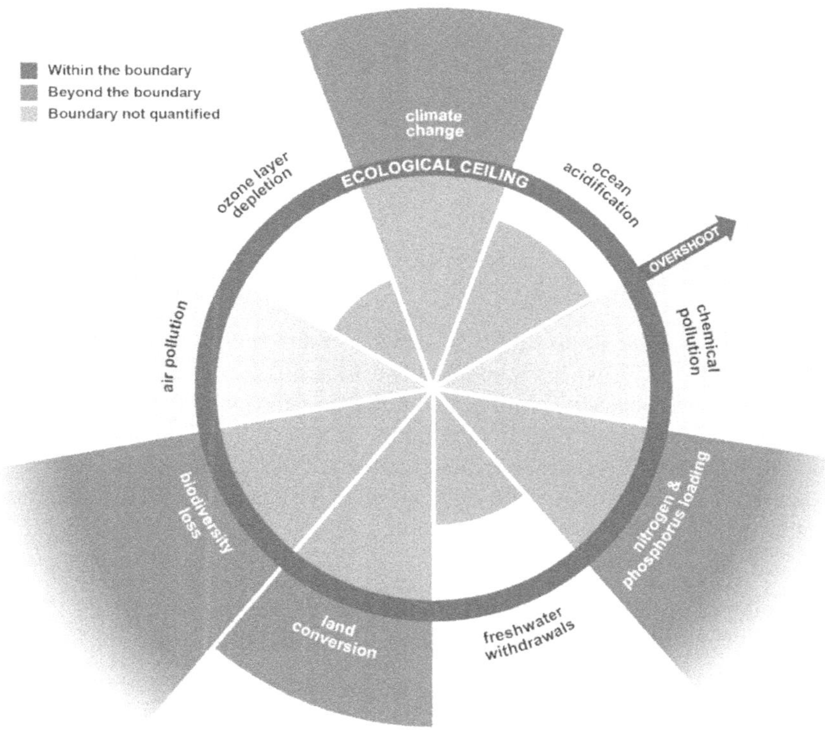

Figure 10.2 Shortfalls and overshoot in Raworth's doughnut

and (2) the internal limits that refer to the social dimension compiled in 11 elements that ensure a safe and dignified life:

> Enough food; clean water and adequate sanitation; access to energy and clean culinary facilities; access to education and health care; a decent home; a minimum income and a decent job; access to information networks and social support networks. In addition, it is necessary that these elements be achieved within a framework of gender equality, social equity, political participation, peace, and justice.
>
> (Raworth, 2017, p. 54)

Not exceeding planetary and social boundaries would place the human being in a safe zone of comfort, diminishing the risk of resource deprivations that endanger human wellbeing (Leach et al., 2013; Raworth, 2017). Raworth's argument is in a similar line of the analysis of Max-Neef for whom climate change (one of the planetary limits) is more than an environmental problem, it impacts on the life of people: desertification advances creating poverty, malnutrition, wars for natural resources, or climate displaced persons who leave everything behind to survive.

Giving this theoretical affinity, in Table 10.1, we integrate the 11 social needs of Raworth's doughnut scheme into the 9 fundamental human needs of Max-Neef's matrix. In the first column, we list the social needs of Raworth and integrate them into four human needs of Max-Neef, listed in the second column. In the third column, we list the remaining five human needs of Max-Neef, convinced that they enrich our understanding of the social needs in Raworth's scheme. In the fourth column, we summarise the principles and philosophy that support the theoretical affinity between these two approaches, considering it as a tool to better understand the ecological crisis and the limits that cannot be transgressed if we expect to live in a safe and sustainable world.

Integrating these two perspectives allows us to combine the macro dimension (the external/physical boundaries) which can be addressed with quantitative methodologies, with the micro dimension (internal/social boundaries) that can be studied either with qualitative or quantitative methodologies. This combination opens the door for interdisciplinary (Leach et al., 2013) and transdisciplinary (Max-Neef, 2005a) analyses of CC and its consequences.

> This means moving beyond simply producing knowledge for instrumental purpose (…) This points to the importance of reflexive knowledge-making which engages critically with the assumptions of science and social science.
>
> (Leach et al., 2013, p. 88)

This interpretation of the conceptual and philosophical affinity, between Max-Neef and Raworth, leads us to the fields of ethics and transdiscipline, so fundamental in the understanding the double crisis.

Table 10.1 Integration of Raworth's 11 social needs into Max-Neef's 9 fundamental human needs

Internal boundaries or social needs in Raworth's scheme	*Fundamental human needs in Max-Neef's matrix*	*Dimensions of Max-Neef's matrix to enrich Raworth scheme*	*Principles and philosophical affinity*
1. Enough food and clean water; 2. adequate sanitation; 3. access to energy and culinary facilities; 4. access to education and health care; 5. decent home; 6. a minimum income and a decent job	1. Subsistence	5. Affection; 6. creation; 7. idleness	**Max-Neef**: a new economy will be based on fundamental postulates and principles. "Development is about people not about objects"; "No economy is possible in the absence of ecosystem services"; "The economy is to serve people, and not the people to serve economy" (Smith & Max-Neef, 2011, pp. 203, 204)
7. Access to information networks and social support networks	2. Understanding		
8. Gender equality; 9. social equity; 10. peace, and justice	3. Protection	8. Identity. 9. Freedom	**Raworth**: environmental change and enduring poverty and social inequity need for conceptual approaches that enable these challenges to be addressed together so that options for pathways to equitable and sustainable development can be identified and debatable Leach et al. (2013, p. 84)
11. Political participation	4. Participation		

Ethics and transdiscipline to address climate change

Several of the reasons for which Max-Neef has been considered a philosopher rather than an economist are his transdisciplinary approach, where ethics and qualitative methodology have a preponderant place. It means an approach closer to social sciences rather than mathematics. In his collaborative book *Economics Unmasked* (Smith & Max-Neef, 2011), they were convinced that we face an absurd situation, an economy, and lifestyles that act as if we had five planets. Even more, faced with the scientific evidence on planetary boundaries and climate change politicians, at international as well as national level, act like recognising the seriousness of the problem, without tackling the problem. This could have, at least, a two-sided explanation. On the one hand, a prevailing shallow ecology in the analyses prevents us of getting to the root of the ecological and social problems. On the other hand, all the international summits and agreements are not binding for the national/local governments! Therefore, we are subject to the supposed "good faith" in our governments in matters of climate change.

If the goal is to overcome this absurd situation, Max-Neef argued that we need to develop a new economic paradigm, based on an ethical and biocentric perspective. At the heart of this moral principle lays an extended ethics (Leopold, 1949), in which life (human and non-human) has intrinsic value. And an extended ethics which compels us to ask fundamental questions like "Do we, human beings, have the rights to deplete nature in name of our own welfare?" "What impacts do human practices have on nature?" "What is our moral obligation to 'the lives of others' (human and non-human entities)?". This is an ethical proposal in line with the eco-philosophy of the Deep Ecology of Arne Næss that,

> Goes beyond the present and the immediate. It aims at generations yet to come at the planet as a whole, at an economy as if people matter. While making explicit a global concern for the human species and life in general, the organizing language–as suggested by Schultz–should be some kind of deep ecology.
>
> (Max-Neef, 2005a, p. 8)

Although there is a whole conceptual discussion around whether to call this a biocentric or ecocentric ethics, the fundamental point in Max-Neef's thought is an ethic that goes beyond anthropocentrism to integrate nature and all forms of life (human and non-human) inhabiting the planet. From such an ethical perspective, we can argue that CC puts us in front of a dilemma. What to do with the CC in a world where the economic system preaches individualism and consumerism, pushing, day by day, the planetary boundaries at a point that jeopardises life in the entire planet? It is a dilemma equated with what Garrett Hardin (1968) called "the tragedy of the common":

> Picture a pasture open to all (...) Therein is the tragedy. Each man is locked into a system that compels him to increase his herd without limit in a world that

> is limited. Ruin is the destination toward which all men rush, each pursuing his own best interest in a society that believes in the freedom of the commons.
>
> (Hardin, 1968, pp. 1243–1244)

In a more contemporary context, climate change is also a "tragedy of the commons" with no technical solution. Smith and Max-Neef (2011) argue that the solutions to clean the biosphere from pollutants, in particular CO2, are completely unknown. But, despite this hopeless scenario, from the experiences that Max-Neef had with communities around the world, we can renew our hopes. And these hopes come from social movements that are committed with different economic and democratic systems.

> The world is a system, and it will soon be a very different world, driven by millions of communities who believe that democracy and restoration are grassroots movements that connect us to values that we hold in common.
>
> (Smith and Max-Neef, 2011, p. 170)

In a similar vein, Dobson (2010) argues that we need the implementation of a cosmopolitan democracy where the hierarchy would be inverted. That is a democracy from the bottom up in which policies of commons could be developed. Regarding the problems of CC, for the philosopher Carmen Velayos (2015), is it essential that all agreements became binding-mandatory for governments, so that respect for environmental standards and respect for common goods became a "categorical imperative", in a Kantian sense (Kant, 2007, 2022). Hence the need to transcend the anthropocentric ethics that characterise Western thought and move towards other ethics that conceive nature as that space in which all life is configured.

To change the ways CC is analysed and to overcome the epistemological reductionisms, Max-Neef is convinced that we need a transdisciplinary approach. Transdiscipline is a methodological frame with four levels of analysis intimately interrelated. The first level refers to "to what exists", a level where the factual sciences are concentrated, and which predominate in the elaboration of planetary limits and in the preparation of the matrix of Max-Neef. In the second level is placed the question of "what we are capable of doing?". At this level are technical professions such as engineering, architecture and that would help implement more sustainable modes of production. At the third level, we are faced with the normative dimension that would limit modes of production and lifestyles, with regulations consistent with sustainability. At the fourth level is the ethical dimension. And it is so because without principles and values consistent with sustainability, the resolution of the problem of CC and PB (social and physical) would not be successful. The fundamental role of ethics is also present in Raworth's proposal, since the social dimension refers to the fundamental human rights, which we also consider a moral principle.

> Planetary boundaries propose the outer limits of pressure that humanity should place on critical Earth system in other to protect human well-being.

> Yet at the same time, human well-being also depends upon each person having access to the resources needed to meet their human rights such as food, water, health, and energy.
>
> (Leach et al., 2013, p. 85)

Science and policymakers need holistic approaches, integrating social and natural dimensions, under the guide of ethic and values if they aim to comprehend and solve the problem.

Conclusion

In this chapter, we highlighted the contribution of Max-Neef's perspective in addressing CC, as one of the PB which humanity have already exceeded (as the scientific studies of the Stockholm Resilience Centre show). In particular, his holistic approach of the ecological problems and the biocentric perspective are key epistemological tools to have a better understanding of the double crisis and overcome the reductionisms that characterise the current studies of CC and PB. Even though CC was not at the forefront of Max-Neef's work, the connection among economy, nature, and society established the foundations to elaborate a critical argument on the causes of this planetary problem. In particular, his perspective on the principles over which the economy should be governed and the transdisciplinary methodology provide us enough guide to approach this global problem, a "tragedy of the commons", with no technical solution.

In the chapter, we tried to offer some answers to two interrelated questions: (1) How this complex problem could be tackled? (2) Why is a real solution not yet offered? With this goal in mind, we also searched for other holistic perspectives like the one which Kate Raworth (2012, 2017) offers on the PB, transcending the natural/physical dimensions to introduce the social foundation/needs. These social needs must be guaranteed; they are limits we cannot exceed if we aim to ensure a safe and dignified life. From our understanding, the work of Raworth is in a similar conceptual and philosophical line with Max-Neef's perspective. For this reason, we integrate these two analyses to mutually enrich them and underline the importance of critical and holistic approaches in addressing CC. Even more importantly, we underline the fact that there is no possibility of having comprehensive understanding of CC problems, unless we take into consideration the dimension of ethics and values. In particular, the ethics and values dominate conventional economics, modern societies, and development models.

References

Agar, N. (2001). *Life's intrinsic value: Science, ethics, and nature*. Columbia University Press.

Attfield, R. (2016). Biocentrism. *The international encyclopedia of ethics*. https://onlinelibrary.wiley.com/doi/book/10.1002/9781444367072

Brundtland, G. H. (1987). *Our common future. Report of the world commission on environment and development*. Oxford University Press.

Bugallo, A. I. (2015). *Filosofía ambiental y ecosofías. Arne Naess, Spinoza y James*. Prometeo.
Dobson, A. (2010). *Ciudadanía y medio ambiente*. Proteus.
Francis, P. (2015). *Laudato si*. Vatican Press.
Gates, B. (2021). *Cómo evitar un desastre climático. Las soluciones que ya tenemos y los avancez que aún necesitamos*. Penguin Random House.
Gore, A. (2006). *An inconvenient truth: The planetary emergency of global warming and what we can do about it*. Rodale.
Hardin, G. (1968). The tragedy of the commons: The population problem has no technical solution: It requires a fundamental extension in morality. *Science*, *162*(3859), 1243–1248. https://www.jstor.org/stable/1724745
IPCC, I. S. (2018). *IPCC special report*. https://www.ipcc.ch/site/assets/uploads/sites/2/2019/06/SR15_Full_Report_High_Res.pdf
Jolibert, C., Max-Neef, M., Rauschmayer, F., & Paavola, J. (2011). Should we care about the needs of non-humans? Needs assessment: A tool for environmental conflict resolution and sustainable organization of living beings. *Environmental Policy and Governance*, *21*(4), 259–269. https://doi.org/10.1002/eet.578
Kant, I. [1781] (2007). *Grundlegung zur Metaphysik der Sitten*. Suhrkamp.
Kant, I. [1795] (2022). *Zum ewigen Frieden Ein philosophischer Entwurf*. Otbebookpublishing.
Lanz, R. (2010). Diez preguntas sobre Transdisciplina. *RET. Revista de estudios transdisciplinarios*, *2*(1), 11–21. https://doi.org/10.1177/1049732312468251
Leach, M., Raworth, K., & Rockström, J. (2013). Between social and planetary boundaries: Navigating pathways in the safe and just space for humanity. In *World social science report. Changing global environments* (pp. 84–89). ISSC, UNESCO.
Leopold, A. (1949). *A sand county almanac*. Oxford University Press.
Max-Neef, M. (1992). *From the outside looking in: Experiences in barefoot economics*. Zed Books Ltd.
Max-Neef, M. (2003). Transdisciplina para pasar del saber al comprender. *Revista Debates*, Universidad de Antioquia, (36), 21–33.
Max-Neef, M. (2005a). Foundations of transdisciplinarity. *Ecological Economics*, *53*(1), 5–16. https://doi.org/10.1016/j.ecolecon.2005.01.014
Max-Neef, M. (2005b). Del saber al comprender. *Revista Facultad de Ciencias Económicas*, *13*(2), 6–12. https://doi.org/10.1177/1049732312468251
Max-Neef, M. (2010). The world on a collision course and the need for a new economy. *Ambio*, *39*(3), 200–210. https://doi.org/10.1007%2Fs13280-010-0028-1
Max-Neef, M. (2014). The good is the bad that we don't do: Economic crimes against humanity: A proposal. *Ecological Economics*, *104*, 152–154. https://doi.org/10.1016/j.ecolecon.2014.02.011
Max-Neef, M. (2016). Philosophy of ecological economics. *International Journal of Economics & Management Sciences*, *5*(5), 1–5. http://doi.org/10.4172/2162-6359.1000366
Max-Neef, M., & Smith, P. B. (2014). *La Economía Desenmascarada, Del Poder y la Codicia*. Icaria editorial.
Naess, A. (1973). The shallow and the deep, long-range ecology movement. A summary. *Inquiry*, *16*(1–4), 95–100. https://doi.org/10.1080/00201747308601682
Olivé, L. (2011). Interdisciplina y transdisciplina desde la filosofía. *Ludus Vitalis*, *19*(35), 251–256. https://doi.org/10.1177/1049732312468251
Persson, L., Carney Almroth, B. M., Collins, C. D., Cornell, S., de Wit, C. A., Diamond, M. L., & Hauschild, M. Z. (2022). Outside the safe operating space of the planetary

boundary for novel entities. *Environmental Science & Technology*, *56*(3), 1510–1521. https://doi.org/10.1021/acs.est.1c04158
Raworth, K. (2012). A safe and just space for humanity: Can we live within the doughnut? *Oxfam Discussion Paper*.
Raworth, K. (2017). *Doughnut economics: Seven ways to think like a 21st-century economist*. Green Publishing.
Rockström, J., Steffen, W., Noone, K., Persson, Å., Chapin, F. S., III, Lambin, E., Lenton, T. M., Scheffer, M., Folke, C., Schellnhuber, H. J., Nykvist, B., de Wit, C. A., Hughes, T., van der Leeuw, S., Rodhe, H., Sörlin, S., Snyder, P. K., Costanza, R., Svedin, U., Falkenmark, M., … (2009). Planetary boundaries: Exploring the safe operating space for humanity. *Ecology and Society*, *14*(2), 32. https://www.ecologyandsociety.org/vol14/iss2/art32/
Rolston III, H. (1989). Environmental justice. *Between the Species*, *5*(3), 147–153. https://doi.org/10.15368/bts.1989v5n3.5
Schweitzer, A. (1923). *Civilization & ethics: The philosophy of civilization*. Black.
Sessions, G., & Naess, A. (1986). The basic principles of deep ecology. *The Trumpeter*, *3*(4), 14. https://doi.org/10.1177/1049732312468251
Smith, P. B., & Max-Neef, M. (2011). *Economics unmasked: From power and greed to compassion and the common good*. Green Books.
Steffen, W., Richardson, K., Rockström, J., Cornell, S. E., Fetzer, I., Bennett, E. M., Biggs, R., Carpenter, S. R., de Vries, W., de Wit, C. A., Folke, C., Gerten, D., Heinke, J., Mace, G. M., Persson, L. M., Ramanathan, V., Reyers, B., & Sörlin, S. (2015). Planetary boundaries: Guiding human development on a changing planet. *Science*, *347*(6223). https://science.sciencemag.org/content/347/6223/1259855
Taylor, P. W. (1983). In defense of biocentrism. *Environmental Ethics*, *5*(3), 237–243. https://doi.org/10.5840/enviroethics19835322
Velayos, C. (2015). *El cambio climático y los límites del individualismo*. Horsori.
Wang-Erlandsson, L., Tobian, A., van der Ent, R. J., Fetzer, I., te Wierik, S., Porkka, M., Staal, A., Jaramillo, F., Dahlmann, H., Singh, C., Greve, P., Gerten, D., Keys, P. W., Gleeson, T., Cornell, S. E., Steffen, W., Bai, X., & Rockström, J. (2022). A planetary boundary for green water. *Nature Reviews: Earth and Environment*, *3*(6), 380–392. https://doi.org/10.1038/s43017-022-00287-8

11 Demand-side, socio-cultural and systemic solutions

The contributions of Max-Neef's work for climate change and sustainability

Lina Brand-Correa

Introduction

In recent years, Max-Neef's work, and in particular his distinction among human needs, satisfiers and economic goods, has impacted the way the climate change and sustainability scholars think about environmental issues in general, and climate change in particular. Max-Neef's work has influenced the way these academic communities consider issues of demand, of consumption and of the role of the economic system.

In his seminal book *Human Scale Development. Conception, application, and further reflections*, Max-Neef et al. (1991, p. 27) explain that it is valid to talk about a set of socio-universal human needs, despite it being impossible to collect empirical evidence to prove with absolute certainty that a particular set of human needs is (and will be) historically and culturally constant. The validity of talking about a particular set of human needs comes from the fact that these vary at a very slow rate. The rhythm of change of human needs, according to Max-Neef, is akin to the rhythms of evolution. This is consistent with other needs theories, which recognise that there are certain dimensions of well-being that are common to people across cultures due to our shared humanity (Alkire, 2002; Doyal & Gough, 1991). This chapter does not go into discussions about the specifics of what a certain set of human needs should or should not include, nor how it should or should not be structured.[1] For this chapter, it is enough to acknowledge the importance of Max-Neef's contribution in relation to human needs: it is valid to speak of a set of universal human needs, which is distinct from the specific elements that contribute to the actualisation of human needs themselves: satisfiers.

Satisfiers "are related instead to everything which [...] contributes to the actualization of human needs" (Max-Neef et al., 1991, p. 24). Satisfiers are culturally, historically and geographically specific, "they are modified according to the rhythm of history and vary according to culture and circumstance" and "are forms of Being, Having, Doing and Interacting related to structures" (Max-Neef et al., 1991, p. 28). Satisfiers are not economic goods. The latter are simply objects or artefacts that influence the way satisfiers help or hinder need actualisation. Our current social and economic order has elevated economic goods to a level where they have become ends in themselves, rather than means towards need actualisation.

DOI: 10.4324/9781003381143-13

Therefore, the capitalist socio-economic system places life "at the service of artifacts, rather than artifacts at the service of life" (Max-Neef et al., 1991, p. 25).

The key thing to understand about the importance of Max-Neef's distinction among human needs, satisfiers and economic goods is that it opens the space to critique our current economic system from the perspective of a truly humanistic political position. Needs can relate to states of both deprivation and potential. When seen as mere deprivation, needs can lead to paternalism and dependency. But when seen also as potential, human needs can mobilise communities and lead to self-reliance. Moreover, satisfiers are the products of history and culture, created by people and thus can be re-created, re-invented and re-imagined. Here, David Graeber's quote seems to appropriately capture the spirit of what this chapter intends to highlight of Max-Neef's work: "The ultimate, hidden truth of the world is that it is something that we make and could just as easily make differently" (Graeber, 2015). Or paraphrasing the quote above but using Max-Neef's terminology: satisfiers are something that we make and could just as easily remake differently powered by the potential of human need actualisation.

Considering the above distinction, there are three ways in which Max-Neef's thought has and is contributing to considering climate change and sustainability thinking. In this chapter, these will be referred to as demand-side solutions, socio-cultural solutions and systemic solutions. In relation to demand-side solutions, Max-Neef's thought has been part of the efforts to include demand-side climate change mitigation strategies. Considering issues of well-being has allowed climate change scholars to question the reign of economic goods, and the role of ever-increasing consumption (demand) in actualising human needs. In relation to socio-cultural solutions, Max-Neef's thought has contributed to the understanding of lifestyle changes as changes in the way we satisfy needs. Here, relating social practices (a sociological concept) to need satisfiers has proved useful in the area of sustainable consumption studies (see e.g. Sahakian & Anantharaman, 2020). And in relation to socio-cultural solutions, Max-Neef's thought has been associated with studying the provisioning systems that lead to certain configurations of need satisfiers that are hard to escape. This approach is in line with political economy thinking and takes a systemic perspective (see e.g. Brand-Correa et al., 2020). This chapter will explore and synthesise these three avenues in which Max-Neef's thought has been taken forward in relation to climate change and sustainability. It will also put forward some preliminary ideas on how the three avenues logically lead to an anti-capitalist environmental political agenda.[2]

Demand-side solutions: Satisfiers and demand reduction for a 1.5-degree world

Researchers in the area of climate change, whose academic work is periodically synthesised by the IPCC (Intergovernmental Panel on Climate Change), have acknowledged that, in order to stay "well below 1.5 degrees of global warming", "rapid and far-reaching transitions" are required (Allen et al., 2018). Such transformations will include changes in the levels of resource use, both by producers *and* consumers, and the role of demand-side reductions has been highlighted (Creutzig et al., 2018). It is tempting to think that calls for demand-side measures are a way of eliminating the systemic roots and impacts of climate change, by focusing on individual decisions made by atomised actors. However, many calls for demand-side measures state that they are not an attempt to put the responsibility of climate change on the shoulders of individuals, but rather to recognise that the scale of the climate change challenge will require deep lifestyle changes (Newell et al., 2021).

It is increasingly common to see appeals for "lifestyle changes" or "behavioural changes" within plans to tackle climate change. For example, the Committee on Climate Change (The CCC) in the UK reports that for their "further ambition scenario" over 60% of measures contain an element of societal and behavioural changes (The CCC, 2019). These changes include things like a "reduction in the consumption of beef, lamb and dairy which is replaced by an increase in the consumption of pork, poultry and plant-based products" (The CCC, 2019, p. 147), and reductions in the demand for aviation. In short, appeals for lifestyle or behavioural changes always have an element of demand reduction. And these demand reductions are important because they will lead to reductions in greenhouse gas emissions, be it from land use changes or from energy demand reductions.

At this point, it is important to make a pause for clarification. When talking about (energy) demand reductions, the implication is that these apply to affluent portions of the population, both globally and within countries (Wiedmann et al., 2020). The reasons for this should be fairly self-explanatory, given the highly unequally distributed historical responsibility for greenhouse gas emissions by countries from the Global North (Hickel, 2020) and the extremely unequal current distribution of carbon footprints (Oswald et al., 2020).

Modelling and scenario work for future emission pathways have only recently started to even consider the possibility of low (energy) demand futures (Grubler et al., 2018; Nieto et al., 2020; Nikas et al., 2020; Vita et al., 2019). The dominant approach to dealing with economic growth (as measured by GDP) and (energy) demand[3] in climate change research was to leave them unquestioned. According to Keyβer and Lenzen (Keyßer & Lenzen, 2021, p. 2), "none of the 222 scenarios in the IPCC SR1.5 [Special Report on the impacts of global warming of 1.5 degrees above pre-industrial levels] and none of the shared socioeconomic pathways projects a declining GDP trajectory". This is still the case in Chapter 3 of the most recent IPCC report [6th Assessment Report, Working Group 3] (IPCC, 2022). However, a low energy demand scenario is included as one of the options to effectively limit global warming below 1.5 degrees.

Considering the above, the appearance of an increasing number of appeals for lifestyle changes and modelling efforts that include (energy) demand reductions is very significant. In particular, Max-Neef's conceptual proposal of distinguishing between needs and satisfiers opens the possibility to question consumption and demand. Even if not explicitly referring to Max-Neef's work, questioning of demand and consumption options within the climate change community has been influenced by his work, through the contributions of the ecological economics and degrowth communities more generally. For instance, Grubler's et al. (2018) low energy demand scenario refers to "human needs", and the work of Narasimha Rao and colleagues (Rao & Baer, 2012; Rao & Min, 2017) uses "Decent Living", which considers human needs as a building block and the underlying understanding of well-being is very much in line with Max-Neef's. Moreover, the work of Julia Steinberger and colleagues has explicitly taken forward the ideas of Max-Neef, as well as those of Doyal and Gough (1991), around human needs and satisfiers to argue for and model low energy futures.

By moving away from the conventional wisdom than "more is better", and that development happens due to a "trickle-down" effect where the gains from economic growth eventually reach the poorest in society, Max-Neef provided powerful interrogations of the desirability of economic growth (Max-Neef, 2014, 2016; Smith & Max-Neef, 2011). This critique did not only point out the environmental and ecological consequences of constant growth (or the problem scale, as he put it), but also the deep detrimental effects on the social fabric and well-being of communities. In Barefoot Economics (Max-Neef, 1982, p. 133), he stated "it should thus be clear that the constant increase in the scale of economic activity alienates those participating in it and destroys the human element in the surrounding framework". He diagnosed this as an issue where "[economic] growth is forced on us, willy-nilly, by the custom of measuring wealth in terms of money" (Smith & Max-Neef, 2011, p. 74), for which of course his solution was to move towards measuring wealth (and debt) in real physical units (like joules of energy) (Smith & Max-Neef, 2011, pp. 74–81), and to work with people in defining what wealth/development/well-being actually means for them rather than having it imposed from the top, the West or the Global North (Max-Neef et al., 1991).

Socio-cultural solutions: Satisfiers and sustainable consumption for a 1.5-degree world

At a more granular level, Max-Neef considers issues of consumption and demand (in economics terms) through the lens of satisfiers: "economic goods are objects or artifacts which affect the efficiency of a satisfiers, thus altering the threshold of actualization of a need, either in a positive or a negative sense" (Max-Neef et al., 1991, p. 30). Thus, Max-Neef's HSD (Human Scale Development) framework for holistically analysing a particular configuration of satisfiers (either the "negative" or the "utopian" matrix for a specific community) also implicitly questions issues around consumption and demand. In other words, the fact that economic goods affect the ways in which satisfiers contribute or hinder human needs actualisation means that issues around consumption and demand (of economic goods) are necessarily addressed in any HSD process.

Here, Max-Neef's categorisation of satisfiers into negative (inhibiting, destroyers or violators and pseudo-satisfiers) and positive (singular and synergetic) satisfiers is particularly helpful. Negative satisfiers are those that hinder, either directly or indirectly, human need actualisation. Conversely, positive satisfiers contribute to human need satisfaction, either in a single- or multi-dimensional way.

It is not difficult to see how ways of being, having, doing and interacting that promote overconsumption can be associated with negative satisfiers. Max-Neef himself points towards things like fashions, status symbols, exploitation of natural resources, commercial television, Taylorist-type production and others, as examples of negative satisfiers. And in negative matrices developed by communities, it is not uncommon to find things like wastefulness, consumerism, polluted spaces and selfishness – all associated with overconsumption.

Monica Guillen-Royo's (2016) seminal book *Sustainability and Wellbeing: Human Scale Development in Practice* explores the ways in which Max-Neef's HSD approach can contribute to sustainability. This questioning might be indirect, through the lens of needs and satisfiers, but Guillen-Royo argues that HSD processes lead to sustainable outcomes or utopian matrices that are more sustainable. There are two main ways in which that happens, according to Guillen-Royo (2016, p. 176): "synergetic satisfiers are 1) not harmful to any other human as they would then by qualified as *violators* or *inhibiting*; and 2) not harmful to the natural environment, as by destroying nature they would limit the possibilities to meet human needs now and in the future". Therefore, it can be argued that pursuing HSD-type processes provides a space and framework for communities to question their levels of demand and consumption practices and lead to moves towards reduced levels of demand.

The emerging field of sustainable consumption corridors, pioneered by Di Giulio and Fuchs (2014), has also embraced Max-Neef's conceptualisation of human needs and his distinction between needs and satisfiers in order to conceptualise consumption corridors themselves. For sustainable consumption corridors, the concept of needs is pivotal to connecting sustainability to consumption: "to define sustainable consumption, therefore, it seems reasonable to deduce a concept of needs from the notion of good life in the context of sustainability and apply it to consumption [by defining minima and maxima levels of consumption]" (Di Giulio & Fuchs, 2014, p. 187). Therefore, sustainable consumption "should be consumption allowing individuals to live a fulfilled life and at the same time it should be consumption which contributes to the improvement of the chances of others to live a fulfilled life, now and in the future (or at least not hurt these changes)" (Di Giulio & Fuchs, 2014, p. 187).

Another area of overlap between the sustainable consumption corridors literature and Max-Neef's contributions is around the importance of transdisciplinarity. Max-Neef was an advocate for the true involvement of people and communities in their own development, and sustainable consumption corridors people are also advocates for truly participatory process for the definition of consumption corridors.

Empirically, sustainable consumption scholars have used Max-Neef's categorisation of satisfiers to analyse certain social practices. Recently, Sahakian and Anantharaman studied the use of parks in the Indian city of Chennai, conceptualising them as "inclusive areas for synergistic need satisfaction" (Sahakian & Anantharaman, 2020). Although social practice theories have not been directly drawn from Max-Neef's work or vice versa, it is interesting to note the conceptual overlap between certain elements of social practice theories and how Max-Neef described satisfiers.

The main elements of social practices are threefold: social norms and other meanings, material arrangements and artefacts and skills and competences. Max-Neef seems to have been aware of social practices, and certainly of the social norms and physical configurations that lead to people behaving in a certain way. "Satisifers may include, among other things, forms of organization, political structures, *social practices*, subjective conditions, *values and norms, spaces*, contexts, modes, types of behaviours and attitudes, all of which are in a permanent spate of tension between consolidation and change" (Max-Neef et al., 1991, p. 24 own emphasis).

Systemic solutions: Satisfiers and provisioning systems for a 1.5-degree world

Not only does the HSD framework allows communities to question what they consume, but also under which institutional, attitudinal, temporal and geographical circumstances they do so. Max-Neef's different categorisations of satisfiers also allow for the critical examination of socio-technical provisioning systems. Through the exploration of satisfiers (mainly) as ways of "having" and "interacting", the HSD framework centres participant's thinking around the ways in which need satisfiers are provisioned. Therefore, the analysis is not only on whether needs are actualised or not but also on *how* they are actualised (or not), and the impact of the broader socio-technical provisioning systems on communities' well-being.

The important role of provisioning systems has also been related to need satisfiers conceptually and empirically (Max-Neef et al., 1991, p. 24 own emphasis). By analysing the role of the private car in need satisfaction, the authors above have highlighted the key role that broader economic structures of provisioning play in determining the range of available satisfiers for human need satisfaction. In the case of cars, the political economy of the car industry, urban planning, public transport provision and cultures of car use (Mattioli et al., 2020) determine a situation in which driving a private car becomes almost the only feasible mobility option for need satisfaction.

Max-Neef's further categorisation of satisfiers as endogenous or exogenous opens the space for critically engaging communities in issues of governance and incentivises them to work towards governance systems that are more self-reliant, and arguably more democratic and participatory.[4] In this sense, Max-Neef's work is also revolutionary and an empowering call to action at all levels, by all of us, to tackle climate change and environmental degradation at a human level.

From negative to synergetic satisfiers for a 1.5-degree world

Considering the arguments made around demand-side solutions, socio-cultural solutions and systemic solutions, Max-Neef's contributions to climate change mitigation and sustainability can be understood as anti-capitalist,[5] and leading to a policy agenda that is necessarily anti-capitalist. The argument would go like this:

Our current economic system (the current institutional, political and cultural structures that we "have"[6]) leads to increased demand and unsustainable consumption practices. That is why the science of climate change and sustainability is increasingly tackling the issue of demand (in particular energy demand) and unsustainable consumption.

Increased demand and unsustainable consumption practices will impede need actualisation for ourselves and others in the future, given the level of environmental degradation and destruction of climate stability they lead to.

Satisfiers that impede need actualisation now and in the future is the definition of negative satisfiers. Therefore, our current economic system is necessarily a constellation of mainly negative satisfiers. Most likely pseudo-satisfiers, given that we are often not aware of their destructive potential, and are content with the apparent or momentary satisfaction they provide.

As such, we should strive to change our economic system to one comprised of synergetic satisfiers. This change would certainly require tackling issues of demand, moving away from the relentless pursuit of economic growth, a key engine of capitalism.

Concluding remarks

The scholarly and applied work of Manfred Max-Neef has permeated current discourses around climate change and sustainability. It can be argued that distinguishing between needs and satisfiers has had a liberating effect when it comes to thinking about climate mitigation pathways and sustainable consumption. This liberation has mainly been from mainstream economics, and its modern political incarnation as neoliberalism, where prosperity is tied to ever-increasing production and consumption and where means become confused with ends.

However, Max-Neef's work is often not cited directly but is present implicitly in the most recent ideas around climate change mitigation and sustainability, or present through the citation of work that has in turn built on Max-Neef. Moreover, his ideas are sometimes superficially referred to (e.g. "human needs" and "satisifers"), without a deep understanding of what they mean, what they do not mean and how they are different from each other. This lack of direct engagement with Max-Neef's work could be explained by the complexity of the matrix of satisfiers in the HSD framework. The size of the matrix and the participatory nature of exploring needs and satisfiers *a la* Max-Neef are both the biggest strength and the biggest weakness of his work. It is also not so amenable to international scale quantitative work, which dominates current climate change mitigation research.

Nonetheless, Max-Neef's work has thus opened conceptual and empirical possibilities to reduce consumption while maintaining a good life (Millward-Hopkins et al., 2020; Rao & Min, 2017). These have not yet translated into widespread political and economic possibilities. The complexity of Max-Neef's thought, as described above, could be a contributing element, as is the presence of competing views on well-being, not only from a mainstream economics point of view but also from a more heterodox perspective. The latter include Amartya Sen's and Martha Nussbaum's ideas around capabilities (Nussbaum, 2001; Sen, 1999) and, even more closely related to Max-Neef, Len Doyal and Ian Gough's theory of human needs (which also includes the concept of satisfiers) (Doyal & Gough, 1991).

Despite challenges, there are encouraging signs that there might be momentum building around this agenda. For instance, the growing reach of the Wellbeing Economic Alliance (Coscieme et al., 2019) and of Kate Raworth's "doughnut economics" (Raworth, 2017), with national governments and city municipalities adopting their ideas around well-being and social foundations as a way forward.

We can only hope Max-Neef's ideas, and not neoliberal ideas, will guide our way out of this climate and ecological crisis, by continuing to provide the basis for a critical and transformative view on climate change and sustainability solutions: demand-side solutions, socio-cultural solutions and systemic solutions. The distinction between needs and satisfiers seems to be the key in moving this agenda forward.

Notes

1 Chapters 3 and 4 of this volume explore Max-Neef's ideas around human needs in detail.
2 This idea does not come from Max-Neef's though directly, but rather from the contributions that have taken Max-Neef's work forward and how those contributions come together in a way that contradicts some core tenants of capitalism.
3 Given the tight coupling between energy demand and economic growth (Haberl et al., 2020; Wiedenhofer et al., 2020), it is not unreasonable to assume that if Gross Domestic Product is projected to grow, energy demand will also grow. This is explained by the rebound effect, and the role of energy efficiency improvements in driving economic growth (Ayres & Voudouris, 2014; Brockway et al., 2017).
4 Most examples where the HSD approach has been implemented lead to somewhat improved self-reliance, or at the very least empowered self-awareness. See, for instance, Brand-Correa et al. (2018) and the many examples in Guillen-Royo (2016).
5 In his own work, Max-Neef does not refer to his view as being anti-capitalist. Instead, Max-Neef considers his position to be "counter-hegemonic", as the capacity to subvert power relations and change them from being top-down to being bottom-up.
6 "Have" as an existential category.

References

Alkire, S. (2002). Dimensions of human development. *World Development*, *30*(2), 181–205. https://doi.org/10.1016/S0305-750X(01)00109-7

Allen, M., Babiker, M., Chen, Y., de Coninck, H., Connors, S., van Diemen, R., Dube, O. P., Ebi, K., Engelbrecht, F., Ferrat, M., Ford, J., Forster, P., Fuss, S., Guillen, T., Harold, J., Hoegh-Guldberg, O., Hourcade, J.-C., Huppmann, D., Jacob, D., … Zickfeld, K. (2018). Summary for policymakers. In *Global warming of 1.5°C: An IPCC special report on the impacts of global warming of 1.5°C above pre-industrial levels and related global greenhouse gas emissions pathways, in the context of strengthening the global response to the threat of climate change*. Cambridge University Press.

Ayres, R. U., & Voudouris, V. (2014). The economic growth enigma: Capital, labour, and useful energy? *Energy Policy*, *64*, 16–28. https://doi.org/10.1016/j.enpol.2013.06.001

Brand-Correa, L. I., Martin-Ortega, J., & Steinberger, J. K. (2018). Human scale energy services: Untangling a 'golden thread'. *Energy Research and Social Science*, *38*(January), 178–187. https://doi.org/10.1016/j.erss.2018.01.008

Brand-Correa, L. I., Mattioli, G., Lamb, W. F., & Steinberger, J. K. (2020). Understanding (and tackling) need satisfier escalation. *Sustainability: Science, Practice, and Policy*, *16*(1). https://doi.org/10.1080/15487733.2020.1816026

Brockway, P. E., Saunders, H., Heun, M. K., Foxon, T. J., Steinberger, J. K., Barrett, J. R., & Sorrell, S. (2017). Energy rebound as a potential threat to a low-carbon future: Findings from a new exergy-based national-level rebound approach. *Energies*, *10*(1), 1–24. https://doi.org/10.3390/en10010051

Coscieme, L., Sutton, P., Mortensen, L. F., Kubiszewski, I., Costanza, R., Trebeck, K., Pulselli, F. M., Giannetti, B. F., & Fioramonti, L. (2019). Overcoming the myths of mainstream economics to enable a new wellbeing economy. *Sustainability*, *11*(16), 4374. https://doi.org/10.3390/su11164374

Creutzig, F., Roy, J., Lamb, W. F., Azevedo, I. M. L., de Bruin, W. B., Dalkmann, H., Edelenbosch, O. Y., Geels, F. W., Grübler, A., Hepburn, C., Hertwich, E., Khosla, R., Mattauch, L., Minx, J. C., Ramakrishnan, A., Rao, N. D., Steinberger, J. K., Tavoni, M., Ürge-Vorsatz, D., & Weber, E. U. (2018). Towards demand-side solutions for mitigating climate change. *Nature Climate Change*, *8*(April). https://doi.org/10.1038/s41558-018-0121-1

Di Giulio, A., & Fuchs, D. (2014). Sustainable consumption corridors: Concept, objections, and responses. *Gaia*, *23*, 184–192. https://doi.org/10.14512/gaia.23.S1.6

Doyal, L., & Gough, I. (1991). *A theory of human need*. The Macmillan Press.

Graeber, D. (2015). *The utopia of rules: On technology, stupidity, and the secret joys of bureaucracy*. Melville House.

Grubler, A., Wilson, C., Bento, N., Boza-Kiss, B., Krey, V., McCollum, D. L., Rao, N. D., Riahi, K., Rogelj, J., de Stercke, S., Cullen, J., Frank, S., Fricko, O., Guo, F., Gidden, M., Havlík, P., Huppmann, D., Kiesewetter, G., Rafaj, P., & Valin, H. (2018). A low energy demand scenario for meeting the 1.5 °C target and sustainable development goals without negative emission technologies. *Nature Energy*, *3*(6), 515–527. https://doi.org/10.1038/s41560-018-0172-6

Guillén-Royo, M. (2016). *Sustainability and wellbeing: Human-scale development in practice*. Routledge.

Haberl, H., Wiedenhofer, D., Virág, D., Kalt, G., Plank, B., Brockway, P., Fishman, T., Hausknost, D., Krausmann, F., Leon-Gruchalski, B., Mayer, A., Pichler, M., Schaffartzik, A., Sousa, T., Streeck, J., & Creutzig, F. (2020). A systematic review of the evidence on decoupling of GDP, resource use and GHG emissions, part II: Synthesizing the insights. *Environmental Research Letters*, *15*(6), 065003. https://doi.org/10.1088/1748-9326/ab842a

Hickel, J. (2020). Quantifying national responsibility for climate breakdown: An equality-based attribution approach for carbon dioxide emissions in excess of the planetary boundary. *The Lancet Planetary Health*, *4*(9), e399–e404. https://doi.org/10.1016/S2542-5196(20)30196-0

IPCC (2022). *Climate change 2022: Mitigation of climate change*.

Keyßer, L. T., & Lenzen, M. (2021). 1.5 °C degrowth scenarios suggest the need for new mitigation pathways. *Nature Communications*, *12*(1), 1–16. https://doi.org/10.1038/s41467-021-22884-9

Mattioli, G., Roberts, C., Steinberger, J. K., & Brown, A. (2020). The political economy of car dependence: A systems of provision approach. *Energy Research and Social Science*, *66*, 101486. https://doi.org/10.1016/j.erss.2020.101486

Max-Neef, M. (1982). *From the outside looking in: Experiences in barefoot economics*. Zed Books Ltd.

Max-Neef, M. (2014). The good is the bad that we don't do. *Ecological Economics*, *104*, 152–154. https://doi.org/10.1016/j.ecolecon.2014.02.011

Max-Neef, M. (2016). Philosophy of ecological economics. *International Journal of Economics & Management Sciences*, *5*(5). https://doi.org/10.4172/2162-6359.1000366

Max-Neef, M., Elizalde, A., & Hopenhayn, M. (1991). *Human scale development: Conception application and further reflections*. Apex Press.

Millward-Hopkins, J., Steinberger, J. K., Rao, N. D., & Oswald, Y. (2020). Providing decent living with minimum energy: A global scenario. *Global Environmental Change*, *65* (August), 102168. https://doi.org/10.1016/j.gloenvcha.2020.102168

Newell, P., Daley, F., & Twena, M. (2021). *The Cambridge sustainability commission on scaling behaviour change*. https://www.rapidtransition.org/wp-content/uploads/2021/04/Cambridge-Sustainability-Commission-on-Scaling-behaviour-change-report.pdf

Nieto, J., Carpintero, Ó., Miguel, L. J., & de Blas, I. (2020). Macroeconomic modelling under energy constraints: Global low carbon transition scenarios. *Energy Policy*, *137*, 111090. https://doi.org/10.1016/j.enpol.2019.111090

Nikas, A., Lieu, J., Sorman, A., Gambhir, A., Turhan, E., Baptista, B. V., & Doukas, H. (2020). The desirability of transitions in demand: Incorporating behavioural and societal transformations into energy modelling. *Energy Research & Social Science*, *70*, 101780. https://doi.org/10.1016/j.erss.2020.101780

Nussbaum, M. C. (2001). Symposium on Amartya Sen's philosophy: 5 adaptive preferences and women's options. *Economics and Philosophy*, *17*, 67–88. https://doi.org/10.1017/S0266267101000116

Oswald, Y., Owen, A., & Steinberger, J. K. (2020). Large inequality in international and intranational energy footprints between income groups and across consumption categories. *Nature Energy*, *5*(3), 231–239. https://doi.org/10.1038/s41560-020-0579-8

Rao, N. D., & Baer, P. (2012). "Decent living" emissions: A conceptual framework. *Sustainability*, *4*, 656–681. https://doi.org/10.3390/su4040656

Rao, N. D., & Min, J. (2017). Decent living standards: Material prerequisites for human wellbeing. *Social Indicators Research*, 1–20. https://doi.org/10.1007/s11205-017-1650-0

Raworth, K. (2017). *Doughnut economics: Seven ways to think like a 21st-century economist*. Penguin Random House.

Sahakian, M., & Anantharaman, M. (2020). What space for public parks in sustainable consumption corridors? Conceptual reflections on need satisfaction through social practices. *Sustainability: Science, Practice, and Policy*, *16*(1), 128–142. https://doi.org/10.1080/15487733.2020.1788697

Sen, A. K. (1999). *Development as freedom*. Oxford University Press.

Smith, P. B., & Max-Neef, M. (2011). *Economics unmasked: From power and greed to compassion and the common good*. Green Books.

The CCC (2019). *Net Zero: The UK's contribution to stopping global warming*. *May*, 277. https://www.theccc.org.uk/publication/net-zero-the-uks-contribution-to-stopping-global-warming/%0Awww.theccc.org.uk/publications

Vita, G., Lundström, J. R., Hertwich, E. G., Quist, J., Ivanova, D., Stadler, K., & Wood, R. (2019). The environmental impact of green consumption and sufficiency lifestyles scenarios in Europe: Connecting local sustainability visions to global consequences. *Ecological Economics*, *164*, 106322. https://doi.org/10.1016/J.ECOLECON.2019.05.002

Wiedenhofer, D., Virág, D., Kalt, G., Plank, B., Streeck, J., Pichler, M., Mayer, A., Krausmann, F., Brockway, P., Schaffartzik, A., Fishman, T., Hausknost, D., Leon-Gruchalski, B., Sousa, T., Creutzig, F., & Haberl, H. (2020). A systematic review of the evidence on decoupling of GDP, resource use and GHG emissions, part I: Bibliometric and conceptual mapping. *Environmental Research Letters*, *15*(6), 063002. https://doi.org/10.1088/1748-9326/ab8429

Wiedmann, T., Lenzen, M., Keyßer, L. T., & Steinberger, J. K. (2020). Scientists' warning on affluence. *Nature Communications*, *11*(1). https://doi.org/10.1038/s41467-020-16941-y

12 Human scale sustainable development

Where Max-Neef's fundamental human needs meet sustainability

Gibrán Vita

Introduction

Popular wisdom dictates 'we care about what we measure, and measure what we care about'. In the early 1990s, Max-Neef (hereafter MN) proposed a framework called Human Scale Development (HSD) as a participatory tool to design development strategies that meet people's fundamental needs directly, rather than through proxies such as economic growth. MN's goal with HSD was to push for social and economic development that enhances human well-being, understood by him as the satisfaction of nine fundamental biological, social and psychological needs (see Chapters 3 and 4 in this volume).

HSD main goal was not environmental sustainability as such, but to empower citizens to pursue well-being through direct democracy. However, empirical work on HSD is abundant with examples in which human well-being depends on the healthy natural systems that support it (Max-Neef et al., 1991). One could argue that a careful reading of HSD theory and practice suggests that environmental stewardship is a prerequisite for well-being and thus HSD strategies.

In this chapter, I focus on making the environmental sustainability dimension of HSD more explicit and thus relevant to contemporary sustainability goals. I begin by depicting an augmented version of HSD with more explicit prominence on sustainability, a version that I call 'human scale sustainable development' (HSSD). Noteworthy that I do not claim HSSD to be an entirely new framework, but rather a 'sustainability explicit' version of the original HSD. In this version, the goal of the framework is not only well-being, but 'sustainable well-being', i.e., meeting all fundamental needs within planetary boundaries.

HSSD differs from HSD in three main aspects. First, the expansion of HSD system boundaries to consider the life cycle of satisfiers. Second, I expand HSD with components of the theory of capitals by sociologist Pierre Bourdieu and with the paradigm of socio-economic metabolism, an interdisciplinary concept from the disciplines of Social Ecology and Industrial Ecology that characterise socio-ecological systems in terms of the extraction, flow, accumulation and environmental impact of natural resources that derive from socio-economic activity. I depict a visual representation of the HSSD to ease grasping and communication of the framework, highlighting its connection to the sustainability paradigm. Finally,

DOI: 10.4324/9781003381143-14

I provide examples on how to operationalise HSSD into current sustainability agendas by monitoring, embedding, innovating and enacting policies following an HSSD lens.

This chapter is an exploratory proposal with the intention to leverage on MN's legacy. The proposal of HSSD and examples are mere illustrations and not to be taken as prescriptions or conclusions, but rather to spark dialogue. The examples are provided irrespective of how realistic or unrealistic they might appear through the lens of current cultural, legal, academic or economic paradigms.

The spirit of HSD is self-determination to envision the ideal satisfiers for a given context and to enact (or ignore) the outcomes of an HSD/HSSD process. As a transformative process, HSD/HSSD functions as a mirror to reflect upon our current systems and discern the true satisfiers from the false satisfiers. As any transformative process, the conclusions might confront us to face the habits, culture and behaviours that are detrimental, yet self-preserving.

The examples here might appear to at odds with mainstream modern lifestyles and consumption-oriented conceptions of freedom. To that end, I examine the challenges of implementing HSSD and strive to reconcile the goals of HSSD and the worldviews of individualised freedom of consumer choice, so precious in Western democracies.

The chapter is divided as follows: the second section describes the context of the surplus economy as a support for upscaling HSSD, the third section discussed premises and proposal of the HSSD vis-à-vis HSD, and the fourth section depicts the operationalisation of HSSD: diagnose and monitor; embed, apply and innovate; and enact. Finally, I discuss the limitations. The discussion is supported by literature but also articulated around open questions and thought experiments to dialogue with MN's thought about contemporary issues.

The surplus economy: The time is ripe for a sustainability centred Human Scale Development

The premise of mainstream economic theory is that resources are scarce and human wants infinite (Jackson, 2005). To MN, this principle assumes the world as mechanical and nature as a sub-system of the economy, translated to the political pursuit of quantitative goals, such as economic growth (Victor, 2010). This development philosophy, he argues, is disconnected from the human experience and therefore leads to policies that – regardless of their intention – can often be seen as economic crimes against humanity due to the hardships they create for those that it allegedly intends to uplift (Max-Neef, 2014).

In support of MN's proposal, recent evidence reveals that the Global North lives in a surplus economy, as indicated by the over-consumption of commodities, food surplus and the electronic waste generated (Fanning et al., 2021; Hiç et al., 2016; Robinson, 2009). Similarly, the threshold hypothesis (Max-Neef, 1995), to a large extent supported by recent empirical evidence, suggests steady or even declining well-being metric after reaching certain level of wealth (see the introduction in Vita et al., 2019a and Chapter 13 in this volume for a discussion on recent evidence).

The material bonanza of the Global North and the Global Wealthy indirectly jeopardise development for the rest by depleting resources, degrading their local environment and exacerbating inequalities which allow for an exploitative master-servant relationship (Robinson, 2009; Vita et al., 2019b). This power imbalance can also be seen as an economic crime against humanity (Max-Neef, 2014).

The current growth-centric development paradigm relies disproportionately on natural capital to sustain a hungry socio-economic metabolism – regardless of whether it creates satisfiers or not. Against mounting empirical evidence, neo-classical economics embedded in dominant development narratives assume that individuals maximise their utility (satisfy needs) as long as income is available (Stiglitz et al., 2010). Data-driven analyses reveal the paradox of our days: we enjoy unprecedented material standards at the expense of nature's destruction, but that is not even a guarantee of satisfied basic needs (Rao et al., 2017) nor of healthy minds, bodies and communities (Vita et al., 2019a).

The notions that ever-increasing resource use and affluence are a necessary development pathway to resolve socio-ecological problems, as proposed by modernisation theories, such as environmental Kuznets curves and neo-classical economics, are not supported by evidence (Wiedmann et al., 2020). Following MN, we can conclude that any development paradigm that degrades all capitals while failing to satisfy or obstructing need satisfaction is a crime against humanity (Max-Neef, 2014).

A needs-centred economy confronts the 'premise of scarcity' embedded in capitalist and socialist economic thinking alike, where human wants are infinite and resources are limited, and thus best distributed by markets or central planning (Wiedmann et al., 2020). A needs-based economy implies 'sufficiency', where needs are satiable (finite) and material resources have an important, yet limited, contribution to well-being. In HSD, non-material and non-market satisfiers, such as social practices and lifestyles, also play an equally important role (Max-Neef, 1992; Sirgy et al., 2006).

In sum, a system that relies on ever-rising consumption to function is an obstacle to the regeneration of underlying natural and social capitals. Over-consumption and waste not only undermine natural capital, but they directly threaten social capital by reducing it to mere labour force, while systematically repressing other types of labour such as reproductive, self-development, care, social learning, household production, community work and participation in democracy (Haug, 2016).

Moreover, reducing lifestyles to working-earning-spending cycles encourages materialistic worldviews, which are consistently associated with lower well-being and obstruct sustainability policies (Andersson et al., 2014; Kasser, 2002; Vita et al., 2020).

Human scale sustainable development: Core premises and theoretical expansion of HSD

HSD provides a template that directs natural and human resources to satisfy fundamental human needs in a bottom-up fashion. HSD is the counter-proposal to the predominant (often paternalistic and inadequate) top-down development that focuses on supplying objects and inputs such as housing, clothes, apparatus and income with little regard to the subjective human experience (Max-Neef, 1992). HSD main premises are as follows: (1) development should be about people, not about objects or economic growth (Max-Neef, 2014); (2) fundamental human needs are finite (satiable), limited in number and classifiable; and (3) fundamental human needs are relatively constant across cultures and time, while need satisfiers are distinct from human needs and therefore subject to change and up for discussion. For more details on HSD and fundamental needs postulates, see the original work by Max-Neef et al. (1991) and Chapters 3 and 4 in this volume.

HSD embeds specific assumptions about the purpose of the economy. First, satisfying human needs is the ultimate driver of all human endeavours. Second, 'the purpose of the economy is to serve the people, and not the people to serve the economy' (Max-Neef et al., 1991, p. 4).

The HSSD versions add three extra premises. Third, environmental impact is the result of the strategies employed to satisfy needs (Max-Neef et al., 1991; Vita et al., 2019a). Fourth, policy should enhance the creation of satisfiers that prove effective and synergistic need satisfiers while regenerating the underlying natural, cultural and social capitals. Fifth, sustainability policy should aim to limit or phase out false satisfiers that do not enhance well-being but deplete underlying capitals: natural, social and cultural capital (Figure 12.1).

Figure 12.1 is a visual representation of the integrated framework HSSD. Natural capital is the world's stocks of natural assets which include all abiotic and biotic factors that keep ecosystems in balance, thereby enabling human life by the services it provides directly (clear air, water, landscape etc.) and indirectly (via materials). Cultural capital is the accumulation of knowledge, behaviours and skills that a person can tap into to demonstrate one's cultural competence and social status. Social capital is the social fabric or 'the networks of relationships among people who live

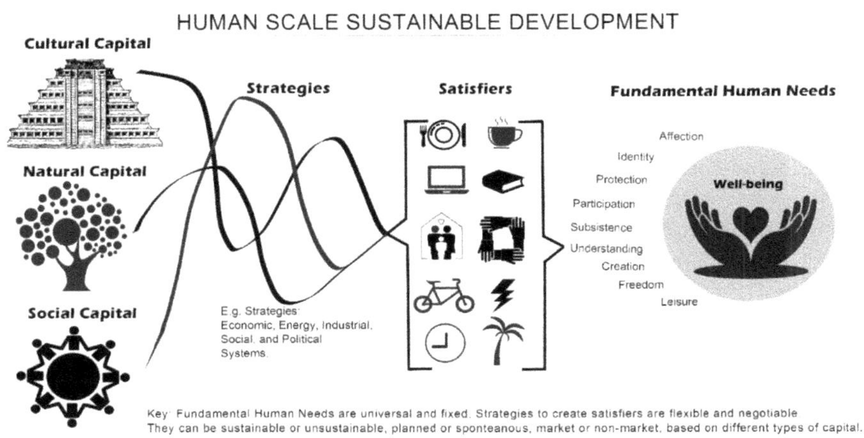

Figure 12.1 Human scale sustainable development

and work in a particular society, enabling that society to function effectively'. See Bourdieu (1986) for more detail on the forms of capital. All other capitals, such as physical and economic, are seen as derived from these three in HSSD.

In HSSD, Figure 12.1 shows that the system boundaries and geographical scope expand beyond the local to consider the full life cycle of satisfiers, from their creation the extraction of raw materials and labour they require, to their socio-ecological impact, i.e., whether the choice of a given satisfiers depletes or regenerates capitals. We call this a 'cradle to grave' perspective.

I depict HSSD as a visual framework to ease the grasping of the concept and pinpoint the inter-connections among well-being, sustainability and the underlying capitals. In this visual model, it becomes more clear that environmental stewardship is (implicitly) one of the cornerstones of HSD.

It should be noted that the HSSD is not only a graphical representation of HSD, but also a conceptual expansion of HSD to better serve sustainability agendas. The HSD framework is expanded by incorporating concepts from fields that deal with complex socio-ecological systems. First, the concept of capitals from Bourdieu, second a life cycle perspective and expanded systems boundaries to think about satisfiers from 'cradle to grave', i.e., from raw materials, to production and all the way to their end of life. Third, the concept of socio-economic metabolism[1] provides an indication of the sustainability implications of our development and satisfiers, i.e., assess whether these are extractive or regenerative of underlying capitals.

If the premises above are accepted, then a new paradigm of HSSD emerges as portrayed in Figure 12.1, linking the underlying capitals, to the strategies that provide satisfiers, the satisfiers produced and the social outcomes (need satisfaction). By strategies I mean those 'systems of provision' of satisfiers which can take not only the shape of systems of productions, economic systems, but also political systems, educational systems, technological systems and infrastructures (physical capitals), all of which influence the lifestyles reproduced by the majority.

Figure 12.1 is intended to feed imagination towards operationalising HSSD. The framework on Figure 12.1, emphasising the interconnection between social well-being and environmental sustainability through *socio-economic metabolism*, could be considered for every action or policy. In this view, HSSD can be seen as a system's thinking framework to aid the design of synergistic satisfiers that also enrich underlying capitals.

The game-changer proposed by MN is to differentiate *needs* from *satisfiers*. While needs are embedded in our human nature and we cannot change them, the ways we choose to satisfy needs are embedded in our culture and systems – and we can change those. To do so, we draw on available resources to create satisfiers. As Figure 12.1 shows, we have nature (natural capital); we have networks, time, skills and institutions (social capital); we have heritage, idiosyncrasies and ingenuity (cultural capital); we each have our inner worlds, motivations, values and intelligence (lifestyles as satisfiers discussed earlier). Such a lens opens up possibilities to decouple satisfiers from natural resources and markets. The difference with HSD is that HSSD makes an explicit consideration of socio-ecological systems through a broader life cycle lens, thus placing more prominence on environmental stewardship. We could say that HSSD adds another variant of satisfier: *eco-efficient satisfier*, which is one of those satisfiers that efficiently satisfy needs at a minimum environmental cost.

Operationalising human scale sustainable development

Operationalising HSSD has two main prerequisites. First, similar to HSD, is to deploy a democratic participatory approach where citizens and stakeholders have a voice in self-diagnosing on current status and collectively design the most synergistic satisfiers to improve well-being. Second, which is not explicit in HSD, is to validate the diagnosis and monitor outcomes (need satisfaction) with a third-party system of indicators that correspond with the fundamental human needs, as proposed by previous research (Costanza et al., 2007; Vita et al., 2019a). The assessment of social outcomes should be complemented with an assessment of environmental impact of such satisfiers.

The path to HSSD is to satisfy human needs with satisfiers that yield the best social outcomes at minimum environmental cost (eco-efficient satisfiers). To measure progress towards this end, need satisfaction has to be measured as directly as possible and not by input proxies such as investments, jobs and income – which are no guarantee of outcomes of need satisfaction (Stiglitz et al., 2010).

How can individuals, communities, nations and firms embed an HSSD approach in daily actions, livelihoods, products, policies and plans for the future? The answer is to place our fundamental human needs at the core of everything we do, in other words, prioritising the psychological, social, biological and spiritual building blocks that associate with a flourishing life (Büchs & Koch, 2017).

Thus, outcomes of HSSD would compel us to spare resources from false satisfiers, prioritise capital-regenerative satisfiers and limit the appropriation by the global rich so the global poor can dispose of natural capital too.

In the following section, I dwell upon several dimensions that pertain the implementation of HSSD, and implications to diagnose and monitor HSSD, how to embed HSSD in current decision-making and innovation, and implications to enact the outcomes of an HSSD process.

Diagnose and monitor

HSSD-based strategy departs from diagnosing current society-wide levels of need satisfaction and stating minimum decent living thresholds (O'Neill et al., 2018; Rao & Min, 2019), while also considering the subjective opinion (or subjective satisfaction) of the bearers of policy with respect to current levels and future goals (Brand-Correa et al., 2018; Lindellee et al., 2021).

Contrary to the assumption that inputs (monetary or resources) contribute to quality of life *per se*, an HSSD approach addresses and evaluates societal outcomes in terms of need satisfaction directly without assuming 'the more inputs the better' (Vita et al., 2019a). HSSD, thus, is more flexible to pursue well-being beyond economic and natural resources, but also by re-designing certain strategies that influence our lifestyles.

Indicators

Since sustainable lifestyles are multidimensional, an adequate framework to study them requires multiple indicators of wellbeing and environmental impact (Costanza et al., 2007; OECD, 2015). A challenge to operationalise HSD is the unclarity on how to assess the effectiveness or progress towards HSD goals. One could assume that HSD assumes an on-going process where the community continuously assesses the effectiveness of their satisfiers. Such an approach is ideal at the local but limits the application and influence of HSD into wider scope agendas.

Here, I propose a combination of objective and subjective – qualitative and quantitative – indicators to monitor the progress towards 'HSSD', in terms of need satisfaction. Objective indicators are evaluations carried out by a third party to inform objective outcomes, ideally presented with granularity (spatially explicit, or micro data) to capture nuances and heterogeneity across populations. Subjective indicators are judgements made by the study subjects and indicate the experience and satisfaction with respect to a certain need (e.g., free time and satisfaction with the neighbourhood) (Büchs & Koch, 2017). Ideally, diverse indicators of a particular need should converge; else, it might indicate deficient satisfiers or measurement issues.

Well-being indicators are vast and varied, which can be classified as follows:

- Objective or subjective
- Inputs or outcomes
- Single or composite
- Unidimensional or multidimensional

Table 12.1 provides an overview of subjective and objective indicators commonly used in well-being research and policy, depending on the school of thought. In short, hedonic well-being is concerned with pleasurable mental states and minimised pain. While a eudemonic approach focuses on the activities, abilities or functionings that set the basis for human flourishing, where flourishing can be understood as a balanced satisfaction of the nine fundamental human needs proposed by MN.

The indicator types that are most compatible with monitoring HSSD are those classifiable as eudemonic well-being and outcome oriented.

The most popular indicators for well-being are objective, single or composite. Single indicators such as life expectancy are powerful, yet a narrow view on well-being (Steinberger et al., 2020). Composite indicators, such as the human development index (HDI), obscure drivers of change (Sagar & Najam, 1998). Objective indicators measure the level to which human needs are met but ignore peoples' subjective satisfaction with respect to such levels (Costanza et al., 2007). Aside from life satisfaction or happiness, subjective indicators are absent in the policy arena – including the SDGs.

Dashboards should balance inputs and outcomes. Measuring only inputs can be misleading, e.g., national energy access that obscures distributional aspects and ignores appliances required to use energy (Vita et al., 2021). Outcomes are a more direct measure of well-being (e.g., healthy people rather than investments in health) (Stiglitz et al., 2010).

Table 12.1 Types of well-being measures and example indicators of their subjective and objective accounts. The indicator types that are most compatible with monitoring HSSD are those within the eudemonic well-being and outcome oriented

Type of measure	*Subjective self-report*	*Third-party objective report*
Measures of hedonic well-being	*Self-reports on emotions (anger, anxiety, happiness) or overall life satisfaction (evaluative)*	*Objective measurement of feelings and emotions (neuro-physiological monitoring of brainwaves, pulse, cortisol, etc.)*
Measures of eudemonic and evaluative well-being	*Self-reported satisfaction with respect to dimensions related to life dimensions and mastery, agency etc., e.g., 'I am satisfied with my health, community, work, skills, freedom, autonomy, finances, leisure, social life, etc.'*	*Objective measures of specific dimensions, e.g., health care, political freedom, work conditions, skill level, financial freedom, leisure time, social contact etc.*
Measures of objective 'general' well-being	*Objective self-report (e.g., 'I have good health')*	*Third-party objective (medical evaluation)*
Inputs	*Self-reported income, free time etc.*	*Actual disposable income, actual residual free time*
Outcomes	*Self-report on several dimensions: enough food, housing, make ends meet, safety etc.*	*Objective measures of several dimensions: food, housing, safety*
Overarching indicators	*Unidimensional: 'I am satisfied with my life'*	*Unidimensional: Life expectancy*
	Composite: national happiness index	*Composite: Human development index*

Note: Determinants of well-being should be controlled to characterise the effect of contextual factors and compare differences across individuals or groups, e.g., income, health status, social contact, employment, education, age, personality type, culture etc. See Tay and Diener (2011) and Vita et al. (2020).

Comprehensive outcome-oriented dashboards are key to grasp multidimensional well-being. Initiatives such as the Better Life Index (OECD, 2015) or the Social Progress Index (Porter et al., 2013) demonstrate the policy usefulness of integrating multiple – objective and subjective – indicators to measure the good life (Costanza et al., 2007).

An HSSD dashboard would jointly track material inputs, environmental outputs (footprints or impact) and well-being outcomes centred on human need satisfaction. Objective lists can capture inputs (socio-economic metabolism and satisfiers) that constitute material satisfiers which are a prerequisite for a decent life (Rao & Min, 2019). However, deploying HSSD requires to give less importance to objective inputs (expenditure in health, education etc.) and prioritise (objective and subjective) outcomes (health of people, understanding etc.) (Stiglitz et al., 2010). Monitoring outcomes would consider the qualitative and subjective experiences with satisfiers and the status need satisfaction (Vita et al., 2019a).

Besides third-party indicators, MN left ample examples on how to facilitate a process where people can discuss the satisfiers and their linkage to needs bottom-up (Max-Neef et al., 1991). Few empirical works link needs to resources. Guillen-Royo (2020) conducted workshops to understand the need satisfaction related to ICT technologies. Brand-Correa et al. worked with communities to identify energy services in their relation to specific needs (2018). Vita et al. (2019a) connected HSD to global consumption and emissions (inputs), as well as objective and subjective indicators of need satisfaction. Murata and Kobayashi (2019) identify barriers to sustainable consumption and production in Vietnam. Implementing this participatory process at a larger scale is still a challenge to be solved, but information and blockchain technologies are ripe to facilitate such as a large-scale process, as shown recently by Murata et al. (2021).

Previous efforts on a multidimensional monitoring dashboard of well-being clearly reveal the limitations of material inputs to satisfy all needs, and thereby open up space for the contribution of non-market and non-material factors to well-being (Costanza et al., 2007; O'Neill et al., 2018; Vita et al., 2019a). The measurement and tracking of these aspects remain open for debate. Issues such as time use, urban spaces, social support, etc. are available but more careful identification of key non-market satisfiers would be necessary.

To track the environmental impacts (in function of the flows and stocks of socio-economic metabolism), consumption-based footprint, life cycle assessment or material flow analysis are the best available indicators to capture impact at high resolution, in connection with the products and provisioning systems that drive impact (Vita et al., 2019b, 2020). To this end, the field of industrial ecology keeps developing state-of-the-art methods devoted to characterising and managing the socio-economic metabolism (Vita, 2018).

Embed, apply and innovate

Once a diagnosis and monitoring system is in place, the next step is to identify which satisfiers to remove and regulate and which to create or enhance. Ideally, satisfiers are designed optimising for the capitals they demand and how synergistic they are (Figure 12.1). A natural step is to elicit the views and experiences from the population in tandem with an iterative process to co-design the most synergistic/utopian and eco-efficient satisfiers.

Identifying and embedding synergistic and utopian satisfiers in decision-making

The key to implement HSSD is to assess every activity, policy, investment, lifestyle etc. in terms of their environmental costs with respect to their well-being they yield. To identify and reach consensus on strategies, it is necessary that the communities engage in linking needs to their most ideal (*utopian or synergistic*) satisfiers and reflect on the types of capital that they require. In this way, societies can better judge the adequacy of the strategies and amount of capital(s) devoted to each need (O'Neill et al., 2018; Vita, 2016).

In other words, communities must collectively reflect on whether resources are contributing to need satisfaction or simply feeding economic inertia. Some of the guiding questions to assist satisfier design are as follows: could we spare resources and regenerate capitals by employing different strategies? Can we redirect resources to areas where they have proven societal benefits? Such a view broadens the operating space for options of change beyond the classic dogmas of 'consume better, produce efficiently' (Akenji, 2014; Vita, 2016).

For example, the need to *participate* and to *create* in a given community might require commuting in order to interact, work and engage with others. Satisfiers can come in the shape of private or public vehicles, motorised or active transport, and resource-intensive or nature-based infrastructures. However, deploying more capital does not guarantee more or better satisfaction of these needs. If the urban design is poor, the distances long, the proximity with cars unbearable, rude drivers, or the air unbreathable, then rising the resources allocated to transport does not ensure that people can *participate* and *create* better in their communities, and perhaps non-material solutions are needed (Kalt et al., 2019).

Moreover, energy-hungry transport can be driven by unnecessary commute, inefficient transport infrastructure, poor urban planning and car lobbies – not by the intention to satisfy needs. In other words, we can rise energy use but without increasing well-being or even lowering it. Further, if a rising energy bill implies more pollution, more traffic and less pedestrian space, then the energy-intensive strategy inhibits/violates the satisfaction of all other needs such as protection, freedom and leisure (Brand-Correa et al., 2020).

Conversely, the choice of satisfier can exclusively address a specific need or synergistically satisfy multiple needs. For example, urban design for cycling and walking additionally enhance *freedom*, *leisure* and *protection* (safety and health) (Max-Neef et al., 1991).

Take a leisure evening as an example. We can gather with neighbours to play sports and board games, binge watch TV or drive to a shopping mall. Which option would provide the highest quality leisure at the lowest environmental cost?

Which one is most synergistic, meaning it simultaneously satisfies several needs? With relatively low impact, playing with neighbours may satisfy participation and understanding as we engage in conversation and social learning. It may satisfy creation as we polish our tactics and skill. It may even address protection and affection as we nourish our friendships.

The same reasoning applies to all needs. For example, to satisfy the need to 'create', we might rely on our paid or household work, write blogs, start a community garden etc. To feel protected, we can rely on our family, therapy group, our friends, security systems, social policy or private insurances. To show and feel affection, we can give gifts or spend quality time. To survive and be healthy, we can eat highly processed foods or organic produce. To participate, we can spend time on social media or volunteering. To understand, we might pursue formal education, self-study or informal learning with peers. To satisfy our identity, we can rely on our profession, nationality, fashion and house decoration or on our values, deeds and ancestry.

In this sense, lifestyles themselves can become a strategy that provides synergistic satisfiers (see Chapter 11 in this volume). Some examples are household production instead of market consumption (Ironmonger, 1987), trading surplus income for time (Schor, 2001), doing inner 'mental' work such as mindfulness, self-development or self-inquiry that helps to decouple well-being from social comparison, material standards or consumption (Kasser, 2002) etc. However, the individuals might not be entirely free to take such decisions given the inertia of the system to disfavour alternative lifestyles.

In sum, a sustainable good life comes from addressing all needs while regenerating (rather than consuming) our underlying capitals (Figure 12.1). A useful exercise is to envision or identify the most utopian satisfiers that address several needs effectively and with minimum impact. Some exist already, which we must endorse and upscale. Some we might need to co-create.

Transformative innovation of socio-technical satisfiers

A needs-centred approach is perhaps the most underestimated yet most promising solution to many of our socio-environmental challenges. A needs approach welcomes technical and policy innovation, but not always vice versa. Relying on techno-political fixes usually precludes questioning options and choices of satisfiers. Technical progress is constrained by thermodynamics, while consumption is virtually unrestricted. As we witness socio-environmental breakdown, it becomes increasingly risky to place large bets exclusively on technology.

Figure 12.2 depicts the framework by Donella Meadows, which describes the effectiveness of different leverage points to transform socio-ecological systems (Abson et al., 2017; Meadows, 1999). Most policy efforts focus on the most shallow and ineffective leverage points such as **parameters** (subsidies, taxes, size of stocks and flows in the socio-economic metabolism) or the **feedbacks** (delaying the impact or strength of a reaction, such as climate targets).

Not by coincidence, MN's proposal of HSD inherently focuses on the deepest leverage points. HSD calls for socio-technical and political innovations with the

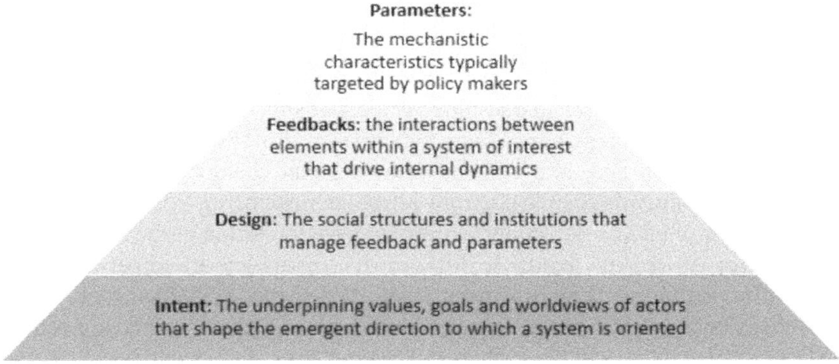

Figure 12.2 The four leverage realms where system-changing interventions and innovations can occur

power to change the **design** of the systems' rules, structure and governance; as well as the **intent** of the system, such as goals of the economy, its epistemology and the underlying paradigms that drive society (Max-Neef, 2014).

Innovations in democracy

Democratic debate centred on needs is more promising than feeding the polarising strategies by parties and media, as it has proven to promote more of a 'systems thinking' approach, which eases consensus across ideologies (Ballew et al., 2019).

Participatory processes are key to identify the status of needs (situational matrix) and satisfiers envisioned by the communities (propositional matrix) (Cruz et al., 2009). Besides the work by MN, a handful of examples are available in the literature. Guillen-Royo (2010) implemented HSD workshops at the city level. Lindellee et al. (2021) ran a series of citizens' forums to discuss potential utopian satisfiers ad hoc to current challenges and resources in Sweden. Brand-Correa et al. (2018) engaged communities in identifying the energy services which are more synergistic. Murata et al. (2021), due to the pandemic, proposed an online system that could be upscaled for mass participation.

Non-material and non-human scale interventions

In this section, we discuss the potential of non-material and non-human scale action such as non-material satisfiers, editing consumer choices to favour synergistic and eco-efficient satisfiers and the role of changing the systemic lock-ins that favour current mainstream lifestyles.

HSSD considers the potential of non-material satisfiers – such as time, care, public and community spaces, social fabric, urban nature etc. Embedding HSSD into policy and innovation could potentially spare significant natural capital while enhancing well-being and enriching social capital.

Editing consumer choices to disfavour false satisfiers and favour synergistic satisfiers is a seldom discussed strategy. While placing needs at the core of all human affairs, we must not fall prey to consumer scapegoatism (Akenji, 2014). Consumer scapegoatism is the strategy of polluting industries to shift responsibility for changing away from them and unto citizens, knowing that changing one individual's behaviour has a limited effect in a nature-intensive system.

The illusion of choice is a major barrier for transformation at the human scale. The lifestyles 'by-design' available in the current paradigm are rather narrow, as they revolve around work-earn-consume and debt cycles (D'Alisa et al., 2015). While these default lifestyles may prove a hindrance to satisfy needs and achieve HSSD, deviating from this prescribed path comes with an extensive risk of need deprivation, such as financial, health and housing insecurities, that in turn affect social life and self-image. In sum, human agency is reduced to choosing between the lesser evils, whether politicians, jobs or commodities, rather than being able to choose the most utopian or synergistic satisfiers (Haug, 2016).

Non-human scale action would address the systematic and structural inertia that lies beyond the agency of the individual but that nevertheless influences an individual's lifestyle by imposing restrictions, or limiting choices. Examples of such inertias are built into our time-use (work week), financial institutions (interests rates), ownership structures (income inequalities and housing crises) etc.

Serious non-human scale action centred on needs would prioritise need satisfaction above economic goals. Such action would open up difficult, but long due, conversations about the drivers of need in satisfaction and natures' degradation.

Enact HSSD: Minimising false satisfiers

The case of inefficient or wasteful use of natural resources which do not yield need satisfaction is covered by the pseudo satisfiers concept in HSD (Max-Neef, 1992), i.e., satisfiers that intend to satisfy needs but fall short, inhibit or seriously violate need satisfaction. The purposeless use of resource that yields no social benefit resonates with the macro-theory of 'treadmills of production' theory of environmental sociology (Vita et al., 2019a), which predicts that the rising level of energy and resource use in society are simply a product of path-dependency of previous usage, regardless of social outcomes.

Implementing HSSD requires us to actively detect false satisfiers, i.e., the use of resources with little or null social benefit. This concept is also called 'defensive expenditure' elsewhere, i.e., using resources that are regrettably necessary to maintain the status quo or prevent further harm, but without really adding to a flourishing life (Stiglitz et al., 2010), for example, spending on safety or commuting to work. In a peaceful society with proper urban planning, such resources would be spared.

The current system is plagued with false satisfiers that add to our environmental bill without yielding satisfaction. All those things that promise or attempt to satisfy needs but actually fail to do so or even backfire on us. For example, the arms race seeks to protect but actually creates panic. Junk food claims to nourish but damages health. Energy sources supposedly enable the quality of life by enabling work but with side-effects that damage all other dimensions of life. Leisure time on social media might create unease and solitude rather than restoration and connectedness. Satisfying creation through excessive work might lead to burnout and jeopardise other needs. Transformation requires individuals, policy makers and society to honestly reflect on false satisfiers and plan for their downscale, replacement or phase out.

This would require consulting the public and a wide range of experts on activities, artefacts, goods, laws, institutions, social practices etc. that do not prove effective at satisfying needs but do consume resources. Would politicians embrace this new development paradigm in the face of current socio-ecological breakdown? Doing so would require to systematically phase out all resource usage that does not demonstrably satisfies needs. The implications to freedom are discussed in the next section.

Limitations and drawbacks of upscaling HSSD

Upscaling HSSD faces several challenges. First, my proposal to upscale HSSD might antagonise the inception of HSD. Second, challenges of implementation such as the tensions between optimising for individual freedom versus the common good, and related to that, the challenge to upscale HSSD to the wider society as a truly participatory process. Lastly, some challenges remain regarding the transition speed required to change the intent and rules of the system to support HSSD.

My rationale for developing the HSSD version is that the HSD doesn't make environmental sustainability prominent enough and its micro-scale focus limits its influence over global sustainability agendas. One could argue that MN conceived HSD to be applied at the micro-scale (community level) to ensure participatory decision-making, in the spirit of what he called 'barefoot economics', which is economic development grounded in local knowledge and resources. Contrary to the rule of experts or elites, MN believed that regular citizens are well equipped to act in their best interests and build thriving communities. In my view, limiting HSD to be applied at the micro-level limits its influence on how we think about sustainability globally.

A further challenge to enact HSSD is that capitalistic systems are plagued with false satisfiers, as the goal is to make money, not to satisfy needs or regenerate capitals. In accordance to capitalistic economies, the Western concept of freedom is that one should be free to choose how to spend money and time, regardless if this is a virtuous act or harmful for oneself, the environment or others. Naturally, enacting HSSD by regulating false satisfiers and favouring synergistic ones can create social unrest. To this I argue that restrictions are already in place where authorities ban risky or harmful activities (gambling, antibiotics, drugs, guns etc.). It would be a matter of expanding this mandate to more subtle ways of self-harm (video games, junk food, excessive working hours etc.). Nevertheless, a shifting worldview on freedom, away from materialism, and understood as health, freedom of expression, liveable cities and more free time would support the enacting of HSSD.

Finally, is it realistic to change the underlying rules and intent (Figure 12.2) quick enough to support HSSD process in response to our global socio-ecological crises? In a way, during the COVID pandemic, global goals shifted overnight towards preserving life above economic interests. If we are to be consistent with how we handle existential crises, it is not outrageous to think that the goals, intent and underlying values of our systems could change quickly to support HSSD.

Conclusion

HSSD is as suitable for institutions, governments, international organisations, as for communities, families and individuals. Any entity can use HSD/HSSD to think about decision-making and practices in policies, production, consumption, leisure time, urban-planning etc. Establishing a monitoring dashboard of indicators would be a key step in mainstreaming HSSD.

Lifestyles changes – by choice and by design – require balancing between individual changes and systematic (non-human) action, as they reinforce each other. Those (bad) decisions beyond the control of regular individuals, such as laws, energy systems, infrastructures, car-domination, working hours, privatisation, junk food etc. would have to be strictly assessed under an HSSD lens.

Pearls can be found in operationalising HSSD in all dimensions of all life. In the worst case, we might find more democratic and human ways to manage our socio-economic metabolism. In the best, we find ways to flourish with less impact. In any case, upholding and mainstreaming the thought of MN and HSD is an asymmetric bet, and there is much more to win and not much more to lose.

Note

1 Socio-economic metabolism refers to the flow and accumulation of energy, materials and resources through society, and the impact of this flow on the environment, economy and society.

References

Abson, D. J., Fischer, J., Leventon, J., Newig, J., Schomerus, T., Vilsmaier, U., von Wehrden, H., Abernethy, P., Ives, C. D., Jager, N. W., & Lang, D. J. (2017). Leverage points for sustainability transformation. *AMBIO: A Journal of the Human Environment*, *46*, 30–39. https://doi.org/10.1007/s13280-016-0800-y

Akenji, L. (2014). Consumer scapegoatism and limits to green consumerism. *Journal of Cleaner Production*, *63*, 13–23. https://doi.org/10.1016/j.jclepro.2013.05.022

Andersson, D., Nässén, J., Larsson, J., & Holmberg, J. (2014). Greenhouse gas emissions and subjective wellbeing: An analysis of Swedish households. *Ecological Economics*, *102*, 75–82. https://doi.org/10.1016/j.ecolecon.2014.03.018

Ballew, M. T., Goldberg, M. H., Rosenthal, S. A., Gustafson, A., & Leiserowitz, A. (2019). Systems thinking as a pathway to global warming beliefs and attitudes through an ecological worldview. *Proceedings of the National Academy of Sciences*, *116*, 8214–8219. https://doi.org/10.1073/pnas.1819310116

Bourdieu, P. (1986). The forms of capital. In *Handbook of theory and research for the sociology of education* (pp. 241–258). https://doi.org/10.1002/9780470755679.ch15

Brand-Correa, L. I., Martin-Ortega, J., & Steinberger, J. K. (2018). Human scale energy services: Untangling a "golden thread". *Energy Research & Social Science*, *38*, 178–187. https://doi.org/10.1016/j.erss.2018.01.008

Brand-Correa, L. I., Mattioli, G., Lamb, W. F., & Steinberger, J. K. (2020). Understanding (and tackling) need satisfier escalation. *Sustainability: Science, Practice and Policy*, *16*, 309–325. https://doi.org/10.1080/15487733.2020.1816026

Büchs, M., & Koch, M., (2017). *Postgrowth and wellbeing: Challenges to sustainable welfare*. Palgrave Macmillan, Lund University. https://doi.org/10.1007/978-3-319-59903-8

Costanza, R., Fisher, B., Ali, S., Bond, C., Boumans, L., Danigelis, R., Dickinson, N. L., Elliott, J., Farley, C., Gayer, J., Glenn, D. E., Hudspeth, L. M., Mahoney, T., McCahill, D., McIntosh, L., Reed, B., Rizvi, B., Rizzo, S. A. T., Simpatico, D. M., & Snapp, T. (2007). Quality of life: An approach integrating opportunities, human needs, and subjective wellbeing. *Ecological Economics*, *61*, 267–276. https://doi.org/10.1016/j.ecolecon.2006.02.023

Cruz, I., Stahel, A., & Max-Neef, M. (2009). Towards a systemic development approach: Building on the human-scale development paradigm. *Ecological Economics*, *68*, 2021–2030. https://doi.org/10.1016/j.ecolecon.2009.02.004

D'Alisa, G., Demaria, F., Kallis, G., & Nelson, S. K. (2015). *Degrowth a vocabulary for a new era*. Routledge.

Fanning, A. L., O'Neill, D. W., Hickel, J., & Roux, N. (2021). The social shortfall and ecological overshoot of nations. *Nature Sustainability*, 26–36. https://doi.org/10.1038/s41893-021-00799-z

Guillen-Royo, M. (2010). Realising the "wellbeing dividend": An exploratory study using the human scale development approach. *Ecological Economics*, *70*, 384–393. https://doi.org/10.1016/j.ecolecon.2010.09.010

Guillen-Royo, M. (2020). Applying the fundamental human needs approach to sustainable consumption corridors: Participatory workshops involving information and communication technologies. *Sustainability: Science, Practice, & Policy*, *16*, 114–127. https://doi.org/10.1080/15487733.2020.1787311

Haug, F., (2016). The "Four-in-One Perspective": A manifesto for a more just life. *Socialism and Democracy*, *23*(1), 119–123. https://doi.org/10.1080/08854300802635932

Hiç, C., Pradhan, P., Rybski, D., & Kropp, J. P. (2016). Food surplus and its climate burdens. *Environmental Science & Technology*, *50*, 4269–4277. https://doi.org/10.1021/acs.est.5b05088

Ironmonger, D. (1987). *Household productive activities*. University of Melbourne.

Jackson, T. (2005). Live better by consuming less? Is there a "double dividend" in sustainable consumption? *Journal of Industrial Ecology*, *9*, 19–36. https://doi.org/10.1162/1088198054084734

Kalt, G., Wiedenhofer, D., Görg, C., & Haberl, H. (2019). Conceptualizing energy services: A review of energy and wellbeing along the energy service cascade. *Energy Research & Social Science*, *53*, 47–58. https://doi.org/10.1016/j.erss.2019.02.026

Kasser, T. (2002). *The high price of materialism*. The MIT Press.

Lindellee, J., Alkan Olsson, J., & Koch, M. (2021). Operationalizing sustainable welfare and co-developing eco-social policies by prioritizing human needs. *Global Social Policy*, *21*, 328–331. https://doi.org/10.1177/14680181211019164

Max-Neef, M. (1992). Development and human needs. In M. Max-Neef & P. Ekins (Eds.), *Real life economics* (pp. 197–214). Routledge.

Max-Neef, M. (1995). Economic growth and quality of life: A threshold hypothesis. *Ecological Economics*, *15*, 115–118. https://doi.org/10.1016/0921-8009(95)00064-X

Max-Neef, M. (2014). The good is the bad that we don't do: Economic crimes against humanity: A proposal. *Ecological Economics*, 152–154. https://doi.org/10.1016/j.ecolecon.2014.02.011

Max-Neef, M. A., Hopenhayn, M., & Elizalde, A. (1991). *Human scale development: Conception, application and further reflections* (2nd ed.). The Apex Press.

Meadows D. H. (1999). *Leverage points: places to intervene in a system*. Sustainability Institute.

Murata, H., Horio, S., & Kobayashi, H. (2021). Development of online needs-based workshop support system in a pandemic. *Frontiers in Sustainability*, *2*, 1–14. https://doi.org/10.3389/frsus.2021.687754

Murata, H., & Kobayashi, H. (2019). Needs-based workshops for sustainable consumption and production in Vietnam. In *Proceedings of the 6th international conference on sustainable design and manufacturing* (KES-SDM 19). Springer, Singapore.

O'Neill, D. W., Fanning, A. L., Lamb, W. F., & Steinberger, J. K. (2018). A good life for all within planetary boundaries. *Nature Sustainability*, *1*, 88–95. https://doi.org/10.1038/s41893-018-0021-4

OECD (2015). *How's life? Measuring wellbeing*. https://doi.org/10.1787/how_life-2015-en

Oxfam (2015). *Extreme carbon inequality*. Oxfam Media Brief.

Porter, M. E., Stern, S., & Artavia Loría, R. (2013). *Social progress index 2013*.

Rao, N. D., & Min, J. (2019). Decent living standards: Material prerequisites for human wellbeing. *Social Indicators Research*, *138*, 225–244. https://doi.org/10.1007/s11205-017-1650-0

Rao, N. D., Van Ruijven, B. J., Riahi, K., & Bosetti, V. (2017). Improving poverty and inequality modeling in climate research. *Nature Climate Change*, *7*, 857–862. https://doi.org/10.1038/s41558-017-0004-x

Reader, S. (2005). Aristotle on necessities and needs. *Royal Institute of Philosophy Supplement*, *57*, 113–135. https://doi.org/10.1017/S1358246100009176

Robinson, B. H. (2009). E-waste: An assessment of global production and environmental impacts. *Science of the Total Environment*, 183–191. https://doi.org/10.1016/j.scitotenv.2009.09.044

Sagar, A. D., & Najam, A. (1998). The human development index: A critical review. *Ecological Economics*, *25*(3), 249–264. https://doi.org/10.1016/S0921-8009(97)00168-7

Schor, J. B. (2001). *Why do we consume so much?* Clemens lecture series. Saint John's University.

Sirgy, M. J., Michalos, A. C., Ferriss, A. L., Easterlin, R. A., Patrick, D., & Pavot, W. (2006). The quality-of-life (QOL) research movement: Past present and future. *Social Indicators Research: An International and Interdisciplinary Journal for Quality-Of-Life Measurement*, *76*(3), 343–466.

Steinberger, J. K., Lamb, W. F., & Sakai, M. (2020). Your money or your life? The carbon-development paradox. *Environmental Research Letters*, https://doi.org/10.1088/1748-9326/ab7461

Stiglitz, J. E., Sen, A., & Fitoussi, J.-P. (2010). *Mismeasuring our lives: Why GDP doesn't add up*. New Press.

Tay, L., & Diener, E. (2011). Needs and subjective well-being around the world. *Journal of Personality and Social Psychology*, *101*(2), 354–365. https://doi.org/10.1037/a0023779
Victor, P. (2010). Questioning economic growth. *Nature*, *468*, 370–371. https://doi.org/10.1038/468370a
Vita, G. (2016). Smart city or ecovillage? An industrial ecology approach. *The Current Global Affairs Review*. Fox Hedgehog.
Vita, G. (2018). *The environmental impacts of human needs and lifestyles: Connecting the global economy, natural resources, and human wellbeing* (1st ed.). Norwegian University of Science and Technology. https://doi.org/http://hdl.handle.net/11250/2578271
Vita, G., Ivanova, D., Dumitru, A., García-Mira, R., Carrus, G., Stadler, K., Krause, K., Wood, R., & Hertwich, E. G., (2020). Happier with less? Members of European environmental grassroots initiatives reconcile lower carbon footprints with higher life satisfaction and income increases. *Energy Research & Social Science*, *60*. https://doi.org/10.1016/j.erss.2019.101329
Vita, G., Hertwich, E. G., Stadler, K., & Wood, R. (2019a). Connecting global emissions to fundamental human needs and their satisfaction. *Environmental Research Letters*, *14*, 014002. https://doi.org/10.1088/1748-9326/AAE6E0
Vita, G., Lundström, J. R., Hertwich, E. G., Quist, J., Ivanova, D., Stadler, K., & Wood, R. (2019b). The environmental impact of green consumption and sufficiency lifestyles scenarios in Europe: Connecting local sustainability visions to global consequences. *Ecological Economics*, *164*, 106322. https://doi.org/10.1016/j.ecolecon.2019.05.002
Vita, G., Rao, N. D., Usubiaga-Liaño, A., Min, J., & Wood, R. (2021). Durable goods drive two-thirds of global households' final energy footprints. *Environmental Science & Technology*. https://doi.org/10.1021/acs.est.0c03890
Wiedmann, T., Lenzen, M., Keyßer, L. T., & Steinberger, J. K. (2020). Scientists' warning on affluence. *Nature Communications*, *11*, 3107. https://doi.org/10.1038/s41467-020-16941-y

13 Economic growth and well-being

Examining Max-Neef's "threshold hypothesis"

Luis Valenzuela

Introduction

In April 1995, a distinguished group of academics from varied disciplines and countries published a short article in Science, challenging the view that economic growth would in itself solve existing environmental problems – a view entrenched in the so-called Environmental Kuznets Curve (EKC; an inverted U-shaped relationship between environmental quality and GDP). The article was then reprinted in three academic journals, *Ecological Economics* (November 1995), *Ecological Applications* (February 1996), and *Environment and Development Economics* (February 1996), together with a series of brief reactions by invited authors. One of the invitees was Manfred Max-Neef (MMN henceforth).

In his short response (three pages long), published in Ecological Economics, MMN agreed with the original Science article, but he goes further by proposing what he calls the "threshold hypothesis":

> … for every society there seems to be a period in which economic growth (as conventionally measured) brings about an improvement in the quality of life, but only up to a point – the threshold point – beyond which, if there is more economic growth, quality of life may begin to deteriorate.
>
> (Max-Neef, 1995, p. 117)

He then included a figure showing the correlation between the Index of Sustainable Economic Welfare and Gross National Product for five developed countries, as tentative evidence in support for his hypothesis.

This chapter explores this paper in more detail, which is MMN's second most cited academic paper (after his work on transdisciplinarity, Max-Neef, 2005). In particular, it shows that MMN's proposal derived naturally from his previous intellectual contributions (particularly in relation to his work on fundamental human needs as well as his analysis of the scale of economic activity). It also connected well with the thoughts of other economists and scientists of the time, many of whom were references to MMN.

DOI: 10.4324/9781003381143-15

The article provided no formalisation nor even some rough theorisation of the hypothesis itself. The evidence presented was interesting in its time but was not explored very rigorously either. Even though one cannot expect much from a three-page document, framed as a response to another publication, follow-up developments (or rather, the lack of them) confirm MMN's lack of interest in formalisation, theorisation and quantitative appraisal of this hypothesis, even when he later on considered it to be "a robust hypothesis that has become fundamental in the field of ecological economics" (Max-Neef, 2010, p. 206). The article is an example of MMN's preferred approach to science: intuitive, tentative, even reluctant, one might argue. True to himself, Max-Neef was a barefoot economist.

The merit of the article is in providing a new language that read quite well the "sign of the times", at least around the field of ecological economics. This is confirmed by the solid citation record. However, the idea did not permeate beyond heterodox fields, let alone mainstream economics.

Empirically, the evidence today does not seem to validate the hypothesis. Yet, if one is to stick to the conceptualisation used by MMN (that of quality of life as satisfaction of fundamental human needs), then we must conclude that the hypothesis has not yet been tested. Moreover, its theoretical foundations have not been developed either. There is thus an opportunity to explore further the issues raised by Max-Neef more than 20 years ago.

The chapter continues as follows. The "The context" section provides the context Max-Neef's 1995 article. The "The 'threshold hypothesis'" section presents the threshold hypothesis as stated in the original article. The "Relation to Max-Neef's previous work" section relates the threshold to MMN's previous work. The "Other influences" section explores other sources that might have been relevant for MMN. The "Mechanisms" section explores the mechanisms that could give rise to the threshold, in light of MMN's earlier thought. The "Impact on academia and beyond" section explores the impact of the article in academia and beyond. The "Current standing" section explores its current empirical standing. The "Final words" section concludes.

The context

The academic debate about the relationship between the environment and economic growth was not new in 1995 (the publication date of the article under discussion). Although pre-dating the 1970s, the debate was formally boosted in that decade by a series of major publications, critical to the contemporary model of development. Perhaps the most well-known is *The Limits to Growth*, published by the think-tank Club of Rome in 1972.[1] In a nutshell, the book presented simulations of the world economy, highlighting the risks of business as usual for humanity in terms of raw materials and food scarcity, and ultimately economic and population "collapse". The message was grim: current development patterns were unsustainable. Since these publications, research on the sustainability of production and consumption patterns exploded (together with associated environmental activism). Ecological economics as a heterodox field of research was born.[2]

On the other ideological side was mainstream economics, which in the early 1990s proposed the now-called EKC (Grossman & Krueger, 1991, 1995; Selden & Daqing, 1994; Shafik, 1994). This is an inverted U-shaped relationship between environmental quality and GDP, capturing the idea that economic growth initially expands pollution, deforestation and related problems, but this same growth would later on provide the incentives as well as the technology for reducing its environmental "side effects".[3] Both camps acknowledge the existence of environmental "bads" but differ about the solution. The heterodox field is pessimistic (or at least doubtful) about economic growth self-correcting its problems, thereby calling for change (with different degrees of radicality). The mainstream field is optimistic that *more* growth is the answer (or at least growth is not the problem *per se*). This divide persists until today.

Amid this context is that, in April 1995, a multidisciplinary and ideologically diverse group of 11 academics published a short piece in Science calling to question the empirical and theoretical validity of the EKC as a general guide to sustainability (Arrow et al., 1995). They argue that economic growth is not sufficient for environmental sustainability, nor has to be a problem *per se*. What matters are "proper" environmental institutions and policies. MMN was invited by the heterodox journal Ecological Economics to respond to this piece.

The "threshold hypothesis"

In his article, MMN agreed with the general ideas in Arrow et al. (1995) but moves forward to propose a new hypothesis:

> … for every society there seems to be a period in which economic growth (as conventionally measured) brings about an improvement in the quality of life, but only up to a point – the threshold point – beyond which, if there is more economic growth, quality of life may begin to deteriorate.
>
> (Max-Neef, 1995, p. 117)

The hypothesis had two interesting novelties. First, it moved beyond the environmental dimension to that of *quality of life*, which, as argued later, was only natural to MMN given his previous work. Second, it connected the macro (GDP) with the micro (quality of life, an intuitively individual dimension). Both innovations tried to refresh a debate that was essentially at the macro level only and preoccupied with issues such as which pollutant was or was not empirically favourable to the EKC. There was also the new (to the field) and catchy language of a threshold, a direct competition to the concept of EKC, which helped to promote debate and further research.

In his article, MMN argued that the hypothesis was inspired by earlier work of himself – qualitative work based on interviews of individuals from 19 countries, rich and poor, regarding the satisfaction of their needs (more specifically, MMN's Matrix of Needs, a sub-product of his theory of needs and satisfiers; see Chapter 3 and 4 of this volume). It must be noted that this work was not representative at any level. Complementary, the article presented a graph for five rich countries contrasting GNP with the recently defined Index of Sustainable Economic Welfare, or ISEW (Daly & Cobb, 1989). This index is built around the National Accounts measure of personal consumption, adding and subtracting a range of different components to, in principle, better reflect personal welfare.[4] The data itself was taken from other authors.[5] The graph, reproduced in Figure 13.1, reveals for each country a GNP level after which more growth does not correlate with higher ISEW. For Germany and much more dramatically for the UK, ISEW even falls continually after its peak, suggesting a worsening of aggregate welfare. It is interesting to notice that all authors from which data was obtained also contrasted ISEW with GNP (or GDP), but none went far enough in proposing a broader underlying phenomenon such as a threshold. MMN's contribution is then providing a narrative that united them under a common thread; the threshold hypothesis.

Finally, it must be noticed that the definition of the hypothesis is qualified by the verb *may*. That is, quality of life may either decrease or remain at the threshold point, respectively. In a sense, this is a weak version of the hypothesis, which contrasts with clear demarcation of the EKC. As mentioned later, MMN never developed this hypothesis further, either theoretically or empirically, an example of his usual preference for remaining at the intuitive level.

Relation to Max-Neef's previous work

MMN's research agenda was already well developed by the publication of the article (potentially a reason for why he was invited to write a reply). As argued next, considering his main work as well as his influences and intellectual developments of the time, one is not surprised by his proposal.

Max-Neef (1991)

This is MMN's most well-known book, published in several editions and languages (see Chapter 3 in this volume). The reason for starting with this work is because, according to MMN (1995), this is where the threshold hypothesis was first proposed:

> During the late 1980s, using a methodology designed in the Development Alternatives Centre in Chile which I headed at the time, we carried out studies in 19 countries, both rich and poor, in order to assess elements and conditions that inhibited peoples' possibilities of adequately satisfying their desired personal well-being and collective welfare (Max-Neef, 1991). Without going into a description of the methodology here, the result was that, having detected among people in rich countries a growing feeling that they were part of an overall deteriorating system that affected them both at the personal and collective levels, **we were led to propose a "Threshold Hypothesis"**.
>
> (Max-Neef, 1995, pp. 115–117, emphasis added)

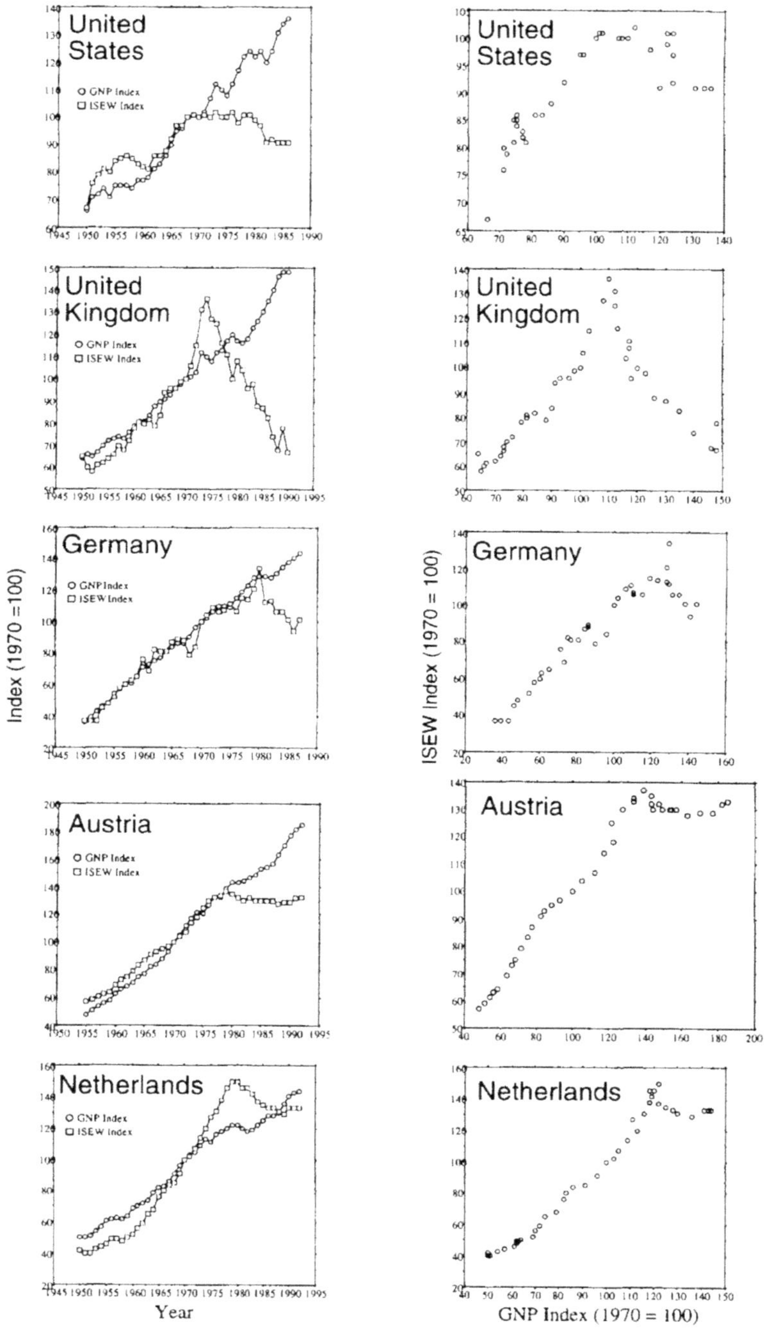

Figure 13.1 Index of Sustainable Economic Welfare and GNP for selected countries

Unfortunately, I was not able to find an explicit mention of such hypothesis. Perhaps MMN was referring to the following paragraph:

> Although much more work has to be completed in order to confine some probable tendencies, it is already clear that unsuspected yet significant findings will come to light. One of the most interesting may be the fact that **no correlation seems to exist between achieved levels of economic growth and relative happiness of the people concerned**.
>
> (Max-Neef, 1991, p. 43, emphasis added)

Two comments can be made about this statement. First, this definition is not equivalent to that of the threshold, not even implicitly. For a start, mathematically, zero correlation between two variables does not imply a threshold type of relationship. The correlation between series in Figure 13.1 is clearly not zero for any case. Second, the suggested empirical analysis carried out in 19 countries is not available in the document (nor anywhere else, it seems), except for accounts of needs satisfaction for 5 individuals from 5 different countries. How these examples, let alone all of the surveys, are indicative of such zero correlation is not clear. Moreover, the methodology itself does not allow us to safely propose country-level conclusions from individual data (which number is not stated either). All in all, the conclusion that "*we were led to propose a 'Threshold Hypothesis'*" based on previous qualitative research seems not to be available and feels unsupported by the evidence available in the referred book or elsewhere.

Max-Neef (1982)

This is MMN' second most well-known book, *From the Outside Looking In. Experiences in 'Barefoot Economics'*. The book includes anecdotal as well as theoretical reflections on development, based on his first-hand experiences of poverty and (under)development in different Latin American countries during the 1960s and 1970s.[6] Although more will be said later, for now, it suffices to comment on MMN's reflections regarding the "dogma of unlimited growth", which can be directly connected with the idea of a threshold. He traces the origin of this dogma to the Judaeo-Christian-Muslim "culture of expansion and submission of nature" (based on his reading of Genesis 1:28), suggesting this culture was later on adopted by conservatism, liberalism and socialism alike, particularly at the advent of the technological advancements of the Industrial Revolution: "In this manner the myths of Genesis and Prometheus become one single equation" (p. 40). He also refers to the scepticism of John Stuart Mill regarding the "supposed advantages of indefinite growth of production and population as advocated by liberalism" (p. 40).

Later on, MMN highlights per capita gross national product as a "highly misleading indicator of the standard and quality of life, as it includes any activity, regardless of whether or not it is beneficial to society" (p. 133). Then, he cites an article in Science that presents evidence that[7]:

> … the improvement of living standards (basic needs and luxuries) constitutes a diminishing fraction of each new unit of increased per capita GNP; the rest is spent on the structural changes required by growth itself, on its side effects and on managing its wastes. (p. 133)

In other words, traditional growth is characterised by diminishing returns to the quality of life. Across MMN's most important work, this is the closest to a definition of a threshold before his 1995 article.

Other influences

There is a plethora of ideological and intellectual developments that might have been influential, to different degrees, in MMN's ideas regarding the threshold hypothesis. Here I will focus on a positive and a negative influence: limits to growth and happiness studies, respectively. A more comprehensive review escapes the purpose and length of this chapter.[8]

Limits to growth

Although the threshold does not contain an explicit mention of the limits to growth (more on this later), the potentially negative consequences of economic growth (its "side effects and wastes") can affect future economic growth and well-being. This is partly the tenet of a significant part of the "limits to growth" literature. Three well-known works on the area are *The Entropy Law and the Economic Process*, by Nicholas Georgescu-Roegen (1971), *A Blueprint for Survival*, by a collection of authors (1972), and perhaps the most famous work on the topic, *The Limits to Growth*, by the Club of Rome (1972). The later book highlights the "catastrophic" consequences of business as usual in terms of collapse of population, industrial output and food per capita, due to either the scarcity of non-renewable resources or too much pollution affecting productivity of resources. The projections do not focus on human needs or quality of life (aspects of particular interest to MMN) but rather on issues such as consumption and poverty.

Although I found no reference to this work in MMN's work, it must have been relevant for him, as it was for many other development and environmental thinkers of the period. Moreover, between 1977 and 1979, MMN worked at *Fundación Bariloche,* a left-wing research centre in Argentina that in 1977 published the Latin American World Model, an alternative model to that in *The Limits to Growth*. The analysis included a critique to "overconsumption" in rich countries, as well as a discussion on the "alienation" of the masses in these countries, due to "the existence of a system of social and international organization that is directed towards competitive accumulation of wealth, lacking any spirit of international harmony and goodwill, and which, by reducing people to mere tools of production, precludes any possibility of integral human development" (p. 23). Importantly, the new model focused directly on the satisfaction of human needs (based on the work that Carlos Mallmann was producing on the topic; Mallmann, 1972). MMN referred to his experience at *Fundación Bariloche* in other publications and also co-authored some research with Mallmann and others (see Chapter 18 at the end of this volume for Max-Neef's complete bibliography). It is very likely then that this experience stimulated his thinking in terms of the limits to "integral human development" across rich countries.

An important critic to the traditional economic growth paradigm, often cited by MMN, was Herman Daly (e.g., 1973, 1974, 1989, and, 1993, co-authored with Cobb). Daly's (1974), for instance, entitled *The Economics of Steady-State*, suggested an alternative model for an economy in a steady state, built upon population control, depletion quotas and distribution of income. This now well-known concept of the steady state economy is explicitly cited by MMN in the 1995 article under study:

> In fact, if the Threshold Hypothesis stands, it may mean, among other things, the late vindication of John Stuart Mill's stationary state (Mill, 1848) or of Herman Daly's earlier concept of the steady-state economy (Daly, 1974). Or, it may reveal the existence of a point in a country's economic evolution where quantitative growth must be metamorphosed into qualitative development. (p. 117)

The distinction between quantitative and qualitative growth, intuitively related to the threshold, as MMN states above, is also present in Daly's thought. For instance:

> We need, however, to shift the emphasis toward ecological adaptation, that is, to accept natural limits to the size and dominion of the human household, to concentrate on moral growth and qualitative improvement rather than on the quantitative imperialist expansion of man's dominion.
>
> (Daly, 1993 [1977], p. 12)

In a later document, MMN would make the link between these two types of growth and the threshold explicit, stating that "we can identify the pre-threshold period as a quantitative economy and the post-threshold as a qualitative economy" (Max-Neef, 2010, p. 208). Daly (1999) defined the term "uneconomic growth" as precisely the economic growth which decreases the quality of life.

Happiness studies

During the 1970s, research on the topic of happiness boomed. Within economics, Richard Easterly, an economics professor at the University of Pennsylvania, was the first to link data from surveys on happiness to macroeconomic variables like GNP. In his first paper (Easterlin, 1974), he finds almost no correlation between GNPs per capita an happiness across a sample of 19 countries across the income spectrum. The same lack of evident trend is also found for the one country where he has a sufficiently long time series, the US. Although not evidence *per se* of a threshold, it certainly shows a significant limitation of economic growth in terms of raising subjective well-being.

It could be that MMN was unaware of Easterlin's research, but this is very unlikely given that MMN spent almost one year (1975/1976) as a Visiting Senior Fellow at the Faculty of Arts and Sciences of the University of Pennsylvania, the same faculty where Easterlin worked. Moreover, Easterlin's work inspired a myriad of subsequent papers, many confirming Easterlin's results.[9] Even MMN himself found such lack of correlation between happiness and growth, as cited already above (Max-Neef, 1991, p. 43), yet providing no reference to Easterlin's previous findings. An alternative explanation for the omission might be that Easterlin's research allowed no scope for criticism of the development process.[10] In effect, the interpretation given by Easterlin himself of his results was that of a "consumption norm", a point of reference to which all individuals compare, and a norm which tends to rise with the general level of income or consumption. The argument was accompanied with a neat neoclassical model. Perhaps, from MMN's point of view, it might have seemed that no critical development theory or analysis could be thought of in terms of eliminating the mechanisms impairing "happiness growth", let alone discussing the usual "bads" of economic growth (like pollution).[11,12]

Mechanisms

What can explain the existence of a threshold hypothesis? What is the dynamic behind it? MMN's article was brief and did not offer many insights on this. In fact, he did not oversell the importance of the results, as he stated:

> In the face of expanding new evidence and challenging new research possibilities, it would be a serious mistake to overrate presumptions that are based on precise yet restricted information. ... To attribute to them [the results] more than what they actually reveal may lead to the discrediting of otherwise helpful tools.
>
> (Max-Neef, 1995, p. 117)

Perhaps better data would prove the hypothesis to be false. But if not, "new research possibilities" open up (which Manfred himself did not pursue, by the way).[13] He asked, for instance[14]:

> What indicators must be designed to reveal how close a given economy may be to its threshold point? How does income inequality (not per capita GNP) correlate with environmental deterioration? How must development and environmental policies differ if applied before or after the threshold point? Can a threshold point only be reached in a so-called wealthy economy? Is it always the same combination of elements that determines the threshold point? And so forth.
>
> (Max-Neef, 1995, p. 117)

The definition of the threshold hypothesis reveals three interesting suppositions by MMN. First, the hypothesis goes beyond a mere correlation suggesting a causal effect, from economic growth to quality of life. In effect, the hypothesis states that before the threshold "economic growth ... **brings about** an improvement in the quality of life", but after it, "**if** there is more economic growth, quality of life may begin to deteriorate". Naturally, the mechanisms underlying the causal link are to be uncovered. Second, the post-threshold behaviour is ambiguous, since "quality of life **may** begin to deteriorate". This is of course consistent with the data presented in the article (Figure 13.1 here), which shows that after the threshold ISEW can remain flat, go down, or both. This ambiguity highlights that the mechanisms at play can be quite complex. Third, the threshold point exists "for every society" (as stated in the hypothesis). This universality resonates with MMN's wider thoughts on the universality of needs.

Ultimately, the threshold hypothesis is a bridge between the macro (economic growth) and the micro (quality of life *a-la* Max-Neef, that is, in terms of fundamental human needs). The real challenge for the theoretical foundation of the threshold is to provide the causal mechanisms behind such a macro-micro link – a non-trivial challenge indeed. Unfortunately, this theoretical foundation is not explicitly found in MMN's work. Still, some indirect insights can be deduced from his wider work.

To see this, let us consider MMN's theory of fundamental human needs and satisfiers (Max-Neef, 1991). In a nutshell, MMN defined a taxonomy of nine fundamental human needs – finite (unlike economics' traditional understanding), unordered (unlike Maslow's paradigm) and common to all societies and ages.[15] Satisfiers are the "means" used to satisfy needs – diverse and culturally dependent. To MMN, a high quality of life consisted of the "adequate satisfaction" of all these needs, and development exists *solely* with increased satisfaction of these needs. Thus, economic growth can enable a higher quality of life, since goods and services can act as proper satisfiers, but not all needs depend on economic growth since some satisfiers are provided by the family, the community, or more generally, outside the scope of the economy. Moreover, "bads" associated with economic growth could dampen the satisfaction of needs. Under this theory, one can define the threshold to represent the point where satisfiers, even though might still increase in quantity, start to reduce their quality. Rather than being singular or synergic (that is, to affect positively a certain need alone or also other needs, respectively), they become pseudo-satisfiers (not actually solving the need), or even worse, destructive satisfiers (that is, destroying any possibility of satisfaction of certain or all needs). As he states:

> In the eyes of many, development consists of achieving the material living standards of the most industrialized countries in order for people to have access to a growing array of goods (artifacts) which become increasingly more diversified. It may be asked to what extent such attempts at emulation make any sense at all. First, there is no evidence that people in those countries experience their needs in an integrated manner. Second, in the rich countries, the abundance of goods and economic resources has not proved to be

> a sufficient condition for solving the problem of alienation. … fundamental human needs can and must be realized **from the outset and throughout the entire process of development**. In this manner, the realization of needs becomes, instead of a goal, the motor of development itself. This is possible only if the development strategy proves to be capable of stimulating the permanent generation of synergic satisfiers.
>
> (Max-Neef, 1991, p. 53, emphasis in original)

As shown earlier, MMN speculates that the threshold point might represent the point "*where quantitative growth must be metamorphosed into qualitative development*" (Max-Neef, 1995, p. 117). Qualitative development is then characterised by "the permanent generation of synergic satisfiers". Conversely, rich countries in a process of underdevelopment (or under-developing countries, as he called them) are those past the threshold point, where needs are not being satisfied synergistically. As he states:

> It no longer makes sense to talk about developed and developing countries, unless we add an additional category: **the under-developing countries or countries in a process of underdevelopment**. This would be the category to fit most of the presently rich countries, where peoples' quality of life is deteriorating at an alarming speed.
>
> (Max-Neef, 1991, p. 111, emphasis added)

Here we can also consider the issue of **scale**. The threshold might represent the point in the system where there is a structural change in the link between growth and the quantity and quality of satisfiers. As the system grows in scale, some problems begin to arise which impede the proper satisfaction of needs. The threshold is thus the point in which the system moves beyond its optimal scale. MMN's earlier book *Barefoot Economics* (1982) offer many insights that can support the above theorisation. It is worth quoting *in extenso* the connection MMN sees between growth (in terms of scale of economic activity) and individual well-being:

> Since the scale of economic activity has a direct influence on the scale of other systems such as cities, let me go back and analyse its implications a little further. Economics has worshipped efficiency, and on its behalf we have evolved from economies of scale to what I would like to call "diseconomies of uncontrollable dimensions". The economic efficiency of this process is incontestable and so is its power to pillage natural resources, its capacity to pollute and its contribution to the rise in heart attacks and hypertension. And once dimensions of large scale have been consolidated, their evolution is possible only in terms of becoming even larger. The system no longer expands to meet the consumption needs of people; it is people who consume in order to meet the system's requirements of growth. As long as alienation, boredom, dissatisfaction, rural and urban decay, pollution, insecurity, anxiety and, finally, dehumanisation are not measured as costs of the process,

> it will continue to be seen as positive, efficient and successful in terms of the traditional criteria by which it is judged. … It should thus be clear that the constant increase in the scale of economic activity alienates those participating in it and destroys the human element in the surrounding framework. (pp. 132–133)

To conclude, MMN was not explicit on the mechanism or theoretical aspects producing the threshold. Yet, as done above, one can make sense of some of them from his main work. This of course does not replace a proper foundation, which he did not pursue, nor has it been produced so far. As MMN suggested when proposing the hypothesis, new research possibilities are there to be explored and remain so 20 years later.[16]

Impact on academia and beyond

To assess its impact, let us consider first the quantitative dimension of academic impact, narrow as this is. Citations of Max-Neef (1995) average around 13 per year (314 in total).[17] It received 6 citations in the first 3 years, and 11 in the first 4 years, which is significantly above the average in Ecological Economics (1.3 in 1999, when data first available; 5.6 in 2020).[18] These numbers are not too far off from top mainstream economic journals. Average citations in the first 4 years in the American Economic Review were 2.7 in 1999 and 7.4 in 2020, below MMN's article.[19] Only the Quarterly Journal of Economics, the top economic journal, has average citations above MMN's article.[20] In other words, for being a short article in a heterodox journal, it performed and still performs quite well.[21]

All in all, the ideological influence of MMN's article (which seems to be true for the rest of his research) does not cross towards the mainstream side of economics. I could find no mainstream journal citing the article.[22] Around 16% of the citations come from Ecological Economics. Around 80% come from environmental or ecological journals. The rest are mostly on well-being and social indicators, with just five citations (1.6%) on pure economic journals. The article was once cited in Nature (15 May 1997). It is also referred to in several handbooks of ecological economics and sustainable development by heterodox publishers (Edward Elgar and Routledge, for instance), but none, it seems, by mainstream ones (North Holland, Taylor & Francis). This reaffirms the deep ideological divide MMN could not bridge (and, one would argue, did not actively attempt to bridge).

This ideological divide also means there is virtually no critique to the threshold hypothesis. Critiques can be found mostly concerning ISEW. In effect, as stated before, Max-Neef (1995) was the first article in Ecological Economics directly focusing on ISEW.[23] It had the merit of bringing together all ISEW estimates to date and teasing out its relation. The (unintended) provocativeness of the hypothesis proposed by MMN contributed to its impact. Lack of critiques might also be a consequence of the lack of theoretical motivation and explicit foundations in the paper.

Beyond academia, references to the hypothesis are found all over the heterodox world, often in the context of critics to GDP. A Google search for *threshold hypothesis Max-Neef* reveals the diversity of arenas where MMN's ideas have found tribune.

Overall, disregarding the lack of take-up within mainstream economics (a challenge not many heterodox economists have been able to tackle), the academic impact for such a short article is quite remarkable. This is more relevant considering he was not a strong marketeer. He was not even a very academic person (not even in the heterodox world), having been disappointed of academia quite early.[24] These contrasts sharply for instance with Herman Daly, who coined and quite successfully "exploited" the phrase "steady-state economics", as well as other terms like "uneconomic growth".

Before concluding, let us to consider MMN's own assessment of the impact his article (and hypothesis) made in academia. We can find this in the only other article, to the best of my knowledge, where MMN mentions the threshold hypothesis (Max-Neef, 2010; emphasis added):

> A few months after we proposed the hypothesis, based on our qualitative analysis, a study was published by Daly and Cobb (1989), in which a new indicator called Index of Sustainable Economic Welfare, where positives and negatives are disaggregated, was proposed. [...] As a result of our proposed hypothesis and the paper of Daly and Cobb, a number of groups got organized in different countries in order to repeat the studies using the methodology of the US paper. The threshold begun to appear in practically all cases, provoking a great debate between many economists. Several of them dismissed the findings as methodological errors, while others made constructive suggestions in order to improve the index.
>
> After 20 years, improvements have been made, and the indicator has changed name, becoming the Genuine Progress Indicator. Many more studies were carried out, confirming the threshold. Although there are still some economists that dismiss the results, it can be stated that **the threshold hypothesis is a robust hypothesis that has become fundamental in the field of ecological economics**. (p. 206)

This reveals a considerable appreciation from his own part to the ultimate relevance of the hypothesis on the heterodox field. It is possible to concur with this, but with some caveats. MMN ascribes partial inspiration in his proposed hypothesis to the pioneering work by Daly and Cobb (1989) as well as subsequent estimations of ISEW. Unfortunately, as mentioned previously, MMN is light on references and does not provide any on this respect in the quoted paragraphs. To evaluate such influence, I searched in the articles producing ISEW estimations, cited by him in the 1995 paper (see footnote 5 in this chapter). Daly and Cobb (1989), Diefenbacher (1994) and Stockhammer et al. (1997) make no reference to Max-Neef's work or his threshold hypothesis. Jackson and Marks (1994) do mention MMN in the acknowledgement, also citing his 1991 book but not in the context of the threshold (book which I have argued earlier does not explicitly introduces the threshold, contrary to what MMN suggested). I could not obtain access to Rosenberg and Oegema (1995).

Is MMN over-appreciating his earlier influence on the development of ISEW? In light of this, it seems so. Yet, as discussed next, his article did provoke some healthy criticism regarding ISEW as a measure of well-being. MMN's 1995 article was the first in Ecological Economics properly discussing ISEW, and as such it quickly became a standard reference in discussions about such indicator (and its follow-up, Genuine Progress Indicator, GPI), as well as broader welfare measurement issues. A combination of attractive terminology with right timing and MMN's knowledge of the literature merited the article to be placed in a privileged spot.

Current standing

So, is there a threshold? Is the hypothesis robust, as MMN concluded in 2010? Many metrics could be used to analyse this. It is beyond the scope of this section to provide a comprehensive review of the literature on the correlation between welfare and GDP. The focus will be on a few key indicators.

Let us start with the ISEW and its upgraded version, the Genuine Progress Index (GPI), which is the metric used in Max-Neef (1995). Long and Ji (2019) summarise all previous studies calculating the ISEW/GPI. To this we should add their own results for China, as well as the newer work by Kenny et al. (2019) for Australia and Cook and Davíðsdóttir (2021) for Iceland. Overall, 10 papers find a clear threshold, 12 papers find weak evidence of it and 15 papers find no evidence of threshold. At first, one could think the inconsistent evidence might reflect different stages of development (given that the threshold is supposed to become binding at a certain level of development). Yet, among the 37 papers mentioned above, no particular pattern exists in terms of threshold and income of the country. In fact, papers finding weak or no threshold tend to be newer (perhaps reflecting improved methodology and/or greater data availability). There are also contradictory results for some countries across studies. This is not surprising, given that GPI has no official methodology. Each study adds and subtracts whatever it considers appropriate, a decision also based on data availability, which changes over time. As such, the comparison of results across papers must be taken with care. But at least we can conclude that the evidence in favour of the threshold is not as robust as MMN argued in 2010.

Among the sharpest critics of ISEW/GPI is Neumayer (2000), who calling into question the threshold hypothesis itself, states:

> … proponents of ISEW/GPI consider their results too easily as evidence for the "threshold hypothesis". … as far as depletion of non-renewable resources and long-term environmental damage contribute to the widening gap between ISEW/GPI and GNP, this gap might be the artefact of highly contestable methodological assumptions. … variables related to the environment do not provide evidence for the "threshold hypothesis". They only do so if a widening gap between ISEW/GPI and GNP is artificially created via the

> introduction of the 3% cost escalation factor and the accumulation of long-term environmental damage. … the threshold, if existent, is not due to factors related to the environment. (pp. 358–359)

Particularly relevant is the critique that ISEW/GPI does not measure human development or quality of life – which is what Max-Neef had in mind regarding the threshold. For example, Fox and Erickson (2020) found no bi-variate correlation between GPI per person and a subjective measure of well-being across US states. One of the reasons is that GPI, being a monetary variable, can only consider what can be measured in monetary terms, either using market prices or shadow prices. In the end, GPI is nothing but a set of additions and subtractions to personal consumption. Daly and Cobb (1989), for instance, explain the observed gap between ISEW and GNP in the US in terms of resource depletion, long-term environmental damage and greater income inequality.

Perhaps a more suitable indicator for the task at hand is the Human Development Index, a composite index, including GNI per capita, life expectancy at birth, expected years of schooling and mean years of schooling. Theoretically this index is far from proxying MMN's quality of life. Also, it includes GNI as one of its components. Still, if one were to look at the evidence, it is clear there is no threshold, neither across countries nor across time.[25] In effect, looking at the 1990–2021 period (the data available at the writing of this chapter), the index has trended upward among most countries in the world. Those with net negative trajectories are all poorer countries.

Other indicators attempting to measure well-being focus on subjective metrics. Among these, the most common one is happiness. Essentially, happiness is taken from surveys to individuals (like World Values Survey) asking to rate their life satisfaction between two extreme values. The long list of research on happiness will not be provided here, but it is clear from most of the literature, covering wide periods and countries, that there is a threshold in terms of happiness and GDP *at the cross-section level but not at the time-series level*.[26] That is, at the cross-section level, happiness is positively correlated with income for poorer countries, but uncorrelated with income for richer countries. Similarly, poorer individuals tend to report lower happiness than richer individuals. Conversely, at the time-series level, individuals do not show higher happiness levels as their country grows. This apparent discrepancy between the cross-section and the time-series patterns is what has been called the *Easterlin Paradox*, as it was originally pointed out by Easterlin (1974). The most common explanation for this paradox is the "reference level" proposition, stating that individuals value their well-being in relation to the rest of society, informally referred to as "keeping up with the Joneses" (e.g., see Easterlin & O'Connor, 2020).

Thus, in terms of happiness research, the evidence on the paradox is robust, whereas that on the threshold hypothesis is not. This is because the latter is primarily presented as a time-series phenomenon (see its definition and the theorisation about potential mechanisms discussed in the previous section), precisely where such evidence is lacking. Moreover, if the threshold were to be retained only as a cross-section phenomenon, it is hard to see how MMN's *universal* theory of needs and satisfiers could compete with the "reference level" explanation mentioned before. Henceforth, it would lose most of its critical power against the current economic system, as originally intended.

Having said all the above, what MMN was ultimately concerned with in terms of the hypothesis is quality of life, which, according to his view, was based on the satisfaction of a defined set of fundamental human needs. Therefore, the proper assessment of the threshold hypothesis requires a comprehensive, representative, standardised application of the matrix of needs to individuals across countries and over time. Such a dataset is long overdue.[27]

Final words

Although the threshold hypothesis was presented in the context of ISEW (and that is where its impact has mostly been felt), it should be disentangled from it. First, because the debate about the measurement of ISEW/GPI (which is far from being settled) is muddy and not evidently related to quality of life *a la* Max-Neef. Second, because the evidence in terms of ISEW/GPI does not support the threshold.

More broadly, the evidence presented here does not suggest the threshold is as empirically robust as Max-Neef thought so to be (in fact, one would expect, as more countries hit the threshold, to become more and more robust over time). If anything, competing hypothesis, like the Easterlin Paradox, or even the EKC, seem to retain more weight than the threshold hypothesis.

Ultimately, available metrics are not fully capturing MMN's definition of quality of life. If one is to stand by MMN's theory of needs, then we do not yet have the proper data to test the threshold hypothesis.

The theoretical foundations of the hypothesis were not explicitly developed by MMN but can be partly deduced from MMN's wider thought on fundamental human needs and the scale of economic activity. Still, much remains to be done to provide a proper foundation – perhaps even a mathematical model.

The relevance of MMN's contribution was, among others, to provide a new language to test and challenge reality. Yet, almost 20 years later, many open questions remain. Hopefully, this chapter will motivate researchers to provide some answers.

Notes

1 The other three are *The Entropy Law and the Economic Process*, by Nicholas Georgescu-Roegen (1971); *A Blueprint for Survival*, by several authors (1972); and *Steady-State Economics*, by Herman Daly (1977), a culmination of work carried out by the same author and published several times during the 1970s.

2 Environmental economics as a mainstream field of research exists at least since Ronald Coase's seminal article *The Problems of Social Costs* (1960). This field initially tended to focus specific issues like local externalities, abatement technology and costs, taxation and subsidies, and other aspects related to the efficiency of the market. Ecological economics tends to be more critical of the development model and economic system as a whole.

3 The original Kuznets curve refers to the inverted U-shape relationship between inequality and GDP (Kuznets, 1955).

4 Components change across implementations but common added components are "public non-defensive expenditures", "capital formation", "services from domestic labour". Common subtracted ones are "private defensive expenditures", "costs of environmental degradation", and "depreciation of natural capital".
5 Daly and Cobb (1990 [1989]) (US); Jackson and Marks (1994) (United Kingdom); Diefenbacher (1994) (Germany); Rosenberg and Oegema (1995) (Netherlands); Stockhammer et al. (1997), cited as Obermayr et al. (1994) (Austria).
6 It was because of this work, collated in that book, that MMN received the Right Livelihood Award (or "Alternative Nobel Prize", as it is sometimes referred to), a recognition given annually since 1980 by the Swedish foundation Right Livelihood. This prize catapulted MMN to the international stage across heterodox development circles.
7 "Energy and Resources", Bent Sørensen, Science (1975, pp. 255–256)
8 For example, Schumacher's *Small is Beautiful* (1973) was also a constant reference for Max-Neef. For more details, see Chapter 8 in this volume.
9 For a recent survey, see Clark et al. (2008); for Easterlin's latest update, see Easterlin and O'Connor (2020).
10 It also seems MMN had a significant aversion for all things mainstream economics, critical as he was of it. He might have had a personal policy of minimising references to them. In effect, to my experience it is rare to find explicit citations to mainstream economists in MMN's broad work, even as points of departures for critiques. This is not likely because of ignorance but because of active omission. More generally, he did have a tendency to be thin on references.
11 Yet, in terms of MMN's matrix of needs, one could think of consumption norms, reinforced through marketing and other means, as a type of pseudo-satisfactor for needs like identity or leisure.
12 A further reason could be the distinction between eudaimonic and hedonic happiness. According to Unaune (Chapter 5 in this volume), MMN thought of happiness as the former, whereas self-reported life satisfaction metrics are more akin of the second kind.
13 Fifteen years later, endorsing the threshold hypothesis as "fundamental in the field of economics", MMN makes similar call for further research regarding the threshold (Max-Neef, 2010, pp. 206–207).
14 Noticing the timing of the threshold, he concludes the article also asking whether the decline in ISEW could be "caused by the influence of Thatcher-Reagan neoliberal principles" (p. 118). This idea is not developed further.
15 For details, see Chapter 3 and 4 in this volume. The needs are subsistence, protection, affection, understanding, participation, leisure, creation, identity and freedom.
16 Research is starting on this front though. For example, Vita et al. (2019) is the first to directly connect the satisfaction of fundamental human needs *a la* Max-Neef with energy consumption and carbon footprint.
17 Based on https://plu.mx/plum/a/?doi=10.1016/0921-8009(95)00064-X
18 Based on "Citations per document", https://www.scimagojr.com/journalsearch.php?q=20290&tip=sid
19 Based on https://www.scimagojr.com/journalsearch.php?q=22697&tip=sid&clean=0
20 Based on https://www.scimagojr.com/journalsearch.php?q=29431&tip=sid&clean=0
21 For reference, the most cited *paper* by MMN seems to be his 2005 article *Foundations of Transdisciplinarity*, also in Ecological Economics, which has 31 citations per year over the period. Based on https://plu.mx/plum/a/?doi=10.1016/j.ecolecon.2005.01.014
22 Full list of citations is available at https://www.scopus.com/results/citedbyresults.uri?sort=plf-f&cite=2-s2.0-0029200880&src=s&imp=t&sid=6ced98b9e30d7defbb02ff3585400b08&sot=cite&sdt=a&sl=0&origin=inward&editSaveSearch=&txGid=5ba738c466a0996359e516ce36534239
23 Previously, Daly and Goodland (1994) had made a brief reference to Daly and Cobb's (1989) results regarding ISEW, but in a paper exploring the implications of deregulation of trade under GATT.

24 Here is a very clear passage from his book *From the Outside Looking In* (1982): "After a number of years, the enthusiasm and optimism with which I had worked as an economist for several international organizations, gave way to a growing uneasiness. To continue being engaged, whether as a witness or as a direct participant, in efforts to *diagnose poverty*, to *measure* it and to *devise indicators* in order to set up a statistical or conceptual threshold beyond which a percentage may reveal the numerical magnitude of those to be classified as the extremely poor; and then to participate in costly seminars and even costlier conferences in order to communicate the findings, interpret the meaning of the findings (my God!!), criticize the methodologies behind the findings, express our deep concern (often during cocktails) for what the findings show, and, finally, end up with recommendations to the effect that what must urgently be done is to allocate more funds for further research into the subject to be discussed again in other meetings – made me feel at a certain point that I was happily participating in a rather obscene ritual" (p. 20).

25 Graphical analysis is available here: https://hdr.undp.org/data-center/human-development-index#/indicies/HDI

26 For recent updates, see Easterlin et al. (2010), Proto and Rustichini (2013), De Neve et al. (2018) and Easterlin and O'Connor (2020). The latter seems to be the most comprehensive study in terms of coverage of years and countries.

27 A middle point in between this "ideal" method and the current one is to evaluate *individual* needs with a set of metrics (e.g., Vita et al., 2019). It must be stated that this "ideal" approach is not without problems. Two important ones are the quantification of need satisfaction from text responses and the aggregation of the latter across needs to produce a single index of need satisfaction.

References

Arrow, K., Bolin, B., Costanza, R., Dasgupta, P., Folke, C., Holling, C. S., Jansson, B., Levin, S., Maler, K., Perrings, C., & Pimentel, D. (1995). Economic growth, carrying capacity, and the environment. *Science*, *268*(5210), 520–521. https://doi.org/10.1126/science.268.5210.520

Clark, A. E., Frijters, P., & Shields, M. A. (2008). Relative income, happiness, and utility: An explanation for the Easterlin Paradox and other puzzles. *Journal of Economic Literature*, *46*(1), 95–144.

Cook, D., & Davíðsdóttir, B. (2021). An estimate of the genuine progress indicator for Iceland, 2000–2019. *Ecological Economics*, *189*, 1–13. https://doi.org/10.1016/j.ecolecon.2021.107154

Daly, H. E. (1973). *Toward a steady-state economy*. W.H. Freeman.

Daly, H. E. (1974). The economics of the steady state. *American Economic Review*, *64*(2), 15–21. http://www.jstor.org/stable/1816010

Daly, H. E. (1993 [1977]). *Steady-state economics: Second edition with new essays*. Island Press.

Daly, H. E. (1999). *Uneconomic growth in theory and in fact* [The First Annual Feasta Lecture], *Feasta Review*. Trinity College, Dublin. http://www.feasta.org/documents/feastareview/daly.htm

Daly, H., & Cobb, J. (1989). *For the common good*. Beacon Press.

Daly, H., & Goodland, R. (1994). An ecological-economic assessment of deregulation of international commerce under GATT. *Ecological Economics*, *9*(1), 73–92. https://doi.org/10.1016/0921-8009(94)90017-5

De Neve, J.-E., Ward, G., De Keulenaer, F., Van Landeghem, B., Kavetsos, G., & Norton, M. I. (2018). The asymmetric experience of positive and negative economic growth: Global evidence using subjective well-being data. *The Review of Economics and Statistics*, *100*(2), 362–375. https://doi.org/10.1162/REST_a_00697

Diefenbacher, H. (1994). The index of sustainable economic welfare: A case study of the Federal Republic of Germany. In: C. Cobb & J. Cobb (Eds.), *The green national product: A proposed index of sustainable economic welfare*. University Press of America.

Easterlin, R. A. (1974). Does economic growth improve the human lot? Some empirical evidence. In: Paul A. David & Melvin W. Reder (Eds.), *Nations and households in economic growth: Essays in honor of Moses Abramovitz* (pp. 89–125). Academic Press. https://doi.org/10.1016/B978-0-12-205050-3.50008-7

Easterlin, R. A., McVey, L. A., Switek, M., Sawangfa, O., & Zweig, J. S. (2010). The happiness-income paradox revisited. *Proceedings of the National Academy of Sciences of the United States of America*, *107*(52), 22463–22468. https://doi.org/10.1073/pnas.1015962107

Easterlin, R. A., & O'Connor, K. J. (2020). *The Easterlin Paradox* (IZA Discussion Papers 13923). Institute of Labor Economics (IZA).

Fox, M.-J. V., & Erickson, J. D. (2020). Design and meaning of the genuine progress indicator: A statistical analysis of the U.S. fifty-state model. *Ecological Economics*, *167*, 1–11. https://doi.org/10.1016/j.ecolecon.2019.106441

Grossman, G. M., & Krueger, A. B. (1991). *Environmental impacts of a North American Free Trade Agreement* [NBER Working Papers, No 3914]. National Bureau of Economic Research, Inc. https://doi.org/10.3386%2Fw3914

Grossman, G. M., & Krueger, A. B. (1995). Economic growth and the environment. *The Quarterly Journal of Economics*, *110*(2), 353–377. https://doi.org/10.2307/2118443

Jackson, T., & Marks, N. (1994). *Measuring sustainable economic welfare – A pilot index: 1950–1990*. Stockholm Environment Institute.

Kenny, D. C., Costanza, R., Dowsley, T., Jackson, N., Josol, J., Kubiszewski, I., Narulla, H., Sese, S., Sutanto, A., & Thompson, J. (2019). Australia's genuine progress indicator revisited (1962–2013). *Ecological Economics*, *158*, 1–10. https://doi.org/10.1016/j.ecolecon.2018.11.025

Kuznets, S. (1955). Economic growth and income inequality. *The American Economic Review*, *45*(1), 1–28. http://www.jstor.org/stable/1811581

Long, X., & Ji, X. (2019). Economic growth quality, environmental sustainability, and social welfare in China – Provincial assessment based on genuine progress indicator (GPI). *Ecological Economics*, *159*, 157–176. https://doi.org/10.1016/j.ecolecon.2019.01.002

Mallmann, C. (1972). *Sobre las necesidades del ser humano y su relación con las teorías del mundo*. Fundación Bariloche.

Max-Neef, M. (1982). *From the outside looking in. Experiences in "Barefoot Economics"*. Dag Hammarskjöld Foundation.

Max-Neef, M. (1991). *Human scale development: Conception, application and further reflections*. The Apex Press.

Max-Neef, M. (1995). Economic growth and quality of life: A threshold hypothesis. *Ecological Economics*, *15*(2), 115–118. https://doi.org/10.1016/0921-8009(95)00064-X

Max-Neef, M. (2005). Foundations of transdisciplinarity, *Ecological Economics*, *53*(1), 5–16. https://doi.org/10.1016/j.ecolecon.2005.01.014

Max-Neef, M. (2010). The world on a collision course and the need for a new economy. *Ambio*, *39*(3), 200–210. https://doi.org/10.1007/s13280-010-0028-1

Neumayer, E. (2000). On the methodology of ISEW, GPI and related measures: Some constructive comments and some doubt on the "threshold" hypothesis. *Ecological Economics*, *34*(3), 347–361. https://doi.org/10.1016/S0921-8009(00)00192-0

Obermayr, B., Steiner, K., Stockhammer, E., & Hockrieber, H. (1994). *Die Entwicklung des ISEW in Oesterreich von 1955 bis 1992*.

Proto, E., & Rustichini, A. (2013). A reassessment of the relationship between GDP and life satisfaction. *PLOS ONE*, *8*(11), e79358. https://doi.org/10.1371/journal.pone.0079358
Rosenberg, D., & Oegema, T. (1995). *A pilot index of sustainable economic welfare for the Netherlands, 1950-1992*. Institute for Environment and Systems Analysis, Amsterdam.
Selden, T. M., & Daqing, S. (1994). Environmental quality and development: Is there a Kuznets Curve for air pollution emissions? *Journal of Environmental Economics and Management*, *27*(2), 147–162. https://doi.org/10.1006/jeem.1994.1031
Shafik, N. (1994). Economic development and environmental quality: An econometric analysis. *Oxford Economic Papers*, *46*, 757–773. http://www.jstor.org/stable/2663498
Stockhammer, E., Hochreiter, H., Obermayr, B., & Steiner, K. (1997). The index of sustainable economic welfare (ISEW) as an alternative to GDP in measuring economic welfare. The results of the Austrian (revised) ISEW calculation 1955–1992, *Ecological Economics*, *21*(1), 19–34. https://doi.org/10.1016/S0921-8009(96)00088-2
Vita, G., Hertwich, E. G., Stadler, K., & Wood, R. (2019). Connecting global emissions to fundamental human needs and their satisfaction. *Environmental Research Letters*, 14(1), 014002. https://doi.org/10.1088/1748-9326/aae6e0

Part III

Methodology of economics

14 The thinking of Manfred Max-Neef and the challenge to neoclassic economics and policy orthodoxy

Andrés Solimano

Introduction

Manfred Max-Neef (MMN for short) was a remarkable economist and a highly cultivated person. His broad range of interests included economics, history, music, ecology, international relations, culture, ethics, and other topics. Given the wide breadth of his knowledge, it is not surprising that he felt uneasy with theoretical constructs that reduce human beings to the role of cold calculators of costs and benefits in a relentless process of maximising individual satisfaction and monetary profits. He was aware of the dangers of understanding economics as a self-contained system rather than a sub-system embedded in broader systems such as society and the physical environment. He warned that an approach of a self-contained economic system, disregarding wider social impacts, would eventually lead to the adoption of economic policies that create inequality, social conflict, and ecological crises and exacerbate adverse shocks. Endless material growth can be inconsistent with planetary boundaries. Regarding issues of methodology in economics MMN favoured transdisciplinary exploration and dismissed static analysis that compare one stationary equilibrium with another. In turn, he promoted ethical considerations in economic policy arguing that focusing only on efficiency issues, material growth, and the promotion of private consumption constituted a limited agenda of comprehensive development.

Max-Neef was not an ivory tower academic. Early in his career, facing the opportunity of a rewarding career in international organisations and private corporations, he preferred the more austere and financially less lucrative choice of a 'barefoot economist' devoted to teaching, research, and social activism. At maturity, MMN runs for president of Chile in the presidential elections of 1993. Then he became rector of the Universidad Austral de Chile in Valdivia. He participated in different international initiatives in favour of sustainable development, leaned against austerity and promoted more fair adjustment policies by international financial organisations. In the aftermath of the financial crisis of 2008–09, he was also appalled by the fact that public money went to save banks rather than people. He was chilled by the magnitude of existing hunger and poverty around the world amid conditions of affluence and prosperity. Unequal wealth and income distribution was an important concern for him. As a personal note, I was lucky of having

DOI: 10.4324/9781003381143-17

known, personally, MMN and being a guest in his home. I can testify his genuine humanism, keen intelligence, social sensibility, and warm personality.

This chapter will focus on MMN's main themes of his research and advocacy agenda, including issues of methodology and the nature of economics (second section), human wants and the good life (third section), globalisation, neoliberalism, and economic austerity (fourth section), economic crimes (fifth section), ecological economics, multiple crises, decoupling, and sustainable economic development (from sixth section to eighth section). The chapter seeks to place MMN's ideas and writings in the broader context of the history of social thought encompassing elements of economics, psychology, philosophy, and ecology. It also identifies aspects of Max-Neef's research that, in my view, would need further clarification and extension. Attention is devoted to how his views were intended to be an alternative to neoclassic economics and policy orthodoxy (neoliberalism) at the national and international scale.

Methodological issues: The need for an expanded approach to economics

Neoclassic economics, and variants, is the dominant approach in economics currently taught in most universities around the world.[1] This approach combines Alfred Marshall's partial equilibrium analysis – say the market of oranges, the labour market, the market for cars – with 'general equilibrium'. The latter follows the tradition of Leon Walras in which several markets are treated simultaneously, and their interactions are considered to reach a full equilibrium of the whole system. Non-linearities, multiple and unstable equilibrium are often not considered relevant in that analysis although these features do exist in the real world.

Macroeconomic analysis, in turn, as developed by Keynes and subsequent formulations starts from the 'circular flow' that connects firms with workers and the respective flows of labour services, wages payments, total sales, and total demand. Injections (consumption, investment, exports) and outflows (savings, taxes, and imports) alter the circular flow and the equilibrium levels of output, employment, and savings. The budget constraints that are derived from the supply and demand side formed the basis for the preparation of national accounts and input-output tables.

The teaching and practice of economics is, in the mainstream, that of a closed system, not explicitly embedded in a larger system that embeds social and physical frameworks that go beyond markets. Max-Neef (2010) and Daly (2022) view the economy as a sub-system of: (i) society (with institutions, culture, history) and (ii) the physical environment (biosphere).

Political economy traditions and institutional economics are all concerned with the impact of institutions and politics on economic outcomes. More recently, ecological economics (see Daly, 2022 for a good description of the field) has gained more influence since around the 1990s. This approach integrates the use of material inputs and energy of an economic system into a broader ecological and physical, natural, system (Common & Stagl, 2005; Daly, 2022). Max-Neef (2010, 2016) emphasised the impact of growing production levels and rapid capital accumulation on the environment, eco-system services, and planetary boundaries therefore contributing to the development of an ecological view of economics.

A main message of ecological economics, with policy implications, is that infinite economic growth that consumes natural resources and burn fossil fuels is, ultimately, incompatible with the resource constraints posed by a finite planet. This leads to the question of how to address the fundamental contradiction between the drive of a capitalist economy to endless capital accumulation to maximise profits and the fact that natural resources and energy that support accumulation and growth are finite and exhaustible? In eighth section, we deal with this issue and make a distinction between 'weak decoupling' and 'strong decoupling' as possible responses to this dilemma or contradiction. In this context, an economic organisation is faced with at least two broad choices: (i) either to slow-down (or halt) GDP growth as it is practised now to reduce the use of natural capital and energy and/or[2] (ii) to adopt new technologies that reduce or prescind altogether of fossil fuels replacing them by renewable sources of energy such as solar and wind. In other words, to avoid collision between growth and the environment, it is necessary to reduce the *energy-intensity*, particularly of fossil fuels, and reduce the extraction rate of exhaustible natural resources. Otherwise, human civilisation goes in the way of *collision*, using MMN words. By the way, evidence of ecological destabilisation is already happening witness the increased frequency of severe storms, acidification of the ocean, rising temperatures, the melting of ice, all with dire consequences for human life in the planet (see IPCC, 2022).

Max-Neef actively warned, though his lifetime, about these issues. Part of these concerns gradually became, in a certain way, mainstream (at least at a rhetoric level) and some national governments and international bodies have incorporated the environmental dimension into their programmes and actions (see, for example, the development of the Index of Sustainable Economic Welfare or the Gross National Happiness Index).

In his home country, Chile, Manfred was an early critic of national growth strategies that relied too heavily on the exploitation – in some cases to near exhaustion – of the natural resource base of the country such as copper, iron ore, lithium, fishery, and forestry resources. He warned of the undesirable consequences of this (unsustainable) strategy of economic development. Perhaps the sense of urgency of these predictions and warning in the 1960s and 1970s (when MMN produced his early work) were less dramatic than in the third decade of the 21st century.

Human needs and the good life: Max-Neef and other literature

In the book *Human Scale Development*,[3] Max-Neef and his collaborators, Antonio Elizalde and Martin Hopenhayn, engaged in a reflection on human needs and the quality of life. The authors identified needs and satisfiers with a distinction between *existential* needs and *axiological* (the study of values) needs. Existential needs include subsistence, protection, affection, understanding, participation, idleness, identity, creation, and freedom. The list is large and combines physiological needs (subsistence), socially bounded needs (participation), and psychological needs (affection, freedom). Social needs include a quest for recognition from peers and support from the family, friends, and colleagues. Axiological needs, in turn, are defined by the concepts of being (qualities), having (things), doing (actions), and interacting (settings).

In contrast to the more psychologically oriented work of Abraham Maslow (Maslow, 1943), for Max-Neef et al., there are no hierarchies among needs. They are 'organic' and 'systemic' and can be interactive, simultaneous, and complementary to each other. In Max-Neef (1991, 2010), a human needs matrix is presented with rows representing existential needs and columns reflecting axiological needs. The resulting matrix (cells) in Max-Neef (1991) although suggestive is bound to be affected by *over-determinacies and redundancies* given the complexity of the multiple interactions between existential and axiological needs.

In Max-Neef's scheme things such as food, homes, and shelter, the possibility of undertaking artistic and literary works are satisfiers. Moreover, education is also a satisfier of the need of understanding reality.

The economic system plays a central role in the production and distribution of a variety of satisfiers such as food, clothing, homes, and durable goods like electronics, computers, cars, and so on. However, modern capitalism – exacerbated in the individualistic societies of late neoliberal capitalism – has turned into a 'consumption society' that engages in the *over-production of goods*, say satisfiers (personal consumption goods, pseudo-satisfiers) using scarce resources with an opportunity cost and an environmental impact. The other side of the coin is an *under supply* of collective goods (parks, hospitals, preservation areas, stadiums, concert halls).

How to put MMN (and his colleagues) theory of needs in the perspective of *other* theories of well-being and the good life? Unfortunately, MMN had a certain tendency in his writings of refraining from citing related contributions on the subject, particularly those coming from schools of thought he did not agree with. For example, in MMN (1991, 2010), no systematic overview of the relevant literature on the good life (utilitarianism, Marx, Maslow, Sen's capability approach) is presented to help the reader to trace where their theory really comes from. Differences with Maslow and neoclassic theory are mentioned at times. We noted differences between the pyramid of needs in Maslow (1943) and Max-Neef et al. matrix and utilitarianism postulates that human well-being is directly derived from pleasure and pain (or utility) associated with consumption (or the lack of it).

A formulation that conveys some similarities with MMN's matrix is the capabilities approach developed by Amartya Sen and Martha Nussbaum (see Sen, 2009). In Sen's scheme, capabilities refer to the ability of people to do things that he or she has reason to value. The focus is on the *freedom of people* to undertake actions considered valuable.[4]

The capability approach focuses on human life and the quality of life rather than objects, income, and wealth as the main criteria to judge human success as in utilitarian analysis and neoclassical theory (Sen, 2009). The focus is shifted from the means of living (resources) to the actual opportunities of living. Sen's aim is to transform goods and actions into outcomes (the ability to perform certain ends). This looks somewhat like Max-Neef's satisfiers.

Another view of the good life is provided by Karl Marx.[5] Marx, as interpreted by Elster (1985, 1990), stressed that *self-realisation* – the full and free actualisation of the powers and abilities of the individual – was more important than the passive consumption of goods and services for assessing the quality of life of individuals. Self-realisation may include a variety of activities such as playing tennis, cooking a meal, writing a book, painting a canvas, playing piano, organising a political campaign, and proving a mathematical theorem. In Marxist terms, self-realisation is a concept more transcendent than consumption (by its nature a short-lived experience). In other words, consumption (say eating a meal or reading a book) and social interactions (talking to a friend) do not render, necessarily, for self-realisation. Consumption produces satisfaction (utility) but it is not oriented to pursue a certain goal or purpose that contributes, significantly, to the realisation of human potential and capacities. In principle, Marx self-realisation can be attained, through *productive work*. In contrast, in neoclassic theory, it is leisure that generates utility and not directly work.

Marx emphasised that capitalism tends to fragment the sense of community by promoting individualism. In particular, he noted, with force, that the capitalist factory structured around the division of labour produces *alienation* that goes against self-realisation. So, one of his fundamental critiques (along with Engels) of the capitalist factory system was that through the division of labour and the control by capital oriented to extract a maximum of labour power (surplus value) from workers, labour was alienated or separated from an identification with the final product of his/her work. This was a difference with the pre-capitalist craft system.

Max-Neef's treatment of the complex issues of the 'good life' was rather intuitive and eclectic using pieces of different theories while emphasising the need to take the community (a critique of individualism) seriously making a case for the need to promote local development and more humane cities in which people could interact safely and in rewarding fashion with each other.

An important and influential view on the meaning of the good life was provided by British philosopher G.E. Moore in its *Principia Ethica* published in 1903. In that tract, Moore went at length in opposing the utilitarian logic of identifying the good life with pleasure and the attainment of utility: watching a drama play may, at times, produce sadness and certain displeasure, but the good life requires a reading of Shakespeare. Moore's view said that it was very difficult to define what is 'good' in life: there were puzzles and impossibilities in the subject of human happiness and welfare.[6] Still, he entertained the notion that living a good and enlightened life required more than a cold calculation of pleasures and pains, leaning to an appreciation of goods, aesthetic values, beauty, and a high-spirited behaviour. Moore's philosophical stance exerted an important influence on the thinking of the economist John Maynard Keynes and of philosophers Bertrand Russell and Ludwig Wittgenstein, working at the time on analytical philosophy at Cambridge University in Britain. Moore's philosophical outlook was compatible with individualism combined with concerns for solidarity and empathy for others, respect for democracy, and the promotion of personal and national autonomy.

Globalisation, neoliberalism and economic austerity

At the level of economic and development policy, MMN was an early critic of free market economics and the neoliberal policy model that has dominated, to a significant extent, global economic policymaking in developing nations and advanced capitalist countries since the 1980s. In his writings for the Royal Swedish Academy of Sciences in 2010 and his contribution to the *Manifesto on Global Economic Transitions*[7] presented prior to the global crisis of 2008–09, Manfred took task of highlighting feeble assertions and 'myths' accompanying the process of neoliberal globalisation based on unrestricted international trade and capital mobility, restraints on the international mobility of labour, the priority of financial capital and multinational corporations, and the primacy of profits over people.[8]

MMN listed various assertions on the benefits of neoliberal globalisation that, in his view, were more wishful thinking than claims with a strong backing in hard empirical evidence. The assertions are as follows: (i) globalisation leads to an acceleration of economic growth. He showed that comparing economic growth between the period 1960 and 1980 (pre-globalisation) with 1980 and 2000 (globalisation) average economic growth across countries *declined* rather than accelerated; (ii) globalisation leads to a lasting reduction in (multi-dimensional) global poverty. Although by some income measures of global poverty have declined in the last 30 years (mainly in China), these declines may be transitory rather than robust; (iii) static comparative advantage is a key criterion for trade policy. MMN, among others, argued that comparative advantages must be seen in *dynamic terms* and should be complemented by an active concern with trade patterns that comply with environmental standards and labour rights; (iv) globalisation leads to solid job creation. On the contrary, jobs became outsourced to countries with low wages, precarious occupations, and weak labour standards; (iv) the International organisations (WTO) overseeing international trade is a neutral policy body. In contrast, MMN argued that WTO was strongly affected by the views and interests of big corporations and that more transparency in their decisions was needed, (vi) globalisation is close to a deterministic and inevitable process. On this last point, Max-Neef was sceptical of the dictums of 'Third Way' leaders of the global north such as Bill Clinton and Tony Blair who claimed that 'globalisation was irreversible and irresistible'. This criticism also extended to former UK's Prime Minister Margaret Thatcher's motto of 'there is no alternative (TINA)' to a market economy in a post-soviet world.

MMN also noted that main central banks during the crisis of 2008–09 managed to provide large sums of money to bail-out private commercial banks in distress but this monetary help was not reaching workers and poor people. 'Save the people not the banks' was his recommendation, noting that it was a worrying distortion of policy priorities doing just the opposite: save the banks not the people. MMN derided the notion that those pointing to this alteration of priorities were 'populists and irresponsible individuals', while those favouring protecting the financial system (Wall Street) over the rank and file of society (Main Street) were 'serious people'.

Max-Neef was highly sceptical of the possibilities to attain genuine and sustainable development based on the unrestricted operation of markets, the prevalence of the profit motive in all activities and the retreat of the state in its roles of producer of public goods and regulator of the private sector.

The evidence on economic performance in Latin America, Africa, and East Asia in the 1970–2010 period, argued Max-Neef, was not supportive of simplistic predictions that by dismantling trade barriers, enabling international financial integration, deregulating, and privatising business, countries would automatically jump to a higher circular flow of economic prosperity, job creation, lower poverty, and enhanced national happiness.

MMN was also critic of the asymmetry of the international financial architecture that operates more actively in forcing adjustment in deficit countries (often in the global south) than in encouraging corrections to balance of payments surpluses or deficits (in the global north). In some of his presentations for international audiences, he was particularly critic of the costs imposed by austerity programs endorsed by the IMF (also the European Central Bank and the European Commission) in the countries of southern Europe such as Greece in the aftermath of the financial crisis of 2008–09 that led to near a decade of output stagnation, high unemployment, and massive emigration in this country (Solimano, 2020).

Economic crimes

We have mentioned that *ethical considerations* in economic policy were important for MMN. Outraged by decades of economic turmoil and austerity induced by national governments with the backing of international financial organisations, MMN went as far as claiming the need to establish an international tribunal for 'economic crime' in developing countries (Max-Neef, 2014a, 2014b). There was a precedent that inspired his initiative, and this was the International War Crimes Tribunal better known as the 'Russell Tribunal',[9] an entity formed to evaluate and assess the impact of the American military intervention in Vietnam in the 1960s. It was set up in 1966 and convened twice: first in 1967 in Stockholm and a second time in Roskilde, Denmark. The Tribunal was composed by personalities such as Bertrand Russell, Jean-Paul Sartre, Simone de Beauvoir, Tarik Ali, Julio Cortazar, Lazaro Cardenas, and others.

Max-Neef's notion of economic crime amounted to unnecessary pain imposed on vulnerable groups (children, the poor, ageing population, workers, foreign migrants) in countries experiencing externally imposed economic policies. The economic costs of these policies can be measured in loses of employment, cuts in real wages, increased poverty, reduction in social spending in health and education, and adverse effects on nutrition and mental health. The implementation of policies resisted by the population can lead also to the violation of human rights besides political repression to curb 'food riots' and 'transport riots' at times of economic hardship (Solimano, 2022). The agents of repression are often the national police, the army, and secret service agents. In turn, policies that led to repressive acts were associated with the harsh conditionality imposed by international financial institutions such as the IMF, the World Bank, the European Central Bank in exchange for loans and technical assistance.

His criticism was not only centred on the restrictive measures embedded in loan conditionality (taxes hikes, cuts in public sector employment, rises in food prices and public utility fares) but also focused on the accountability of international financial institutions imposing harsh polices on indebted nations.

This proposal, although never implemented, in its original format probably influenced the United Nations Human Rights Council, which has, in recent years, developed covenants and methodologies to evaluate the impact of economic adjustment on human rights and related social costs.[10] Moreover, the indictments of a possible 'tribunal on economic crimes' would be more in terms of conscience objections and denunciation rather than seeking legal responsibilities over the staff/senior managers of international institutions making these loans. To be fair, responsibility must be extended also to national governments and parliaments that sign/endorse financial operations with policy conditionality without a careful analysis of their possible impact on the poor and the most vulnerable members of society as well as effects on the stability of democracy and respect of human rights (civic/political and economic/social).

Is contemporary capitalism in collision course?

Around the time of the 2008–09 crisis, Max-Neef endorsed the idea that we were living in a period of *multiple crises*. The concept incorporates not only a crisis of the financial system, perhaps intermingled with a fiscal crisis, into advanced capitalist economies and emerging economies but also an ecological crisis and a social crisis (Solimano, 2020). We could also add the existence of 'governance crises' that stretches the ability of the democratic system to adequately deal with various systemic crises happening at the same time. The result of weak governance can be a slide into authoritarian tendencies, violence, and even war.

The ecological crisis is often manifested in a rising trend in temperatures and 'global warming' that is producing the melting of ice in the north and southern pole, sudden and violent storms, droughts, heavy rainfall, increases in the level of the ocean, and so on. Clearly, planetary boundaries were stretched with very damaging potential consequences for human security. Vividly, MMN stated that we were on the 'road to catastrophe' meaning by that, chiefly, ecological destabilisation besides social and political disruption accompanied by geopolitical tensions, including the risk of nuclear war and chemical war. This ugly combination of intervening factors can be lethal indeed.

The slide into an ecological crisis was the consequence of several factors often building up in a cumulative way over several decades: the reliance on fossil fuels as the main source of energy to sustain production and consumption of goods and services, the dominance of private corporate interests in the oil and gas industry that opposed a shift to cleaner energies based on wind, biomass and solar energy, the neglect of the fact that the economy is a sub-system of a larger system of the biosphere in which the injections and outflows of energy and waste disposal and composed of natural capital and eco-systems that sustained human life and economic activity.

Max-Neef pointed that the multiple crises scenario was rather unique in the history of mankind. Before the industrial revolution, the size of global population and the scale of economic activity were relatively small compared with the resources of nature to affect, in a significant way, world eco-systems and undermine planetary boundaries. However, around the 1950s, this started to change. Advanced capitalist countries were in a 'golden age of capitalism' featuring rapid growth rates that relied on the intensive use of raw material, fossil fuels, and natural resources. This expanded, dramatically, the absolute size of economic activity harming natural eco-systems. This dominance of the human on the nature is called the Anthropocene Era. One dimension of the ecological threat is the *intergenerational democratic deficit* associated with the absence of mechanisms that consider the interests of *future generations* in the decisions of current generations regarding the rate of growth of output, and the use of exhaustible natural resources and fossil fuel energy.

Humanistic and sustainable development

In response to the deficiencies of prevailing development models based on material growth, consumerism, and profit-driven accumulation, Max-Neef articulated several principles and a value proposition for an alternative development framework[11]:

1 The economy is to serve people and not people to serve the economy
2 Development must be centred on people and not on objects
3 Growth is not the same as development and development does not require growth
4 No economic system can function without adequate eco-services
5 The economy is a sub-system of the biosphere, and its physical laws and constraints must be respected. Endless growth is incompatible with a finite planet
6 Value proposition: no economic interest must be above the respect for life

MMN approach, in line with the spirit of ecological economics, was critical of material growth as a main mean for attaining genuine social welfare. This is a strong departure from the perspective of both neoclassic economics and to some extent Keynesian economics. As mentioned, the premise of economic orthodoxy is that individual utility depends on the amount of consumption goods available to a person or household: the amount of food, clothing, cigars, the use of cars and houses, TV sets, travelling services, and so on. In the aggregate, the social welfare function is the sum, across all individuals, of the level of utility of everyone. This is yardstick of the good life in the tradition of Jevons, Bentham, Edgeworth, and other thinkers in the utilitarian tradition. The maximisation of social welfare through the aggregation of individual preferences is not easy as it fails to satisfy certain basic conditions that rule out the imposition of dictatorial preferences, transitivity, and irrelevance to third conditions, posing complex issues for political theory and social choice theory based on the maximisation of social welfare (Solimano [2022] examines the underpinnings of impossibility theorems in social choice theory).

Returning to the topic of how to measure economic development, mainstream economics uses a predominantly *object-based* metric of development. An increase in personal and family welfare is identified as having more goods and services: larger homes, more sophisticated cars, more visits to the 'shopping mall', better TV sets, and so on. Max-Neef was aware of the 'commodification' of economic life under capitalism and he was also critical of material product measures of welfare in centrally planned economies a tendency largely incompatible with a more humanist conception of development. His leaning was for 'people-centred development' – as an alternative to 'commodity-centred development' – putting more emphasis on addressing the complex needs of people, both existential and axiological, rather than simply the consumption of commodities as a way to maximise utility.

On the other hand, Keynesian economics was, in a sense, 'pro-growth' – or more precisely *anti-stagnation* – but for different reasons. Keynes reasoned that as capitalism was affected by a chronic tendency of insufficient aggregate demand, unemployment, and the under-utilisation of productive capital, then aggregate demand and production must be stimulated by fiscal policy (through higher public spending and/or lower taxes). At the same time, Keynes postulated that monetary stimulus was less effective than fiscal policy in a situation of liquidity traps (an infinitely elastic demand for money at a low interest rate). In the Keynesian tradition, stagnation, and the fact that labour and capital are not put fully into productive uses, leads to waste which is not only economically inefficient but also can lead to social disarray and political instability.

Weak and strong decoupling

A decoupling between a broader concept of development (sustainable and socially fair) and the objective of economic growth is a potential way out to the contradiction between endless growth and a finite planet. Here a distinction can be made between:

a Weak decoupling
b Strong decoupling

Weak decoupling can be thought as an approach in which growth is recognised as important for increasing employment, real wages, and consumption, but that growth should not be at the expense of damaging eco-systems and threatening planetary boundaries, a process already underway. Thus, the emphasis is in using technologies in production that reduce the reliance on fossil fuels and an excessive exploitation of natural resources. In addition, there is a need of active government regulations that impede the execution of 'development' projects in areas that damage forests, deplete natural resources, contaminate air and water, and displace local populations and ethnic groups.

Strong decoupling can be viewed as 'zero-growth development' (or minimal growth) with mechanisms for ensuring a basic living standard to everyone. This view is often associated with the *de-growth analysis*. Nonetheless, this approach does *not* advocate for a sort of permanent recession or protracted economic contraction but for a medium-run, planned, scale-down of the economy in terms of energy use and a change in the composition of production in favour of social and collective goods rather than luxury goods and other considerations.[12] It is unclear, however, what was the exact position held by Max-Neef on decoupling in seminars, public lectures, and writings.

The zero-growth stance poses both analytical and practical challenges. This is for various reasons: no GDP growth in a society with positive population growth implies a path of shrinking GDP per person with adverse consequences on poverty and living standards, particularly in middle- and low-income countries. Moreover, it is not simple to envisage how to curb the various forces that account for dynamism in a capitalist economy: these forces can be the 'animal spirits' of investors highlighted by Maynard Keynes, the process of 'creative destruction' of Joseph Schumpeter, and the drive for endless capital accumulation and the search for profits underscored by Karl Marx. In other words, a post-growth economy may probably require a post-capitalist system.

From the perspective of attaining the 'good life', it is not entirely clear that dispensing of material growth altogether will not enter in collision with self-realisation through work. Marx, as said before, was critical of the ability of achieving, at least for the workers, self-realisation in the capitalist factory in (19th century) capitalism with rapid mechanisation, and the division of labour. In these circumstances, the most likely result is alienation rather than self-realisation. In an economy without many jobs, the practical result can be lack of incomes, poverty, and frustration, probably leading to emigration to countries with higher per capita incomes and better job opportunities.

Max-Neef had a critical stance towards the supposed existence of an environmental equivalent of the Kuznets curve[13] in which at low levels of economic development growth deteriorates the environment through pollution and other effects but after a certain point of per capita income more economic growth can lead to an improvement in the quality of the environment (a sort of inverted U-shape curve along a GDP growth/environmental index plane). MMN established, *contrary* to the optimist message of the environmental Kuznets curve, that, based on different prices of empirical evidence, after a certain threshold is reached, additional growth will *deteriorate* the environment and worsen living standards therefore impairing both ecological sustainability and human development. These thresholds vary across time and space (see Max-Neef, 1995, 2010 and Chapter 13 in this volume).

Another possible extension of this hypothesis is that beyond certain threshold of basic needs (food, shelter, basic transport, clothing), objects may fail to satisfy the individual demand for social integration, belonging, emotional attachment, solidarity, self-fulfilment through creative work, and so on.

The commodification of economic life and the deleterious effects of endless material growth on the quality of life (congestion, deterioration of the sense of community, environmental degradation) were all features of society that were stressed by Max-Neef. This is, in line with, the tradition of critics of capitalism such as Marx, Engels, and Polanyi, to cite the most prominent names in this literature.

These authors highlighted that capitalism tends to turn relations between humans as near equivalent to relations between objects. This is the case, for example, of the creation of modern labour markets after the industrial revolution in which the workers sell their labour power (equivalent to a commodity) in exchange for a salary in the capitalist factory system. This is in contrast to the more personal relation developed between master and apprentices and trainees in handcraft production in pre-capitalist orders.

Nonetheless, MMN also pointed that soviet-type of socialist economies were not environmentally friendly as did not have incentives to economise energy in production and investment. These economies were also affected by the syndrome of the 'shortage economies' with 'soft budget constraints' in the words of the late Hungarian economist Janos Kornai suffering chronic supply shortages of consumer goods (from food to durable goods, Kornai, 1992).

Max-Neef (2010) proposes that an alternative economic system to capitalism should replace greed, competition, and accumulation by cooperation, solidarity, and compassion. This is an important ethical and motivational point. Capitalism is based on the operation of the first set of values although the variant of regulated capitalism and the welfare state can dampen its most adverse effects on the family and social cohesion. However, neoliberal capitalism based on deregulation, the dismantling of the welfare state, and the application of the profits' motive to education, health, pension management exacerbates greed, commodification, and competition with serious adverse social and environmental consequences.

There is a need to alternatives here and models of economic democracy can open spaces for cooperation, solidarity, and companion to play a significant role in the coordination of economic activities (Solimano, 2014, 2022).

MMN also elaborated on the need to keep money circulating near the sectors we wanted to support in the economy: for example, small- and medium-scale enterprises, the poor and marginalised, local communities (Max-Neef, 2014a, 2014b). This relates to financial inclusion and more democratic ways of conducting monetary policies, opposite perhaps to the modalities of 'independent central banks' that largely insulate the production of money and its distribution from social needs, and the democratic process. He also stressed the need for a local and regional approach to economic development, with bottom-up development taking the priority. Manfred advocated the taxing of pollution, the use of dirty energy, and generally the production of 'negative goods'. He also connected democracy with genuine development.

Concluding remarks

Max-Neef was a creative and iconoclast thinker who sought original answers for the complex problems of our time. He was deeply sceptical that adequate responses to human development are to be found in the realm of neoclassic economics offering a view of the economy based on assumptions of methodological individualism, utility/profit maximisation, atomistic markets, and the social optimality of general equilibrium. In this view of the world, economic outcomes are largely devoid from the influences of history, institutions, the physical environment, and political developments. MMN favoured transdisciplinary analysis and believed in a holistic, organic, and historically oriented study of socio-economic phenomena. He developed an early appreciation of the central role played by natural resources and planetary boundaries in shaping economic outcomes, highlighting the multiplicity of ecological, financial, and social crises the world is heading to. In line with his ethical concerns extended to government action and international financial institutions, Max-Neef entertained the notion of 'economic crimes', supported by an international tribunal along the lines of the Russell Tribunal of the 1960s. MMN associated economic crime with economic policies that impinge undue social costs to the population and harm human rights during austerity policies, privatisation, and the retrenchment of social spending. The proposed economic tribunal was to be more an ethical device than a legal court. Max-Neef was also critical of neoliberal globalisation, the bail-out of central banks to the financial system, the asymmetries of current financial architecture for developing countries and emerging economies, and the deleterious effect of austerity promoted by international financial institutions and some first-world governments to ensure bank loan repayments. Looking ahead there is a need for more dialogue between mainstream development views and alternative schools of the sort of Max-Neef contributed to create. There is certainly much more environmental awareness these days than a few decades ago and work on sustainable development and ecological economics contributed to this. However, inertia and entrenched interests make difficult to handle the transition to more environmentally friendly economy and comply with targets on global warming. Also, Max-Neef's work on human needs is probably better appreciated today than in the past. Further, his emphasis on the importance of ethics in economics must be considered more strongly today.

Notes

1 See Keen (2021).
2 On the de-growth approach, see Hickel (2020).
3 Max-Neef et al. (1991).
4 Freedom plays a central role in Sen's theory and appears as an existential need in Max-Neef. The capabilities approach also uses axiological categories in its analysis. Expanding the scope for individual freedom is essential and alternative arrangements and local situations are evaluated in terms of the contribution to freedom (one of Sen's most important books is entitled precisely *Development as Freedom*).
5 Chapter 16 in this volume elaborates on the links among David Ricardo, Marx, and Max-Neef thoughts.
6 Solimano (2022) reviews various impossibility theorems in the field of collective choice and social welfare.
7 The Manifesto was prepared under the auspices of the International Forum on Globalization, the Institute for Policy Studies, and the Institute for Economic Transition.
8 Max-Neef (2010) and Solimano (2017).
9 In the Russell Tribunal, there were no official delegates from the US and Vietnam. Funding largely came from North Vietnam following a direct request from Bertrand Russell to Ho Chi Minh.
10 See Nolan and Bohoslavsky (2020) and Bohoslawsky and Cantamutto (2020–2021).

11 Max-Neef (2010) and Cruz et al. (2009).
12 See Hickel (2020).
13 The Kuznets curve is an inverted U-shape relation between inequality and GDP growth. At low levels of development, growth will deteriorate income distribution but after a threshold the relation changes sign and additional growth would reduce inequality. The existence of this relation, based on US data for the first half of the 20th century, as an almost universal law, has been widely questioned.

References

Bohoslawsky, J. P., & Cantamutto, F., Editores Invitados. (2020–2021). Edicion Especial: Fondo Monetario Internacional y Derechos Humanos. *Revista Derechos en Accion*, año 6, *18*, 8.

Common, M., & Stagl, S. (2005). *Ecological economics. An introduction*. Cambridge University Press.

Cruz, I., Stahel, A., & Max-Neef, M. (2009). Towards a systemic development approach: Building on the human-scale development paradigm. *Ecological Economics*, *68*(7), 2021–2030. https://doi.org/10.1016/j.ecolecon.2009.02.004

Daly, H. (2022). Ecological economics in four parables. *Real-World Economics Review*, *102*, 2–15.

Elster, J. (1985). *Making sense of Marx. Studies in Marxism and Social Theory*. Cambridge University Press.

Elster, J. (1990). Self-realization in work and politics: The Marxist conception of the good life. In J. Elster & K. Ove Moene (Eds.), *Alternative to capitalism, studies in Marxism and social theory* (Chapter 8). Cambridge University Press.

Hickel, J. (2020). *Less is more. How de-growth will save the world*. Penguin, Random House.

IPCC (2022). *Climate Change 2022: Impacts, Adaptation, and Vulnerability*. Contribution of Working Group II to the Sixth Assessment Report of the Intergovernmental Panel on Climate Change [H.-O. Pörtner, D.C. Roberts, M. Tignor, E.S. Poloczanska, K. Mintenbeck, A. Alegría, M. Craig, S. Langsdorf, S. Löschke, V. Möller, A. Okem, B. Rama (eds.)].Cambridge University Press, 3056 pp.

Keen, S. (2021). *The new economics: A manifesto*. Polity Press.

Kornai, J. (1992). *The socialist system. The political economy of communism*. Princeton University Press.

Maslow, A. (1943). A theory of human motivation. *Psychological Review*, *50*(4), 370–396. https://psycnet.apa.org/doi/10.1037/h0054346

Max-Neef, M. (1991) with A. Elizalde and M. Hopenheym. *Human scale development. Conception, reflection and further elaboration*. Dag Hammarskjold Foundation, The Apex Press.

Max-Neef, M. (1995). Economic growth and quality of life: A threshold hypothesis. *Ecological Economics*, *15*(2), 115–118. https://doi.org/10.1016/0921-8009(95)00064-x

Max-Neef, M. (2010). The world on collision course and the need for a new economy. Contribution to the 2009 royal colloquium. *Ambio*, *39*(3), 200–210. https://www.jstor.org/stable/40730901

Max-Neef, M. (2014a). Local money as solution to capitalist global financial crises. In M. Pirson, U. Steinvorth, C. Largacha-Martinez, & C. Dierksmeier (Eds.), *From capitalism to humanistic business. Humanism in business series*. Palgrave Macmillan. https://doi.org/10.1057/9781137468208_11

Max-Neef, M. (2014b). The good is the bad that we don't do: Economic crimes against humanity: A proposal. *Ecological Economics*, *104*, 152–154. https://doi.org/10.1016/j.ecolecon.2014.02.011

Max-Neef, M. (2016). Philosophy of ecological economics. *International Journal of Economics & Management Sciences*, *5*(5), 1–5.

Nolan, A., & Bohoslavsky, J. P. (2020). Human rights and economic policy reform. *The International Journal of Human Rights*, *24*(9), 1400–1428. https://doi.org/10.1080/13642987.2020.1823638

Sen, A. (2009). *The idea of justice*. The Belknap Press of Oxford University Press.

Solimano, A. (2014). *Economic elites, crises and democracy*. Oxford University Press.

Solimano, A. (2017). *Global capitalism in disarray. Inequality, debt and austerity*. Oxford University Press.

Solimano, A. (2020). *A history of big recessions in the long 20th century*. Cambridge University Press.

Solimano, A. (2022). *Economic and political democracy in complex times*. Routledge.

15 The *Gustibus est Disputandum*

Building a bridge between mainstream economics and Max-Neef's Theory of Fundamental Needs

Roberto Pastén

Introduction

Manfred Max-Neef (MMN henceforth) and several other authors challenged a cornerstone idea of neoclassical economics, namely that material consumption is the only determinant of social well-being. Starting from Ramsey (1928), models of economic growth considered a univariate utility function that only depends on consumption (Kaldor, 1957; Solow, 1956; Swan, 1956). Thus, there was an increasing relation between well-being and economic growth. At some time, leisure was included as a second good in economic growth models (Wilenski, 1961), but the main point remains, that the welfare of a society depends only on consumption. In order to assure positive economic growth in the long-run, it was necessary to impose the technical assumption of non-satiability in preferences. However, this technical assumption became an undisputed matter of fact for orthodox economists: for thousands of students, the first thing that they learn in introductory classes of economics is that resources are finite, while needs are unlimited and non-satiable. After the impressive period of high rates of economic growth that followed the Second World War, other social pressing issues started to emerge; i.e., climate change, environmental issues, unequal distribution of wealth, and many others. Recent models that include these emerging issues have consistently shown that a sustainable path of economic growth only emerges by lifting the assumption of non-satiability (Copeland & Taylor, 2004; McConnell, 1997; Pastén & Figueroa, 2012; Stokey, 1998).

Moreover, when a myriad of studies showed that happiness is not necessarily correlated with material consumption (measured by GDP per capita), a new framework to understand the determinants of well-being was necessary. The subjective well-being (SWB) approach and the objective well-being (OWB) were two of these frameworks. In short, the SWB pioneered by Easterlin is devoted to the understanding of the main determinants of self-reported happiness.

The OWB, pioneered, among others by MMN, is the idea that satisfaction of needs is the means to a good life, and unlike desires, needs are universal, stable, and above all, identifiable. Moreover, MMN's theory of fundamental human needs addresses a fundamental difference between needs and their satisfiers: satisfiers are the means by which needs are satisfied (see Chapters 3 and 4 in this volume).

DOI: 10.4324/9781003381143-18

So what is the relationship of economic goods to this complex interplay of needs and satisfiers? It is perhaps the most complex question raised by the needs-based critique of conventional development and is far from being answered. In this chapter, I present a conceptual framework to integrate the neoclassical theory of preferences and MMN's Theory of Fundamental Needs. This framework provides a limited contribution towards understanding the issues involved in answering the question raised at the outset. Given the contemporaneous validity of Manfred's ideas, this is a necessary step.

Are preferences exogenous or endogenous?

Manfred's ideas are in some way related to the analytical framework of the Environmental Kuznets Curve (EKC). This empirical relationship shows that pollution increases with income up to a turning point and then starts to decrease. The idea of the EKC is in absolute contrast with the threshold hypothesis postulated by MMN stating that things get worse rather than better when income is high (see Valenzuela, 2023). Therefore, what is, analytically, the source of the difference? MMN's Theory of Fundamental Needs (Max-Neef et al., 1991) is related to the old debate started by Stigler and Becker about whether preferences (or tastes, desires) are exogenous or endogenous, i.e., if they are given or are the same across people and time.

Even though classical economics assumes that preferences are exogenous, the theoretical work shows that the EKC is incompatible with exogenous preferences,[1] and this is valid for any non-monotonic relationship between income and pollution (including MMN's threshold hypothesis), exogenous preferences give rise to monotonic relationships, endogenous preferences to nonlinear relationships such as the EKC or the threshold hypothesis. The theoretical models that explain the relationship between economic growth and the environment rest on endogenous changes either in technology or on changes in social preferences (Pastén & Figueroa, 2012). Models based on technology explain sustainable growth by the reduction of the costs of environmentally clean technologies as the economy grows. For unchanging preferences, at some point in the process of development, improving abatement technologies make the cost of cleaning the environment cheaper and therefore economic development is accompanied by better not by worse environmental quality. By contrast, if preferences – not technologies – are endogenous, it is the change in preferences between consumption and environmental quality which explain the sustainable path in the economy. At some level of income, material needs are already satisfied, and consumption is less valued in relation to non-material needs, thus, richer societies grow with clean environments because society demands it (Copeland & Taylor, 2004; McConnell, 1997; Stokey, 1998). However, modelling technologies rather than preferences is at the core of mainstream economics. Perhaps because costs and prices are intrinsic values are not subject to the subjective nature of tastes; nevertheless, it is difficult to explain why technologies improve without resorting to changing preferences that demand such improvements.

In the debate about whether preferences are exogenous or endogenous, Stigler and Becker (1977) argue that preferences are constant and immutable across individuals and time. They propose a theory, called Z theory of human behaviour. Z theory consists of the following three statements: (i) Z goods enter the utility function; (ii) the relation between physical commodities (X goods) and Z goods can be represented by a household production function; and (iii) preferences for Z goods are constant across time and people (Cowen, 1989). Stigler and Becker (1977, SB henceforth) explain their theory by the example of addictive consumption. They postulate that relying on preferences is unnecessary. For example, Z theory assumes that people listen to music because it produces enjoyment, which is valuable. Enjoyment enters directly into the utility function and is produced by a household production function made of time devoted to listening music and human capital. Music affects the stock of human capital that changes the structure of the household production function making enjoyment easier to obtain trough music. In other words, hours of listening to music affect the stock of human capital that increases the marginal productivity of music in the production of enjoyment, which makes listening to music desirable and so on. Therefore, according to SB, it is unnecessary to restore an explanation based on changes in preferences, which are assumed given and constant across people.

However, after Stigler and Becker, a myriad of studies seems to put into question the exogenous preferences theory (Hogan & Ones, 1997; McCrae & Costa, 1997; Piedmont, 1998). Today psychologists, sociologists, and neuroscientists have developed a deeper understanding of how preferences emerge, to the extent that preference-based explanations have ceased to be a 'black box'. Even accepting that there is some evidence that preferences are stable (McCrae & Costa, 1990), the view that preferences are identical is more challenging (Costa & McCrae, 1995; Johnson, 1997; Piedmont, 1998). In economics, however, exogenous preferences remain as part of the foundation of the discipline, and economic phenomena are better explained by changing prices, income, etc., than by changing behaviour. Moreover, neoclassical economists in general tend to consider the emerging field of economic behaviour as *soft science*. Exogeneity of preferences, together with the assumptions of rationality and insatiability are assumptions at the core of mainstream economics (Guillen-Royo, 2007).

Exogenous preferences and the Theory of Fundamental Needs

It may seem at odds with the line of thought of MMN that in the debate between exogenous and endogenous preferences, he meets two icons of the Chicago School, but I will argue that Z theory resembles the theory of fundamental human needs of MMN. Indeed, in both, the Z theory and MMN's Theory of Fundamental Needs, preferences (or fundamental needs), are stable, universal, and the same across individuals. Moreover, in both cases, these needs are satisfied (or intended to be) through satisfiers (or the equivalent to SB household production function). Satisfiers (similar to household production functions) may include forms of organisation, political structures, social practices, values and norms, spaces, types of behaviour and attitudes. For example, listening to music can be a satisfier of the need for enjoyment (or leisure), but also playing cards or other games, consuming drugs, etc. While the need for enjoyment is stable and constant across individuals, the form of satisfying is not. It is possible to interpret satisfiers as inputs in a household production function, like in Stigler and Becker, which helps to fulfil the common need for leisure. Is in this respect, the universality of needs and the role of satisfiers in the Theory of Fundamental Needs resembles Z theory.

However, there is one fundamental difference between the view of MMN and the conventional view based on the ideas of SB; neoclassical economics neglects to address the question of human needs but instead prefers to characterise human well-being exclusively in terms of preferences for material goods that in the market would be expressed in monetary terms. The conventional idea is very well expressed by Allen (1982):

> Economics can say much which is useful about desires, preferences and demands.... But the assertion of absolute economic need – in contrast to desire, preference and demand – is nonsense'. (p. 23)

Neoclassical economics, therefore, equates needs with subjective desires. The satisfaction of these individualistic preferences, is argued, is best achieved through the mechanism of consumer choice in open markets. This is precisely what allows theorising that well-being increases with economic consumption. However, there are several reasons to dub this assertion (Lutz & Lux, 1988; Sagoff, 1994). In the first place, it does not help us to understand why empirically consumption seems to be not the only one determinant of happiness, well-being or a life worth of living. Moreover, there are certain kinds of entities – peace, tranquillity, freedom, creativity, friendship, for example – that are not traded, and probably will never be tradable, on the market. It would surely be short-sighted to forego the possibility that some of these entities might be the object of human need.

By contrast, there is an essential distinction – present in the writings of the old philosophers like Aristotle concerned with humankind's optimal well-being – between needs (desires) which are only subjectively felt and whose satisfaction leads to momentary pleasure' and 'objectively valid needs' which are deeply ingrained in human nature and whose realisation is conducive to a life of plenitude. If this distinction is valid, it raises two important questions. Firstly, what are these 'objectively fundamental needs?' Secondly, what is the relationship between these fundamental needs to the orthodox idea in economics that needs (or more specifically wants or desires) are infinite, insatiable, and potentially expressed through the market?

Objective and subjective well-being

In the utilitarian tradition, consumption is considered either to fulfil consumers' desires or to contribute to their happiness (Sen, 1985), and consumption is thought to be related to individual well-being. Alternative approaches to well-being, such as the SWB and OWB traditions, while rejecting most of the assumptions of neoclassical economics, do not support the direct positive link between consumption and well-being.

SWB studies by analysing the correlation between income and happiness claim that income is weakly correlated with SWB. Even though people in richer countries declare themselves to be on average happier than people in poorer countries (Diener & Biswas-Diener, 2002), the causes appear not to be related to higher levels of income. Moreover, after a given level of income, economic growth seems not to be associated with increases in SWB (Diener & Biswas-Diener, 2002; Diener & Oishi, 2000; Easterlin, 1995; Frey & Stutzer, 2002). Thus, SWB's studies provide the empirical evidence against the neoclassical assumption that consumption is equivalent to well-being.

Easterlin is one of the first to notice that a happiness indicator and GDP per capita are not correlated. In what is becoming known as the *Easterly paradox* he shows that while GDP per capita is growing through the time, happiness seems to be stationary. Since Easterlin (1974), there has been an increasing literature about happiness research in the economic realm. Beginning with the relationship between income (absolute and relative) and happiness, nowadays economists are studying several other variables. Among them are age, number of kids, marital status, employment status, and inflation (Di Tella et al., 2007; Easterlin, 2001; Frey & Stutzer, 2002). The threshold hypothesis proposed by MMN draws similar conclusions. These results support the idea that income (or consumption) is not the only argument in utility functions. On the other hand, psychological science has typically conceptualised a good life in terms of either hedonic or eudaimonic well-being. In this line of research, psychological richness is another neglected aspect of what people consider a good life. Different to happy or meaningful lives, psychologically rich lives are best characterised by a variety of interesting and perspective-changing experiences. Oishi and Westgate (2022) present empirical evidence that happiness, meaning, and psychological richness are related but distinct and desirable aspects of a good life, with unique causes and correlates. In doing so, they show that a non-trivial number of people around the world report they would choose a psychologically rich life at the expense of a happy or meaningful life, and that approximately a third of them say that undoing their life's biggest regret would have made their lives psychologically richer. Furthermore, they propose that the predictors of a psychologically rich life are different from those of a happy life or a meaningful life and report evidence suggesting that people leading psychologically rich lives tend to be more curious, think more holistically, and lean more politically liberal.

Maslow and Max-Neef developed an objective theory of well-being (OWB). Maslow's pyramid is often portrayed with the most fundamental needs at the bottom (the basic or material needs), and higher order needs – with the need for self-actualisation and transcendence – at the top. Therefore, the idea is that the most basic needs must be met before they become motivated to achieve higher order needs. The most fundamental needs for Maslow are esteem, friendship and love, security, and physical needs. If these needs are not satisfied, not only physical but also psychological pain in the form of anxiety, stress, etc. may be felt.

Maslow suggests that the most basic levels of needs must first be met so that only then does the individual become focused or motivated to achieve higher order needs. Maslow coined the term 'meta motivation' which is required in those cases where motivation goes beyond reaching the satisfaction of basic needs and is in a continuous stage of searching for fulfilment. The human brain, he argues, is a complex system working in parallel implying that many different motivations in Maslow's hierarchy can occur at the same time. Rather than claiming that the individual is focused on a certain need at any given time, as conventional economics postulates, Maslow recognised the possibility that different levels of motivation could occur at any moment in the human mind but focused on identifying the basic types of motivation and the order in which they would tend to be fulfilled.

MMN on the other hand, in his theory of fundamental human needs, addresses a fundamental difference between needs and their satisfiers. Satisfiers are the means by which needs are satisfied, for example, forms of organisation, political structures, social practices, values and norms, spaces, types of behaviour and attitudes, and so on. A house can be a satisfier of the need for protection, as also a family can be so. In addition, one cannot say that a need is 'satisfied' or not. It is better to say that needs are satisfied to a greater or lesser extent.

In fact, Max-Neef distinguished five different kinds of satisfiers as follows: destroyers or violators occupy the paradoxical position of failing completely to satisfy the need towards which they are directed; pseudo-satisfiers generate a false sense of satisfaction of the need; inhibiting satisfiers satisfy one need to which they are directed but tend to inhibit the satisfaction of other needs; singular satisfiers manage to satisfy a single category of need without affecting satisfaction elsewhere; and synergistic satisfiers manage simultaneously to satisfy several different kinds of needs. This approach also allows for a much more complex and multifaceted model of development than is provided by the unidimensional concept of economic growth. Using the characterisation outlined above, the provision of welfare can be represented as the process of satisfying underlying needs. Poverty, by contrast, can be seen as the failure to satisfy needs. Therefore, there is no one single concept of poverty but a multiplicity of poverties corresponding to failures to satisfy different kinds of needs.[2] The converse of this is that it is no longer possible to expect economic growth necessarily to alleviate poverty, since poverty is not only in purely monetary terms.

Cultural change, in the context of Human Scale Development is the evolution of satisfiers, which can also be seen as individual or collective potential strengths. Fundamental human needs is a system where all fundamental human needs are interrelated and interactive. With the exception of basic needs necessary to stay alive, there is no hierarchy in the system. On the other hand, simultaneities, complementarities, and trade-offs are characteristics of the process of satisfying needs. There is no one-to-one correspondence between needs and satisfiers, they can simultaneously contribute to the satisfaction of different needs or, conversely, a need may require different satisfiers to be satisfied. The quality and intensity of the levels, and within the contexts, will depend on time, location, and circumstances. All this also means that every fundamental human need that is not sufficiently satisfied produces loss of well-being. Some examples are poverty of living (due to insufficient food), of protection (due to bad health conditions), of affection (due to involuntary emigration), of understanding (because censorship or indoctrination), of participation (because dictatorship and oppression), and of identity (due to ideological interpretation of the history).

In the following section, I present a structural framework that accepts the notion that fundamental needs are universal and stable. Moreover, fundamental needs are a target reached with low probability, but we challenge the exogenous preferences doctrine by proposing that preferences change according to the (quantitative or qualitative) distance from this target, an idea in line with MMN's theory fundamental needs. There is empirical support for this idea. For example, studies show that the needs for appreciation that can be satisfied by social relationships have an increasing negative effect on people as the difference between expectations and realities increases, but this effect is lower for old people than for young people. Here I show that if the need for appreciation does not change across people and space, when this need is totally fulfilled (the Valhalla), welfare is maximised. Moreover, social relationships increase and the distance with Valhalla decreases if labour productivity increases. However, if we lift the assumption that the need for subsistence is fixed but increasing in income, social interaction decreases, hours of work increase, and the necessity of appreciation is unsatisfactory creating a group of pathologies and giving rise to the Easterlin Paradox where material well-being increases but quality of life either decreases or remains constant.

Even though there have been attempts to integrate the perspective of fundamental needs into neoclassical economics (Baucells & Zhao, 2021; Lades, 2013; Seeley, 1992; Woersdorfer, 2010), this is the first time a compressive model of the fundamental needs theory of MMN is built.

A sketch of a model to bridge mainstream economics and MMN theory

In the model proposed and following Lades (2013) and Pastén (2023), I assume that poverty alleviation of fundamental needs is the main driver of agent's behaviour. Moreover, following MMN, individuals have nine fundamental needs that may be satiated by the technology $z_{ki}(x_1, x_2, \dots \dots x_n)$, where $x_j \epsilon (0, n)$ are the satisfiers of a given need, where for each fundamental need, the level of complete satiation is $\theta_k = 1$. Similar to Lades (2013), need deprivation is defined as the degree in which the fundamental need is not fulfilled, that is, $1 - z_{ki}(x_1, x_2, \dots\dots x_n)$ for $k = 1, \dots 9$. Total well-being for person i is a function of need deprivation.

$$U_i = U_i\left(1 - z_{1i}\left(x_1, x_2, \dots\dots x_n\right); \dots\dots\dots\dots 1 - z_{9i}\left(x_1, x_2, \dots\dots\dots x_n\right)\right)$$

with z_{ji} for $j = 1, \dots 9$ is the production structure by which the satisfiers $x_1 \dots\dots x_n$ interact (the household production function), which is culturally specified. Deprivation of need k, $1 - z_{ki}$, is an indicator of poverty not constrained to be a quantitative measure, rather it is an indicator of the degree of insufficiency to meet the fundamental needs (poverty over the nine dimensions), $\partial U / \partial z_k \geq 0$, $\partial^2 U / \partial z_k^2 < 0$, and $U_i(0) - U_i(\theta_k - z_{ki})$ are the degree of pain associated to be unable to meet fundamental needs. While the θ_k are fixed across individuals and time, satisfiers are not fixed (n can be any number and eventually infinite), and culturally determined. And not necessarily, the n satisfiers enter in each z_{ki}, and more than one satisfier may enter in more than one z_{ki}.[3]

If we think for example of consumption of material thinks as a satisfier for the basic need of subsistence, time spent in earning a salary implies less time available to the satisfaction of other fundamental needs. On the other hand, in the case of addition to music, enjoyment is satisfied through the household production function $z_k(x_1, x_2)$, where x_1 is time devoted to listening music and x_2 is human capital to listen music (knowing about progressive rock, having peers that enjoy similar type of music, and so on), an increase in human capital increases the marginal product of hours listening music if both goods are complementary. This makes it more desirable to increase time spent listening to music (this is similar to a substitution effect), on the other hand, more time listening to music decreases its marginal utility making it less valuable. Pastén (2023) shows that if human capital and time listening to music are highly complementary, and utility of enjoyment is unbounded, time devoted to it increases through time.

An example including the basic need for affection

If we assume that one form of satisfaction of material needs is through work, this also reduces time spent with family and friends, which is important for the satisfaction of affection. If working longer hours is welfare improving, then material needs is a need of first order in comparison with the need for affection. On the contrary, if actual welfare decreases, working longer hours is an inhibiting satisfier. Below, I consider three applications of the proposed model.

The effect of a raise in labour productivity

If there is a raise in labour productivity, given by an increase in wages, more time is left available to be spent with friends and less hours of work are necessary (with less material consumption) if material goods and relational goods are complementary. This effect runs again standard neoclassical economics (and explains the decreasing part of the threshold hypothesis). High complementarity, given by a low elasticity of substitution between consumption and relational goods, is equivalent to a high elasticity of marginal utility of material good (in fact higher than one), and this is equivalent to satiation in consumption, which is valid by construction if fundamental needs are exogenous. However, it is also possible to show that if people associate needs with wants or desires, and wants increase with affluence, then time spent with family decreases as income grows. According to Lades (2013), this is in fact the case under the idea of 'Keeping up with the Joneses', i.e., when a group of peers spend as a manner to signal their status (Charles et al., 2009; Heffetz, 2011; Kaus, 2013).

Cooperative versus non-cooperative behaviour

Regarding the model, it is also possible to show that working longer hours is a pseudo-satisfier if the decision-maker does not consider the external effect on social relations. Thus, this creates a negative externality in others that decreases overall well-being. This is simply because social relations are similar to a public good where the marginal benefits depend on the number of people engaged in the relationship. When the individual does not consider his effects in others, spends more time in the job and less time building significant relationships. As is well known, under certainty, cooperative solutions yield more well-being than the Nash equilibrium solution, thus working longer hours is a pseudo-satisfier.

The effect of uncertainty

It is possible to show that if there is uncertainty about the degree of commitment of others, affection deprivation increases, and this effect is overcompensated by more hours of work and more consumption. This effect relates to the concept of prudence coined by Kimball (1989) and risk aversion (Pratt, 1964). If people are prudent (given by the third derivative of the utility function in the relational good), more effort is exerted to build a relation in which outcome is uncertain. But if the agent is risk averse, putting more effort in an uncertain relationship increases the overall risk and this effect is undesirable, thus the agent prefers to devote more time working longer hours and less to building a relationship.

Conclusions

The main object of this chapter is to present the basis of a formal model to bridge mainstream economics with the Theory of Fundamental Needs of MMN. There is no doubt that the concept of fundamental needs against standard preference theory is more realistic and more adequate explaining the pressing issues of our time. However, the theory lacks a formal conceptual framework leading to a field of general and intuitive ideas disconnected between them. It is true that MMN had a rather critical attitude to formalisation in economics, but in the last years, several limitations of mainstream economics have been surpassed. By adapting economic theory and building on it rather than throwing away the whole building of knowledge new insights have appeared. A formal theoretical framework allows a better understanding of gaps, links, and so on and leads to new lines of research, theoretically, empirically, and experimentally. I do not pretend in this chapter to build the whole bridge between MMN Theory and neoclassical economics, it is a first stepping-stone and much more work is needed. Nevertheless, given the actuality of the ideas set forth by Manfred this endeavour is more than necessary.

I started this chapter by putting forward the idea that there is a similarity between Stigler and Becker the *gustibulus est non disputandum* and MMN's Theory of Fundamental Needs. In both cases, it is assumed that preferences are stable and universal and the way in which preferences are satisfied (the household production function in Stigler and Becker and the satisfier in MMN Theory of Fundamental

Needs) is different between agents. But there are differences in both frameworks, Becker and Stigler focus on market goods with given prices, while MMN focuses in the satisfaction of fundamental needs by satisfiers not necessarily expressed through prices in the market.

After a revision of the most well-known theories of subjective and OWB, I develop a simple model to adapt neoclassical theory of preferences to the ideas contained in the Theory of Fundamental Needs. The simple model accommodates several aspects of fundamental needs theory, the idea that fundamental needs are universal and stable, and the existence of satisfiers and a production structure aimed to reach the objectives of fundamental needs. In the model of the fundamental need of affection, I derive several results that are consistent with the model, i.e., increasing labour productivity decreases time devoted to fulfil material needs and increases the production of relational goods whenever material and relational goods are gross complements, thus helping to explain the disentanglement between material affluence and well-being. In addition, under the standard assumption that the elasticity of substitution is decreasing (increasing) in income, it is possible to show that the EKC (the threshold curve) arises. Because the slope of the elasticity of substitution is an empirical fact to be unveiled (perhaps by experimental economics), there is not a priori elements to disregard one or the other theory. We have also shown that under a non-cooperative Nash equilibrium, time devoted to relational goods is lower and time devoted to material goods is higher than under cooperative equilibrium. In addition, because it is well known that total well-being is higher under cooperative than under non-cooperative equilibrium, it is safe to state that working longer hours is a pseudo-satisfier in this case. Finally, we show that under uncertainty in the outcome of production of relational goods (building a relationship), time destined to working to procure material goods increases for risk-averse agents.

Notes

1 Nonlinear preferences and decreasing marginal abatement costs are other explanations. However, nonlinear preferences can be modelled as endogenous preferences (see Kahneman & Tversky, 2013), and decreasing marginal abatement costs is standard in models of endogenous technologies rather than preferences (but see Pastén & Figueroa, 2012, showing that better technologies are preferred if preferences demand them and for that an increasing valuation of the environment is required).

2 There is a broad literature in multidimensional poverty that follows this line of research. See, for example, the Oxford Poverty and Human Development Initiative (OPHI) https://ophi.org.uk. See also Alkire and Summer (2013).

3 Regarding the five types of satisfiers, it is possible to point that for a destroyer or violator $\partial z_{ki}/\partial x_j < 0$; inhibit satisfiers $\partial z_{ki}/\partial x_j > 0$ and $\partial z_{-ki}/\partial x_j < 0$; singular satisfiers $\partial z_{ki}/\partial x_j > 0$ and $\partial z_{-ki}/\partial x_j = 0$; synergetic satisfiers $\partial z_{ki}/\partial x_j > 0$ and $\partial z_{-ki}/\partial x_j > 0$. Pseudo-satisfier is more difficult to characterise but can be assumed as low efficient satisfiers that are pseudo-compensated by increasing other satisfiers.

References

Alkire, S., & Sumner, A. (2013). Multidimensional poverty and the post-2015 MDGs. *Development*, *56*(1), 46–51. https://doi.org/10.1057/dev.2013.6

Allen, W. (1982). *Midnight economist: Broadcast essays III*. International Institute for Economic Research.

Baucells, M., & Zhao, L. (2021). Goods and needs: A satiation approach. *Darden Business School Working Paper*. 2017/01 SSRN http://dx.doi.org/10.2139/ssrn.3811976

Charles, K. K., Hurst, E., & Roussanov, N. (2009). Conspicuous consumption and race. *Quarterly Journal of Economics*, *124*(2), 425–467. https://doi.org/10.1162/qjec.2009.124.2.425

Copeland, B. R., & Taylor, M. S. (2004). Trade, growth, and the environment. *Journal of Economic Literature*, *42*(1), 7–71. http://doi.org/10.1257/002205104773558047

Costa, P., & McCrae, R., (1995). Domains and facets: Hierarchical personality assessment using the revised neo personality inventory. *Journal of Personality Assessment*, 64, 21–50. https://psycnet.apa.org/doi/10.1207/s15327752jpa6401_2

Cowen, T. (1989). Are all tastes constant and identical? A critique of Stigler and Becker. *Journal of Economic Behavior & Organization*, *11*(1), 127–135. https://doi.org/10.1016/0167-2681(89)90067-X

Diener, E., & Biswas-Diener, R. (2002). Will money increase subjective well-being? A literature review and guide to needed research. *Social Indicators Research*, *57*, 119–169.

Diener, E., & Oishi, S. (2000). Money and happiness: Income and subjective well-being across nations. In E. Diener, & E. M. Suh (Eds.), *Culture and subjective well-being* (pp. 185–218). The MIT Press.

Di Tella, R., Haisken-DeNew, J. P., & MacCulloch, R. (2004). Happiness adaptation to income and to status in an individual panel. *SSRN eLibrary*. https://papers.ssrn.com/sol3/papers.cfm?abstract_id=760368

Easterlin, R. A. (1974). Does economic growth improve the human lot? In P. A. David, & M. W. Reder (Eds.), *Nations and households in economic growth: Essays in honour of moses abramovitz*. Academic Press Inc.

Easterlin, R. A. (1995). Will raising the incomes of all increase the happiness of all? *Journal of Economic Behavior and Organization*, *27*(1), 35–47. https://doi.org/10.1016/0167-2681(95)00003-B

Easterlin, R. A. (2001). Income and happiness: Towards a unified theory. *Economic Journal*, *111*(473), 465–484. https://doi.org/10.1111/1468-0297.00646

Frey, B. S., & Stutzer, A. (2002). *Happiness and economics: How the economy and institutions affect human well-being*. Princeton University Press.

Guillen-Royo, M. (2007). Well-being and consumption: Towards a theoretical approach based on human needs satisfaction. In L. Bruni & P. L. Porta (Eds.), *Handbook on the economics of happiness*, Edward Elgar Publishing, 151–169.

Heffetz, O. (2011). A test of conspicuous consumption: Visibility and income elasticities. *Review of Economics and Statistics*, *93*(4), 1101–1117. https://doi.org/10.1162/REST_a_00116

Hogan, J., & Ones, D. S. (1997). Conscientiousness and integrity at work. In R. Hogan, J. Johnson, & S. Briggs (Eds.), *Handbook of personality psychology* (pp. 849–870). Academic Press.

Johnson, J. (1997). Units of analysis for the description and explanation of personality. In R. Hogan, J. Johnson, & S. Briggs (Eds.), *Handbook of personality psychology* (pp. 73–93). Academic Press.

Kahneman, D., & Tversky, A. (2013). Prospect theory: An analysis of decision under risk. In L. C. MacLean, & W. T. Ziemba (Eds.), *Handbook of the fundamentals of financial decision making: Part I* (pp. 99–127). World Scientific Publishing Co. Pte. Ltd.

Kaldor, N. (1957). A model of economic growth. *The Economic Journal*, *67*(268), 591–624. https://doi.org/10.2307/2227704

Kaus, W. (2013). Conspicuous consumption and the race: Evidence from South Africa. *Journal of Develompent Economics*, *100*(1), 63–73. https://doi.org/10.1016/j.jdeveco.2012.07.004

Kimball, M. S. (1989). Precautionary saving in the small and in the large. *Econometrica*, *58*(1), 53–73.

Lades, L. K. (2013). Explaining shapes of Engel curves: The impact of differential satiation dynamics on consumer behavior. *Journal of Evolutionary Economics*, *23*(5), 1023–1045. https://doi.org/10.1007/s00191-013-0324-6

Lutz, M., & Lux, K. (1988). *Humanistic economics – The new challenge*. Bootstrap Press.

Max-Neef, M., Elizalde, A., & Hopenheym, M. (1991). *Human scale development. Conception, reflection and further elaboration.* Dag Hammarskjold Foundation, The Apex Press.

McConnell, K. E. (1997). Income and the demand for environmental quality. *Environment and Development Economics*, *2*(4), 383–399. https://doi.org/10.1017/S1355770X97000 20X

McCrae, R., & Costa, P. (1990). *Personality in adulthood.* Guilford Press.

McCrae, R., & Costa, P. (1997). Personality trait structure as a human universal. *American Psychologist*, *52*, 509–516. https://doi.org/10.1037//0003-066x.52.5.509

Oishi, S., & Westgate, E. C. (2022). A psychologically rich life: Beyond happiness and meaning. *Psychological Review*, *129*(4), 790. https://psycnet.apa.org/doi/10.1037/rev 0000317

Pasten, R. (2023). *The gustibus est disputandum: Building a bridge between mainstream economics and Max-Neef Theory of Fundamental Needs*. Working Paper, Universidad Austral de Chile.

Pasten, R., & Figueroa, E. (2012). The environmental Kuznets curve: A survey of the theoretical literature. *International Review of Environmental and Resource Economics*, *6*(3), 195–224.

Piedmont, R. (1998). *The revised NEO personality inventory: Clinical and research applications*. Plenum Press.

Pratt, J. W. (1964). Risk aversion in the small and in the large. *Econometrica*, *32*(1/2), 122–136. https://doi.org/10.2307/1913738

Ramsey, F. P. (1928). A mathematical theory of saving. *The Economic Journal*, *38*(152), 543–559. https://doi.org/10.2307/2224098

Sagoff, M. (1994). Should preferences count? *Land Economics*, *70*, 127–145.

Seeley, E. (1992). Human needs and consumer economics: The implications of Maslow's theory of motivation for consumer expenditure patterns. *The Journal of Socioeconomics*, *21*(4), 303–324. https://doi.org/10.1016/1053-5357(92)90002-O

Sen, A. (1985). *Commodities and capabilities*. Elsevier.

Solow, R. M. (1956). A contribution to the theory of economic growth. *The Quarterly Journal of Economics*, *70*(1), 65–94. https://doi.org/10.2307/1884513

Stigler, G. J., & Becker, G. S. (1977). De gustibus non est disputandum. *The American Economic Review*, *67*(2), 76–90.

Stokey, N. L. (1998). Are there limits to growth? *International Economic Review*, *39*(1), 1–31. https://doi.org/10.2307/2527228

Swan, T. W. (1956). Economic growth and capital accumulation. *Economic Record*, *32*(2), 334–361. https://doi.org/10.1111/j.1475-4932.1956.tb00434.x

Wilenski, H. L. (1961). The uneven distribution of leisure: The impact of economic growth on free time. *Social Problems*, *9(1)*, 32–55. https://doi.org/10.2307/799420
Woersdorfer, J. S. (2010). Consumer needs and their satiation properties as drivers of the rebound effect. The case of energy efficient washing machines. *Papers on Economics & Evolution,* 2010–16 https://nbn-resolving.org/urn:nbn:de:gbv:27-20110628-150519-4

16 Manfred Max-Neef and heterodox economics

Influences, and links with Piero Sraffa

Jean Pierre Doussoulin and Yoann Verger

Introduction

Manfred Max-Neef made many contributions to economic discussion; through the discussion of transdisciplinary analysis of economic development (Max-Neef, 2005), the fundamentals of the 'barefoot economy' adapted to poor and developing countries (Max-Neef, 1982), and his thinking on economic growth and quality of life proposed by the 'threshold hypothesis' (Max-Neef, 1995). His seminal work was *Human Scale Development* (Max-Neef, 1991; Max-Neef et al., 1986), which proposed a critique of the current economic development model.

Manfred Max-Neef's work was highly original in the economic sphere. His rejection of economic theory leads him to develop a redefinition of what the aim of science, development politics and economics should be. He introduced the idea that efficiency can be achieved through 'organised smallness', promoted 'self-reliance' for people as well as states and an 'ecological humanism'. These 'barefoot economics' are directed towards the satisfaction of human needs and to achieve a *Human Scale Development*.

His project was new and revolutionary, it rose from a rejection of both mainstream and heterodox economic theory. This chapter will present the reasons why Max-Neef was critical of heterodox theories, discuss his rationale and identify whether some bridges could be built between the two.

The heterodox theories considered here are Marxist, Keynesianism and post-Keynesianism, neo-Austrian and ecological economics. While often highly critical of heterodox economics, Manfred Max-Neef made connections with some heterodox theories. We assess whether more fruitful relations can be made, especially with the work of Piero Sraffa.

In the second section, we will present Max-Neef's key contributions to economics. In the third section, we will show the different criticisms Max-Neef raised against heterodox economics. In the fourth section, we will see the connections which might be established between Max-Neef and heterodox theories. And finally, in the fifth section, we will focus on the possible links with Sraffa that can be highlighted.

DOI: 10.4324/9781003381143-19

Max-Neef's key contributions to economics

For Max-Neef, the human development model is based on a development that takes into account the satisfaction of fundamental human needs, the generation of levels of self-dependence and in the articulation between people and nature using levels of technology. The achievement of higher levels of well-being depends fundamentally on the management of the common good by humans. To move from the person as an object to a person as a subject of transformation, a paradigm shift in terms of scale is necessary. This idea responds to the specific context in which Max-Neef's *Human Scale Development* book (Max-Neef, 1991; Max-Neef et al., 1986) was written. This was a watershed moment in the heterodox Latin American economy's thinking and might also represent the start of a specific vision of economic and human progress, as well as the notion of sustainability. It raises, despite its simplicity, issues that are revolutionary and based on a critical view of the prevailing theories of economic growth (Cruz et al., 2009). Within these ideas is a 'humanistic vision'; putting the human being at the centre and analysing the satisfaction of their needs based on the notion of scale.

The notion of scale has been applied in the dimensions of human development and polycentrism by Elinor Ostrom and colleagues (Gibson et al., 2000; Ostrom, 1998). Authors such as Daly, Van den Bergh and Martinez-Alier from ecological economics have studied the relationship between scale and sustainable development (Daly, 2007; Van den Bergh, 2001) and in the notion of scale and pollution (Muradian et al., 2002). Annis (1987) made an application of the notion of small-scale development in Latin America.

Max-Neef also develops this notion in his book written in Spanish *The Lost Dimension* (Max-Neef, 2007); in which he reflects on the impossibility of unlimited human growth, taking as an example the growth of large cities as large systems. This analysis makes a dissociation between the vital space of people and the space that we build as societies. This difficulty of scale observation might in fact be related to Jurgen Habermas' dimension of the world of living (Baxter, 1987).

It is relevant to understand the context from which this theory comes. Max-Neef, after working for several years in development cooperation in Latin America, made a proposal for alternative models for development. Max-Neef travelled to Sweden to write his work on these alternative development models. This first book 'looked from the outside in' on this development and questioned from practice the way in which economists have constructed their way of seeing development (Max-Neef, 1982). The process of building an alternative paradigm for development was carried out in a Latin American context where there is an exhaustion of development models, the establishment of neoliberalism and more monetarist views. In this sense, Chile (Max-Neef's home country) was part of the experiment of the neoliberal installation. In this vision, the way in which peripheral countries can achieve development is questioned. In this institutional and geopolitical context, Max-Neef and his colleagues wrote *Human Scale Development* (Max-Neef, 1991; Max-Neef et al., 1986).

Some of the intellectual confluences that Max-Neef used to design his theory consider a barefoot economy. In this, all the 'invisible' are visible, those that are not being accounted for in the GDP, such as domestic work at home. This contribution makes visible the contribution of all those invisible actors to macro-economic theory, which represent a sample of actors and leaderships, not explicitly contained in the prevailing economic theory. This is part of the discussion of the scale of development and that 'small is beautiful' (Schumacher, 1973). This is also part of the dimension of space on a human scale proposed by Le Corbusier and reworked by Heidi Weber (Weber, 2008). This notion of scale is related to the limits of economic growth proposed by the Club of Rome (Meadows et al., 1972). Meadows's book condenses the critique of productivism as limitless and the search for a model that anticipates the depletion of resources. It proposes that those resources that were defined as unlimited will no longer be proposing planetary and territorial consequences. The foundation of the idea of sustainability begins in part of this critical view of resource depletion and was formally incorporated into modelling after the oil crisis of the 1970s (Machado et al., 2020). The analysis questions the development model based on cheap oil; arguing that resources will not be unlimited and that they depend on geopolitical situations which the centres of production and consumption will not be able to manage.

The theory of development on a *human scale* is built from the dialogues carried out by Max-Neef, Antonio Elizalde and Martín Hopenhayn amongst others at the CEPAUR centre (Max-Neef et al., 1986). These dialogues catalysed the proposition of a paradigm shift in development. In this sense, development on a human scale is a conceptual model of reality, which is not exempt from a strong normative vision of how it should be.

Why Max-Neef was critical of heterodox theories

For Max-Neef, heterodox economists suffer partly from the same kind of problem as orthodox economists. First, of a language that can be too technical and closed to itself, with no connection with the real world. Second, a desire to solve the problems affecting humanity from above, with top-down solutions. Third, an admiration for gigantism and big solutions. Fourth, an obsession with measurements and quantifiers. Fifth, a mechanistic approach to economic problems with almost no reference to the environment, and sixth, a bias towards economic problems of the North – overlooking what happens in the South.

For instance, because stagflation never occurs in the North, this concept was considered impossible:

> in all economic theories, beginning with Cantillon and Adam Smith and continuing with Ricardo, Marx and all the way through Keynes and Phillips (with his beautiful curves), something identified in the modern jargon as stagflation (inflation with growing unemployment) simply could not occur.
>
> (Max-Neef, 1991, p. 98)

But it was very common in the South to have stagflation. The fact that stagflation was not possible in economic theories was then due to the blindness concerning economic problems of the South:

> we may describe stagflation as a situation characterized by high and rising prices together with insufficient jobs. This is surprising, because that is precisely one of the characteristics that has prevailed in more countries. With Northern thinking (and with this kind by Southern economists as well), something like stagflation could only be discovered and so acquire legitimate existence if, and only if, it appeared in the North. The fact that it was to be found everywhere in the South simply went unnoticed. After all, a poor country that is expensive for its own inhabitants is normally dismissed as very inexpensive by all its Northern visitors. Cases like this – and there are many more – should invite deep critical reflection.
>
> (Max-Neef, 1991, pp. 98–99)

But some heterodox theories are criticised as such. Marx and Trotsky are criticised because they point towards growth and technology as a solution for the economic problems, overlooking the environmental question:

> The thinking of Marx (1818–1883) reflects the belief in the possibilities of unlimited growth and of the victory of mankind over nature, aided and influenced by a fully realized and developed technology. For Trotsky (1879–1940) it is technology, among other things, that will make it possible for socialist man to become 'superman', capable of moving mountains and altering his surroundings as he pleases.
>
> (Max-Neef, 1982, pp. 40–41)

Their modelling is also criticised because they follow the way Ricardo described nature, i.e. only through the notion of land:

> The relationship established by these models with the environment is confined to David Ricardo's (1772–1823) notion of land, which is no more than a synonym for space, immune to any qualitative change. 'Marx's diagrams of economic reproduction do not include even this colourless coordinate'.
>
> (Max-Neef, 1982, p. 41)

Developmentalism is also criticised. Its application to Latin America failed because concepts such as 'development' come from ideologies that do not consider the relation with the environment, as well as the social crisis that was prevalent since the mid-1970s. In this context, Max-Neef studies local solutions to development:

> The possibilities for the poor to improve their living conditions as a consequence of the nationally designed development strategies, has proved, in the great majority of cases, to be nil. The only – alarmingly few – exceptions to

> be found are in countries where regional and local autonomies have really been enhanced.
>
> (Max-Neef, 1982, p. 116)

> What we have now is a language based on the enthusiasm of unlimited economic growth and expansion faced with a reality of social and ecological collapse.
>
> (Max-Neef, 1991, p. 109)

Finally, Max-Neef criticises the fact that all different economic theories have not been able to overcome the distinction between a micro and a macro level. The classical school, as well as the neoclassical school and the neo-Austrian school, focuses on the micro level, whereas Keynesianism focuses on the macro level, but no economic theory successfully describes the articulation between the two:

> The first 'world view' of economics as a discipline as such – mercantilism – was a macroeconomic view. The aftermath of the crisis of mercantilism determined that the three ensuing economic revolutions, represented in succession by the physiocrats, the classical school and the neo-classical school, should correspond to micro-economic views, the differences among them being in the main determined by diverging criteria as to the notion of value. [...] The fourth revolution – Keynesianism – again envisaged economics as macroeconomics. [...] post-Keynesians, neo-Keynesians and present-day monetarists, no matter how much they endeavour to rid themselves of their immediate past, are still dwelling in the macro-economic abode that Keynes erected. [...] The problem of micro-macro articulation, unresolved by economic theory, has therefore not met with a visible solution in development processes either.
>
> (Max-Neef, 1991, pp. 87–88)

But as we will see in the next section, Manfred Max-Neef was not rejecting all heterodox theories at once. He used their insights to develop his own theory, such as the articulation between the micro and the macro level, where he builds partly upon the neo-Austrian School:

> The economists from the neo Austrian School, committed to 'methodological individualism,' hold that every type of behaviour can only be understood in individual terms and that, consequently, there are no collective entities, such as communities, societies and governments, the attributes of which are different from those of individuals. [...] Without purporting to come up with an eclectic solution, it is necessary to acknowledge, in our opinion, that there exist sound and persuasive elements in the [...] arguments that we have chosen as extreme examples. It seems sensible to admit, on the one hand, that observable and understandable behaviour does in fact occur at the level of the individual, that is to say, at the micro-level.
>
> (Max-Neef, 1991, pp. 88–89)

Bridges that could be built with heterodox theories

Many bridges can still be built between Max-Neef and traditional or current heterodox theories. Manfred himself showed his debt to some of them, such as the work of economists who made 'systematic studies of poverty', 'Oscar Lewis in Mexico and Gunnar Myrdal in Asia' (Max-Neef, 1982, p. 3). This section reviews some of these bridges.

Keynes

The goal of Keynes was to provide an economic theory of macro-economic relationships amongst employment, money and interest rates. The importance of Keynes in the theory of Max-Neef's economic thought is acknowledged by Max-Neef: 'Keynesianism [...] gave rise, among many other contributions which are difficult to discard, to the notion of aggregate indicators' (Max-Neef, 1991, p. 88).

But Max-Neef was not a macro-economic theoretician. He was looking for practical answers to solve real economic problems at the local level. Hence, he did not use Keynes' theory in his writings. On the other hand, he borrowed from Keynes his detachment and ironic glance on the world of the economists. For instance, he was sympathetic to 'Lord Keynes warning to the effect that the importance of economic problems should not be over-estimated with the result that matters of higher and more permanent significance are sacrificed to its supposed necessities' (Max-Neef, 1982, p. 19).

What could be built between Keynes and Max-Neef? Not much, but the notion that the aggregation of individual actions can have unintended effects is shared between both, so the study of this articulation between the micro and the macro level can be investigated.

Critical realism, genetic structuralism, constructivism, old institutionalism

Critical realism is a philosophic research programme mainly directed by Tony Lawson (see, for instance, Lawson, 2003), which aims to redefine the ontology of the social world so that social sciences can use appropriate tools to analyse and understand social phenomena. Typically, it rejects the use of mathematical tools used to describe equilibrium solutions of neoclassical models because the social world is not composed of closed systems. On the contrary, social reality is open, which means that not all events are predictable. And it is also structured, which means that there exist forces that can explain the events actually happening in the social reality.

Max-Neef was also certain that the social reality is such that mechanical reasoning should be avoided:

> The impossibility of making mechanical predictions about human systems compels us to devote energy to dealing with such notions [such as] instability, chance, uncertainty, choice, thresholds of different types and catastrophes.
> (Max-Neef, 1991, pp. 89–90)

And, like critical realism, he tried to rebuild economics by starting to find new foundations:

> The integral problematic displayed before us, like a fan which upon opening reveals more and more surprises because of all the novelty it holds, is not only a crisis as such, but, in addition, calls for equally integral reformulations. The 'crisis of the foundations' which, at the beginning of the century, brought down a good part of classical mathematics and mechanics, takes its turn, at the end of the century, at toppling the economic theories.
>
> (Max-Neef, 1982, p. 37)

He was very sensitive to social complexity, to historical processes and structures that shape social reality. Hence his theory of needs, satisfiers and economic goods was not disconnected from the society at large, its structure and its history:

> In a critical theory of society, it is not sufficient to specify the predominant satisfiers and economic goods produced within that society. They must be understood as products which are the result of historical factors and, consequently, liable to change. Thus, it is necessary to retrace the process of reflection and creation that conditions the interaction between needs, satisfiers and economic goods.
>
> (Max-Neef, 1991, p. 26)

In this way, his theory can be integrated into the critical realism programme of research. Links with the genetic structuralism of Bourdieu or with the constructivism of Piaget can also be attempted, as well as with the old institutionalism of Thorstein Veblen. Indeed, while looking at the reasons why economic goods, needs and satisfiers change over time and space, Max-Neef explains these changes by saying that 'they are modified according to episodic rhythms (vogues, fashions) and diversify according to cultures and, within those cultures, according to social strata' (Max-Neef, 1991, p. 28). Hence the study of their appearance, of the domination of certain needs or satisfiers or economic goods upon others can be investigated following these kind of theories.

Marx

Marx developed a famous analysis of the social world as the result of the class conflict. Max-Neef was not using the economic model developed by Marx, and was not referring to himself as a Marxist, but very often uses Marx's notions and descriptions of society, which shows that he considered Marx and the Marxist literature. Notions such as exploitation, capitalism, alienation, accumulation and superstructure can be found in Max-Neef. He clearly describes the relations between social groups as conflicting ones, and his engagement to make visible the invisible parallel Marx's political writings aiming at the emancipation of the working class:

> The invisible sectors are marked by precarious living and working conditions, the consequences of a permanent lack of security imposed by the

> competitive market that creates disadvantages for these sectors where productivity is low. All this is aggravated by the fact that the invisible world becomes very useful to a capitalism which is unable to generate sufficient jobs in the formal economy.
>
> (Max-Neef, 1991, p. 66)

Finally, Max-Neef explicitly accepts Marx's heritage when working on his theory of needs: 'To approach the human being through needs enables us to build a bridge between a philosophical anthropology and a political option; this appears to have been the motivation behind the intellectual efforts of, for example, Karl Marx and Abraham Maslow' (Max-Neef, 1991, p. 24). So his theory seems to be the continuation of Marx's analysis of the society.

However, as we have seen earlier, Max-Neef was critical of the industrial-oriented solutions developed by Marx (and Trotsky), and upon the fact that the environment was not represented in Marx's analyses. On this last point, the Marxist literature since the 1990s attempted to show that Marx was actually an ecologist. For instance, Paul Burkett (1999) or John Bellamy Foster (2000) developed a reinterpretation of Marx's and Engels' writings, showing that they were very aware of the relationships between nature and the production of wealth, and the risk that this relationship could be destroyed by industrial development. Max-Neef himself acknowledged that at least Engels 'in his capacity as a more complete scientist than his colleagues, gives warning on the dangers involved in the indiscriminate conquest of nature' (Max-Neef, 1982, p. 41).

So Max-Neef follows the Marxist traditions and very interesting developments can be made by taking the two theoretical frameworks together.

Critical history and geography

Critical historical studies and critical geography attempted to develop analysis which reveals how exploitation and domination were constructed historically in various parts of the world. The history of colonisation is highlighted, and the dependence between the different countries and the exploitation of some regions by other regions are described. Theories of centre-periphery of the world economy and of unequal exchanges derive from this new way of undertaking history and geography. Famous authors are Arghiri Emmanuel (1972), Immanuel Wallerstein (1979) and Samir Amin (1976).

Max-Neef was aware of this literature and was eager to integrate it into his analysis of the economic, social and ecological situation in Latin America. For him, economics should have a sense of history and he was aware that 'some modern historical research is taking a sociological turn', i.e. trying to make visible the invisible to classical history. His analysis of the relations between the United States and the rest of the world, and of the constraints imposed on Latin American countries by the International Monetary Fund and the Northern countries follow these kinds of research. For instance, reflecting on the dependence that should be broken between industrial countries and Latin America, Max-Neef was writing this:

> To break away from imitative consumption patterns not only frees us from the spell of cultural dependence, but also creates the conditions for a more efficient use of the resources generated in the periphery. It further lessens the negative impact of protectionist policies that industrial countries put into practice to shelter their own products. The various forms of dependence reinforce one another. The different domains of dependence – economic, financial, technological, cultural, and political – cannot be viewed in isolation from one another, since the power of one is derived from the support it receives from the other domains.
>
> (Max-Neef, 1991, p. 56)

His whole theory of Human Scale Development and of needs is based on the idea that dependence on other countries, and even other regions of a same country, should be avoided:

> By lessening economic dependence, subsistence is safeguarded, since economic fluctuations (recessions, depressions) cause greater damage when a centre-periphery structure prevails.
>
> (Max-Neef, 1991, p. 65)

But to construct independent local spaces requires time and policies that are also concerning the large-scale:

> Alternative policies central to Human Scale Development are needed in order to empower social actors to initiate autonomous, self-sustaining and harmonious development in the different domains. This does not imply, of course, that Human Scale Development is solely concerned with small social and physical spaces. The impact of the international recession on Latin American countries and the structural imbalances of peripheral capitalism make it obvious that development in local spaces is inadequate unless it is complemented by global policies to alleviate the precarious conditions of the dispossessed masses.
>
> (Max-Neef, 1991, p. 63)

Following this last idea that Human Scale Development should also be concerned with the development of policies at the level of a country, links between Max-Neef and French regulation school, or with history of economic facts made by Piketty, can be attempted. These are schools or researchers that are concerned with macroeconomic policies, with an historical stance. Fruitful developments can thus be made.

Ecological economics

Røpke (2004) traces back the theoretical origins of ecological economics as a field of research to the physiocrats, who first saw the link between land production and economic production, and to the development of thermodynamics in the middle of 19th century, which allows economic processes to be described in a physical way, as transfers of energy and matter. One of the main contributors to the development of economics as a part thermodynamic science is Georgescu-Roegen (1971), but other authors, such as chemical researchers Soddy (1926) and Ostwald (1908), also tried to establish a link between physical and social sciences. This naturalisation of economic processes expresses one of the core beliefs of ecological economics (Røpke, 2005), which is that economy and the production of economic value cannot be separated from its physical natural basis:

> The basic observation in ecological economics is banal and difficult to disagree with: the human economy is embedded in nature, and economic processes are also always natural processes in the sense that they can be seen as biological, physical and chemical processes and transformations.
>
> (Ropke, 2004)

This echoes Max-Neef's theoretical point of view. For him:

> Humans, who may conceivably abstract themselves from technology to a large degree in order to live, cannot, however, disengage themselves from nature. Nature, however, needs neither one nor the other to fulfil its evolutionary program. Such an organic hierarchy should not be broken, if it is to evolve under conditions of dynamic equilibrium. It requires a form of integration in which the rules of interdependence have primacy over those of competition.
>
> (Max-Neef, 1982, p. 35)

For Max-Neef, humans should integrate nature and should develop a form of humility in front of this fact that our link with nature is a link of dependence. He cites John Stuart Mill as one of the first to develop the idea of a controlled growth:

> John Stuart Mill (1806–1873), a little bit more than a century after the death of Locke, stated his concern about the damage done by man to nature, and became sceptical of the advantages of indefinite growth of production and population as advocated by liberalism.
>
> (Max-Neef, 1982, p. 40)

He himself was sceptical on the advantages of modern technologies (Max-Neef, 1991, p. 58).

Furthermore, his 'threshold hypothesis', i.e., that growth does not improve well-being above a certain level, makes his theory possibly open to a connection with degrowth theory of Georgescu-Roegen or Herman Daly, or low-growth analyses developed by Timothy Jackson (2009) (see Chapters 8 and 13 in this volume).

Sraffa and Max-Neef: A case study

Piero Sraffa could be considered an unusual heterodox economist: while he did not write extensively, his work had a major impact on economic and philosophic research. In 1925, he published an article in which he criticised partial equilibrium theory. Following this, the neoclassical theory had to be abandoned in this field of research and turned into general equilibrium analyses (Sraffa, 1926, 1925). His controversy with Hayek made the latter abandon the field of the theory of value and concentrated on the philosophy of society (Keynes, 1931; Sraffa, 1932a, 1932b; von Hayek, 1932). His interaction with Wittgenstein generated a turn from formal to anthropological analyses for the philosopher. And the publication of his only book in 1960 had a major impact on the theory of distribution and capital (Sraffa, 1960).

Despite the fact that Max-Neef and Sraffa are revolutionary in the history of economic theory, and despite the fact that their legacy is critical to the contemporary economy's development, their works are scarcely taught in undergraduate courses in economics. These are often relegated to specialised master's or doctorate courses and are not part of the baggage that an economist should handle when leaving college. Hence, we find it interesting to find out if there can be some kind of connection between Sraffa and Max-Neef, following what we have learned in the previous section.

Sraffa was a friend of Keynes, but he borrowed little from him, and as we have seen, Max-Neef did likewise.

Sraffa developed a theory of value which is an accounting theory, i.e. it allows someone to find the prices just by looking at what has been exchanged in the market during the previous year, at the methods of production and at the level of the wages or of the rate of profits. It is not a theory which allows mechanical predictions: it is concerned with what just happened. Hence, it can be integrated into the critical realism research programme. Furthermore, the study of the reason for exchanges and the production of luxury goods instead of basic goods can be studied, following for instance insights from Bourdieu or Veblen.

Sraffa was a close friend of Gramsci, he wrote some articles in the journal of the Italian communist party and he was an expert of Marx's theory of value. His own theory of value can be understood as a solution for the Marxist problem of the transformation of labour values into prices.

However, his theory has no connection with critical history and geography, although one can study how the distribution of the surplus between profits and wages has evolved through time and in different regions of the world.

Finally, Sraffa seems to have little to share with Ecological Economics. But as his theory of value is amongst the rare ones that can be integrated within a non-neoclassical economic framework, his work is often cited in the journal Ecological Economics (Verger, 2016). His idea of a cycle of production, the way he uses input-output matrices and his work on the rent on natural resources, which can be interpreted as the result of a political choice, make his work the source of many inspirations for ecological economics researchers.

We may extend Max-Neef and Sraffa's legacy to new topics of study, such as environmental economics and the issues of environmental care, as well as man's integration as a member of the environment or as a productive component and his transcendence.

In this sense, Patterson (2021) analysed the notion of renewable and non-renewable resources using Sraffa's theory of value and Verger (2017) introduced the notion of circularity through strong sustainability using Sraffa's theory. For his part, Max-Neef proposed that we are heading for a collision if we continue to use the current production system (Max-Neef, 2010). Taking this context into account, the circular economy provides an alternative response to a dominant paradigm, although this virtuous solution can also become an incentive to continue using cheap nature (Doussoulin, 2020).

In industrial processes, the dominant paradigm is to take resources from nature, produce items and then leave them in the trash. In circular economic thinking, it is possible to reuse these wastes. These wastes are not final waste, but rather intermediate products of a production that has not yet finished and that can follow a virtuous loop logic.

The vision of Jason Moore argues that we can neglect the environment to embrace the crisis of natural resource capitalism (Moore, 2015). In this approach, we can deconstruct this circularity into four low-cost inputs: labour, food, energy and raw materials. Existing value relationships in the Sraffian sense are co-produced through a mechanical mechanism that relates humans who can be considered entities outside of nature or entities that are part of nature through a dualistic vision (Juniper, 2021). Therefore, the question is, how we consider the human. This can be ecological nature or extra-human nature. The decisive question, therefore, ignites the relationships that envelop and unfold the successive configurations of human and extra-human nature, symbolically enabled, and materially realised, throughout the long duration of the modern world-system.

The mainstream view of the circular economy only analyses the flow of raw materials and sometimes the creation of energy through waste-to-energy (Adeleke et al., 2021) and the reuse of food (Ada et al., 2021), but in almost no cases the circular flow of work. Analysing only the creation or destruction of jobs in countries through the implementation of laws that support the circular economy (Chateau & Mavroeidi, 2020), we believe that the analysis should go a little further, including the circular flow in the labour economy in the Marxist sense. In this flow, the worker, after each shift, returns home to replace his capital. This flow is aligned with the Marxist sense and can also be classified as the recycling of a productive resource if it is considered a standard commodity in the Sraffa sense, which belongs to the economic system or can be considered external to the system. In this case, we do not take care of it 'depreciation' and therefore it is a type of 'outdated junk' that we have to pay for someone to take care of. The circular economy in this sense could reuse this 'obsolete human waste' by including it in these circular production systems where they can contribute from their life experience.

From a point of view of Max-Neef's theory of needs, this vision of circularity of Jason Moore's 'Four Cheap' would allow it to vary, referring to the need for 'transcendence' in the Max-Neef sense. This broadening of the need for transcendence would cause a 'second life' through reuse or reuse of human beings as productive resources or as part of a community. Clube and Tennant (2020) analysed the relevance of the analysis of the circular economy using the Max-Neef needs matrix; therefore, it would be interesting to deepen the analysis of the need for transcendence of work as one of the 'Four Cheap' of Moore.

So Max-Neef and Sraffa have a lot to share, and their theories, while different, do not contradict themselves. One could try then, through this proximity to develop a heterodox research programme. For instance, Nuno Martins' (2016) attempt to link Sraffa's theory with the capability theory of Sen and Nussbaum. One could investigate how a link can be made between this theory and Max-Neef's theory of fundamental needs, satisfiers and economic goods.

Furthermore, the investigation of the notion of surplus, developed by Sraffa, can help to shed light on some of the developments of Max-Neef, and especially his reflection on the accumulation process and the politics of the distribution of the surplus:

> In contrast with the prevailing economic rationale, Human Scale Development – focused on encouraging self-reliance within the different spaces and domains – does not consider accumulation as an end in itself, or as a panacea that cures all the ills of Third World countries. Although it in no sense minimizes the importance of generating surpluses, its emphasis is on the consolidation of groups, communities and organizations capable of forging self-reliance. Through its expansion and articulation from the micro-spaces to national settings, economic accumulation can eventually help to progressively satisfy the fundamental human needs of people. The capacity of the different groups and individuals to decide how to use and allocate their own resources will ensure a use of surpluses that is neither discriminatory nor restrictive.
>
> (Max-Neef, 1991, p. 62)

Conclusion

We have discussed the interaction between Max-Neef and Sraffa. We are confident that numerous theoretical bridges have been built between these two knowledge providers. Sometimes they are avant-garde, and other times they are economic visionaries.

As we saw in this chapter, Max-Neef and Sraffa have a lot in common, and their ideas, while quite distinct, do not contradict one other. As a result, we believe it would be fascinating to attempt to make use of this proximity in a future paper and the building of a heterodox research programme.

We believe it would be useful to have contributions from other mainstream and heterodox economists in this discussion. As a result, we welcome Marx, Keynes, critical realism critics, genetic structuralism, constructivism, old institutionalism and, of course, the ecological economics debate to the table.

References

Ada, N., Kazancoglu, Y., Sezer, M. D., Ede-Senturk, C., Ozer, I., & Ram, M. (2021). Analyzing barriers of circular food supply chains and proposing industry 4.0 solutions. *Sustainability (Switzerland)*, *13*. https://doi.org/10.3390/su13126812

Adeleke, O., Akinlabi, S. A., Jen, T. C., & Dunmade, I. (2021). Sustainable utilization of energy from waste: A review of potentials and challenges of waste-to-energy in South Africa. *International Journal of Green Energy*, *18*(14), 1550–1564. https://doi.org/10.1080/15435075.2021.1914629

Amin, S. (1976). *Unequal development: An essay on the social formations of peripheral capitalism*. Monthly Review Press.

Annis, S. (1987). Can small-scale development be a large-scale policy? The case of Latin America. *World Development*, *15*, 129–134. https://doi.org/10.1016/0305-750X(87)90151-3

Baxter, H. (1987). System and life-world in Habermas's "Theory of communicative action". *Theory and Society*, *16*(1), 39–86. https://www.jstor.org/stable/657078

Burkett, P. (1999). *Marx and nature: A red and green perspective*. Springer. https://doi.org/10.1057/9780312299651

Chateau, J., & Mavroeidi, E. (2020). The jobs potential of a transition towards a resource efficient and circular economy. *OECD Environment Working Papers*. https://doi.org/10.1787/28e768df-en

Clube, R. K. M., & Tennant, M. (2020). The circular economy and human needs satisfaction: Promising the radical, delivering the familiar. *Ecological Economics*, *177*. https://doi.org/10.1016/j.ecolecon.2020.106772

Cruz, I., Stahel, A., & Max-Neef, M. (2009). Towards a systemic development approach: Building on the human-scale development paradigm. *Ecological Economics*, *68*, 2021–2030. https://doi.org/10.1016/j.ecolecon.2009.02.004

Daly, H. E. (2007). *Ecological economics and sustainable development*. Edward Elgar Publishing.

Doussoulin, J. P. (2020). A paradigm of the circular economy: The end of cheap nature? *Energy, Ecology and Environment*, *5*, 359–368. https://doi.org/10.1007/s40974-019-00145-2

Emmanuel, A. (1972). *Unequal exchange: A study of the imperialism of trade*. Monthly Review Press.

Foster, J. B. (2000). *Marx's ecology: Materialism and nature*. Monthly Review Press.

Georgescu-Roegen, N. (1971). *The entropy law and the economic process*. Harvard University Press.

Gibson, C. C., Ostrom, E., & Ahn, T.-K. (2000). The concept of scale and the human dimensions of global change: A survey. *Ecological Economics*, *32*, 217–239. https://doi.org/10.1016/S0921-8009(99)00092-0

Jackson, T. (2009). *Prosperity without growth?* Sustainable Development Commission.

Juniper, J. (2021). Degrowth and full employment: A modern monetary theory perspective. *Journal of Resilient Economies* (ISSN: 2653-1917), *1*(1). https://doi.org/10.25120/jre.1.1.2021.3831

Keynes, J. M. (1931). The pure theory of money. A reply to Dr. Hayek. *Economica*, *34*, 387–397.

Lawson, T. (2003). *Reorienting economics*. Routledge. https://doi.org/10.4324/9780203929964

Machado, P. G., Mouette, D., Rathmann, R., dos Santos, E., & Peyerl, D. (2020). Is energy planning moving towards sustainable development? A review of energy systems modeling and their focus on sustainability. In W. Leal Filho, P. Borges de Brito, & F. Frankenberger (Eds.), *International business, trade, and institutional sustainability* (pp. 629–644). Springer. https://doi.org/10.1007/978-3-030-26759-9_36

Martins, N. O. (2016). Ecosystems, strong sustainability and the classical circular economy. *Ecological Economics*, *129*, 32–39. https://doi.org/10.1016/j.ecolecon.2016.06.003

Max-Neef, M. A. (1982). *From the outside looking in: Experiences in 'barefoot economics'*. Zed Books Ltd.

Max-Neef, M. A. (1991). *Human scale development: Conception, application, and further reflections*. The Apex Press.

Max-Neef, M. (1995). Economic growth and quality of life: A threshold hypothesis. *Ecological Economics*, *15*, 115–118. https://doi.org/10.1016/0921-8009(95)00064-X

Max-Neef, M. A. (2005). Foundations of transdisciplinarity. *Ecological Economics*, *53*, 5–16. https://doi.org/10.1016/j.ecolecon.2005.01.014

Max-Neef, M. A. (2007). *La dimensión perdida: La deshumanización del gigantismo*. Icaria Editorial.

Max-Neef, M. A. (2010). The world on a collision course and the need for a new economy. *Ambio*, *39*, 200–210. https://doi.org/10.1007/s13280-010-0028-1

Max-Neef, M. A., Elizalde, A., & Hopenhayn, M. (1986). *Desarrollo a Escala Humana. Una Opción para el Futuro*. CEPAUR, Fundación Dag Hammarskjöld.

Meadows, D. H., Randers, J., & Meadows, D. L. (1972). *The limits to growth*. Yale University Press.

Moore, J. (2015). *Capitalism in the web of life: Ecology and the accumulation of capital*. Verso Books.

Muradian, R., O'Connor, M., & Martinez-Alier, J. (2002). Embodied pollution in trade: Estimating the "environmental load displacement" of industrialised countries. *Ecological Economics*, *41*, 51–67. https://doi.org/10.1016/S0921-8009(01)00281-6

Ostrom, E. (1998). Scales, polycentricity, and incentives: Designing complexity to govern complexity. In D. Lakshman, L. D. Guruswamy, & J. A. McNeely (Eds.), *Protection of global biodiversity: Converging strategies* (pp. 149–167). Duke University Press.

Ostwald, W. (1908). *Die Energie*. J. A. Barth.

Patterson, M. G. (2021). Reflection on "Sraffa and the revenue of the owner of nonrenewable natural resources: A note on the literature". In A. Sinha (Ed.), *A reflection on Sraffa's revolution in economic theory* (pp. 550–557). Palgrave Macmillan.

Røpke, I. (2004). The early history of modern ecological economics. *Ecological Economics*, *50*, 293–314. https://doi.org/10.1016/j.ecolecon.2004.02.012

Røpke, I. (2005). Trends in the development of ecological economics from the late 1980s to the early 2000s. *Ecological Economics*, *55*, 262–290. https://doi.org/10.1016/j.ecolecon.2004.10.010

Schumacher, E. F. (1973). *Small is beautiful: Economics as if people mattered*. Blond & Briggs.

Soddy, F. (1926). *Wealth, virtual wealth, and debt: The solution of the economic paradox*. Allen & Unwin.

Sraffa, P. (1925). Sulle relazioni fra costo e quantità prodotta. *Annali di Economia*, *2*, 277–328. https://www.jstor.org/stable/45332010

Sraffa, P. (1926). The laws of returns under competitive conditions. *The Economic Journal*, *36*, 535–550. https://doi.org/10.2307/2959866

Sraffa, P. (1932a). Dr. Hayek on money and capital. *The Economic Journal*, *42*, 42–53. https://doi.org/10.2307/2223822

Sraffa, P. (1932b). [Money and capital]: A rejoinder. *The Economic Journal*, *42*, 249–251. https://doi.org/10.2307/2223735

Sraffa, P. (1960). *Production of commodities by means of commodities: Prelude to a critique of economic theory*. Cambridge University Press.

Van den Bergh, J. C. (2001). Ecological economics: Themes, approaches, and differences with environmental economics. *Regional Environmental Change*, *2*, 13–23. https://doi.org/10.1007/s101130000020

Verger, Y. (2016). *Sraffa and ecological economics: Links and possibilities*. University Paris-Saclay.

Verger, Y. (2017). A basis for Sraffian ecological economics. A comment on Martins' "Ecosystems, strong sustainability and the classical circular economy". *Ecological Economics*, *138*, 249–251. https://doi.org/10.1016/j.ecolecon.2017.03.022

von Hayek, F. A. (1932). Money and capital: A reply. *The Economic Journal*, *42*, 237–249. https://doi.org/10.2307/2223821

Wallerstein, I. (1979). *The capitalist world-economy*. Cambridge University Press.

Weber, N. F. (2008). *Le Corbusier*. Knopf.

17 The methodology of barefoot economics

Patrick Kletzka

Introduction

In the 21st century, the gold standard of economic research comprises methods for evidence-based, causal explanatory modelling (Mireles-Flores, 2018). This current state-of-the-art developed from the formalist turn in economic science that took place in the second half of the 20th century (Ward, 1972). This turn caused economic research to become more formal; i.e., more mathematical, more analytical, more standardised, less historical, less philosophical, and more limited in terms of admissible methods (Hands, 2003). The formalist turn was first and foremost driven by Milton Friedman's 1953 essay, *The Methodology of Positive Economics* (Blaug, 2003; Hutchison, 2000). In that essay, Chicago economist and Nobel laureate Milton Friedman (1912–2006) advocated empirical hypothesis testing for predicting measurable economic phenomena not yet observed. In the aftermath of its publication, Friedman's essay became the most cited and most influential work by far on economic methodology in the 20th century (Hausman, 2008). It became 'the only essay on methodology that a large number, perhaps a majority, of economists have ever read' (ibid., 1992, p. 162). Or, as Deirdre McCloskey (1983) put it: 'a watered down version of Friedman's essay is part of the intellectual equipment of most economists, and its arguments come readily to their lips' (p. 485). The principal reason why Friedman's methodology still serves as a paradigm for economists may be the absence of elaborated alternatives, which is, in fact, a direct consequence of the formalist turn provoked by the methodology of positive economics itself. The formalist banishment of philosophical issues from the realm of economic science led to the death of economic methodology in its original sense, i.e., the study of philosophical frameworks guiding economists in the assessment of ways to conduct research (see Hands, 2001). Instead of considering such fundamental investigations into the scientific legitimacy of their research practice, economists are today primarily concerned with the study of methods as research instruments within a set framework that largely remains unquestioned (see Truc et al., 2021). Consequently, this framework continues to be that of positive economics.

One of the last academically renowned economists who devoted his attention to economic methodology in a sophisticated philosophical manner was the German-Chilean economist Manfred Max-Neef (1932–2019). Max-Neef (1991a [1988],

DOI: 10.4324/9781003381143-20

1991b [1989], 2009) was particularly critical of the disregard shown by positive economics for the epistemological insights of the linguistic turn in philosophy in the early 20th century – according to which 'all philosophy is a "critique of language"' (Wittgenstein, 2001 [1921], p. 23). Aiming to overcome the corresponding epistemological blind spots of economic methodology, Max-Neef (1992 [1982]) outlined a substantially different approach which he named *barefoot economics*. With reference to E. F. Schumacher (2011 [1973]), he characterised barefoot economics as an 'economics as if people mattered' (Max-Neef, 1992 [1982], p. 19); acknowledging that '[w]hen the emphasis is on people, communications problems become paramount' (Schumacher, 2011 [1973], p. 169). To address these problems, economics needs to become 'barefooted' in the sense of taking off the 'shoes' of positive economics and making direct contact with the ground by means of lived experience. Although Max-Neef received the 1983 Alternative Nobel Prize for his practice of barefoot economics during the 1970s (Right Livelihood Foundation, 2021), to date he has been largely ignored by economic scholars (Kletzka, 2021). At best, his work is remembered as a historical footnote to economic science. This chapter aims to rectify this by elaborating Max-Neef's approach into a clear and consistent methodology distinct from the dominant methodology of positive economics. In doing so, this chapter will outline the epistemological reasons why a shift from the methodology of positive economics towards the methodology of barefoot economics may be necessary. Finally, social philosophical reasons will be put forward to explain why such a shift is unlikely to take place in academia at present.

What the shift towards barefoot economics is about

A shift towards the methodology of barefoot economics is factually obliged to take its point of departure from the current prevailing methodological paradigm of economic science, which is the methodology of positive economics. In his 1953 seminal essay, *The Methodology of Positive Economics*, Milton Friedman introduced the notion of positive economics to refer to an 'economics [that] is, or [at least] can be, an "objective" science' (p. 4). In this context, he identified a science as 'objective' to the extent that it is value-free, i.e., 'independent of any particular ethical position or normative judgments' (ibid.). In order to achieve this ideal of scientific objectivity, economics should be concerned with the production of knowledge that is grounded in 'what is given' ('the positive'). Thereby, Friedman suggests – in line with the Vienna Circle's logical empiricism (Schlick, 1948 [1932]) – the existence of unquestionable, empirically observable facts. Moreover, Friedman follows Popper's (1959 [1934]) critical rationalism in arguing that these facts can be applied to falsify hypotheses in an experimental manner. To ensure scientific objectivity throughout the entire process of knowledge production, only formal logical and/or mathematical analyses of facts are considered appropriate (Friedman, 1966 [1953]). Lastly, hypothesising and quantification necessarily involve increased levels of abstraction (ibid.). However, the latter are not considered problematic since resultant economic models should not be judged by the correctness of their assumptions but rather by their usability to derive correct predictions (ibid.).

In contrast, the methodology of barefoot economics takes a very different approach. Max-Neef first introduced the notion of barefoot economics in his 1982 classic *From the Outside Looking In*. In his book, Max-Neef (1992 [1982]) describes how he 'severed [his] ties with the trends imposed by the economic establishment, disengaged [himself] from "objective abstractions", and decided to "step into the mud"' (p. 21). Accordingly, barefoot economics is distinct from positive economics and characterised as the kind of economics that an economist who dares to 'step into the mud' must practice. In this context, the phrase 'stepping into the mud' means 'facing "life as it really is out there"' (p. 71). In more concrete terms, this approach demands that economists conduct fieldwork where they encounter economic phenomena first-hand in their lived experience. The epistemological reasons for gaining such life experiences reveal themselves in the practice of barefoot economics (ibid.). Having 'stepped into the mud', economists are forced to become aware of the naïve subreption objectivism of positive economic reasoning, which manifests itself as a disregard for the scientist as a conscious person (*Subject*). In other words, positive economics fails to admit that '[e]conomics is devised by economists' (Max-Neef, 1992 [1982], p. 34). Ultimately, the methodology of positive economics cannot meet its goal of scientific objectivity because knowledge produced through this approach is subject to the presuppositions and bias of the researcher. In contrast to the simplistic Ciceronian belief in positive economics that 'facts speak for themselves' (*res ipsa loquitur*), barefoot economics acknowledges their dependence on the researcher's language (Max-Neef, 1991a [1988], 1991b [1989], 1992 [1982], 2009). Referencing Wittgenstein (2001 [1921]), Max-Neef (1991b [1989]) argued that language is 'a form of imprisonment' (p. 108) that sets a limit to the expression of thought. Since knowledge – including knowledge that relates to facts – appears as declarative sentences (statements), it is linguistic by its very nature. Therefore, every well-formulated hypothesis, and whatever knowledge is generated due to the methodology of positive economics, will be tied to the linguistic horizons of the economist. According to Max-Neef (1991b [1989]), this is not necessarily problematic; it rather 'boils down to a question of coherence and incoherence' (p. 108). More precisely, the fundamental question to ask is whether the language of the researcher is, or is not, coherent with the object of research, i.e., the phenomenon under investigation (ibid.). In the case of economics, Max-Neef claimed that economists generally do not possess a language that is coherent with economic phenomena and, in particular, with the phenomenon of poverty (ibid.). This incoherence of conventional economic language would particularly become apparent when economists decide to 'step into the mud' and, in doing so, become directly confronted with and personally involved in the phenomena they are talking about. To make this issue of coherence more concrete and tangible, consider the following Wittgensteinian thought experiment:

> Let us imagine a language [...]. The language is meant to serve for communication between a builder A and an assistant B. A is building with building-stones: there are blocks, pillars, slabs and beams. B has to pass the stones, and that in the order in which A needs them. For this purpose they use a language consisting of the words 'block', 'pillar', 'slab', 'beam'. A calls them

> out; – B brings the stone which he has learnt to bring at such-and-such a call. – Conceive this as a complete primitive language.
> (Wittgenstein, 1986 [1953], p. 3)

The imagined primitive language solely consisting of 'shape-words' can be interpreted as a language that is coherent with the phenomenon of 'building'. By way of analogy, it would be possible to imagine a language solely consisting of 'colour-words' as being coherent with the phenomenon of 'painting', or a language solely consisting of 'number words' as being coherent with the phenomenon of 'counting'. The latter two languages, in turn, would be incoherent with the phenomenon of 'building'. As Wittgenstein (1986 [1953]) might have said: a language is coherent with a phenomenon, if it works where the *language-game* is actually played, i.e., where words are inextricably interwoven with practical actions in view of the phenomenon. These actions already presuppose a form of extralinguistic sense-making which Max-Neef (2005) was used to describe by means of the life-philosophical concept of understanding (compare Dilthey, 1977 [1894]):

> Suppose that you know everything that can be known, from philosophical, anthropological, biological, theological and psychological points of view, about a human phenomenon called Love. So, you know everything that can be known about Love; but you will only understand Love, once you fall in love. You can only understand that of which you become a part, when the Subject that searches and observes becomes inseparably integrated with the Object searched and observed. (p. 15)

Knowing and understanding are associated with two different concepts of truth that can be traced back to the pre-Socratic philosophy of the 6th century BCE (Heidegger, 1993 [1964], 1998a [1930], 1998b [1931/32, 1940], 2013 [1931/32]). While knowledge refers to propositional truth, i.e., the correctness of statement, understanding refers to alethic truth, i.e., the disclosure of meaning (ibid.). In order to approach the latter truth, it is necessary to 'go back to the "things themselves"' in a phenomenological sense and live through the phenomena under investigation (Husserl, 2001 [1900/01], p. 168; see also Max-Neef, 1991a [1988], 1991b [1989], 2005, 2009). Thereby, the somatic and extralinguistic moment of cognition (which transcends Cartesian mind-body dualism) is acknowledged. Against this backdrop, understanding – in contrast to knowledge – remains linguistically inexpressible. Put differently, the meaning of a phenomenon cannot be expressed in words as life experiences cannot be transferred from one person to another. In line with Heidegger (2001 [1927]), Max-Neef (1991b [1989]) considered alethic truth as a condition of possibility for the correctness of statements: these can only be correct if they are formulated in a manner that is coherent with the phenomenon under investigation; otherwise, they are nonsensical. Ultimately, coherence can only exist within a language-game that arises mimetically from extralinguistic sense-making, i.e., the understanding of phenomena.

To ensure that the existing language of the researcher does not interfere with the process of understanding in such a manner that it renders the researcher immune to lived experience, it has to be pruned (Max-Neef, 1991a [1988], 1991b [1989]). The pruning of language can be viewed as a form of *linguistic lifeworld epoché*, i.e., a linguistic reduction method that put out of action what is usually taken for granted within everyday life (Husserl, 1970 [1936]). This means banishing those words from the researcher's realm of thought that are related to the phenomenon under investigation (Max-Neef, 1991a [1988]). Hence, the banished words should be selected from the key terminology of the researcher's scientific discourse community (ibid.). To illustrate how such linguistic pruning works, Max-Neef (1991a [1988]) used the allegory of an orchard:

> The principle behind the act of pruning should be clear to anyone who has ever been interested in orchards. Through pruning we will achieve more and better from less. Fewer branches and leaves will allow more light to be absorbed and thus produce better fruits. In the case of a language, the pruning of chosen words will force us inevitably into higher degrees of clarity. (p. 99)

The resultant pruned language facilitates the intuitive understanding of phenomena in lived experience by suspending some of the researcher's linguistic presuppositions. Moreover, from this position of 'speechlessness' vis-à-vis the phenomena under investigation, a mimetic process is activated in which the creation of a more coherent, new language is triggered by the everyday necessity of communication and practical actions in the face of economic phenomena and their related challenges. In light of this, the methodology of barefoot economics can be broken down in terms of a *dialectical movement* (see Max-Neef, 1992 [1982]). In line with Hegel (1977 [1807]), this movement describes the unfolding of truth through the negation of negations. To use Hegel's famous botanical analogy: a plant reaches higher stages of its development by negating the bud due to the blossom and then negating the blossom due to the fruit (ibid.). With respect to the methodology of barefoot economics, the linguisticality of the researcher must first be negated by means of the pruning method. This negation is then itself negated by the mimetic creation of a new language. Within this dialectical movement, the researcher's language is concurrently elevated towards a higher stage of development, i.e., a level of greater coherence.

Why there are no barefoot economists in academia

To explain why the methodology of barefoot economics – despite the epistemological advantages outlined above – is unlikely to be adopted in academia, barefoot economics must be considered in a social philosophical context. The first step is to recognise that Max-Neef (1992 [1982]) conceived the kind of economics that an economist who dares to 'step into the mud' must practice as an economics practised on a *human scale*. This characterisation of barefoot economics is related to Max-Neef et al.'s 1986 Human Scale Development theory, in which Max-Neef et al. (1989 [1986]) emphasise that development is, in part, a problem of scale (compare

Kohr, 1957). Moreover, they associate development with improved needs satisfaction (ibid.). With regard to human beings, the theory ultimately advocates that human needs should be fulfilled by means of human-scale satisfiers. Thereby, the theory defines satisfiers as culturally determined ways of meeting needs, which can be distinguished from tradable economic goods (ibid.). The following example clarifies this conception. Imagine a hungry baby: two different satisfiers can be chosen to meet the baby's needs – breastfeeding and bottle-feeding. These ways of feeding are distinct from the economic goods of breast milk and infant formula milk (since breast milk can also be bottled). While bottle-feeding satisfies the infants' physiological needs, breastfeeding also contributes to the satisfaction of both the infant's and the mother's affective needs. Lastly, in contrast to bottle-feeding, breastfeeding is a satisfier that remains on a human scale, i.e., a satisfier where the human individual is not annulled (ibid.). Against this background, barefoot economics can be classified as a *human-scale satisfier* for the synergic fulfilment of intellectual, participatory, and identity needs. Arguing that scientific insights depend on the individual language and first-hand experiences of the researcher, barefoot economics brings the individual person of the economist to the fore. The intuitive, extralinguistic understanding of phenomena that is supposed to be gained from the unity of *Subject* and *Object* in lived experience is inseparably linked to the particular individual and, thus, inappropriate for intersubjective exchange. In contrast, positive economics can be regarded as a singular satisfier for the need of cognition that exceeds a human-scale dimension (and even potentially inhibits the attainment of understanding). The linguistic knowledge targeted by positive economics can be detached from the particular individual who produced it by sharing it in communication. Furthermore, this knowledge can be commodified into a tradable economic product in accordance with the capitalist logic of market valorisation (Horkheimer & Adorno, 2002 [1944]; Marx, 1906 [1867]). Since academic institutions are under constant pressure to promote marketable outputs in the form of commodified knowledge (Jacob, 2003), there is no space for barefoot economists in academia. The same fate may also strike barefoot sociologists and other kinds of scholars practising their science on a human scale. As Max-Neef (2005) argued, this will ultimately result in not only a scientific language that is largely incoherent with the phenomena it aims to address, but also the emergence of a knowledge society 'in which *we know very much, but understand very little*' (p. 14, emphasis in original).

Conclusion

This chapter has elaborated on the methodology of barefoot economics as a dialectical human-scale phenomenology that can overcome the epistemological obstacles of the current prevailing positive economic methodological paradigm by means of an alethic-mimetic imperative. It has explained the extent to which the methodology of positive economics underestimates the influence of the researcher as a conscious person (*Subject*) and thus fails to achieve its goal of scientific objectivity. As a consequence, scientific knowledge produced by means of the methodology of positive economics may be lost in the labyrinth of language. In order to remedy this, barefoot economic methodology is based on an intuitive, extralinguistic understanding of economic phenomena that extracts meaning from lived experience. For instance, when faced with the phenomenon of poverty, barefoot economic methodology focuses on ensuring that the economists understand what it means to be poor in order to facilitate a language that is coherent with the phenomenon of poverty. Against this backdrop, the pursuit of alethic truth by barefoot economics must be seen as a clear epistemological break with the formalist ideals of positive economics. Furthermore, this chapter has explained how the unfolding of alethic truth through barefoot economics requires a dialectical process of pruning and recreating language mimetically. Put differently, it involves a linguistic-phenomenological dialectic in which the economist has to move from words to the 'things themselves' and back again. Lastly, the attained understanding of economic phenomena is inseparably linked to the particular human individual who gains it first-hand through lived experience. Consequently, in line with Human Scale Development theory, barefoot economics is characterised as a human-scale satisfier that evades the capitalist logic of exchange-value. For this reason, it is unlikely that barefoot economics will be supported by academic institutions in the foreseeable future unless counter-hegemonic societal transformation takes place. Such a transformation may be facilitated by the methodological practice of barefoot economics itself and, therefore, depends on the personal courage of individual economists to 'step into the mud' and live through the phenomena about which they talk.

References

Blaug, M. (2003). The formalist revolution of the 1950s. *Journal of the History of Economic Thought*, *25*(2), 145–156. https://doi.org/10.1080/1042771032000083309

Dilthey, W. (1977 [1894]). Ideas concerning a descriptive and analytic psychology. In *Descriptive psychology and historical understanding* (pp. 21–120). Martinus Nijhoff. https://doi.org/10.1007/978-94-009-9658-8_2

Friedman, M. (1966 [1953]). The methodology of positive economics. In *Essays in positive economics* (pp. 3–43). University of Chicago Press.

Hands, D. W. (2001). Economic methodology is dead – Long live economic methodology: Thirteen theses on the new economic methodology. *Journal of Economic Methodology*, *8*(1), 49–63. https://doi.org/10.1080/13501780010022839

Hands, D. W. (2003). Did Milton Friedman's methodology license the formalist revolution? *Journal of Economic Methodology*, *10*(4), 507–520. https://doi.org/10.1080/1350178032000130493

Hausman, D. M. (2008). *The philosophy of economics: An anthology* (3rd ed.). Cambridge University Press.

Hegel, G. W. F. (1977 [1807]). *Phenomenology of spirit*. Oxford University Press.

Heidegger, M. (1993 [1964]). The end of philosophy and the task of thinking. In D. F. Krell (Ed.), *Basic writings* (2nd ed., pp. 427–449). HarperCollins.

Heidegger, M. (1998a [1930]). On the essence of truth. In W. McNeill (Ed.), *Pathmarks* (pp. 136–154). Cambridge University Press. https://doi.org/10.1017/CBO9780511812637.008

Heidegger, M. (1998b [1931/32, 1940]). Plato's doctrine of truth. In W. McNeill (Ed.), *Pathmarks* (pp. 155–182). Cambridge University Press. https://doi.org/10.1017/CBO9780511812637.009

Heidegger, M. (2001 [1927]). *Being and time*. Blackwell.
Heidegger, M. (2013 [1931/32]). *The essence of truth*. Bloomsbury.
Horkheimer, M., & Adorno, T. W. (2002 [1944]). *Dialectic of enlightenment: Philosophical fragments*. Stanford University Press.
Husserl, E. (1970 [1936]). *The crisis of European sciences and transcendental phenomenology: An introduction to phenomenological philosophy*. Northwestern University Press.
Husserl, E. (2001 [1900/01]). *Logical investigations*. Routledge. https://doi.org/10.4324/9780203879054
Hutchison, T. (2000). *On the methodology of economics and the formalist revolution*. Edward Elgar. https://doi.org/10.4324/9780203879054
Jacob, M. (2003). Rethinking science and commodifying knowledge. *Policy Futures in Education*, *1*(1), 125–142. https://doi.org/10.2304/pfie.2003.1.1.3
Kletzka, P. T. (2021). *Inside barefoot economics*. Logos. https://doi.org/10.30819/5346
Kohr, L. (1957). *The breakdown of nations*. Routledge & Kegan Paul.
Marx, K. (1906 [1867]). *Capital: A critique of political economy*. C.H. Kerr & Company.
Max-Neef, M. A. (1991a [1988]). About the pruning of language (and other unusual exercises) for the understanding of social improvement. In *Human scale development: Conception, application and further reflections* (pp. 93–103). Apex Press.
Max-Neef, M. A. (1991b [1989]). A stupid way of life. In *Human scale development: Conception, application and further reflections* (pp. 105–114). Apex Press.
Max-Neef, M. A. (1992 [1982]). *From the outside looking in. Experiences in 'Barefoot Economics'*. Zed Books.
Max-Neef, M. A. (2005). Foundations of transdisciplinarity. *Ecological Economics*, *53*(1), 5–16. https://doi.org/10.1016/j.ecolecon.2005.01.014
Max-Neef, M. A. (2009). From knowledge to understanding: Navigations and returns. *Development Dialogue*, *1*(52), 15–21. https://doi.org/10.1177/1049732312468251
Max-Neef, M. A., Elizalde, A., & Hopenhayn, M. (1989 [1986]). Human scale development: An option for the future. *Development Dialogue*, *1*(29), 5–81. https://doi.org/10.1177/1049732312468251
McCloskey, D. (1983). The rhetoric of economics. *Journal of Economic Literature*, *21*(2), 481–517. http://www.jstor.org/stable/2724987
Mireles-Flores, L. (2018). Recent trends in economic methodology: A literature review. *Research in the History of Economic Thought and Methodology*, *36A*, 93–126. https://doi.org/10.1108/S0743-41542018000036A008
Popper, K. R. (1959 [1934]). *The logic of scientific discovery*. Hutchinson & Co.
Right Livelihood Foundation (2021). "Manfred Max-Neef/CEPAUR." https://rightlivelihoodaward.org/laureates/manfred-max-neef/
Schlick, M. (1948 [1932]). Positivism and realism. *Synthese*, *7*(6), 478–505. https://doi.org/10.1007/BF00540043
Schumacher, E. F. (2011 [1973]). *Small is beautiful: A study of economics as if people mattered*. Random House.
Truc, A., Claceau, F., & Santerre, O. (2021). Economic methodology: A bibliometric perspective. *Journal of Economic Methodology*, *28*(1), 67–78. https://doi.org/10.1080/1350178X.2020.1868774
Ward, B. (1972). *What's wrong with economics?* Macmillan.
Wittgenstein, L. (1986 [1953]). *Philosophical investigations*. Blackwell.
Wittgenstein, L. (2001 [1921]). *Tractatus logico-philosophicus*. Routledge. https://doi.org/10.4324/9780203010341

18 Max-Neef's complete bibliography

María del Valle Barrera

This chapter provides a complete bibliography of Manfred Max-Neef, compilation not available elsewhere. It is organised in four types of publication: (i) articles in journals, (ii) books, (iii) book chapters, and (iv) public policy research reports and working papers. Each section is ordered by date, from newer to older.

Max-Neef also engaged outside academic forums, like newspapers, TV documentaries, interviews for periodicals, etc., across the world. He also supervised and co-authored a great number of theses. None of these are included in this list.

Articles

1. 2017 Una enseñanza no tóxica de la economía. *Estudios Nueva Economía*, 4(1), 13–20.
2. 2016 Philosophy of Ecological Economics. *International Journal of Economics & Management Sciences*, 5(5), 366. doi: 10.4172/2162-6359.1000366, https://pdfs.semanticscholar.org/3a4b/c2196aa85453f4b369c4ee0d61029716ea54.pdf.
3. 2014 The Good is the Bad that We don't do. Economic Crimes Against Humanity: A Proposal. *Ecological Economics*, 104, 152–154.
4. 2013 Economic Growth and Quality of Life: A Threshold Hypothesis., Victor, *International Library of Critical Writings in Economics*, 275, 268–271.
5. 2012 The Vindication of Triviality: My Relationship with the Dag Hammarskjöld Foundation. *Development Dialogue*, 60, 49–58.
6. 2011 Should We Care about the Needs of Non-humans? Needs Assessment: A Tool for Environmental Conflict Resolution and Sustainable Organization of Living Being. *Environmental Policy and Governance*, 21(4), 259–269. With Jolibert, C., Rauschmayer, F. & Paavola, J., https://doi.org/10.1002/eet.578
7. 2011 Carta Abierta a Sebastián Piñera. *Ecología Política*, 41, 14–15.
8. 2010 The World in a Collision Course and the Need for a New Economy. *Ambio*, 39(3), 200–210.
9. 2010 The 9th Royal Colloquium: Climate Action, Tuning in on Energy, Water and Food Security. *Royal Swedish Academy of Sciences*, Stockholm, Sweden.
10. 2009 From Knowledge to Understanding: Navigations and Return. *Development Dialogue*, 52, 15–22.
11. 2009 Towards a Systemic Development Approach: Building on the Human-Scale Development Paradigm. *Ecological Economics*, 68(7), 2021–2030. With Cruz, I. & Stahel, A., https://doi.org/10.1016/j.ecolecon.2009.02.004

DOI: 10.4324/9781003381143-21

12. 2008 The Forgotten Map. It's Time to Navigate Alternative Routes. *Resurgence*, 247, 6–9.
13. 2007 El niño a quien nadie descubre: educación para un mundo equivocado". *Kikiriki. Cooperación Educativa*, Revista de la Universidad de Deusto, 84, 40–43, https://dialnet.unirioja.es/ejemplar/157595
14. 2007 From Knowledge to Understanding: Navigations and Returns. *Development Dialogue*, 11(52), 15–21. Journal of the Dag Hammarskjöld Foundation.
15. 2006 El poder en la globalización. *Facultad Nacional de Salud Pública: El escenario para la salud pública desde la ciencia*, Vol. 24 (23–29), Universidad de Antioquia, Colombia.
16. 2005 Del Saber al Comprender: Navegaciones y Regresos. *Palimpsestvs*, 5, 93–98, Revista de la Facultad de Ciencias Humanas, Universidad Nacional de Colombia.
17. 2005 Foundations of Transdisciplinarity. (Commentary) *Ecological Economics*, 53(1), 5–16.
18. 2006 El Poder de la Globalización. *Revista Futuros*, 14, 23–29.
19. 2005 Fundamentos de la Transdisciplinaridad. *Cuaderno de la Universidad de Alicante*, España.
20. 2004 Human Ecology: Following Nature's Lead. *Ecological Economics*, 48(4), 490–492.
21. 2004 La Universidad y el Desarrollo Sostenible. *Revista Asuntos Económicos y Administrativos*, 6, 9–21. Revista de la Universidad de Manizales, Colombia.
22. 2004 América Latina y la Deshumanización de la Economía. *Revista Colombiana de Trabajo Social*, 18, 11–24.
23. 2004 El ALCA es un Desastre. *Revista Asuntos Económicos y Administrativos*, 7, 13–16. Revista de la Universidad de Manizales, Colombia.
24. 2003 Transdiciplina, para pasar del saber al comprender. *Debates*, 36, 14–21. Revista de la Universidad de Antioquia, Colombia.
25. 2001 La universidad y el desarrollo sostenible. *Revista Asuntos Económicos* y *Administrativos*, 6, 9–21. Revista de la Universidad de Manizales, Colombia.
26. 2001 Investigación y Creatividad para el Desarrollo Sostenible, *Societas. Revista de Ciencias Sociales y Humanísticas,* Vol. 3, Nr. 2, Revista de la Universidad de Panamá.
27. 2000 El Día después de Trinidad. *Mensaje*, 492, 50–52.
28. 1998 Crecimiento, Sustentabilidad y Eficiencia Energética. *Ambiente y Desarrollo*, 14(1), 31–35.
29. 1997 Orientaciones para un desarrollo sustentable del turismo en el medio rural. *Agroturismo Y Turismo Rural en Chile* (171–179).
30. 1997 Música y arte en los cincuenta: cuando los sueños aún eran posibles. *Revista Musical Chilena*, 51(187), 52–53. Recuperado a partir de https://revistamusicalchilena.uchile.cl/index.php/RMCH/article/view/13057
31. 1996 Desarrollo sin Sentido. *Revista Número*, Bogotá, Colombia.
32. 1996 Human scale development: A perspective on poverty alleviation. *Unisa Latin American Report*, 12(1), 57–59.
33. 1996 El drama de las identidades perdidas (sobre males que hicimos, creyendo que éramos buenos). Instituto Indigenista Interamericano Vol (LVI) 33–39,
34. 1995 Economic Growth and Quality of Life: A Threshold Hypothesis. *Ecological Economics*, 15(2), 115–118.
35. 1995 Ciencia, Certeza y Responsabilidad. *Ambiente y Desarrollo*, 11(1), 37–39.
36. 1993 Biosfera, Biodiversidad, Personas y Economía. *Anuario El Mundo*, España.

37. 1993 Sobre el Saber mucho y el Comprender poco. *Cuadernos de Arquitectura. Habitar el Norte.*; Núm. 2–3, 4–7, Revista de la Universidad Católica del Norte.
38. 1992 Llamarle Desarrollo a un Suicidio Colectivo. *Revista El Canelo*, 34–35.
39. 1991 Follies of Humankind. *Resurgence* Nr. 145, 8–11.
40. 1991 Especulaciones y Reflexiones sobre el Futuro. *Perfiles Liberales* (24) Revista de la Fundación Freidich Naumann.
41. 1990 Human Centred Economics: Environment and Global Sustainability. SID, Rome-Italy. *Society for International Development* (Special edition).
42. 1989 Human Scale Development: An Option for the Future. *Development Dialogue* 1(1), 7–80. Journal of the Dag Hammarskjöld Foundation.
43. 1990 Notes on the Semiology of our Megacrisis. *Development. Journal of the Society for International Development*, 3(4), 5–6.
44. 1989 La Deuda en el Contexto Mundial y el Desarrollo a Escala Humana. *Tópicos 90, Cuaderno de Estudio*. Centro Ecuménico Diego de Medellín. Colombia.
45. 1987 Desde La Concepción Ambientalista a un Enfoque Geonómico: Hacia un Nuevo Paradigma sobre La Vida en nuestro Planeta. *CEPAUR*, Santiago.
46. 1986 Patologías Colectivas. *Revista Colegio de Arquitectos de Chile*, Nr. 44.
47. 1985 Economía, Política y Salud: una Síntesis Ineludible. *Revista Universitaria Nr. XVI*, Revista de la Universidad Católica de Chile.
48. 1985 El Problema de la Dimensión. *Revista Comunidad*, Suecia.
49. 1985 Another Development under the Repressive Rule Development Dialogue Dag Hammarskjöld Foundation, (Special edition). Another Development and the Third System. 1, 30–56.
50. 1984 La Cuestión de los Estilos de Desarrollo. *Revista Comunidad*, Suecia.
51. 1984 Historia, Economía y Algunas Invisibilidades. *Revista Comunidad*, Suecia.
52. 1984 Urban Explosion and the Need for a Development Paradigm Shift. *World Social Prospects Association*, Ginebra.
53. 1981 The Tiradentes Project: An Experience of Revitalization for Self-reliance. *Development Dialogue*, 1, 115–137. Journal of the Dag Hammarskjöld Foundation,
54. 1976 Volver a Humanizarnos: Ecodesarrollo y Estilos de Desarrollo *Apuntes de Ecología*.
55. 1967 Reflexiones sobre el Papel de la Juventud en la Universidad Actual. Universidad Nacional Federico Villarreal, Lima, Perú. (mimeo).
56. 1967 La Irresponsabilidad Intelectual. *Imprenta Ausonia*, Lima, Perú.
57. 1967 Los Mecanismos cibernéticos y su Aplicación para una Teoría de Ia Estética. *Revista Sistema*, Año 2, Nr.3, Universidad del Pacifico, Lima, Perú.
58. 1967 La Planificación integral ante el Reto del Mundo del Mañana. *Revista Comunidad*, Vol 2 Nr.10, Universidad Iberoamericana de México.
59. 1966 El Proyecto Camelot: Intervención Intelectual de los Estados Unidos en A Latina. *Revista Comunidad* Nr.3, Universidad Iberoamericana de México.
60. 1965 Concentración del Poder Económico y Motivación Empresarial: El Caso del Sector Pesquero. *Universidad Nacional Mayor de San Marcos*, Lima-Perú.
61. 1963 International Relations and the Dynamics of Misunderstanding. *Howard Law Journal*, 9 Spring.
62. 1963 Investment Criteria for the Development of Arid Zones in Underdeveloped Countries. Symposium on Arid Lands in Latin America. *American Association for the Advancement of Science*, Cleveland, Ohio.
63. 1954 Consideraciones respecto del Cálculo de la Capacidad para importar. *Revista Economía* Nr 48, Facultad de Economía, Universidad de Chile.

Books

64. 2017 Economía Herética: Treinta y cinco Años a Contracorriente. Icaria, ISBN: 9788498887778
65. 2014 La Economía Desenmascarada: Del Poder y la Codicia a la Compasión y el Bien Común. Icaria with Smith, P.B. ISBN: 9788498885576
66. 2013 Ekonominin Gerçek Yüzü. Yeni İnsan Yayınevi with Smith, P.B. ISBN: 9786055895372
67. 2011 Lo Sviluppo su Scala Umana. Slow Food Editore, ISBN: 9788884992574
68. 2011 La Evolución Sostenible (II): Apuntes para una Salida Razonable Lanki – Club of Rome, Mondragón, España with Azkarraga, J.; Fuders, F. & Altuna, L. Mondragon Unibertsitatea, ISBN: 9788460812449
69. 2011 Economics Unmasked: From Power and Greed to Compassion and the Common Good. Green Books, Cambridge-U.K. with Smith, P.B. ISBN-13978-19003 22706
70. 2010 El Mundo en Ruta de Colisión y otros Escritos. Prensas Universitarias de Zaragoza, ISBN.9788415031284
71. 2008 La Dimensión Perdida: La Deshumanización del Gigantismo. Nordan-Icaria, ISBN: 9788474269871
72. 2007 Ensayos de Manfred Max-Neef. Editorial de la Universidad Santiago de Cali.
73. 1999 Las trampas del lenguaje. Universidad Pedagógica y Tecnológica de Colombia.
74. 1994 Desarrollo a Escala Humana: Conceptos, Aplicaciones y Reflexiones. Editorial Icaria, ISBN 9788474262179
75. 1992 Real Life Economics: Understanding Wealth Creation. **In** Ekins P. (Eds.). Routledge, ISBN 9780415079778
76. 1992 From the Outside Looking In: Experiences in Barefoot Economics. Zed Books, ISBN 978-1856491884
77. 1991 Human Scale Development: Conception, Application and Further Reflections. The Apex Press with Elizalde, A. & Hopenhayn, M. ISBN 978-0945257356
78. 1990 Entwicklung nach menschlichem Mass eine Option für die Zukunft. CEPAUR, ISBN 9783881225861
79. 1989 Sociedad Civil y Cultura Democrática: Mensajes y Paradojas. Nordan-CEPAUR with Elizalde, A.
80. 1987 Desde la Concepción Ambientalista a un Enfoque Genómico: Hacia un Nuevo Paradigma sobre la Vida en nuestro Planeta. ILDIS.
81. 1986 La Economía Descalza: Señales desde el Mundo Invisible. Editorial Nordan, ISBN 9789563902068
82. 1984 Från Andra Sidan: Barfotaekonomiska Försök. Nordan, ISBN 9177020847
83. 1989 Sociedad Civil y Cultura Democrática: Mensajes y Paradojas. Ediciones CEP-AUR-CIID Canadá with Elizalde, A.
84. 1982 From the Outside Looking In: Experiences in Barefoot Economics. Dag Hammarskjöld Foundation, ISBN 978-1856491884
85. 1968 Los Recursos para el Desarrollo. Instituto de Investigaciones Económicas, Universidad Nacional Federico Villarreal.
86. 1967 La Irresponsabilidad Intelectual. El caso de Carlos Malpica. Lima-Perú.
87. 1965 En Torno a una Sociología del Desarrollo. Departamento de Sociología, Universidad Mayor de San Marcos.

Book chapters

88. 2017 A Philosophy of Ecological Economics. **In** Rosa, H., & Henning, C. (Eds.). The Good Life Beyond Growth: New Perspectives (1st ed.). Routledge. https://doi.org/10.4324/9781315542126. ISBN 9781315542126
89. 2014 Local Money as Solution to Capitalist Global Financial Crises Fuders, F. **In** Michael Pirson Pirson, M., Steinvorth, U., Largacha-Martinez, C., & Dierksmeier, C. (Eds.). From Capitalistic to Humanistic Business. Palgrave-Macmillan. https://doi.org/10.1057/9781137468208_11
90. 2013 El Desarrollo Territorial Integrado: Una Estrategia Sustentable de Construcción Social del Territorio a partir del Concepto de Topofilia. (Prólogo) Habitat y Territorio –Universidad Piloto de Colombia, Bogotá-Colombia Yori, C.M. (15–20)
91. 2012 From the Village to a Global Order. Common Ground. **In** Murray, J., Cawthorne, G., Dey, C., & Andrew, C. (Eds.). Enough for All Forever: A Handbook for Learning about Sustainability. Common Ground Research Networks. https://doi.org/10.18848/978-1-61229-015-7/CGP.
92. 2011 Preface: The Death and Rebirth of Economics. **In** Rauschmayer, F., Omann, I., & Frühmann, J. (Eds.). Sustainable Development: Capabilities Needs and Well-Being. Routledge.
93. 2011 El poder en la globalización. **In** Matarán Ruiz, A., & López Castellano, F. (Eds.). La tierra no es muda: diálogos entre el desarrollo sostenible y el postdesarrollo. Editores. Universidad de Granada. (133–148). ISBN 978-84-338-5341-7
94. 2010 Development and Human Needs. **In** Gasper, D., & St. Clair, A. L. (Eds.). A Development Ethic. Routledge. ISBN 9780754628385
95. 2005 Vom Wissen zum Verstehen: Wege und Alternativen. **In** Khor, M., Narain, S., & Wallach, L. (Eds.). Konsum Globalisierung Umwelt. VSA -Verlag. ISBN 3-89965-136-7 1
96. 2005 Stärkung kleiner und mittlerer Gemeinschaften. **In** Streich, J. (Eds.). Vorbilder. Kamphausen Verlag. ISBN 978-3899010572
97. 2003 Das Natürliche ist zu kooperieren. **In** von Lüpke, G. (Eds.). Politik des Herzens. Arun Verlag. ISBN 978-3935581332
98. 2002 Programa y reflexiones para las instituciones del mundo contrahegemónico. **In** L'Ullal, X. (Eds.). Sociedad civil, cultura democrática e inclusión social Xàtiva España. (120–137). ISBN 84-931721-6-2
99. 2001 Las discriminaciones invisibles. **In** Aprender para el futuro: educación a favor de la dignidad humana. Fundación Santillana. Madrid España (95–98). ISBN 84-88295-42-1
100. 1998 Economy, Humanism and Neoliberalism. **In** Fals-Borda, O. (Eds.). People's Participation: Challenges Ahead. The Apex Press. ISBN. 978-1853394454
101. 1998 Economía, Humanismo y Neoliberalismo. **In** Fals Borda, O. (Eds.). Participación Popular: Retos del Futuro. Tercer Mundo Ediciones. (69–86). ISBN 95833673109
102. 1997 Community Empowerment and Alternative Development. **In** Smith, P. Y., & Armin Tenner, A. (Eds.). Dimensions of Sustainability. International Network of Engineers and Scientists for Global Responsibility. Nomos Verlaggesellschaft. ISBN 978-3789048289
103. 1996 Desarrollo sin Sentido. In Disoñadores del Futuro: Un Encuentro en el Sur. Asociación para el Desarrollo Campesino Colombia. (66-75)

104. 1996 Desarrollo a Escala Humana. **In** Valcárcel-Resalt, G., Portillo, M. A., Troitiño Vinuesa, L. C. (Eds.). Desarrollo local y medio ambiente: la iniciativa comunitaria LEADER. Diputación Provincial de Cuenca. Ecuador (17–29). ISBN 84-87319-14-9
105. 1995 Paradoxien des Wachsturns und der Globalisierung. **In** E. Deutscher et. al. (Eds.). Entwicklungsmodelle und Weltbilder. Stiftung für Internationale Entwicklung. ISBN 3797306113
106. 1994 Siempre estamos en Proceso de Redescubrirniento… **In** Basch, M., & Yentzen, E. Imagenes para un Nuevo Mundo: Entrevistas. Ediciones Andrómeda. ISBN 9789562600545
107. 1994 Por qué un Cristo de Plástico acerca más a la Gente a la Divinidad que un Árbol. Planeta. **In** Mendoza, M., & Maturana, H. (Eds.). Todos Queríamos ser Verdes: Chile en la Crisis Ambiental. Planeta. ISBN 9789562471121
108. 1993 The City: Its Size and Rhythm. In Morse, R. M., & Hardoy, J. E. Rethinking the Latin American City. Woodrow Wilson Center Press, Johns Hopkins University Press.
109. 1993 El Medio Ambiente: Condición de todo Desarrollo Sustentable. **In** Brunner, J. (Eds.). Chile: Juventud y Futuro: una Mirada al Siglo XXI. Centro de Estudios de la Realidad Contemporánea (CERC).
110. 1993 El Acto Creativo: Desde Ia Esterilidad de la Certeza hacia la Fecundidad de la Incertidumbre. **In** Ampliando Espacios para Ia Creatividad. Pontificia Universidad Javeriana y COLCIENCIAS.
111. 1992 Development and Human Needs. **In** Ekins, P., & Max-Neef, M. (Eds.). Real Life Economics. Routledge. (197–214).
112. 1992 Región de Utopías. América es lo que no la dejan Ser. **In** "Sobre América", Quinto Centenario. (155–160).
113. 1992 Why "Green Economics? In Ekins, P. (Eds.). Wealth Beyond Measure. An Atlas of New Economics, Gaia Books. Future Series. ISBN 978-1856750509
114. 1991 Del Saber al Comprender: El Desafío de una Economía Ecológica. **In** Schatan, J. (Eds.). Crecimiento y Desarrollo. Friedrich Ebert Foundation.
115. 1987 Economics, Politics and Health: The Challenge of Future Trends (A Think-Piece). **In** Schwefel, D. (Eds.). Indicators and Trends in Health and Health Care. Springer.
116. 1987 Barefoot Economics. **In** Woodhouse, T. (Eds.). People and Planet: Alternative Nobel Prize Speeches. Green Books. ISBN 978-1870098021
117. 1987 El Futuro de los Modelos de Desarrollo: una Alternativa Humanista. **In** Sánchez G., W. (Eds.). Política mundial hacia el siglo XXI. Editorial Universitaria. (159–163). ISBNN 8484402270
118. 1986 Human Scale Economics: The Challenges Ahead. **In** Ekins, P. (Eds.). The Living Economy: A New Economics in the Making. Routledge.
119. 1987. Economics, Politics and Health: The Challenge of Future Trends (A Think-Piece). **In** Schwefel, D. (Eds.). Indicators and Trends in Health and Health Care. Health Systems Research. Springer. (125–131). ISBN 978-3-642-71537-2_12
120. 1985 Reflections on a Paradigm Shift in Economics. **In** Inglis, M., & Kramer, S. (Eds.). The New Economic Agenda. The Findhorn Press. ISBN 9780905249612
121. 1981 Necesidades Humanas y la Mujer: Aspectos Económicos. **In** "Necesidades Humanas y la Mujer". Centro de Estudios del Tercer Mundo (CEESTEM).
122. 1979 Notes on Meaningful and Practical Measures of Health, Satisfaction and Quality of Life. **In** Buchmann, M. A., Dauderstädt, M., & Siegmann, W. (Eds.). Basic Needs Strategy as a Planning Parameter. German Foundation for International Development.

123. 1971 Reflexiones acerca de los Ternas de la Investigación Económica. **In** Max, H. (Eds.). Investigación económica, su metodología y su técnica (3a.). Fondo de cultura económica.
124. 1965 Motivación Empresarial y Concentración del Poder Económico. Instituto de Investigaciones Económicas, Universidad Nacional Federico Villarreal.

Public policy research reports and working papers

125. 1996 The Venice Deliberations: Practical Steps Toward a New Security Culture. Diálogo en Venecia (1994), **UNESCO**, Paris.
126. 1989 Common Understanding for a Common Future: Latin American Perspectives on Global Environmental Change. **HDGC** – Royal Society of Canada, Ottawa-Canada With Valencia, H. & de San José, J.
127. 1979 Quality of Life Oriented Development and Global Social Modelling Part of the Series of Studies on Social Development and Improvement of Quality of Life, UNESCO's Socio-Economic Analysis Division with Mallmann, C. & Nudler, O. (Synergic Developments Group & **Fundación Bariloche**)
128. 1978 On the Mathematical Formalization of Human Subjective Time. Con Carlos Mallmann. **Fundación Bariloche**, Argentina.
129. 1978 La sinergia humana como fundamento ético y estético del desarrollo. With Mallmann C, Aguirre, R. **Fundación Bariloche**, Argentina.
130. 1978 Notes on Meaningful and Practical Measures of Health, Satisfaction and Quality of Life. With Mallmann, CA, MA Max-Neef, M. Nudler **Fundación Bariloche**, Argentina.
131. 1978 Work, Urban Size and Quality of Life. CINTER for **ILO**, Montevideo.
132. 1978 Trabajo, Tamaño Urbano y Calidad de Vida. Publicaciones CINTERFOR/**ILO**. Montevideo.
133. 1977 The Ontologization of Formalized Language and its Usefulness for an Axiomatic Interpretation of Social Structures. Proceedings of the Third International Symposium on Trends in Global Mathematical Modeling, **UNESCO**.
134. 1977 Capacitación Profesional y Calidad de Vida. **CINTERFOR/OIT**, Docref/Sem.141, Montevideo.
135. 1976 Eco-Desarrollo y Estilos de Desarrollo. Oficina de **FAO** para América Latina, RLAT/801/76/9-S.
136. 1976 Dinámica de Sistemas y su Aplicabilidad en in Programación Integrada. Oficina Regional para las Americas, **UNICEF**.
137. 1972 En el Mundo Aparte. División Andina – **OIL**, Ecuador. With Gonzalo Freitas.
138. 1971 La Dinámica del Desarrollo ante la Persistencia de nuestra Alienación. Séptimo Congreso de Bienestar Social, Ecuador.
139. 1969 El Desarrollo Ayer-Hoy. Universidad Nacional del Trabajo, San Ramón, Canelones, Uruguay.
140. 1969 Efectos Económicos de las Deficiencias Estructurales del Sector Agrario: Bases para un Modelo Matemático. Proyecto Regional. Laguna Merin, **FAO**, Uruguay.
141. 1969 Compendio Metodológico 3, Método para Planificar la Distribución y Asentamiento de Recursos Humanos. **FAO**, Uruguay.
142. 1969 Compendio Metodológico 2, El Desarrollo Regional: Opciones, Programación y Asignación de Recursos. **FAO**, Uruguay.

143. 1969 Compendio Metodológico 1. Un Método para estimar la Distribución del Ingreso y sus Efectos. **FAO**, Uruguay.
144. 1966 The Camelot Project: U.S. Intellectual Intervention in South America. **CIF** Reports, 5(22).
145. 1964 El Desarrollo de la Comunidad y la Programación Nacional del desarrollo. **OAS** Department of Social Affairs, Washington, DC, United States.

Index

For Product Safety Concerns and Information please contact our EU
representative GPSR@taylorandfrancis.com
Taylor & Francis Verlag GmbH, Kaufingerstraße 24, 80331 München, Germany

www.ingramcontent.com/pod-product-compliance
Ingram Content Group UK Ltd.
Pitfield, Milton Keynes, MK11 3LW, UK
UKHW020149200926
475702UK00016B/2624
9781032463261